# Rebels and Martyrs

## The Image of the Artist in the Nineteenth Century

Alexander Sturgis
Rupert Christiansen, Lois Oliver and Michael Wilson

National Gallery Company, London
Distributed by Yale University Press

Published to accompany the exhibition *Rebels and Martyrs: The Image of the Artist in the Nineteenth Century* at the National Gallery, London from 28 June – 28 August 2006.

The exhibition is supported by the Corporate Members of the National Gallery.



First published in Great Britain in 2006 by
National Gallery Company Limited
St Vincent House
30 Orange Street
London WC2H 7HH
www.nationalgallery.co.uk

ISBN 10: 1 85709 346 1
ISBN 13: 978 1 85709 346 9
525482

British Library Cataloguing-in-Publication Data
A catalogue record is available from the British Library
Library of Congress Control Number: 2005939891

Project Editor: Claire Young
Editor: Johanna Stephenson
Design: Piccia Neri
Picture Researchers: Suzanne Bosman and Kim Klehmet
Production: Jane Hyne and Penny Le Tissier

Printed and bound in Belgium by Die Keure

All measurements give height before width

Front cover:
Alexandre Abel de Pujol, *Self Portrait* (detail), 1806 (cat. 7).
© Musée des Beaux-Arts de Valenciennes. Photo Claude Thériez

# Contents



## Catalogue

# Director's Foreword

The 'artistic personality' suggests someone who is not just creative, but also often dynamic, passionate and temperamental. In our culture, the artist is usually expected to be a genius and an individualist, apparently untroubled by day-to-day practicalities. So powerful is this archetype that it has dominated the popular perception of creative individuals for some two hundred years.

Of course, there were artists marked by their powerful individuality long before the dawn of the nineteenth century – one only has to think of that wilful genius Michelangelo or the notorious, murderous Caravaggio. However, as *Rebels and Martyrs* so vividly chronicles, only from the late eighteenth century did this archetype gain momentum. During a turbulent, volatile era in Europe, amid widespread disenchantment with the aspirations of Neoclassicism, artists deliberately started to adopt identities driven by essentially Romantic notions of the self and creativity. It was during the nineteenth century that there was a fundamental shift in how artists were perceived, a myth added to and embellished by critics, writers, patrons and popular opinion as well as by the artists themselves.

We are proud that the National Gallery has created the first major exhibition on this theme. Of course this has only been possible with the input and energy of staff here. We owe particular thanks to Alexander Sturgis, whose inspiration this exhibition has been, and to both him and Lois Oliver for all their work in nurturing, forming and curating the exhibition and writing much of the catalogue; but as well to Michael Wilson and Rupert Christiansen, both of whom have enhanced this publication with their expertise. We also would like to thank the following people for their contribution to the development of *Rebels and Martyrs* during its early stages: Ann Dumas, Tamar Garb, MaryAnne Stevens, Belinda Thomson, William Vaughan and Joanna Woodall.

We are indebted to all the lenders for agreeing to part with their works. It is because of their generosity that we are able to form such a distinguished display: Courbet's seminal *The Meeting* (Musée Fabre, Montpellier), Renoir's *The Inn of Mère Antony* (Nationalmuseum, Stockholm) and the works by Schiele, Gerstl and Modersohn-Becker have never been shown in Britain before. Brought together as well for the first time are three masterpieces by Delacroix that reflect on the burden of the solitary genius – the rarely seen *Tasso in the Hospital of St Anne* (Private Collection), *Michelangelo in his Studio* (Musée Fabre, Montpellier), with our own *Ovid among the Scythians*.

We are particularly grateful to the Corporate Members of the National Gallery, whose generous support has enabled us to put on this exhibition.

Charles Saumarez Smith

Director, The National Gallery, London

# Rebels and Martyrs

*Michael Wilson*

In May 1823 the young Eugène Delacroix noted in his Journal, 'fortify yourself against first impressions, maintain your *sang-froid* ... the mask is everything'.[1] In a letter of 1854, Gustave Courbet spoke of his 'laughing mask'.[2] The idea of the mask, of disguise or assumed identity, runs like a leitmotiv through the art of the nineteenth century: this was the period in which the myth of the artist as inspired rebel, battling against a hostile, philistine society, took hold of the popular imagination. As has long been demonstrated, legends of the artist as a melancholic outsider had distant origins, but it was only from the late eighteenth century that artists self-consciously adopted personas derived from this conception. Subsequently artists, writers and critics all helped to consolidate the image of the rebellious artist-hero, isolated and suffering in his genius, and there are few artists who failed to identify at some level with this mythic figure.

The exhibition which this book accompanies explores this myth as it is reflected in painting, in representations of artists – portraits and self portraits, pictures of studio interiors or gatherings of artists and their associates – and in imaginative works in which the painter projects a particular image of the creative artist. It looks at how artists deliberately cast themselves and their fellow artists as outsiders, bohemians, dandies, visionaries and martyrs, and how, in doing so, they contributed to profound shifts in attitudes towards the purpose of art and its role in society.

This myth of the artist, which gained such widespread currency during the Romantic era, has proved to be enduring. It found powerful expression in the lives and work of some of the most celebrated painters of the nineteenth century – Courbet, Van Gogh and Gauguin, for example, and later, Munch and the German Expressionists. The lifestyle of the painters of the New York School in the 1940s and 1950s was self-consciously bohemian, rebellious and high-risk, and their art heroic and revolutionary. The myth still colours the popular view of the artist, as an outsider removed from the concerns of ordinary people, living a life in defiance of convention.

Such a view of the artist is of course a distortion. It is only part of the story. As far as the realities of artistic life in the nineteenth century are concerned, it omits much of consequence. It is very little concerned with the business of art, the practicalities of making, promoting and selling pictures, which developed in new ways during the period. It prefers to focus on the heroic conflict with society and with academies, juries and governments, and on rejection, poverty and even failure, rather than on the success that rewarded the efforts of artists whose work conformed to what was required.

Women artists were also largely excluded from the myth, even though their number grew steadily during the nineteenth century, and many enjoyed successful careers. But convention dictated that they could not readily embrace the bohemianism or other extreme forms of identity of their male counterparts without placing themselves irrevocably beyond the pale of society. The women who inhabited the bohemian world of the artist were models, performers and prostitutes – the types who appear so frequently in the works of Degas and Toulouse-Lautrec. Such women were already excluded from respectable society and their role was to provide inspiration and satisfaction to the male artist (who had the advantage of a far higher degree of social mobility). The painter Suzanne Valadon was a rare exception, who managed to negotiate the prevailing myths about artistic creativity and present herself as a bohemian artist. The illegitimate daughter of a labourer, she became an artist's model in Montmartre and learned to paint from those for whom she posed – among them Renoir and Toulouse-Lautrec. Her self portrait of 1923, *The Blue Room* (fig. 1), is an ironic reworking of the odalisque theme and in particular Manet's *Olympia* (1863; Musée d'Orsay, Paris). She shows herself smoking a cigarette and wearing trousers – defiant, unglamorous and bohemian. But by the 1920s mores were changing and it was becoming increasingly possible for women to challenge conventional behaviour and embrace the myth of the artist.

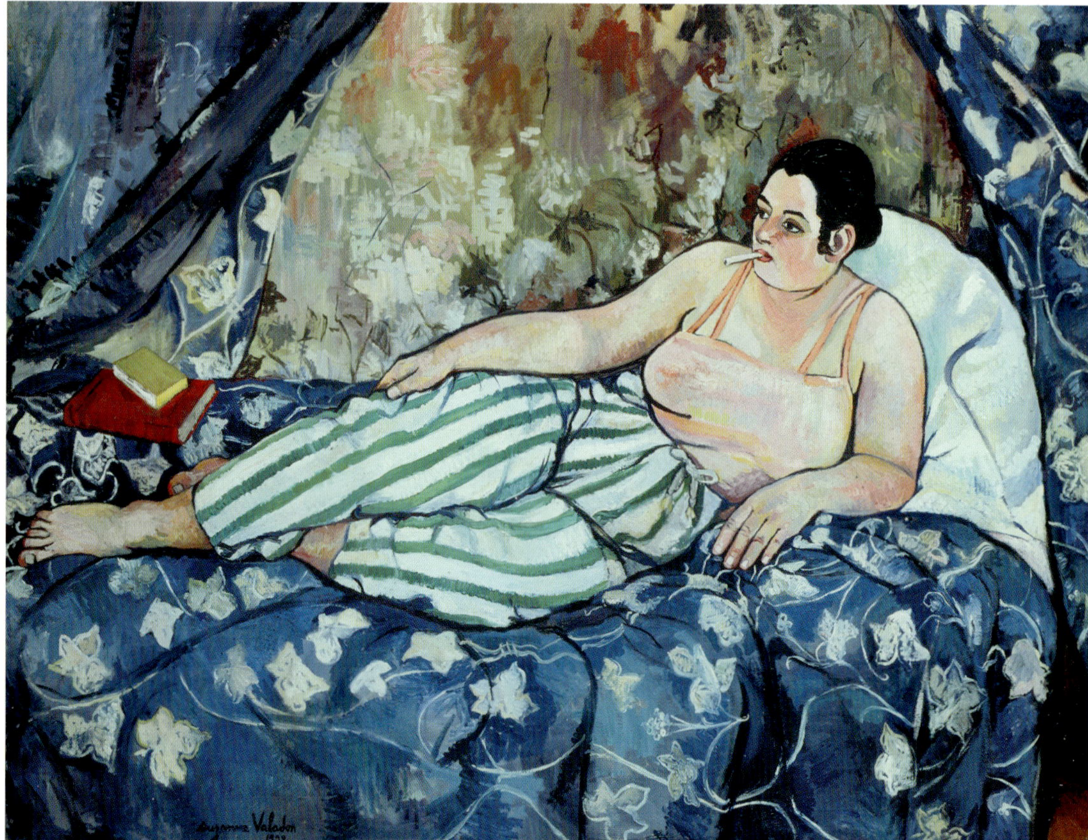


Fig. 1.
Suzanne Valadon
*The Blue Room*, 1923
Oil on canvas, 90 × 116 cm
Centre Georges Pompidou, Musée national d'art moderne/Centre de création industrielle, Paris (LUX.1506P)

The redefinition of the artist that forms the subject of this exhibition was the consequence of new attitudes to art and life that emerged in the last decades of the eighteenth century, to the movement in thought and the arts which came to be known as Romanticism. The question of the status of the artist had been a matter of debate at least since the sixteenth century. Giorgio Vasari in his *Lives of the Artists* (1550) had articulated ideas about artistic genius and claimed for such major painters of his own time, such as Michelangelo, the distinction of the great poets and artists of antiquity. But the reality for most painters in most countries was that they were regarded as little more than skilled artisans. In his *Dictionary* of 1755, Dr Johnson defined the artist as 'the professor of an art, generally an art manual … a skilful man, not a novice'.[3] They were employed by the church, the state and wealthy private patrons to meet a range of specific demands – for portraits, altarpieces, allegories, decorations and furniture pictures. To pursue one's own inspiration in this context would have seemed folly. There were, of course, exceptions. Among the legions of working artists, there were inevitably some who indulged in rebellious and excessive behaviour. Caravaggio's notoriety is due to his violent and unruly career, and because he embodies to a modern audience the Romantic notion of the artistic outlaw. But in the seventeenth century such behaviour was deemed aberrant, not a sign of exceptional gifts.

Certain artists achieved great distinction in the service of kings. Velázquez, Rubens and Van Dyck were all ennobled and decorated for their services and achieved the position of gentlemen. The establishment of academies was also intended to raise the status of the artist, by providing a training based on the study of the great masters of the past and by advocating an elevated, idealising style. Sir Joshua Reynolds, first President of the Royal Academy in London, preached this message to his students in his *Discourses* and himself adopted a grand style for his portraits of the aristocracy. In his own *Self Portrait* of 1780 (cat. 1) he poses, hand on hip, in the gown of a Doctor of Civil Law, with a bust of Michelangelo behind. The rich colouring and deep shadows recall the Venetians and Rembrandt, while the beret is another allusion to the Dutch artist. The message could not be clearer. This is an artist of distinction in the long line of great masters, pursuing a calling of high seriousness.

How different in every respect is Victor Emil Janssen's *Self Portrait* of about 1828 (cat. 12). It is an intimate and private work – painted on paper – and remained in the artist's possession until his death. Janssen shows himself in a plain bedroom, stripped to the waist, at work on the painting we see. He scrutinises himself with a merciless eye, literally laying himself bare in a manner inconceivable to the previous generation. Far from idealising himself, he presents the sunken chest and rounded back of a sick man. The frail body and fixed expression are those of a secular martyr. The same haunting look appears in the *Self Portrait* of the young Samuel Palmer of about 1824–5 (fig. 2). There is a touching openness in the way he gazes out, a youthful innocence, and at the same time an alertness that hints at the visionary intensity

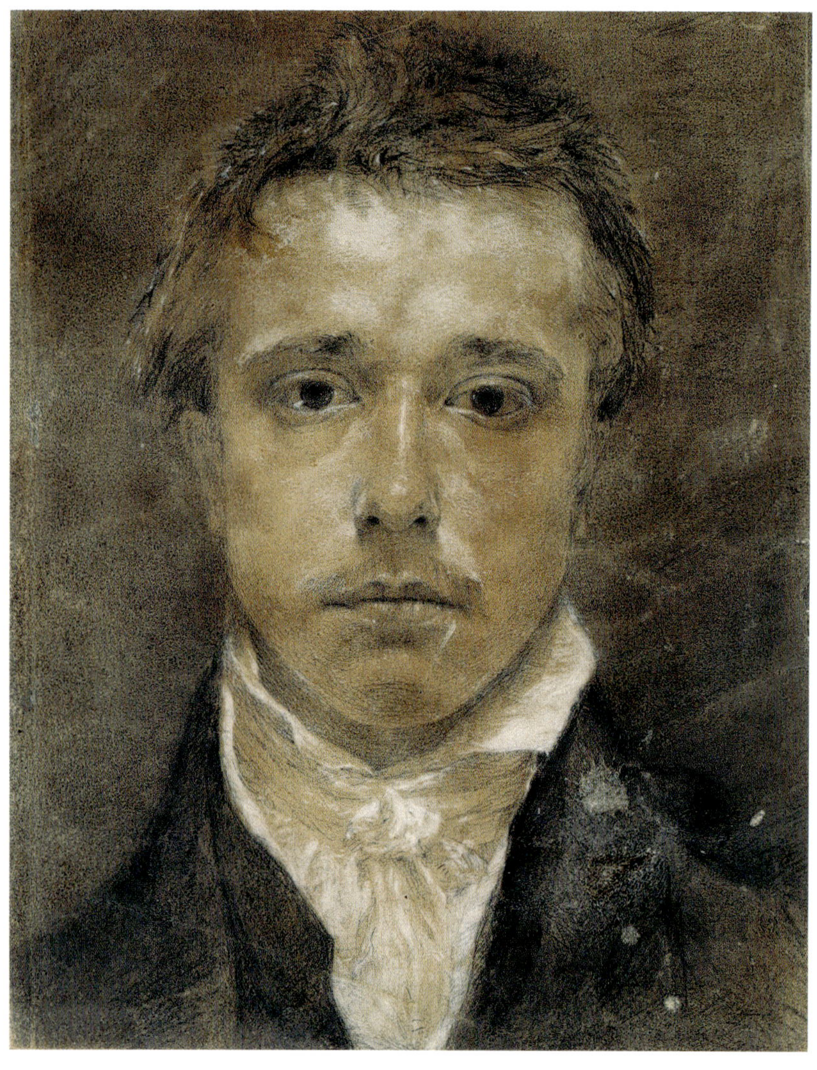

Fig. 2
Samuel Palmer
*Self Portrait*, about 1824–5
Chalk drawing, 29 × 25 cm
The Ashmolean Museum, Oxford (WA1932.211)

with which he came to interpret the natural world. The flicker of black and white chalk on his face and hair is an index of the life within. As William Vaughan has observed, he seems to embody the poet Keats's 'negative capability', 'when man is capable of being in uncertainties, mysteries, doubts, without any irritable reaching after fact and reason'.[4] Palmer, like other Romantic artists, was driven by a sense of his vocation and a need to express a unique vision, independent of tradition and the demands of patrons.

Within a period of a generation, the definition of an artist was transformed – for all time. The notion of genius, enthusiastically adopted by Reynolds and others to give prestige to their art, provided the first step towards elevating the artist above society and its rules. For the Romantic artist subjectivity and introspection replaced the concept of an external ideal of beauty, *le beau idéal*. What counted above all was the artist's sincerity, the authenticity of the emotions expressed. Consequently the artist evolved into an alienated figure, misunderstood and neglected by the world.

What were the causes of this momentous shift? The redefinition of the artist was a part and a consequence of the emergence of Romanticism in the arts, and the causes of this are complex and many. But two factors stand out as paramount: the reaction of philosophers and writers to what they saw as the excessive rationalism and false optimism of Enlightenment thinkers, and the events of the French Revolution and the European wars that followed in its wake. The philosophical reaction to the Enlightenment arose first in Germany. Inspired by the ideas of Kant and Herder, philosophers and writers such as the Schlegel brothers, Schelling and Novalis challenged the eighteenth century's belief in a rationally ordered universe and in the perfectibility of man and society through knowledge and scientific progress. Above all, the religious scepticism of the eighteenth century had left a spiritual void which was now filled by a belief that the mystery of existence could not be comprehended through reason but only grasped by each individual emotionally through the imagination and intuition. Such ideas find early expression in the work of the German painter Caspar David Friedrich, who combined intense religious belief with a yearning melancholy and mysticism. He led a solitary existence, withdrawn from society, and evolved a form of symbolic landscape painting to express his personal search for the divine in nature. His *The Wanderer above the Mists* (fig. 3) shows a frock-coated figure, the artist but also the searcher, perched on a rocky peak, surveying a wild and indeterminate mountain landscape submerged in swirling mists. This image of the solitary pilgrim, conquering the earthly summit and reaching up to what lies beyond, was to haunt the German imagination for decades.

German ideas spread to England where they were embraced by the Lake poets, particularly Coleridge, and to France, largely through the agency of the French-Swiss writer Madame de Staël. But it is unlikely that they would have had such impact without the impetus of the French Revolution. Initially, the overthrow of the monarchy and the liberation of the people were greeted by many with enthusiasm. But the political and social convulsions that followed the events of 1789 confirmed the demise of Enlightenment optimism and filled most of Europe with horror and uncertainty. The time-hallowed institutions of church and state were seen to be fragile and ephemeral, the forces of barbarism and irrationality rampant. Yet in France the rise of Napoleon and the success of the French campaigns gave rise to a new euphoria. The nation and its artists were thrilled by the reports of heroic actions and youthful self-sacrifice. Jacques-Louis David, a painter who participated in the Revolution, has left us a remarkable self portrait from this period (fig. 4), made after the fall of Robespierre when he himself was imprisoned and expected to die. It could be said to fall on the cusp of Classic and Romantic. Properly dressed, seated and holding his palette, he has the typical look of an eighteenth-century artist. But the brushwork is agitated and thin, as in David's other Revolutionary portraits, and the gaze is intense and searching. He does not flatter himself: the growth in his mouth that afflicted him is visible in the bulging right cheek.

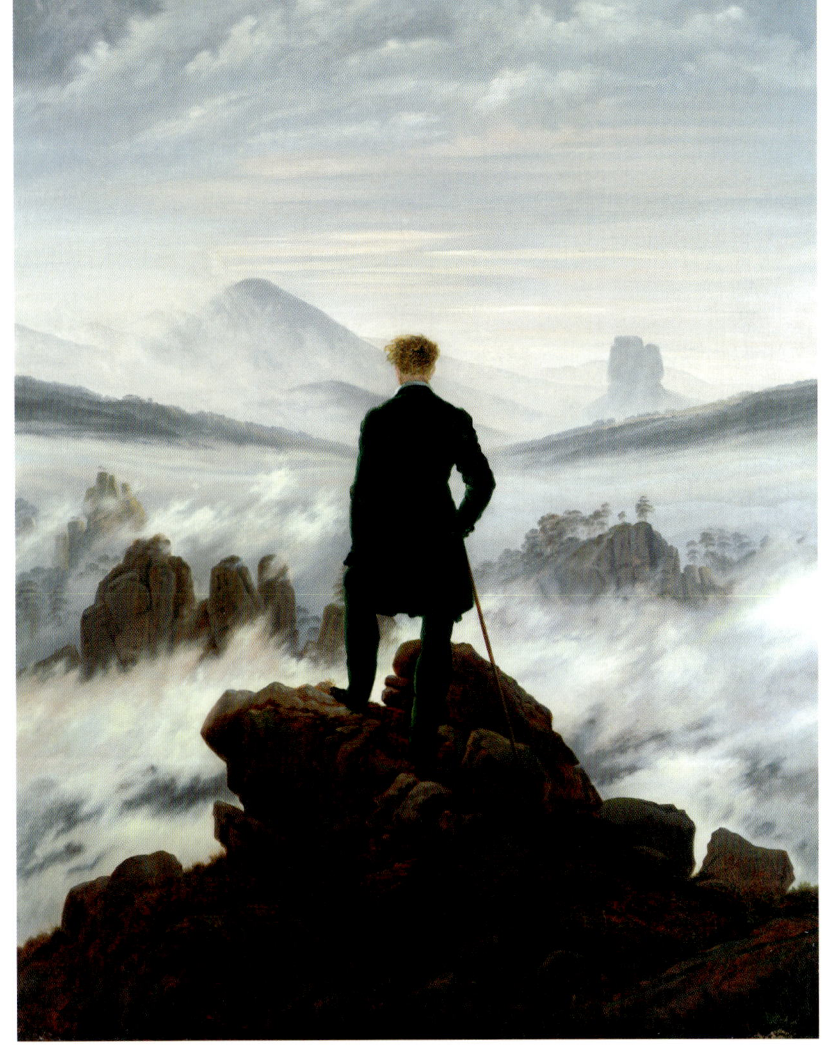

Fig. 3
Caspar David Friedrich
*The Wanderer above the Mists*, about 1817–18
Oil on canvas, 94.8 × 74.8 cm
Kunsthalle, Hamburg (5161)

This is the portrait of a man who is living in the moment, caught up in actual events, no longer intent on establishing a pedigree in the line of tradition.

The defeat of Napoleon in 1815 abruptly terminated the glorious French adventure and gave rise to the *mal du siècle*, the frustration and disillusionment which characterise mature Romanticism. It was felt most acutely by those young men – poets Alfred de Musset and Alfred de Vigny, painters Théodore Géricault and Eugène Delacroix – who had grown up witnessing the heroism of the imperial campaigns only to find that for them the opportunity for heroic action was denied. 'The events I sought were never as great as I needed them to be',[5] lamented Vigny. 'In their heads', Musset wrote, 'they had an entire world; they looked at the earth, the sky, the streets and the pathways, and everything was empty.'[6] The restoration of the Bourbon monarchy, the return of the clergy, and the pretence that the Empire had never been, filled these writers and artists with a profound sense of loss. In 1812 Géricault exhibited a painting of an officer of the Imperial Guard (Musée du Louvre, Paris), sabre in hand, seated on a rearing charger. Vigorously and freely painted, it presents an image of flamboyant and fearless masculinity. Two years later he showed the *Wounded Cuirassier* (1814; Musée du Louvre, Paris). It is an epic portrayal of a defeated soldier leaving the battlefield. Beneath a leaden sky, he restrains his panicked horse and looks back with apprehension. It sounds the note of disillusionment that was to characterise the century.

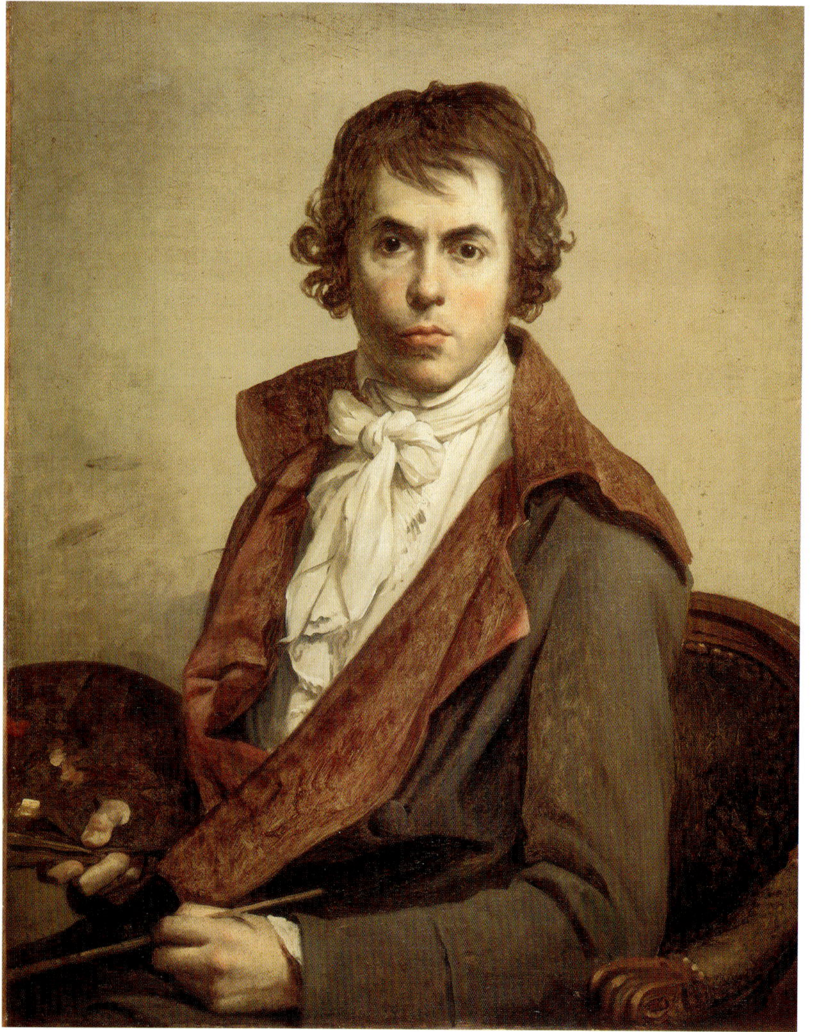

Fig. 4
Jacques-Louis David
*Self Portrait*, 1794
Oil on canvas, 80.5 × 64.1 cm
Musée du Louvre, Paris
(RF 3705)

Especially in France, artists became fixated with the spectacle of defeat and with the image of the victim. Géricault's masterpiece, *The Raft of the 'Medusa'* (1819; Musée du Louvre, Paris), represents on a monumental scale the sufferings of the hopeless survivors of a shipwreck. Delacroix's *Massacre at Chios* (1824; Musée du Louvre, Paris) shows the languid victims of violence without any hint of a consoling message. The same mood can be detected outside France, too. Goya's *Third of May 1808* (1814; Museo del Prado, Madrid) is another massacre of innocents conducted in profound gloom, and a disenchanted commentary on the heroism of David's *Oath of the Horatii* (1784; Musée du Louvre, Paris). The same strain of melancholy permeates Caspar David Friedrich's cool and inhospitable landscapes.

Without the spectacle of heroic events, or the chance to participate in them, artists turned to history and to literature for their subjects, especially the medieval romances of Walter Scott and Byron. Denied the glory of conquerors, they sought glory in the pursuit of their art and greatness as artists. They considered themselves an elite, in Stendhal's words, 'the happy few' or the 'little church of the elect'. While he was working on the *Massacre at Chios*, Delacroix noted in his Journal, 'glory is not a vain word for me'.[7] The attention of the artist is redirected inwards: his inner life – his aspirations, struggles and suffering – becomes his real subject. And painters like Géricault, writers like Stendhal and Balzac, engage with their creation with the frenzy and recklessness of the soldier. 'I live as though on a battlefield',[8] Balzac memorably said. Across the arts – literature, painting and music – autobiography takes on vital importance. The trend is initiated in the eighteenth century with Rousseau's *Confessions* (about 1762; published 1782), and gains momentum with Chateaubriand's *René* (1802), De Quincey's *Confessions of an English Opium Eater* (1821) and Musset's *La Confession d'un enfant du siècle* (1836). Berlioz's *Symphonie Fantastique* (1830) and its sequel, *Lelio* (1831) are described as episodes from the life of the artist and treat his infatuation with Shakespeare and with the English actress Harriet Smithson. Delacroix attempts to dissemble by choosing subjects for his paintings from literature, history and the Bible, but his heroes are his alter egos and the scenarios he depicts driven by personal imperatives. There is no such evasion in the paintings of Courbet, Van Gogh, Gauguin and Munch where the subjects are more often than not drawn directly from the artist's own life.

Indicative of this new fixation on the artist's life and the cult of greatness is the proliferation in the early decades of the nineteenth century of paintings of scenes from the lives of great artists of the past, particularly episodes where power defers to genius. Thus we see Charles V stooping to pick up Titian's paintbrush,[9] and, in Ingres's painting of 1818, Francis I embracing Leonardo on his deathbed (cat. 13). It is also the century of artists' pantheons, from Paul Delaroche's hemicycle in the Ecole des Beaux-Arts in Paris to the Albert Memorial in London. The notion of the specialness of the artist that is cultivated in the nineteenth century (and goes well beyond the status claimed by Reynolds) is projected back on artists of former centuries in order to validate it. In his *Apotheosis of Homer* (fig. 5) of 1827, Ingres shows Homer as the fount of all artistic endeavour surrounded by the great writers, composers and artists of all ages, among them Raphael, Dante, Shakespeare, Poussin, Racine, Molière and Gluck. It is a highly personal and eclectic pantheon. Vigny understood it in Romantic terms as a devotional image for the cult of genius, presenting 'an almost unbroken chain of glorious exiles, of courageous victims of persecution, of thinkers crazed with misery'.[10]

The Romantic genius is usually presented alone, because isolation is part of his condition, a consequence of his introspective tendencies and of his elevation above the ordinary run of mankind, since the Romantic artist was pursuing a higher calling, often in defiance of family and relations, not just a trade or profession. Kersting depicts Friedrich in a bare, cell-like room lit by a single window, contemplating the canvas he is painting (cat. 9). Shut off from the material world, the room is a metaphor for the inner life, and the act of painting the expression of an inner, spiritual vision.

Landscape painting in particular became a vehicle for the expression of a quasi-mystical response to nature, a personal communing with the divine as manifested in God's creation. Initially for English and German poets and painters, and thereafter in France, nature worship filled a void left by the erosion of conventional religion. It has its roots in the Northern Protestant tradition, especially in the nature-mysticism of Jakob Boehme, and places emphasis on the individual's personal experience, unmediated by priest or dogma. A deeply religious man himself, Friedrich pictures his solitary wanderers in such communion with nature (fig. 3). William Blake was one of the first in England to be influenced by this German nature mysticism, and he was soon followed by the Lake poets, especially Wordsworth, who described his 'spots of time' before nature. Samuel Palmer's visionary landscapes painted in the late 1820s are the pictorial equivalent. Above all through the influence of Constable, the gospel of direct

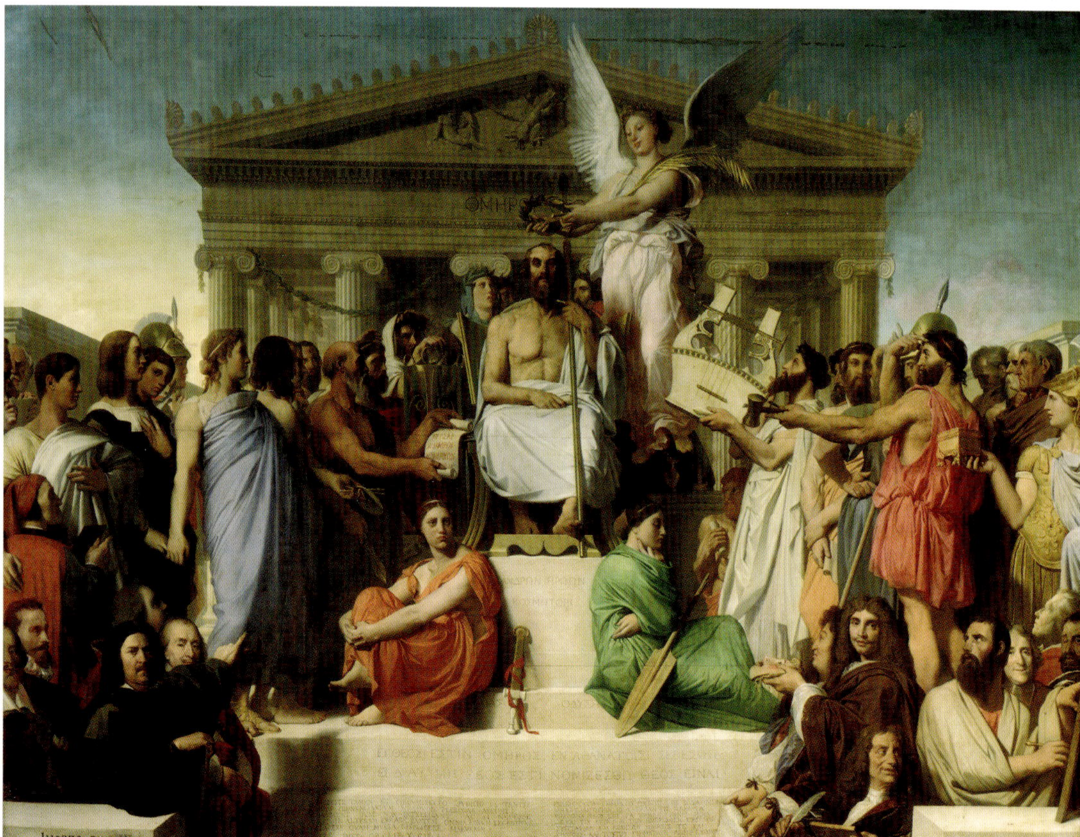

Fig. 5
Jean-Auguste-Dominique Ingres
*The Apotheosis of Homer*, 1827
Oil on canvas, 386 × 512 cm
Musée du Louvre, Paris
(RF 5417)

communion with nature reached France, informing the work of the Barbizon painters, in particular Rousseau and Millet, and through them Van Gogh, who although active in France, had profoundly northern roots. His father was the parson of the parish where he was born in North Brabant and he too trained and worked as a preacher before deciding to be a painter.

The inspiration and vision without which art is lifeless were thought to be most acute in the young. Wordsworth's most intense experiences of nature date from his boyhood, alone among the mountains and lakes. The appreciation of the natural instincts of children has its roots in Rousseau, but the Romantics gave it new emphasis. The child was uncorrupted by society and convention, closer to the mysterious origins of creation. 'Children are what we were', wrote Schiller, 'they are what we should again become.'[11] Consequently a type of painting emerges which stresses the innate genius of the young artist, in whom vision is undimmed. Pierre Henri Révoil is one of many to depict the discovery by Cimabue of the child Giotto drawing his flock – a tale told by Vasari (cat. 14). Arthur Hughes depicts himself as a young poet in rapt communion with nature (cat. 16). The greatest misfortune was to outlive one's inspiration. While Keats, Shelley and Byron all died young, at the peak of their powers, Wordsworth lived into respectable and unexceptional old age. Samuel Palmer could not sustain the visionary intensity by which he transformed the Kent landscape into a primitive Eden, and resorted in later life to a conventional naturalism. The myth of the child genius dying young and neglected is most famously embodied by Thomas Chatterton, immortalised by Wordsworth as 'the marvellous boy, The sleepless soul, that perished in his pride'.[12] A boy poet who wrote a number of poems which purported to be the work of a fifteenth-century monk, Chatterton poisoned himself in 1770 at the age of seventeen in poverty and despair. Henry Wallis shows him in his London garret, elegantly supine and marble-white in death (cat. 21).

Chatterton points to another feature of the Romantic myth: the artist is solitary not only by virtue of the focus on his inner life, but because he is neglected and rejected by the world. This was the period when the term 'philistine' was coined, first in Germany and then in England, to describe the indifference and hostility of those outside the charmed circle of artists, whom Matthew Arnold later called 'the children of light'. Many artists believed they were opposed by a society entirely out of sympathy with their ideals and aspirations, and that they were thus doomed to failure. It is this which underlies the malaise, the *mal du siècle*, which characterises the brooding, melancholic artist. It is nowhere better exemplified than in the portrait of a young artist in his studio formerly attributed to Géricault (fig. 6). With his sensitive features and languid pose, he exudes a nervous lassitude, an air of youthful enthusiasm stifled by an awareness of the futility of endeavour. The alienation and suffering felt by artists was well described by the poet Heinrich Heine: 'when they are not sufferers for the human race, they suffer for their own greatness, for the grand manner of their being, for their hatred of philistinism, for the discomfort they feel among the pretentious commonplaces, the mean trivialities of their surroundings ....'[13]

The emergence of a new and powerful middle class of merchants and entrepreneurs radically affected the demand for art and was viewed with suspicion and dismay by many artists. The traditional patronage of the wealthy aristocracy and the institutions of church and state increasingly gave way to new buyers and new ways of selling. Exhibitions became an important means of promoting work and the picture dealer emerged as a major means of selling. In consequence, artists were freer than ever before to determine their own subjects, but a split occurred between artist and purchaser which widened as the century progressed. And market forces still determined what would sell, so that types of painting that appealed to popular taste more readily found purchasers. In this lies the origin of the division between progressive avant-garde art, by definition beyond the comprehension of the multitude, and art that caters to the market. The term 'vulgarity' was coined by Madame de Staël to describe the debased tastes of the newly enriched class. In a lithograph of 1846 (fig. 7) Honoré Daumier satirises such attitudes in the person of a bourgeois picture-buyer who decides a painting will not do for him, because it is half a cane too narrow. Artists who stooped to appeal to popular tastes were castigated by their more high-minded fellows. Another important factor in this situation was the emergence of the professional art critic who assumed ever-increasing influence over the fate of artists. Although some, like Baudelaire, Zola and Huysmans, championed the new, critics generally greeted new departures in painting with scepticism if not derision, and reinforced public prejudice and the sense of alienation felt by artists.

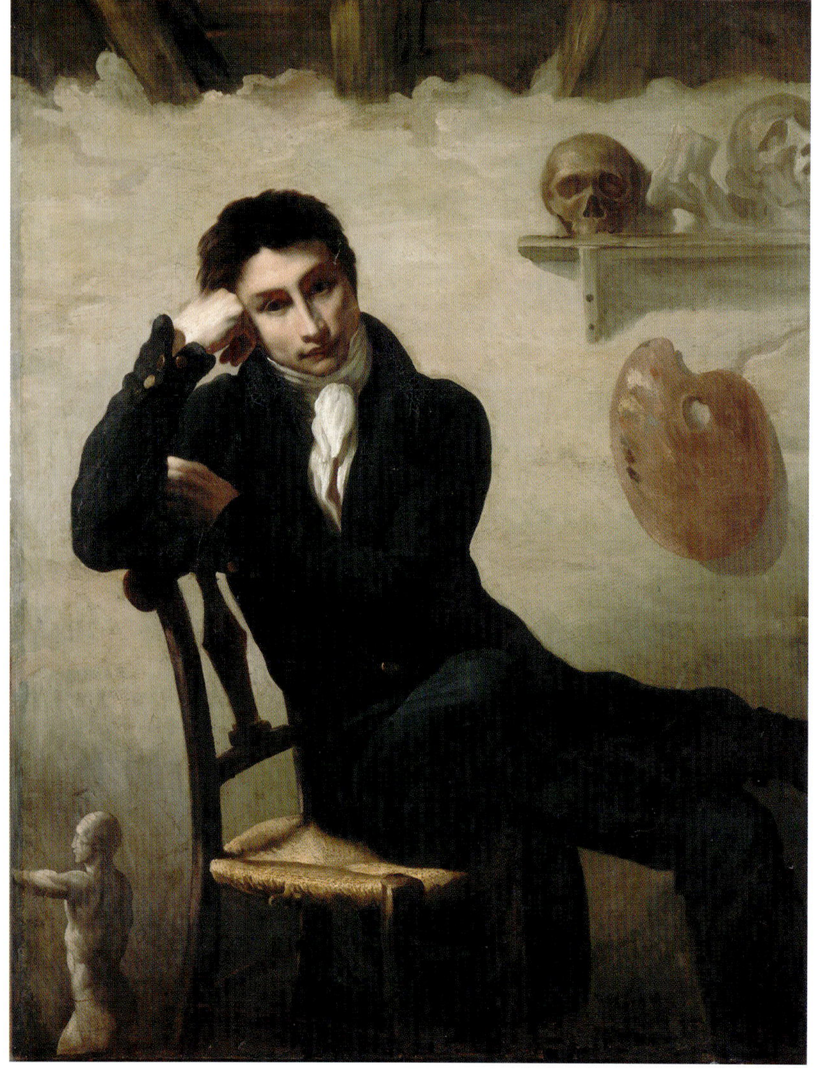

Fig. 6
Formerly attributed to Théodore Géricault
*Portrait of a Young Man in an Artist's Studio*, about 1818–19
Oil on canvas,
146.7 × 101.4 cm
Musée du Louvre, Paris
(RF 1225)

The artist who most clearly exemplifies the Romantic artist's conviction of his superiority and his suffering is Eugène Delacroix. His early career was marked by precocious achievements, violent and turbulent paintings which contravened accepted practice and earned him the reputation of a rebel. In an attempt to mollify his critics and win official approval, he consciously tempered his art, adopting more conventional subject matter while still developing a highly personal form of expression. As he grew older he retreated from society, adopting the pose of the dandy, aristocratic and imperturbable, to distance himself from his critics and from the vulgar crowd – 'a volcanic crater artistically concealed behind bouquets of flowers',[14] as Baudelaire memorably described him. He dismissed notions of social progress through science and found modern city life threatening. To suffer rejection and misunderstanding, as he insists in his essays on Michelangelo, Puget, Poussin and Prud'hon, is part of the burden of genius. 'Not only is the greatest by virtue of his talent, audacity and constancy the most persecuted; he is also exhausted and tormented by the burden of talent and imagination.'[15] But he finds consolation in his superiority and takes solace in his art. 'Who', asks Baudelaire 'has ever had a greater love for his ivory tower?'[16] These attitudes can be seen to determine Delacroix's choice of subjects. In 1830 he wrote an article celebrating Michelangelo as a misunderstood genius, and in 1850 he painted him solitary and brooding in his studio (cat. 18). Nine years later he painted Ovid exiled to the shores of the Black Sea, surrounded by uncomprehending barbarians (cat. 19). The supine figure of the poet bows his head in grief, a poignant image of the isolation and neglect that Delacroix believed was his lot.

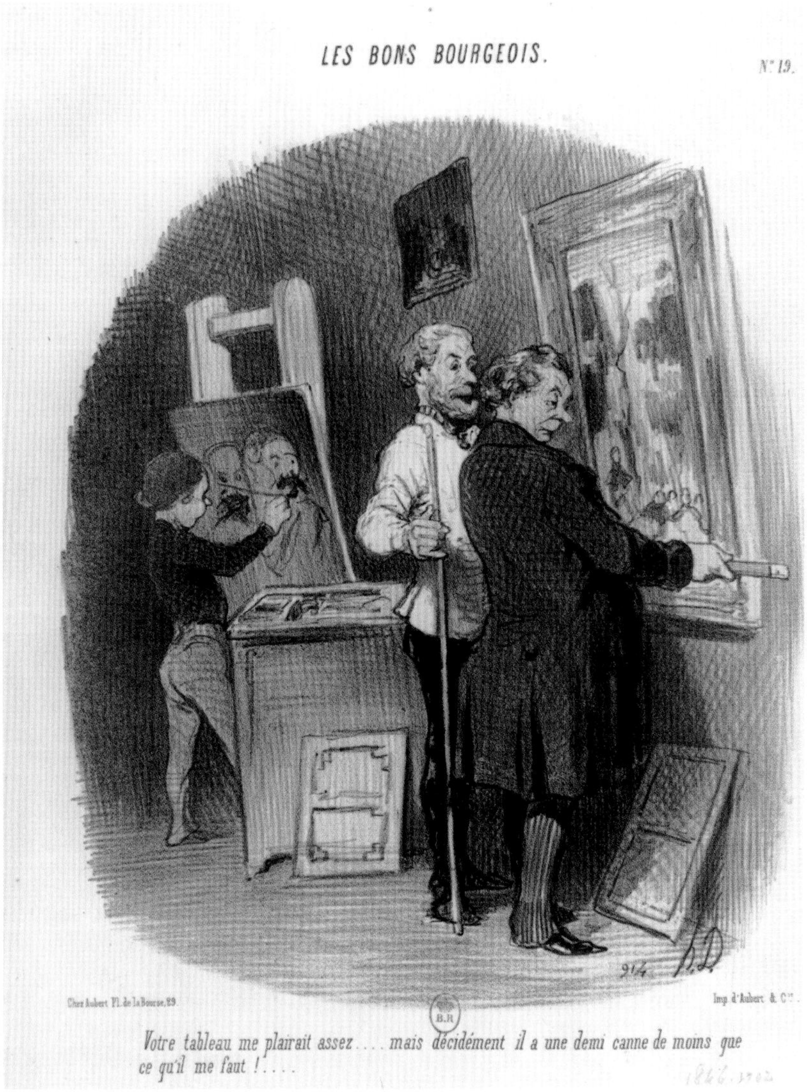

Fig. 7
Honoré-Victorin Daumier
*The painting would do if it were a little wider…*
No. 19 of *Les bons bourgeois*, from *Le Charivari*, 2 October 1846
Bibliothèque Nationale de France, Paris

In reality, most artists were not condemned to solitude. They turned to each other for companionship and confirmation of their ideals. There have always been communities of artists, based usually on guilds and studios, but until the nineteenth century these were primarily practical in purpose, devoted to the business of art. During the nineteenth century groupings of artists proliferated, inspired by shared aims. Among the earliest were the Barbus, a breakaway faction in David's Paris studio who adopted eccentric dress and, as their name suggests, beards; the Lukasbund or Brotherhood of Saint Luke, founded in Vienna, who became known as the Nazarenes after their move to Rome; and the Ancients, the Shoreham group of which Samuel Palmer was a member. Among the best known are the Pre-Raphaelites, the Barbizon painters, the Impressionists, the Pont-Aven group and the Nabis. Some of them, notably the Nazarenes and the Pre-Raphaelites, wanted to reform art by going back to the example of artists of the Renaissance and earlier, before the decadence associated with academies crept in. Others hoped to do so by immersing themselves in unspoilt nature. They were united not just by common aims, but by rejection and by the hostility shown to them by public and critics. It was as a result of his rejection by the Salon Jury and his appearance in the Salon des Refusés in 1863 that Edouard Manet emerged as a leader. The group that gathered round him in the late 1860s, consisting of the young Impressionists and the novelist and critic Emile Zola, is commemorated in Fantin-Latour's group portrait *A Studio in the Batignolles Quarter* (fig. 8). Manet is shown painting the portrait of his friend, the poet and critic Zacharie Astruc, with the others looking on respectfully. They have a solemn air in their dark jackets, in part the result of Fantin's somewhat ponderous brand of realism, but also a reflection of the high seriousness of their undertaking.

The person of the rebellious artist opposed to bourgeois culture and living on the edge of society is best characterised by the bohemian, as famously celebrated in Henri Murger's *Scenes of Bohemian Life* (*Scènes de la vie de Bohème*), a collection of stories revolving round the lives of a small band of writers, painters and musicians, which appeared in instalments from 1845 before being published in book form in 1851. They became hugely popular, were adapted for the stage and became the inspiration for Puccini's opera *La Bohème*. The term 'bohemian' (from the French for gypsy) seems first to have been used to describe an artistic community by the playwright Félix Pyat in 1834, who wrote, 'the ordinary mania of young artists to wish to live outside their time, with other ideas and other customs, isolates them from the world, renders them strange and bizarre, puts them outside the law, banished from society; these are today's Bohemians.'[17] During the 1830s and 1840s this bohemian community became firmly established in Paris. It was centred on the cafés which were the favoured meeting places for artists where art and politics were hotly debated – notably the Brasserie des Martyrs and the Andler Keller where Courbet held forth, the Café Guerbois favoured by Manet in the 1860s, and later the Café Tortoni and the Café de la Nouvelle Athènes.

Fig. 8
Ignace-Henri-Théodore Fantin-Latour
*A Studio in the Batignolles Quarter*, 1870
Oil on canvas, 174 × 208.3 cm
Musée d'Orsay, Paris (RF 729)

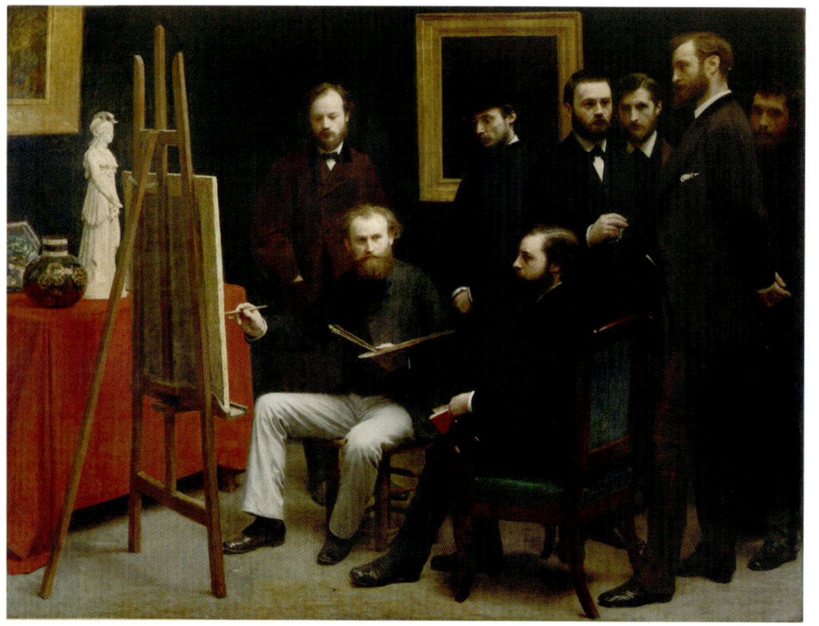

The artist who above all others came to represent the defiant and independent bohemian was Gustave Courbet, confronting the bourgeois with painting which was considered ugly and subversive. In a letter of 1850 he claimed:

> in our oh-so-civilised society it is necessary for me to lead the life of a savage … I must free myself even from governments. My sympathies are with the people, I must speak to them directly, take my science from them and they must provide me with a living. To do that I have just embarked on the great, independent, vagabond life of the Bohemian.[18]

Loudly championing Realism in painting and radicalism in politics, he attracted a group of eager followers. In his person he combined the beer-drinking, pipe-smoking bravado of the urban bohemian with the plain-spoken roughness of the country peasant, and his work celebrates the virtues of rural life. A great deal of it, however, is concerned above all else with his own image and his self-proclaimed independence. In a series of early self portraits he plays with a whole repertoire of identities – a man mad with fear, a desperate man, a wounded man, a lover, a Renaissance artist, and, in *Self Portrait, Man with a Pipe* (fig. 9), the self-assured bohemian. They culminate in the most flagrant statement of artistic independence. *The Meeting* (*'Bonjour Monsieur Courbet!'*) (cat. 29) of 1854 shows Courbet, staff in hand and splendidly bearded like a prophet, encountering his patron Alfred Bruyas and his servant on a country road. It is a secular reworking of Christ meeting his disciples on the road to Emmaus, with the crucial difference that Bruyas has no difficulty recognising the man before him for what he is, doffing his hat in acknowledgement of his greatness. In *The Studio* of 1854–5 (Musée d'Orsay; Paris) he went further. In what he called a 'real allegory', he placed himself at the centre of

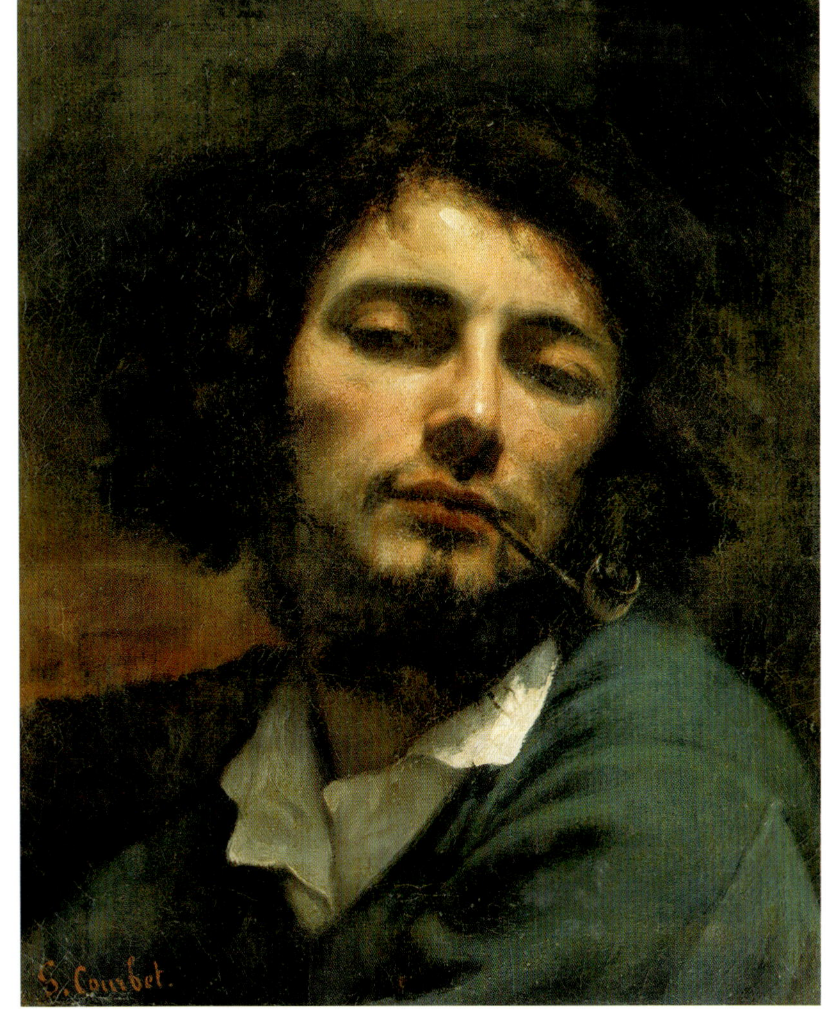


Fig. 9
Jean-Désiré-Gustave Courbet
*Self Portrait, Man with a Pipe*, 1848–9
Oil on canvas, 45 × 37 cm
Musée Fabre, Montpellier
(868.1.18)

a vast canvas, at work on a landscape and surrounded by figures of significance to him, some real, some symbolic, the whole edifice a celebration of his artistic and political principles.

Courbet set out to outrage the establishment, flouting decorum and making personal attacks on the Emperor. In 1855, after *The Studio* was excluded from the Exposition Universelle, Courbet set up his own independent exhibition in defiance of the jury. His friend and supporter novelist Jules Champfleury recognised that his posturing was detracting from his art and in 1863 warned him, 'There is a moral deviation in you which has reached as far as your paintbrush … All rancour should be stripped from your heart, because it acts on your hand, impairs all your faculties, weakens the character of your painting and prevents you from seeing things clearly'.[19] Fate eventually caught up with Courbet. Condemned for his part in the Paris Commune of 1871, he was imprisoned and subsequently driven into exile, where he died a broken man.

In his art and in his person, Courbet was an inspiration to younger artists, in particular to Manet and the Impressionists, who themselves set up their own independent exhibitions in defiance of the art establishment. The self-reliant, peasant-like persona he adopted, pipe in hand, also rubbed off, and became inseparable from the character of the bohemian. It underpins Camille Pissarro's portrait of his friend Paul Cézanne (cat. 34). Not only does Pissarro present Cézanne as a wild-eyed, heavily bearded, shabbily dressed rustic; he also includes above his shoulder a caricature of Courbet himself. However, no less important to the Impressionists and to Cézanne and Van Gogh were the landscape painters of the Barbizon group, especially Rousseau and Millet, who had settled in the Forest of Fontainebleau to immerse themselves in nature. They respected the simple piety of the peasant and were inspired in their painting by a sense of the holiness of rural life. Their chief disciple was Van Gogh, who referred to Millet as 'father Millet'. Like them he retreated to the

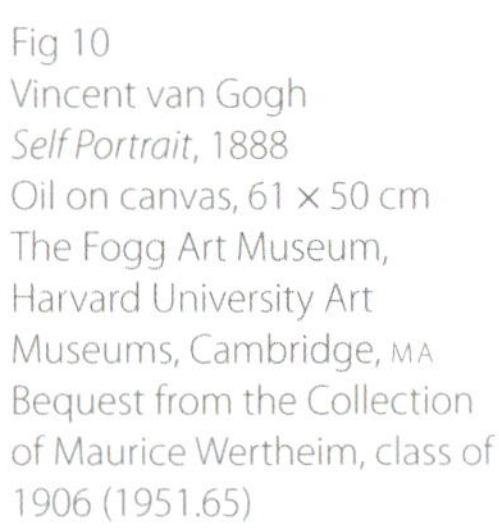

Fig 10
Vincent van Gogh
*Self Portrait*, 1888
Oil on canvas, 61 × 50 cm
The Fogg Art Museum, Harvard University Art Museums, Cambridge, MA
Bequest from the Collection of Maurice Wertheim, class of 1906 (1951.65)

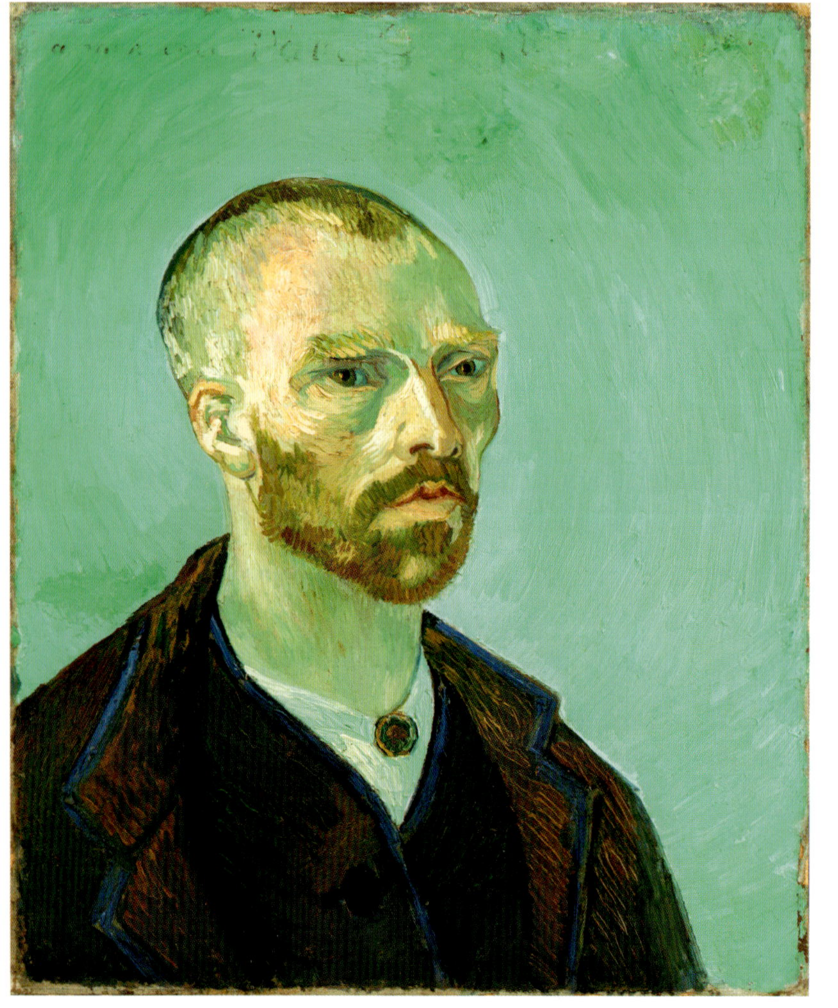

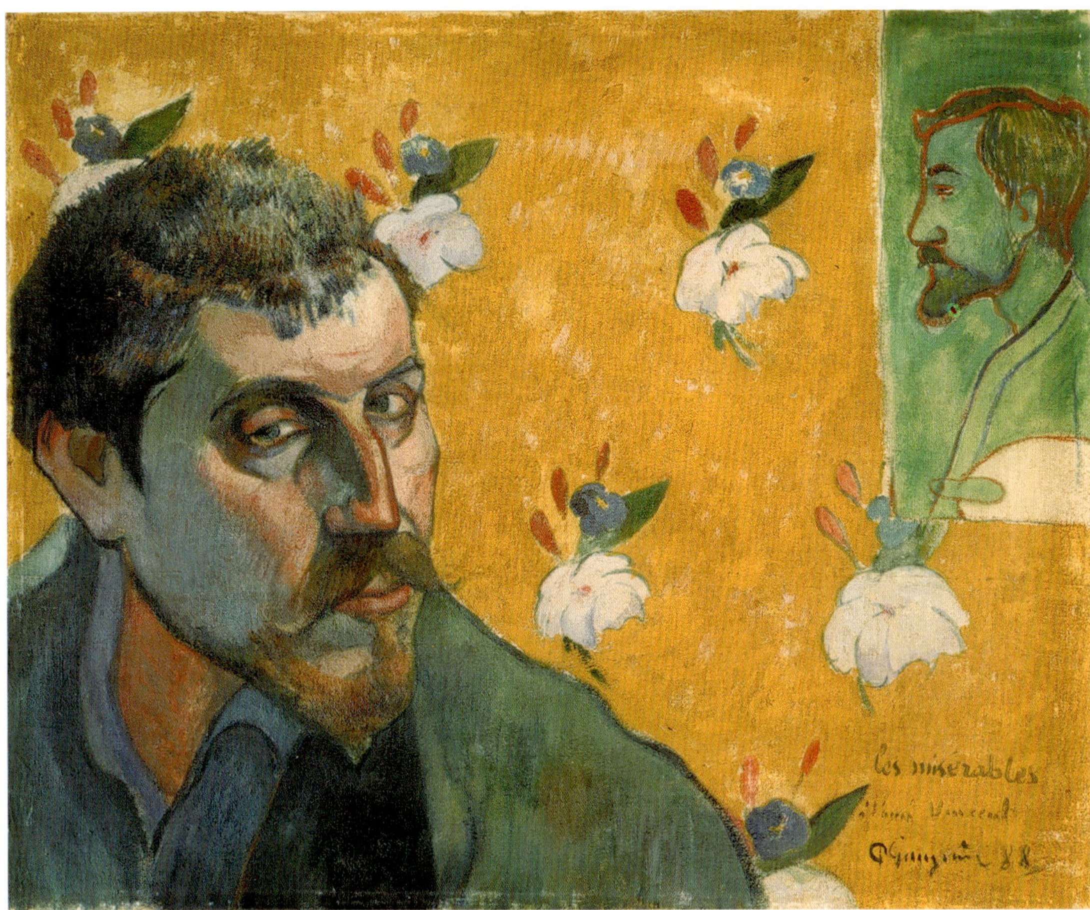


Fig. 11
Paul Gauguin
*Self Portrait with Portrait of Bernard (Les Misérables)*, 1888
Oil on canvas, 45 × 55 cm
Van Gogh Museum, Amsterdam (s 224 V/1962)

country – in his case Provence – and led the life of a peasant. His painting *Van Gogh's Chair* (The National Gallery, London) is in effect a self portrait, the rustic, rush-seated chair standing for himself, and the pipe the enduring symbol of bohemianism.

Van Gogh dreamed of establishing a community of like-minded artists at Arles – a 'Studio of the South' – and Paul Gauguin joined him there for nine ill-fated weeks at the end of 1888. Both of them hated Paris, hankering after an uncorrupted, rural innocence, and Gauguin had spent some months working with other painters at Pont Aven in Brittany. Even before Gauguin joined Van Gogh they had exchanged self portraits. Van Gogh sent him the painting of himself looking gaunt and shaven-headed, a hybrid of monk and convict, certainly an outcast (fig. 10). Gauguin sent the painting known from its inscription as *Les Misérables*, after Victor Hugo's epic novel (fig. 11), in which he emphasises his wild, prominent eyes and hooked nose. His great-grandfather was a Peruvian nobleman and Gauguin liked to boast of his Aztec blood. He described his portrait as 'the face of an outlaw' and asked, 'As for this Jean Valjean [Hugo's hero], whom society has oppressed, cast out – for all his love and vigour – is he not equally a symbol of the contemporary impressionist painter?'[20] Gauguin and Van Gogh, both passionate and wilful personalities, were fated to quarrel. While Van Gogh wanted to paint from nature, Gauguin wanted to work from imagination. They fought. Van Gogh attacked Gauguin and then cut off part of his own ear. They separated – Gauguin for Brittany and Van Gogh for the hospital in Arles and then an asylum at nearby St-Rémy.

The image of the artist as bohemian, the society of the café and the associated lifestyle of excessive drinking and free love proved to be remarkably enduring. Artistic bohemias cropped up in cities throughout Europe, notably in Munch's Christiana (modern-day Oslo), Picasso's Barcelona and Beckmann's Berlin. The Beat poets and abstract painters of the New York School of the 1940s and 1950s self-consciously referred to their Greenwich Village community as 'bohemian', in their assault on the stifling conventions and right-wing politics of American society.

In 1875 Edouard Manet presented the unmistakable image of the bohemian in his painting *The Artist*, a portrait of the painter and printmaker Marcellin Desboutin (cat. 35). The beard, the pipe ('the main tool of my trade', Desboutin quipped), the wide-brimmed hat and the nonchalant pose are trademark. The persona adopted by Manet himself, however, as shown in his portrait by Fantin-Latour of 1867 (cat. 40), could not have been more different. Immaculately and soberly dressed, this is the guise of the dandy. Dandified manners and dress were imported into post-Napoleonic France from England as part of a pervasive Anglomania, and after 1830 developed as a pose of political protest and defiance against the bourgeois monarchy of Louis-Philippe. An early instance in painting is Delacroix's portrait of Louis-Auguste Schwiter (fig. 12), himself a painter, in black evening dress before a brooding landscape. The dandy was famously defined by Baudelaire in his essay *The Painter of Modern Life*: a fastidious aristocrat, eschewing the vulgar and the trivial, who observes the flux of life around him with philosophical detachment. Dandyism is for Baudelaire a critical issue of identity, 'the burning need to create for oneself a personal originality, bounded only by the limits of the proprieties. It is a kind of cult of the self ...'[21] Like Degas, and like the Goncourt brothers, Manet ventured into modern Paris, observing and portraying life on the streets and in the café and the cabaret. In *Music in the Tuileries Gardens* (cat. 41), he includes himself and his friends, among them Baudelaire, each dressed in coat and top hat, mingling in the fashionable crowd. The uniform of the dress-coat and the frock-coat had for Baudelaire their own 'poetic beauty', which is an expression of the loss and disenchantment that lie at the heart of the *mal du siècle*: 'an expression of the public soul – an immense cortège of undertaker's mutes ... We are each of us celebrating some funeral.'[22]

Fig. 12
Ferdinand-Victor-Eugène Delacroix
*Louis-Auguste Schwiter*, 1826–7
Oil on canvas, 218 × 144 cm
The National Gallery, London, (NG 3286)

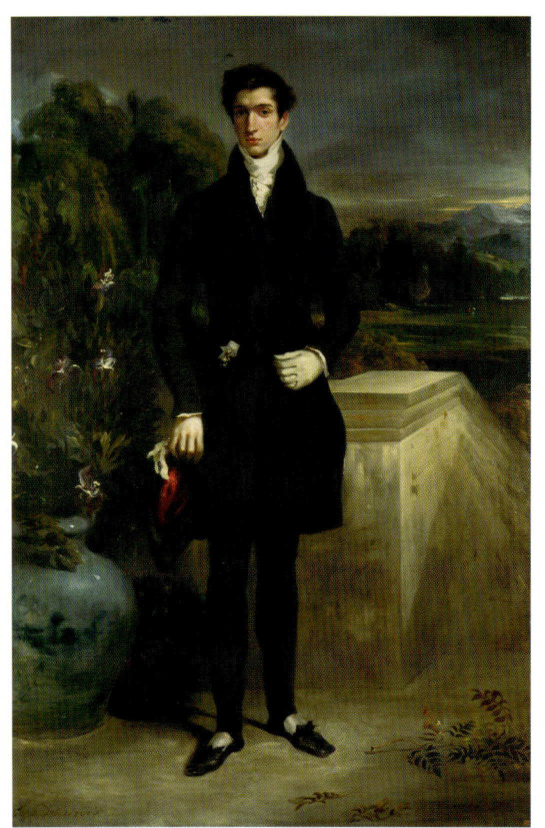

Baudelaire claimed that 'dandyism is the last spark of heroism amid decadence',[23] and it is significant that as the century progresses the dandified artist retreats increasingly into a world of art for art's sake. For Whistler, Beardsley and J.K. Huysmans, the author of the novel *A Rebours* (1884), art is a refuge from a vulgar and materialist society, the antithesis of progress, and true beauty resides in what is useless. The hero of *A Rebours* shuts himself away in a hermetic, artificial world, devoting himself to a life of aesthetic sensations, inspired chiefly by the Symbolist art and literature of the day. Distinguished by his exquisite taste, his refined sensibility and his immaculate dress, the aesthete of the late nineteenth century is a relic of a former, more elegant age, in denial of his time.

The rejection of the modern world was accompanied in the 1880s by a rejection of naturalism. The art of Courbet and the Impressionists came to be seen as a dead end, since it focused on appearances at the expense of the inner life, the eternal subject of the Romantic painter. The Impressionists themselves disbanded and experimented with new ways. Their younger associates – Van Gogh and Gauguin, along with Paul Sérusier, Emile Bernard and others – pursued an art that was non-realist and expressive of the artist's inner feeling. Like those early Romantics at the beginning of the century, painting was for them a sacred calling, the artist a seer or visionary.

In this respect, Delacroix again serves as a crucial link in the evolution of the myth of the artist. Although at the time of his death in 1863 his art seemed to be a closed chapter in French painting, overtaken by Realism, he was passionately revered by younger painters. Cézanne's violent and erotic early work is indebted to him, and Van Gogh continually refers to him in his letters with reverence. Gustave Moreau took his lead from him in his treatment of mythical and exotic subjects, and the young Odilon Redon admired his paintings at the Bordeaux museum. And in the lives and attitudes of these artists can be seen another aspect of the myth of the artist that first finds expression in the person of Delacroix: the idea of the artist as martyr to his art. In spite of the considerable success he enjoyed, Delacroix felt keenly the continued criticisms of his painting, refusing to exhibit at the Salon after 1859. Increasingly he focused on paintings of poets, saints and martyrs and of Christ himself, painted for the most part at his own instigation, emphasising their suffering and rejection by the

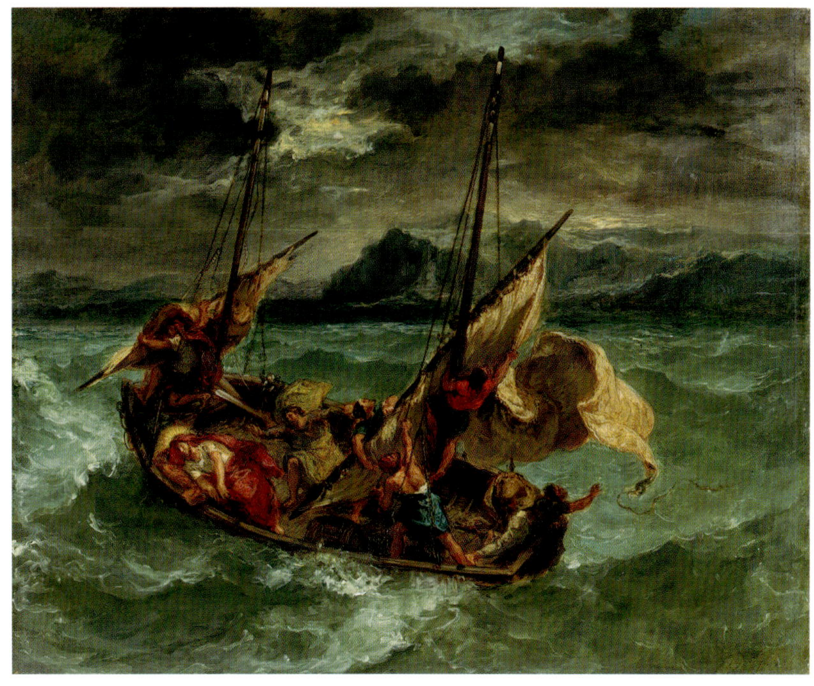

Fig. 13
Ferdinand-Victor-Eugène Delacroix
*Christ on the Sea of Galilee*, 1854
Oil on canvas, 59.8 × 73.3 cm
The Walters Art Gallery, Baltimore (37.186)

people. Baudelaire regarded Delacroix as the greatest religious painter of his day and recognised that his was a 'religion of universal anguish'.[24] An unbeliever himself, Delacroix adopted a stoic philosophy of resignation and indifference: 'Submission to the law of nature, resignation to human suffering, that is the final word of reason.'[25] He sought tranquillity as the ultimate goal. In *Christ on the Sea of Galilee* (fig. 13), a subject he treated repeatedly in his last years, the sleeping Christ is surrounded by turmoil, in the storm-tossed sea, the rippling sails and agitated disciples. He does not take control; eyes closed, he is steeped in oblivion. Likewise *Saint Stephen* (cat. 50), borne away by his distressed followers, is limp with defeat and exhaustion.

The idea of the painter as martyr – and as Christ surrogate – is picked up by Gauguin in his painting of himself as Christ in the *Agony in the Garden* (cat. 51). This subject held a special fascination for the Romantics. It is the subject of a poem by Alfred de Vigny and of works by Blake, Goya and Delacroix. The moment of Christ's inner trial, of his faltering at the prospect of his fate, encapsulated the doubt and pain they felt as artists, confronted, as they saw it, by a hostile world. With extraordinary conceit Gauguin gives Christ his own unmistakable features, casting himself as the rejected saviour. He saw himself as the leader of a new vanguard in painting and was deeply hurt by criticism of his work. 'Let them look carefully at my recent paintings', he wrote to Emile Bernard in 1889, 'and they will see how much there is in them of resigned suffering'.[26] At the asylum at St-Rémy, Van Gogh worked from prints by his favourite artists, Millet and Delacroix. In his treatment of a *Pietà* by Delacroix (cat. 53), he not only responds to the pathos of his source, but seems to give Christ his own features and red hair. Van Gogh certainly regarded his artistic mission as sacred, and in his fits of mental illness came as far as believing himself a Christ-figure. For him the suffering of madness was all too real, and far from cultivating a martyr image, as did Gauguin, Van Gogh sought consolation and hope in nature.

Fig. 14
Maurice Denis
*Homage to Cézanne*, 1900
Oil on canvas,
180.3 × 241.3 cm
Musée d'Orsay, Paris
(RF 1977–137)

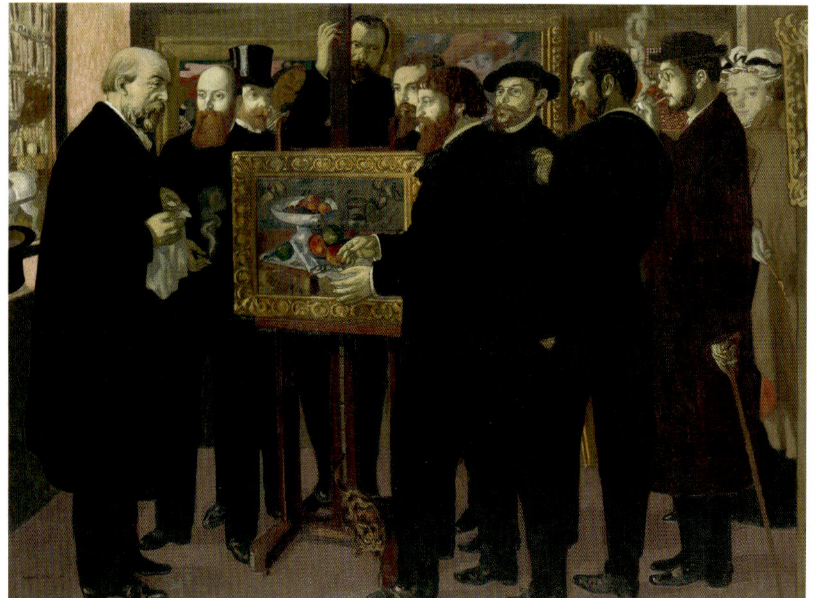

The identification of the artist with Christ became almost commonplace in literature and painting towards the end of the century. In his poem *L'Oeuvre Maudit* of 1889, Albert Aurier describes artists as 'the accursed … of the tribe of Christ and Homer / knowing what it is to be spat upon, knowing Crucifixion'.[27] The Belgian painter James Ensor repeatedly presented himself as Christ, most famously in his massive picture of 1888 (J. Paul Getty Museum, Los Angeles) of Christ entering contemporary Brussels surrounded by a mob of ugly onlookers, a dehumanised sea of masks, frauds, clowns and caricatures. Edvard Munch, in his painting *Golgotha* of 1900 (Munch Museet, Oslo), places himself on the cross above a jeering crowd.

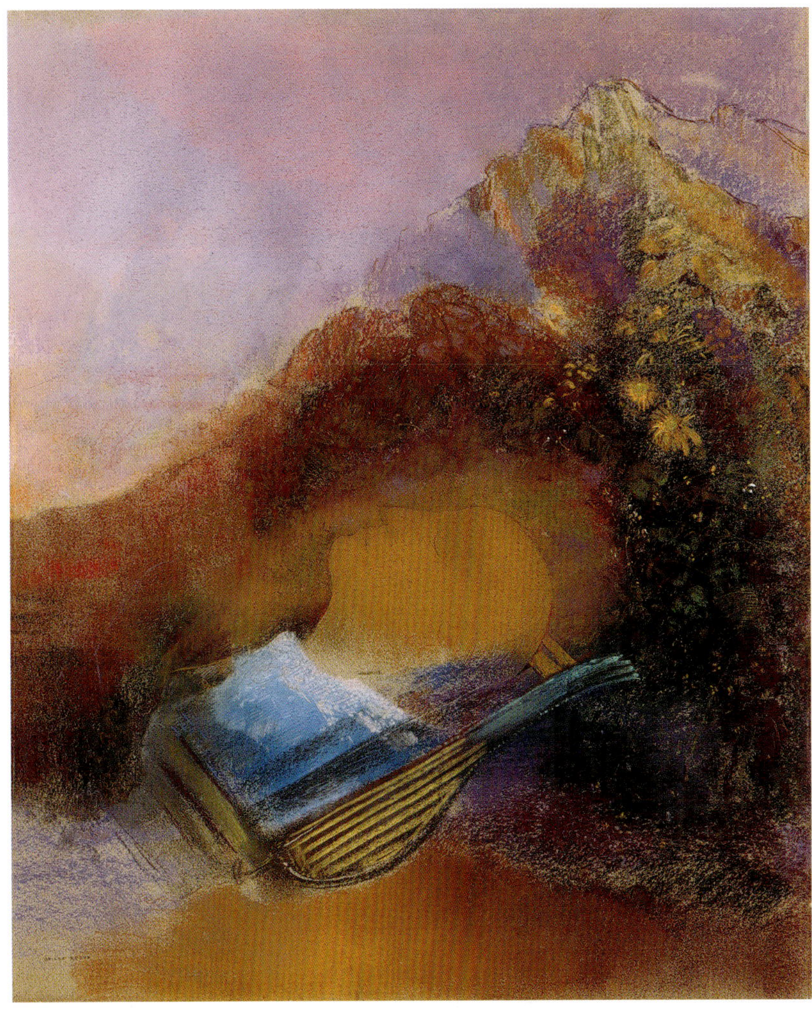

Fig. 15
Odilon Redon
*Orpheus*, about 1903
Pastel, 69.9 × 56.5 cm
Cleveland Museum of Art, Ohio.
Gift from J.H. Wade (1926.25)

The influence of Gauguin's brand of Symbolist painting was crucial to the formation of the Nabis, a group of young painters led by Paul Sérusier and including Maurice Denis, Ker-Xavier Roussel, Paul Ranson, Pierre Bonnard and Edouard Vuillard. They were heavily influenced by the fashionable revival of occult and esoteric cults, believing that their art opened a door to a spiritual realm. The name Nabi, which Sérusier gave the group in 1889, derives from the Arabic and Hebrew word for 'prophet'. Paul Ranson's house became known as 'le Temple' and his wife as 'La Lumière du Temple', and members of the group portrayed each other in priestly robes (cat. 54). In spite of this overtly theatrical element in Nabi art, the inclination towards mysticism is another manifestation of the artist's rejection of decadent bourgeois society, the same impulse that caused Cézanne to retreat to Provence, and led Gauguin to forsake France altogether for the exotic landscape and uncorrupted peoples of the South Seas.

In his painting *Homage to Cézanne* (fig. 14), Maurice Denis shows the Nabis grouped around a still life by Cézanne, but the object of their veneration seems rather to be the elderly figure of the painter Odilon Redon who stands on the left. By 1900, after long years of obscurity, Redon was seen to be in the vanguard of Symbolism. A passionate admirer of Delacroix, he seems to have been untouched by Realism or Impressionism, and devoted himself to purely imaginative visions (celebrated in *A Rebours*). For him the artist is a dreamer and a visionary whose work explores a mysterious inner world. He projects this concept in a number of images of fictional and holy figures, such as Ophelia, Buddha, and *Orpheus* (fig. 15), usually with eyes closed, their sight turned inward. The landscapes he conjures are like visions and the colour preternaturally intense and glowing. According to legend, Orpheus was torn apart by the Thracian women and his head was washed ashore on the island of Lesbos, where it became a famous oracle. Redon's

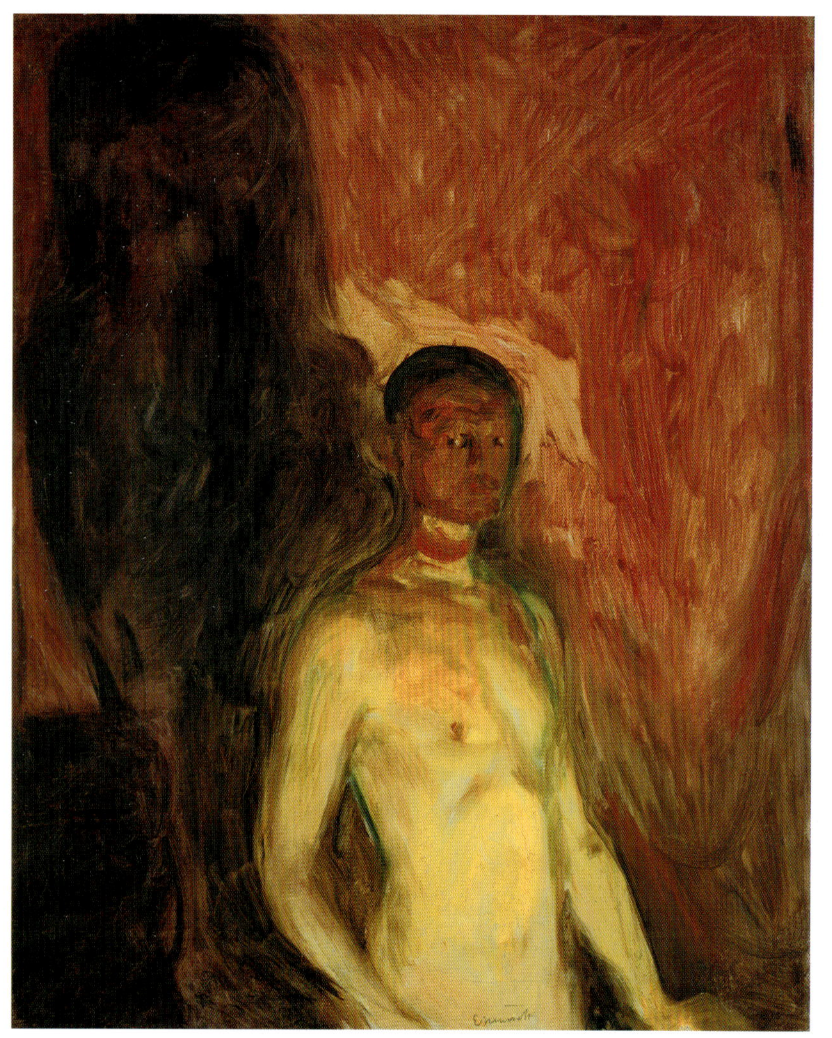

Fig. 16
Edvard Munch
*Self Portrait in Hell*, 1903
Oil on canvas, 85.5 × 61.5cm
Munch Museet, Oslo
(MM. M. 591)

Orpheus is bodiless, immaterial, purely spirit. So too is Gauguin in another remarkable painting by Redon (*Homage to Gauguin*, 1904; Musée d'Orsay, Paris), which shows his head surrounded by a halo of flowers.

While the artist may identify with the divine spark in him and see himself as part of 'the little church of the elect', he is also an outlaw and revels in his rejection of conventional morality. This is the dark side of inspiration, the notion that the artist is driven by malignant and demonic forces. It links back to early superstitions that exceptional skills and knowledge were unnatural and inspired by the devil. But it exerted a special attraction for the Romantic artist who became obsessed with the dark and irrational in himself and others. It explains why, in the wake of Goethe's drama, the Faust myth achieved such popularity in the nineteenth century in literature and painting, inspiring, for example Delacroix's series of etchings (1828) and Berlioz's music-drama, *The Damnation of Faust* (1846). Faust represents the restless artist who, defying society's rules, seeks out experiences and pleasures of all kinds but is never content. The satanic theme is given a novel twist in Oscar Wilde's *The Picture of Dorian Gray* (1891). As the hero pursues his career of vice outwardly untouched, it is his portrait that takes on all the signs of his corruption. Munch liked to emphasise the demonic in his many self-dramatising portraits of himself. In *Self Portrait in Hell* (fig. 16) he shows himself naked against a flame-red background and a looming, threatening shadow. But he is not suffering hell-fire; rather he seems, like Don Juan, to glory in his dark side. Evil is yet another mark of distinction.

It is a short step from divinely inspired utterance to crazed possession, and, like demonism, madness obsessed the Romantic imagination. Goya's paintings of the madhouse and Géricault's portraits of monomaniacs are expressions, albeit very different ones, of this fascination. Delacroix made two paintings based on the story of the Renaissance poet Tasso who was locked up in a madhouse by his enemies (cat. 17), and the tale of Don Quixote gained in popularity with artists, Daumier in particular giving the mad knight errant tragic stature. Illness and suicide were indeed often enough the fate of poets and painters who struggled with both inner demons and indifference to their work. Géricault suffered fits of depression and Gros, feeling that he had betrayed the artistic principles of his exiled master David, drowned himself. Emile Zola's novel, *The Masterpiece* (*L'Oeuvre*; 1886), tells the story of an artist who, despairing at his failure to exhibit what he considers his masterwork but which appears to others nothing but incomprehensible scribbles, hangs himself. Cézanne recognised himself in Zola's description of the painter and consequently broke off relations with his childhood friend. However, it is Van Gogh who has come to stand for the solitary genius overwhelmed by mental illness and driven to take his own life.

The idea that the creative artist lives on the verge of disintegration became integral to the myth of the artist. Munch's work is both obsessively autobiographical and wracked with powerful emotions verging on paranoia. He was tormented by obsessive love affairs and jealousies and exposed them in frankly autobiographical paintings. In *Vampire* (cat. 70), the lover is tempted and seduced by a devouring woman, Munch's incarnation of the femme fatale. Following a destructive relationship with Tulla Larsen,

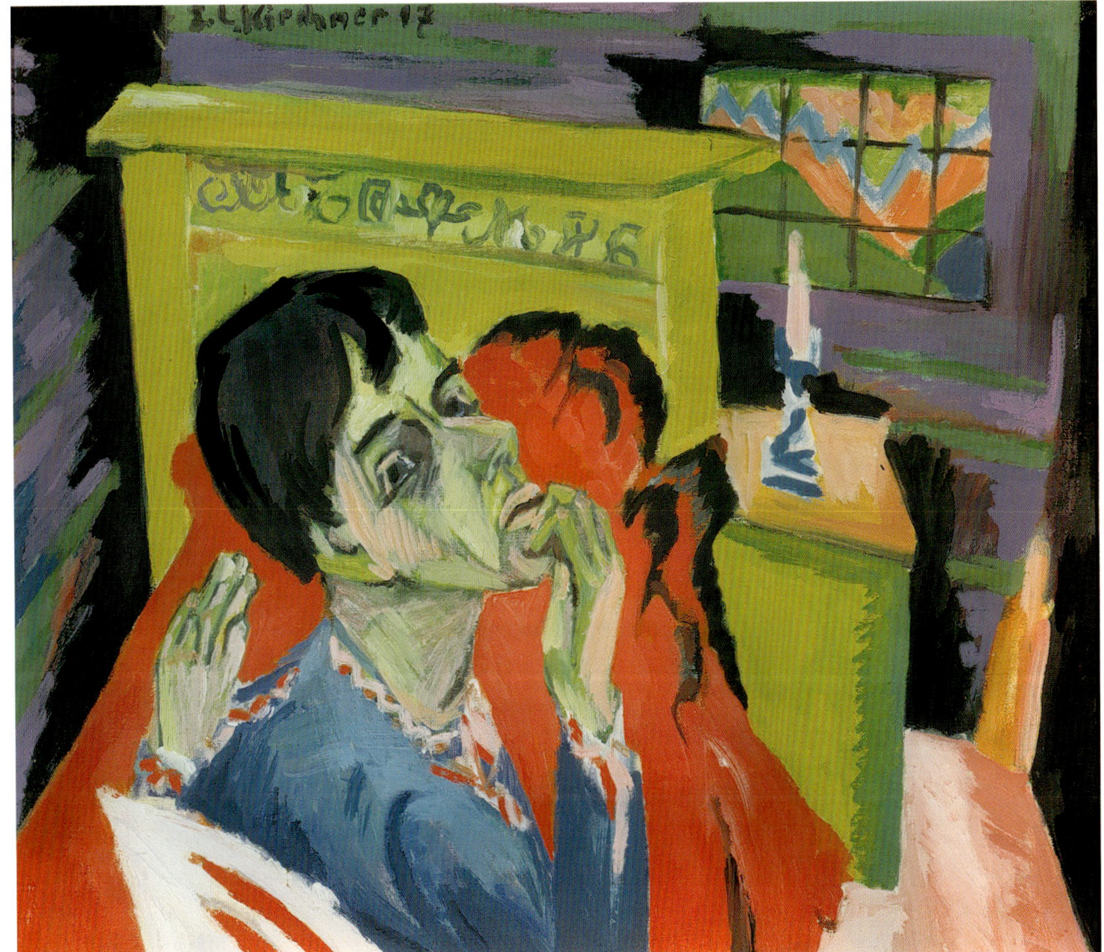


Fig. 17
Ernst Ludvig Kirchner
*Self Portrait as a Sick Man*, 1917
Oil on canvas, 59 × 69.3 cm
Bayerische Staatsgemäldesammlungen, Munich (15580)

Munch shot himself in the hand. He dramatised the incident in the series *The Death of Marat* (1907), took to drink, and in 1908 suffered a nervous breakdown. The theme of insanity also runs through much of the work of his contemporary, the Swedish dramatist August Strindberg. The Viennese Egon Schiele repeatedly represented himself in tortured and tormented nude self portraits, literally stripped bare and cadaver-like (cat. 71). For the German Expressionist painter Ernst Ludwig Kirchner, mental collapse was precipitated by his experience as a soldier in the First World War. He portrayed himself in 1917 as a convalescent in bed, looking terrified and vulnerable (fig. 17). Twenty years later he was to take his own life. In mid-twentieth-century New York, the high-minded experimentation that resulted in Abstract Expressionism was accompanied by a way of life that challenged convention and was personally hazardous. Jackson Pollock died in a car crash; Mark Rothko committed suicide.

The image of the artist that evolved during the nineteenth century has become so firmly established that today it is largely taken for granted. It is often assumed that to be an artist is to be in some sense a rebel or a martyr, removed from the concerns of ordinary people. The gap between contemporary art and the wider public has arguably grown to the point where the artist's work is often considered to be significant only to the initiated, while to the rest it is spectacle. Over recent decades the myth of the artist has extended its range, so that it is now more conspicuous in the provocative behaviour and non-conformist lifestyle of rock singers, football players and film stars. Such posturing is now expected of the celebrity, calculated to win media attention, and goes hand-in-hand with success and wealth. Rebellion, or the pose of rebellion, has become the new orthodoxy, and no longer demands that the artist strike out alone. Since Dada overturned accepted ideas of art, the artist has attacked the once-sacred icons of culture, society and politics so often and so flagrantly that art has all but lost its power to shock. Perhaps these are signs that this once-potent myth of the artist, which arose out of momentous historic events and in response to urgent questions about life, belief and the purpose of art, has truly run its course.

**1** *Journal d'Eugène Delacroix*, 16 May 1823 (Joubin 1950).

**2** Letter dated November 1854, quoted in Clark 1973, p. 24.

**3** Samuel Johnson, *A Dictionary of the English Language*, London 1755, s.v. Artist.

**4** Letter from John Keats to George and Tom Keats, 21 December 1817, quoted in Vaughan 2005, p. 66.

**5** Alfred de Vigny, *Servitude et grandeur militaire*, 1835, quoted in Brookner 2000, pp. 43–4.

**6** Alfred de Musset, *La Confession d'un enfant du siècle*, 1836, quoted in Brookner 2000, p. 46.

**7** *Journal d'Eugène Delacroix*, 29 May 1824.

**8** Quoted in Brookner 2000, p. 48.

**9** The subject of a painting by Pierre Nolasque Bergeret, *Charles V and Titian*, 1808, in the Musée des Beaux-Arts, Bordeaux.

**10** Alfred de Vigny, *'Les Consultations du docteur Noir … 1832'*, quoted in Honour 1981, p. 55.

**11** Friedrich von Schiller, *Über naïve und sentimentalische Dichtung*, 1795–6, quoted in Honour, op. cit. p. 311.

**12** William Wordsworth, *Resolution and Independence*, composed 1802, published 1807.

**13** Heinrich Heine, *Religion and Philosophy in Germany*, 1834, trans. J. Snodgrass, Boston 1959, p. 99.

**14** Charles Baudelaire, 'The Life and Work of Eugène Delacroix' in Baudelaire 1955, p. 57

**15** *Journal d'Eugène Delacroix*, 1 May 1850.

**16** Charles Baudelaire, 'The Life and Work of Eugène Delacroix' in Baudelaire 1955, p. 60.

**17** Félix Pyat, 'Les Artistes' in *Le nouveau tableau de Paris*, IV Paris 1834, pp. 8–9, quoted in Brown 1985, p. 10.

**18** Undated letter from Courbet to Francis Wey, probably written in 1850, quoted in Toussaint and Forges 1977, p. 17.

**19** Letter of 1863 from Champfleury to Courbet, quoted in Toussaint and Forges, op. cit. p. 38.

**20** Letter from Gauguin to Van Gogh 1 October 1888 in Merlhès 1948, no. 166.

**21** Baudelaire 1964a, p. 27.

**22** Charles Baudelaire, 'The Salon of 1846' in Baudelaire 1955, p. 118.

**23** Baudelaire 1964a, p. 28.

**24** Charles Baudelaire, 'The Salon of 1846' in Baudelaire 1955, p. 61.

**25** *Journal d'Eugène Delacroix*, 5 September 1847.

**26** Letter from Gauguin to Emile Bernard, November 1889 in Malingue 1949, XCII.

**27** Poems of Albert Aurier, 1888 and 1889, in *A. Aurier: Oeuvres posthumes*, ed. Rémy de Gourmont, Paris 1893.

# Imagining the Artist: Painters and Sculptors in Nineteenth-Century Literature

*Rupert Christiansen*

In the final act of Shakespeare's *The Winter's Tale*, that 'rare Italian master Giulio Romano' is reported to have carved the miraculously lifelike statue of Hermione.[1] Shakespeare seems to have picked up Vasari's unverified assertion that the historical Giulio Romano was a sculptor as well as a painter, but of course the trick is that it is not a statue at all but the real Hermione. Nevertheless, the reference has its curious significance in this context as the earliest known mention of an actual visual artist in English literature.

It was a long time before anyone else felt the need to name one. In *The Vicar of Wakefield* (1766), for instance, Oliver Goldsmith charts the ups and downs of the innocent Primrose family. At one point in their vacillating fortunes, they make an attempt to keep up with the neighbours by having themselves immortalised by a painter 'who travelled the country and took likenesses for fifteen shillings a head'. He sets to work with 'assiduity and expedition', completing an elaborate allegorical composition specified by the family in four days,[2] but he remains anonymous and totally uncharacterised. Regarded like so many eighteenth-century artists as nothing more than a jobbing craftsman, the question of his artistic identity or individuality does not arise.

At exactly this time, the status of the artist was being debated as Enlightenment intellectuals reassessed all human activities in the light of philosophies of reason. The Royal Academy was founded in London in 1768, elevating the public status of those artists admitted to its ranks as Royal Academicians. One of those who argued that the artist was a special entity was Joshua Reynolds, whose position as first President of the Royal Academy gave him an influential platform from which to deliver his celebrated *Discourses* between 1769 and 1790. Reynolds invoked the authority of the classics to assert that the painter – and the sculptor – displayed exceptional powers of imagination and skill and implied that his status in the world should rise accordingly.

The culture of Revolution and Romanticism which gathered momentum throughout the nineteenth century made even greater claims for the artist. Initially, the Romantics focused on the poet, privileging the word over the image as the most potent element in the crucible. It is significant that during this period we find artists identifying with poets when they examine their own experience – Delacroix, for instance, looks to Tasso's imprisonment and Ovid's exile to represent the crises that he confronted as an artist (cats 17, 19).[3]

But the rhetoric of creativity was established, ready for painters and sculptors to exploit. The artist was not biddable to patrons; he was not a jobbing tradesman. Like a poet, he was someone who worked through a gift of inspiration and imagination to create something 'original' – an inner vision that could then be externally revealed to ordinary mortals. This sense that the artist required independence from ordinary exigencies and belonged to a god-like elite, transforming and illuminating nature rather than merely transferring it on to canvas or into marble by means of manual dexterity and sharpness of eye, soon became one of the cornerstones of nineteenth-century aesthetics and still obtains today.[4] Yet until the mid-nineteenth century this remained an avant-garde position, promoted by intellectuals but not accepted or understood by the middle and commercial classes. To them, a canvas or a bust remained commodities waiting to be bought and sold (an ode or sonnet had by contrast a more transcendent existence). And so a tension grew between the artist's idea that his art was above material transaction, and the public's idea that art was something which had its place, and its market value, alongside the groceries.

Between these two incompatible ideologies swirl a series of conflicts. The desire of Reynolds and other eighteenth-century thinkers to elevate the artisan into the Artist was all very well, but how high should he ascend, and where should he sit when he got there? Could the visual artist be admitted to the rank of 'genius' occupied by, say, Byron or Goethe (as, indeed, had Michelangelo and Raphael in their own day)? Were painting and sculpture to be considered as businesses or callings? And did the visual artist's tendency to stand at a remove from society – observing it, interpreting it, idealising it – inevitably make him a dangerous rebel or a pathetic martyr? These are puzzles that the novel – a literary genre peculiarly suited to the exploration of questions of social mobility – would subtly ponder for the next hundred years in ways that both reflected realities and consolidated stereotypes.

Bypassing such casual amateur sketchers as Goethe's tragic hero Werther and Jane Austen's Emma, whose aim is the unproblematic one of merely reproducing nature (though Werther is a Classicist in reflecting that 'nature alone forms the great artist', and a Romantic in adding that 'any rule is likely to destroy both the true feeling of nature and its true expression'[5]), named visual artists are first encountered in fiction during the 1820s.

Perhaps the first is Frank Tyrrel in *St Ronan's Well* (1823), Walter Scott's drily amusing satire which, like Jane Austen's unfinished novel *Sanditon* (1817), dissects the pretentious vogue for watering-places. Lady Penelope and her friend Lady Binks are excited by some gloomy landscape sketches, and expect to find their creator to be a figure of Byronic allure and misanthropy. On meeting him, they are therefore ironically shocked to find his clothes to be clean and his manners sophisticated (later explained by the revelation that he is the estranged son of an earl). In Lady Binks's eyes, such couthness does not match his apparent status and profession:

> 'There are very well-bred artists,' said Lady Penelope; 'it is the profession of a gentleman.'
>
> 'Certainly,' answered Lady Binks, 'but the poorer class have often to struggle with poverty and dependence. In general society they are like commercial people in presence of their customers, and that is a difficult part to sustain … you seldom see them quite at their ease, and therefore I hold this Mr Tyrrel to be either an artist of the first class, raised completely above the necessity and degradation of patronage, or else to be no professional artist at all.'[6]

The theme of the impossibility of being both an artist and a gentleman recurs repeatedly throughout the nineteenth-century novel, frequently embodied in the figure of an attractive young man, toying with art as part of his superficial youthful rebellion. In Thackeray's *The Newcomes* (1855), for example, Clive Newcome is a member of an *arriviste* family anxious to make its mark in society. Clive is an easygoing, amiable fellow who enjoys associating with artistic types and fancies that it would be fun to make painting his profession. This disgusts his father, who is otherwise happy for him to pursue art as a hobby, and crucially hinders his marital pursuit of Ethel, a banker's daughter. The author comments sardonically:

> The Muse of Painting is a lady whose social station is not altogether recognised with us as yet. The polite world permits a gentleman to amuse himself with her, but to take her for better or worse! Forsake all other chances and cleave unto her! To assume her name! Many a person would be as much shocked at the notion as if his son had married an opera dancer.[7]

The twist is that Clive is not actually a very good or a dedicated painter, and his desire for Ethel and her money wins out. He abandons his lightly held ambition, in contrast to his friend J.J. Ridley, the butler's son, who is a true artist and has no social status to worry about.

Clive's type emerges again in Trollope's *Barchester Towers* (1857), where Bertie Stanhope, the son of a senior cleric, spends two years in a German university, visits Rome, converts to Catholicism and then Judaism, and then takes lodgings in Carrara, where he 'spoilt much marble, and made some few pretty images.'[8] He returns to the cathedral close of Barchester, where his freewheeling ethics, long hair and outlandish garb prove mildly scandalous. But he remains harmless because he plainly does not take his art seriously: sculpture for him is not a vocation or an ideal, but an excuse to avoid addressing life with the earnestness that was so fundamental to the Victorian concept of virtue.

The same could be said of Henry Gowan in Dickens's *Little Dorrit* (1857), whose adoption of painting is motivated by a desire to spite his family: 'He appeared to be an artist by profession, and to have been at Rome sometime; yet he had a slight, careless, amateur way with him – a perceptible limp, both in his devotion to art and his attainments.' The splendidly earnest inventor Daniel Doyce comments, 'He has sauntered into the Arts at a leisurely Pall Mall pace ... and I doubt if they care to be taken quite so coolly.'[9]

Will Ladislaw in George Eliot's *Middlemarch* (1872) has altogether more charm. He too sketches and dallies in Rome, but sheepishly admits that he has neither the talent nor the application to make a career of it. His casual attitude is shown up by his German friend Adolf Naumann, encountered at Heidelberg University, who has both the costume – 'a dove-coloured blouse and a maroon velvet cap'[10] – and the intellectual focus to rank as a genuine painter, indeed as 'one of the chief renovators of Christian art'. (George Eliot is clearly representing Adolf Naumann as one of the artists in the Nazarene circle. Similar Old German costume was worn by Carl Philipp Fohr as a member of the patriotic student society, the Teutonen, when he was a student at Heidelberg University [cats 10, 11]).

Ladislaw and other similar figures in the English novel can be characterised as dilettantes, sophisticates observing society from within, for whom art is part of their insouciant refusal to commit, and an assertion of the claims of the self. But they are merely flirts – their eccentricities can be accommodated within middle-class culture and they do not brave the radical break with social norms made by their cousins the bohemians (see p. 88–117).

Around the latter an altogether more distinct mythology develops, consolidated in ideas drawn from Henri Murger's *Scenes of Bohemian Life (Scènes de la vie de Bohème)*, first serialised in 1845, published in book form in 1851 and much translated and dramatised. This was the major source of a persistent cliché, an artistic subculture, in which male artists – and at this point, even in *La vie de Bohème*, it should be noted that a woman in literature only functions artistically as a muse or a model – mixed with writers in an atmosphere that combined poverty, gaiety, irresponsibility and a devotion to the free love doctrines of George Sand. Bohemians are idealists, writes Murger in his preface, who may need day-to-day money but who are contemptuous of worldly success, 'obstinate dreamers for whom art has remained a faith and not a profession; enthusiastic folk ... whose loyal heart beats high in presence of all that is beautiful'.[11]

Murger's book was hugely influential – the young American artist James Abbott McNeill Whistler was only one of many who felt compelled to visit the French capital as a result of reading it – Rome may have remained the matchless museum of the Antique, but it was in Paris that art was being created.[12] *Scenes of Bohemian Life* did for bohemians what Jack Kerouac's *On the Road* (1957) would do for beatniks a century later, inventing a lifestyle that exuded glamour, even if that involved a period of starving in a garret, as represented by Octave Tassaert's *Artist's Studio* (cat. 28). But it is scarcely a manifesto. Despite the occasional plunge into the sentimental, Murger's tone is lightly comic – nowhere more so than in the pages devoted to the painter Marcel's long-gestating historical canvas *Passage of the Red Sea*, which has been submitted for exhibition at the Salon[13] so often that it 'knew the road to the Louvre well enough to have gone thither of itself'. As it is repeatedly rejected by the judges, Marcel changes a couple of the figures and re-presents it under other titles – *The Passage of the Rubicon*, *The Passage of the Beresina* and *The Passage of the Panoramas* – before selling it in despair to a grocer who needs a shop sign.[14]

The jaunty, Murgeresque community becomes a familiar theme of the English novel in the Naughty Nineties, by which time something of the bohemian spirit of Saint-Germain-des-Près had crossed the English Channel and established a branch on the Thames.[15] Popular naturalistic fiction, much influenced by Zola, is full of naïvely eager young men of artistic inclinations coming to Chelsea and falling for women with a past (or dubious future), whose sexual availability is symbolised by their willingness to model nude. Licence to contemplate the complement of living female flesh, and even to take possession of it, is titillatingly considered one of the perks of the artist's job. Morley Roberts's pretentious potboiler *Immortal Beloved* (1896) is a fair example of this genre.

More endearing is George du Maurier's *Trilby* (1894; fig. 18). This is the tale, drawn on du Maurier's own experience, of 'three musketeers of the brush', who leave stuffy England to live *à la Bohème* in the Paris of the 1850s. They admire the Barbizon School and live it up on next to no money, discussing the merits of Old Masters and young women far into the night. The central figure, nicknamed Little Billee, loves the artless, open-hearted Irish laundress Trilby O'Ferrall, who makes extra money by modelling nude. Because of her loose morals, their marriage is prevented by Little Billee's family. He returns to London, loses his élan and becomes a successful academician whose painting *The Pitcher Goes to the Well* is 'well known to all the world by this time, and sold only last year at Christie's (more than thirty-six years after it was painted) for three thousand pounds'.[16] Such success in the market is considered vulgar: it means losing one's integrity and surrendering to hucksterism. Some years before writing *Trilby* du Maurier had told his mother that 'I want to write about artists for I have met them and see them in a way different to anything that has been written before'. The story was first published as an illustrated serial in the American magazine *Harper's Monthly*, and some instalments appear to have been so close to the author's own experiences as to have caused considerable legal problems for the publishers. Whistler (cats 44, 45), for example, recognised himself in the young art student 'Joe

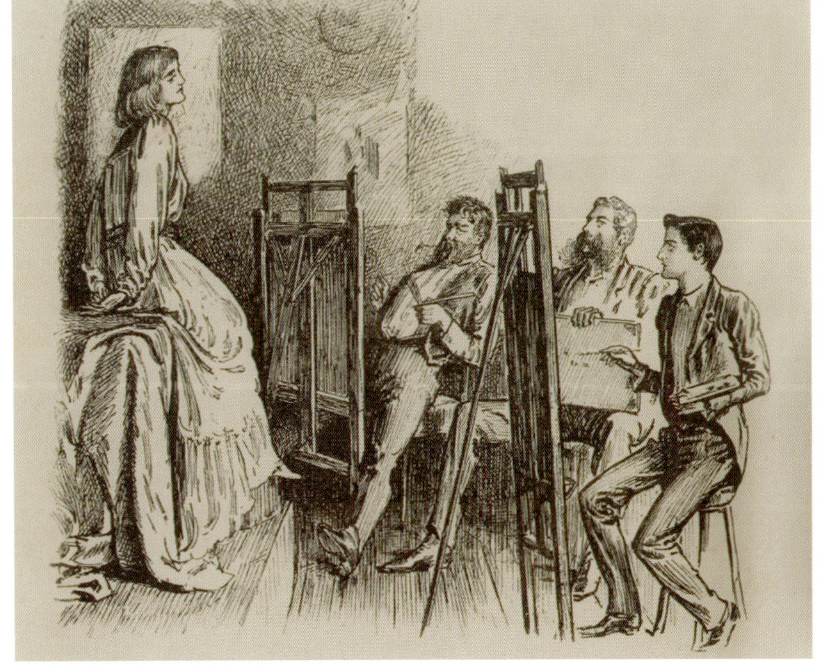

Fig. 18
George du Maurier
'The Soft Eyes'
from *Trilby*, 1894

Sibley', described and illustrated in the March issue; the offending text and illustration were swiftly removed when the book was published.

Between the dilettante and the bohemian, the visual artist is a lightly drawn figure in much of English Victorian fiction, and the novelists who imagine them seem to threaten the jibe of 'pseud' whenever one of them dares to take their work seriously. Yet the power of painting and sculpture – aside from the pretensions of those who created it – is often acknowledged in what to a modern reader seems an almost melodramatic fashion.

The idea of ghostly qualities animating an artistic representation of an individual is a common trope throughout the Gothic novel,[17] recurring in Nathaniel Hawthorne's *The Marble Faun* (1860), in which the mysterious Italian Count Donatello is regarded as the reincarnation of a daemonic sculpture by the Ancient Greek sculptor Praxiteles, and in George Eliot's *Romola* (1863), in which an artist intuitively paints a portrait which reveals the subject's criminal intentions. In Oscar Wilde's penny dreadful *The Picture of Dorian Gray* (1890), the infatuated barrister turned painter Basil Hallward depicts Dorian Gray as 'a young Adonis … made out of ivory and rose leaves',[18] imbuing the painting with an excess of erotic passion that gives it a spiritual life of its own. The narcissistic Dorian makes a Faustian wish 'that he himself might remain young, and the portrait grow old', and the ensuing drama hinges on the way that Dorian's moral decadence manifests itself in the portrait, while he himself remains physically unblemished. The irony is that Hallward himself is described by the Wildean aesthete Lord Henry Wotton as someone rather ordinary. 'Basil had no enemies, and always wore a Waterbury watch … a man can paint like Velázquez and be as dull as possible. Basil was really rather dull.'[19] It is the work of art which has the genius rather than the person who makes it.

Could the visual artist be a hero? Thomas Carlyle thought not, omitting them from his pantheon *On Heroes, Hero-Worship and the Heroic in History* (1841), though this may be due more to ignorance than to prejudice. Yet for John Ruskin, the artist was a hero: his *Modern Painters*, published in five volumes between 1843 and 1860, presented the artist alongside the poet, warrior and law-giver as a maker of society and a changer of lives, possessed by a vision of the world. 'Even if misfortunes fall upon him, such as would make other people religious', he wrote, 'he will not seek for consolation in heaven. He will seek it in his painting room. So long as he can paint, nothing will crush him.'[20] Ruskin had no interest in mere bohemianism for its own sake and he despised the dilettante. The true artist was for him someone isolated and obsessed, half rebel and half martyr. 'Society always has a destructive influence upon an Artist', he pontificated in the third volume of *The Stones of Venice*, published in 1853, 'first, by its sympathy with his meanest powers; secondly, by its chilling want of understanding of his greatest; and thirdly, by its vain occupation of his time and thoughts.'[21]

In parallel to Ruskin's ideas, there developed a similar literary image of the artist – questioning and struggling, tormented and ecstatic. Three of the dramatic monologues in Robert Browning's collection *Men and Women* (1855) illustrate the phenomenon, as well as the growing interest in the history of art, and in particular the Italian Renaissance. 'Pictor Ignotus' is the complaint of an anonymous painter who has shut himself away in a monastery because he cannot bear exposure to commerce and criticism:

If at while my heart sinks, as monotonous I paint
These endless cloisters and eternal aisles
With the same series, Virgin, babe and saint
With the same cold calm beautiful regard
At least no merchant traffics in my heart …

'Andrea del Sarto', in contrast, is the revelation of a lost soul who unashamedly paints for the merchant, prostituting his matchless technical skill for the means to keep his worthless wife happy. 'Fra Lippo Lippi' is motivated by the creative joy that they both lack. He has left the monastery and rejected the repression of the church to roam the streets and countryside to observe:

God's works – paint any one, and count it crime
To let a truth slip.

His is an art that is based in open exuberant experience of life:

The shapes of things, their colours, lights and shades
Changes, surprises.

The phrase echoes Ruskin's insistence that 'nothing exists in the world about him [the painter] that is not beautiful in his eyes in one degree or another … there is no Evil in his eyes; – only Good, and that which displays good'.[22]

Fra Lippo Lippi is one of the few truly triumphant – personally fulfilled and overflowingly creative – visual artists in nineteenth-century literature. Nick Dormer, the hero of Henry James's *The Tragic Muse* (1890), could potentially develop into another one, but the novel is interested in his progress rather than his arrival, and the reader is left to guess at his achievement. Having made a vow to his dying father to follow him into politics, Nick should make the appropriate marriage to the rich, beautiful and influential widow Julia Dallow, who has ambitions to see him as prime minister. But, encouraged by his Wildean friend Gabriel Nash, Nick yearns to pursue his late-flowering talent for portrait painting, in what is described as a 'modern' (presumably Impressionist) style – much to the dismay of his aristocratic Tory family who follow the standard Philistine line, familiar since *The Newcomes* and *Little Dorrit*, that art is all very well as a hobby, but not something for a gentleman to get serious about. Nick has much to learn and understand, and much to sacrifice – his position as a promising member of parliament; his conscience, in terms of the vow he made to his father; and his personal life, in terms of marriage to Julia Dallow. Half-way through the novel, Julia Dallow bursts into his studio while he is drawing a female model. Previously married to a man obsessed with his art collection, she realises that despite their mutual respect, affection and compatibility, Nick's painting drives a wedge between them – 'you love it, you revel in it; that's what you want and that's the only thing you want' – and she breaks off their engagement. The crux is not so much the stain of dilettantism or the association with immoral bohemianism, as the question of commitment – Julia realises that you cannot be both a great artist and a great politician, and as she tells Nick masochistically, 'You must be a great artist.'[23]

That is the deal, James implies. There is no low road or short cut, and the artist, great or not, will be on his own, assailed by doubts, frustrations and disappointments. Nick must also battle with his own facility, 'a damnable suppleness and a gift of immediate response, a readiness to oblige, that made him seem to take up causes which he really left lying … he was too clever by half.'[24] The novel leaves open the question of whether or not Nick will succeed, but there is surely no more sensitive or hopeful picture of an artist in English literature.

With the spiritual stakes raised so high, the risk of failure becomes that much more immediate. A dilettante like Trollope's Bertie Stanhope can wander off, and whether he paints or not makes little difference even to himself; but in what one might call the post-Ruskinian dispensation, the choice becomes decisive. The second half of the nineteenth century thus takes a generally bleaker view of the fate of the visual artist than the first half. He becomes more intensely self-dramatising, more mentally unstable and spiritually isolated – a process delineated in several fictions by Henry James.

James's short story *The Madonna of the Future* (1873) is a re-writing of an earlier *conte* by Honoré de Balzac, 'Le Chef d'oeuvre inconnu' ('The Unknown Masterpiece'), in which the narrator encounters Theobald, an American living in Florence. Theobald seems to know everything about art: he is a brilliant critic of other people's work and has dedicated himself to producing a portrait inspired by a young woman so perfectly beautiful that the painting will rank with the Raphael madonnas. 'I've never sold a picture!' he proclaims proudly. '"At least no merchant traffics in my heart." Do you remember the line in Browning? [from 'Pictor Ignotus']. My little studio has never been profaned by superficial, feverish, mercenary work.'[25] But when the narrator visits him, he finds that the woman is old and rather ordinary and that the masterpiece is a delusion. Paralysed by his ambition and his knowledge, Theobald has painted nothing – the canvas is 'a dead blank, cracked and discolored by time'.[26] He dies in despair.

This failure is something that James relates to what he calls 'the complex fate' of being born American, in a society that has no depth of culture. 'We are the disinherited of art!' Theobald complains. 'We are condemned to be superficial. We are excluded from the magic circle. The soil of American perception is a poor little barren, artificial deposit.' The narrator quietly retorts that 'nothing is so idle as to talk about our want of a nutritive soil, of opportunity, inspiration, and all the rest of it. The worthy part is to do something fine! There's no law in our glorious constitution against that. Invent, create, achieve!'[27] But the American has no native tradition to draw on, and the challenge for an artist is therefore that much stiffer and knottier.

The peculiar difficulties facing the American artist is a theme first taken up in Nathaniel Hawthorne's Gothic allegory *The Marble Faun* (1860), in which two of the four principal characters are young American artists living in Rome. At home, Hilda had been a fresh and original painter, freely inspired by her surroundings, but in Italy she is so overwhelmed by the accumulated art of the past that all she can do is make meticulous copies of details from the Old Masters. The sculptor Kenyon, on the other hand, can only make art that is morally emblematic or symbolic – a trait of his Puritanism, with its insistence that God's will is read in nature. Both are therefore prevented from making the sort of direct emotional engagement with life and people that animates the painting of their European friend Miriam.

Intriguing though it is, *The Marble Faun* remains an obscure and confusing fable that defies reasonable interpretation. In *Roderick Hudson* (1875), Henry James readdresses the same theme in a clearer light. Reared in a small, narrow-minded New England town, the eponymous young sculptor, although raw and uninformed, is full of innocent and enthusiastic ambition, embodied in a bronze he makes entitled 'Thirst'.[28] Taken to Europe by an older man who believes he has genius worth cultivating, Roderick is at first enthralled. But in his hunger for the banquet of culture that France and Italy offer him, 'he was eating all his cake at once and might have none for the morrow'.[29] Gorged, over-stimulated and confused, he becomes arrogant and hysterical, loses his head to a woman, starts to drink, quarrels with his friend, abandons his art and finally falls to a suicidal death 'from a great height'.[30]

In French literature, the artist's vulnerability becomes more extreme and morbid, to the point of a Van Gogh-like masochism, in which success can in itself be a sort of failure, and public recognition a corruption rather than a fulfilment. Those who maintain their ideals go mad and die in poverty; those who sell out despair as their souls rot.

In Jules and Edmond Goncourt's depressing novel *Manette Solomon* (1867), Naz de Coriolis, the idealistic modernist, marries his beautiful Jewish model only to be ruined by her avarice: she fills up the house with her relatives, bullies him to paint only what will sell and finally drives him close to insanity. Emile Zola's *L'Oeuvre* (1886, usually translated as 'The Masterpiece') tells the story of Claude Lantier – a personality largely drawn on the author's friendship with both Manet and Cézanne – whose revolutionary paintings bring him first derision and later acclaim and imitation (fig. 19). As he becomes obsessed with experiments into the rendering of colour and light, his wife Christine becomes ever more jealous of his absorption in art. At the novel's climax, crazed with moral confusion, he curses and spits on his most radically daring canvas, still problematically unfinished. The next day he hangs himself. After the novel was published, Cézanne severed relations with Zola – evidently it hit a raw nerve.

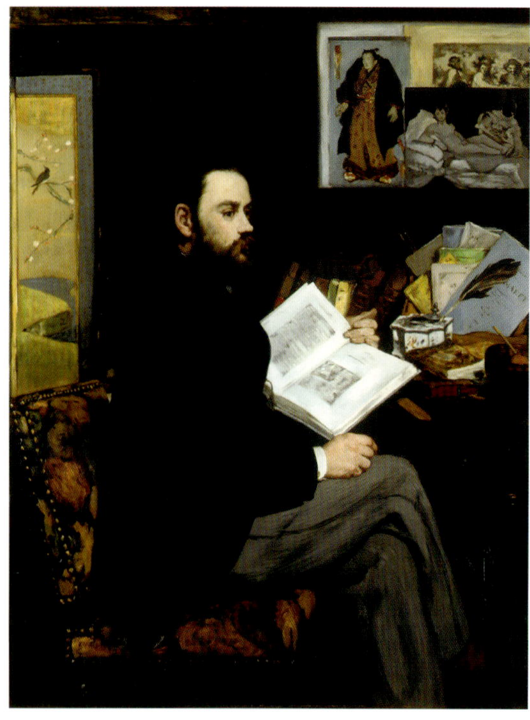

Fig. 19
Edouard Manet
*Portrait of Emile Zola*, 1868
Oil on canvas, 146 × 114 cm
Musee d'Orsay, Paris,
Gift of Mme Emile Zola, 1918
(RF 2205)

More complex in many respects is Rudyard Kipling's underrated *The Light that Failed* (1890), where the naturally adept Dick Heldar's drawings of soldiery and war are brilliantly successful in the newspapers and later in exhibition. Like Browning's Andrea del Sarto, Dick is clear-eyed about his good fortune to the point of cynicism – 'I like the power; I like the fun; I like the fuss; and above all, I like the money', he admits; 'I almost like the people who make the fuss and pay the money'.[31] As an artist, Dick operates on sound technique and fidelity to what he sees; what ultimately destroys him is not his own greed or sensitivity, but physical blindness, a symbolic parallel to his hopeless infatuation with Maisie, the first female painter to feature with any force in English fiction. A student at the Slade, she becomes the pupil of a fashionable French Impressionist and suffers from an ambition which outstrips her craft. Her jealousy of Dick's success and her manipulation of his emotions as she attempts to steal his glory provides Kipling with an opportunity to display all his insight into human nastiness.

While these novels are to a degree either sentimental or melodramatic, Henrik Ibsen's last play, *When We Dead Awaken* (1900), attempts a more grandly tragic statement of the artist's dilemma. The sculptor Rubek has spent his life struggling with marble and stone, working on one summatory epic masterpiece that he cannot complete because of the way he has exploited the woman he loved, who is also its model. In old age he rejects art altogether, lamenting that he set a 'dead clay-image, above the happiness of life – of love!'[32] This is the highest Romantic statement, with a Nietzchean grandeur about its self-abnegation. But Rubek never seems more than a symbolic figure, and to find a portrait of an artist that carries the force of psychological reality, as well as the sense of what it is really like to create visual images, we have to look to Marcel Proust's *A la recherche du temps perdu* (published between 1913 and 1927). Elstir fulfils the Ruskinian definition of the nature of a painter: he is the man 'who made himself deliberately ignorant before sitting down to paint', forgetting 'everything that he knew in his honesty of purpose.'[33] His studio in Balbec is described as 'the laboratory of a sort of new creation of the world,'[34] drawing meaning out of chaos. Proust suggests with marvellous clarity the impressionistic qualities of Elstir's seascapes – 'the charm of each of them lay in a sort of metamorphosis of the objects represented, analogous to what in poetry we call metaphor'[35] – and in particular invents a picture of the harbour of Carquethuit in which land and sea, earth and water magically interpenetrate and partake of each other.

Elstir's status in society remains problematic in sophisticated early twentieth-century Paris, partly because the snobs in the Verdurin salon find his wife boring and coarse, misunderstanding the way she inspires him as his muse. But the fools that other people make of themselves do not matter to him. In the later part of the book, his art simplifies itself to a Chardinesque state of grace, revealing previously unimagined beauty in a bundle of asparagus or a bunch of radishes. Finally, he achieves what no other artist in literature achieves: wisdom. 'We do not receive wisdom', he says: 'we must discover it for ourselves, after a journey through the wilderness, which no one else can make for us, which no one can spare us, for our wisdom is the point of view from which we come at last to regard the world.'[36]

**1** *The Winter's Tale*, Act v, Scene ii.
**2** *The Vicar of Wakefield*, ed. A. Friedman, London 1974, ch. 16, pp. 78–9.
**3** See P.B. Shelley, *A Defence of Poetry*, 1821.
**4** See M.H. Abrams, *The Mirror and the Lamp*, London and New York 1953, and the entry for 'Art' in Raymond Williams, *Keywords*, London 1976.
**5** *The Sorrows of Young Werther*, trans. E. Mayer and L. Bogan, Book 1 (May 26), New York 1971, p. 14.
**6** *St Ronan's Well*, Edinburgh 1995 edn, ch. 7, pp. 58–9.
**7** *The Newcomes*, London 1911 edn, ch. 27, pp. 343–4.
**8** *Barchester Towers*, London 1995 edn, ch. 9, p. 67.
**9** *Little Dorrit*, ed. H.P. Sucksmith, Oxford 1979, book 1, ch. 17, p. 201.
**10** *Middlemarch*, ed. R. Ashton, Harmondsworth 1994, ch. 22, p. 213.
**11** *Scènes de la vie de Bohème*, Paris 1886, Preface, p. 6 (author's translation).
**12** See McMullen 1974, pp. 53–6.
**13** Broadly speaking, an equivalent to the Royal Academy's annual Summer Exhibition, at which artists presented new work and offered it for sale.
**14** *Scènes de la vie de Bohème*, op. cit. [note 11], ch. 16, *passim*. According to the anonymous introduction to *Bohemians of the Latin Quarter*, an 1888 English translation of *Scènes de la vie de Bohème*, Marcel was based on a now-forgotten artist called Tabar, who could not afford to costume the models for his version of *Passage of the Red Sea*, and therefore transformed the composition into *Niobe and her Children Slain.*
**15** See Sturgis 1995, *passim*.
**16** *Trilby*, London 1935 edn, pt 4, p. 208.
**17** See Fredericks 1987.
**18** *The Picture of Dorian Gray*, ed. I. Murray, London 1974, ch. 1, p. 3.
**19** Op. cit. ch. 19, p. 212.
**20** *Modern Painters*, vol. ii, app. 2, quoted in Clark 1964, p. 183.
**21** *The Stones of Venice*, vol. iii, ch. 2, quoted in op. cit. p. 193.
**22** Op. cit. vol. ii, app. 2.
**23** *The Tragic Muse*, ch. 27.
**24** Op. cit. ch. 47, p. 450. This echoes James's opinion of John Singer Sargent, published in *Harper's* magazine in October 1887, while he was writing *The Tragic Muse*: 'There is no greater work of art than a great portrait', but 'the highest result is achieved when to this element of quick perception a certain faculty of brooding reflection is added'. Sargent, in James's opinion lacked the latter.
**25** *Collected Stories*, ed. J. Bayley (2 vols), New York and Toronto 1999, vol. 1, p. 148.
**26** Op. cit. p. 175.
**27** Op. cit. pp. 146–7.
**28** *Roderick Hudson*, Oxford 1980 edn, ch. 1, p. 15.
**29** Op. cit. ch. 5, p. 67.
**30** Op. cit. ch. 26, p. 387.
**31** *The Light that Failed*, London 1907 edn, ch. 4, p. 46.
**32** *When We Dead Awaken*, trans. W. Archer, Act 3, p. 157.
**33** *Remembrance of Things Past*, trans. C.K. Scott Moncrieff and Terence Kilmartin, London 1981, vol. 1, p. 898.
**34** Op. cit. p. 892.
**35** Op. cit. p. 893.
**36** Op. cit. vol. 3, pp. 923–4.

# Catalogue

# Hero of the Establishment; Romantic Hero

The myth of the artist as heroic and rebellious, isolated and suffering emerged as part of what became known as the Romantic movement, that dramatic shift in ideas that was initiated at the end of the eighteenth century, transforming all the arts. Partly in reaction to the Enlightenment emphasis on reason and intellect, and partly in response to the political and social convulsions that followed from the French Revolution, artists placed greater emphasis on personal inspiration and subjective feeling than on the external ideal of beauty, *le beau idéal*, which had been the goal of Neoclassical painters. The artist's own inner life became his most important subject, and in the new bourgeois society that emerged in the early decades of the nineteenth century the frustrated and disillusioned artist felt that his vision went unheeded by the philistine and vulgar crowd. This malaise, *le mal du siècle*, is vividly evoked by Chateaubriand, who lamented, 'imagination is rich, abundant, and marvellous; life poor, sterile and unfulfilling. With a full heart one encounters an empty world, and one is disheartened even at the outset'.[1]

The extent of this shift can be gauged by comparing how artists represented themselves and their fellows in the late eighteenth century, and a generation later, in the early 1800s. One of the chief ambitions of Reynolds and his contemporaries was to raise the status of the artist and achieve official recognition. Until the eighteenth century, most artists were regarded as little more than artisans, producing work on demand for private patrons, the church and the state. Those who, like Rubens and Velázquez, achieved titles and honours were exceptional. So it is that such artists as Reynolds and Roslin working in the late 1700s emphasise the elevated social status they have achieved as painters, Reynolds, by depicting himself in the robes of a Doctor of Civil Law with a bust of Michelangelo behind him (cat. 1), and Roslin in his extravagant court clothes, wearing the Swedish Royal Order of the Vasa (cat. 3). The route to artistic success that Reynolds recommended to the students of the Royal Academy was diligent effort, emulation of the great masters of the past and mastery of the rules of art. 'It must of necessity be', he wrote, 'that even the works of genius, like every other effect, as they must have their cause, must likewise have their rules'.[2]

Genius for the Romantic artist was of another order: innate, untutored and springing from the interior life of an exceptional individual. The portraits and self portraits of Romantic artists show them feverishly seeking ways to understand and express their gifted uniqueness and to set them apart from the run of humanity. While they take as read the status of the artist, they disparage the trappings of worldly success. Alexandre Abel de Pujol adopts an antique toga and hairstyle to vouch for his radical artistic credentials (cat. 7); Overbeck gives his fellow Nazarene, Franz Pforr, Old German costume and long hair to represent his spiritual purity and his rejection of decadent art (cat. 10). If not in costume, they usually show themselves casually attired, alone, with no reference to patrons, to emphasise their independence and the loneliness of their calling. Kersting paints Friedrich alone in a bare studio, focused on his inner vision and the canvas before him (cat. 9). But it is above all in the facial expression that the Romantic myth of the artist is projected, in the intense but distant gaze, concentrating not on the exterior world but on an inner vision, and in the unsmiling mouth and knitted brow that tell of the inner suffering that is the burden of genius. MW

**1** François-René de Chateaubriand, *Le Génie du Christianisme* 1802, quoted in Brookner 2000, p. 42.
**2** Reynolds 1906, p. 80.

## 1. Sir Joshua Reynolds (1723–1792)

*Self Portrait* about 1779–80

Oil on panel, 127 × 101.6 cm

Royal Academy of Arts, London (03/1394)

Sir Joshua Reynolds dominated the British art world in the second half of the eighteenth century. One of the most successful portrait painters of his day, he dined with the most fashionable and influential members of society, and from 1760 lived at one of the smartest addresses in London, 47 Leicester Square. In 1768 he was appointed founding President of the Royal Academy of Arts; he was knighted by George III in April of the following year.

Reynolds's ambitions as an artist are reflected in no fewer than 20 self portraits that he painted over half a century. The artist deliberately sought public recognition, and many of his self portraits are associated with particular honours bestowed on him. This portrait dates from 1779 or 1780, when Reynolds was at the height of his powers. It was painted to hang in the Assembly Room of the Royal Academy's prestigious new premises in Somerset House. Reynolds wears the velvet cap and scarlet robes of a Doctor of Civil Law, the honorary degree conferred on him by Oxford University in 1773. Of all the honours he accrued, Reynolds appears to have valued this most, often portraying himself in his academic robes.

Proclaiming his respect for the great artists of the past, Reynolds stands before a bust of Michelangelo, the artist he admired above all others and repeatedly praised in his *Discourses*. As Nicholas Penny has noted, the bust, by Daniele da Volterra, is probably the 'bust in Plaister of M. Angelo' which was lot 78 at Christie's on 19 May 1821, in the sale of Reynolds's studio contents after his niece's death.[1] His personal seal featured an engraving of Michelangelo's head by Hendrick van der Burch. Reynolds also makes visual allusions to other Old Masters in this portrait. The pose is derived from Van Dyck, and the portrait recalls Rembrandt's self portraits. As David Mannings has observed, the composition echoes Rembrandt's celebrated *Aristotle contemplating a Bust of Homer* (1653; Metropolitan Museum of Art, New York), which by 1815 belonged to Reynolds's friend Sir Abraham Hume.[2] It is uncertain whether Reynolds knew the composition, but as Martin Postle has noted, 'Reynolds would, no doubt, have appreciated the comparison of himself and Michelangelo with Aristotle and Homer'.[3] His prolific output of self portraits often invites comparison with Rembrandt, but while Rembrandt explored his emotions and anxieties in his self portraits, Reynolds presented a public persona.

'Distinction', Reynolds affirmed, 'is what we all seek after, and the world does set a value on them [*sic*]. I go with the great stream of life'.[4] Valentine Green's 1780 engraving of the portrait includes an inscription listing Reynolds's titles: 'Sir Joshua Reynolds, Knight, President of the Royal Academy, Member of the Imperial Academy at Florence, Doctor of Laws of the Universities of Oxford and Dublin, and Fellow of the Royal Society.' LO

**1** Penny 1986, no. 116, pp. 287–8.

**2** Mannings 2000, no. 21, p. 51.

**3** Postle 2005, no. 5, p. 82.

**4** Leslie and Taylor, 1865, vol. 2, p. 611.

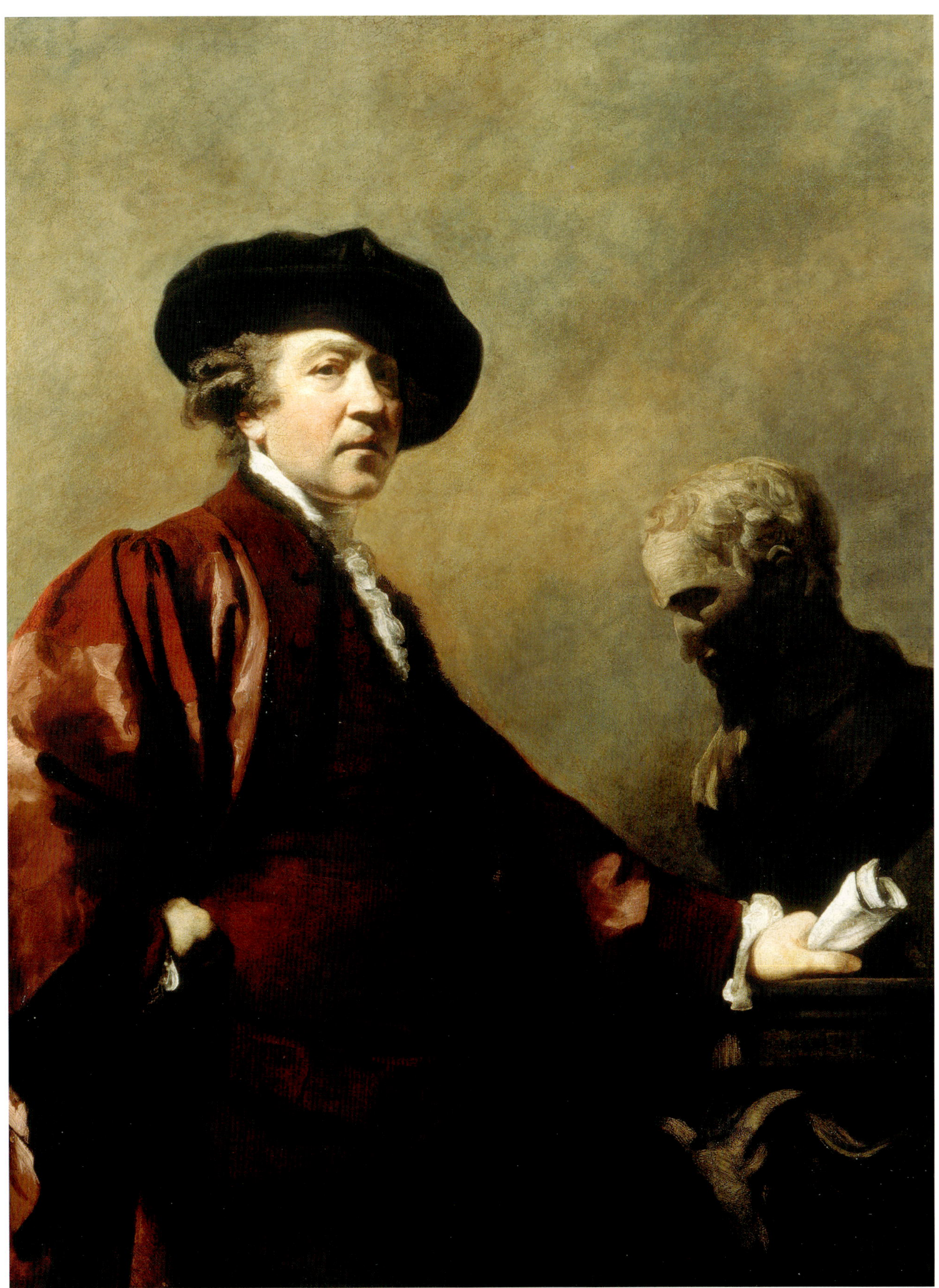

## 2. Elizabeth Louise Vigée Le Brun (1755–1842)
*Self Portrait in a Straw Hat* after 1782

Oil on canvas, 97.8 × 70.5 cm

The National Gallery, London (NG 1653)

Elizabeth Louise Vigée Le Brun earned an international reputation for her stylish portraits of royalty and aristocracy. Born in Paris, she received little formal artistic training as the schools of the Académie Royale de Peinture et de Sculpture were the preserve of men. Precociously talented, she nevertheless established herself as a society painter by the age of 17. She soon became a favourite at the French court, painting some 30 portraits of Queen Marie-Antoinette and the royal children. At the outbreak of the French Revolution in 1789 she went into exile for 12 years, travelling widely through Italy, Austria, Germany and Russia. Wherever she went, she received commissions from a noble clientele. As she recalled in her memoirs: 'My talent, feeble though it might have been compared with the great masters, made me welcome, nay sought after, in all the salons. Sometimes I became the recipient of, how shall I put it, public acclaim.'[1]

This self portrait, one of over 20 by the artist, is an autograph copy of a picture dating from 1782, a pivotal moment in Vigée Le Brun's career. That summer she toured the Low Countries with her husband, the dealer Jean-Baptiste-Pierre Le Brun. In a private collection in Antwerp she saw Rubens's portrait of his sister-in-law, Susanna Lunden (The National Gallery, London). As she wrote in her memoirs, the portrait made such an impression on her that she resolved to paint her own, to capture the same effects of bright sunlight and luminous shadows.[2] The straw hat is a playful reference to the nickname that Rubens's portrait had acquired, *Le Chapeau de Paille*. As an artist closely associated with royalty, it seems appropriate that Vigée Le Brun should have wished to emulate Rubens, whom Sir Dudley Carlton had famously described as 'painter of princes, prince of painters'.

Vigée Le Brun depicts herself as an elegant beauty with her palette and brushes in one hand; the portrait is an advertisement for her artistic talents and for the physical charms that she used to advance her career within elegant society. The original version was acquired by her patron and supposed lover, the Comte de Vaudreuil. In early 1783 it was exhibited at the Salon de la Correspondence where it caused a sensation. As one critic wrote, 'When someone announces that he has just come from the Salon, the first thing he is asked is: Have you seen Madame Le Brun? What do you think of Madame Le Brun? And immediately the answer suggested is: Madame Le Brun, is she not astonishing?'[3] The success of the self portrait at the Salon led to her being proposed for membership of the Académie Royale. There was considerable opposition to her nomination as her husband's position as a commercial art dealer officially disqualified her from membership, but with the crucial backing of Marie-Antoinette she secured one of the four seats reserved for women. LO

**1** *The Memoirs of Elisabeth Vigée Le Brun*, trans. S. Evans, London 1989, p. 24.

**2** Op. cit. p. 38.

**3** Quoted in Baillio 1982, p. 8.

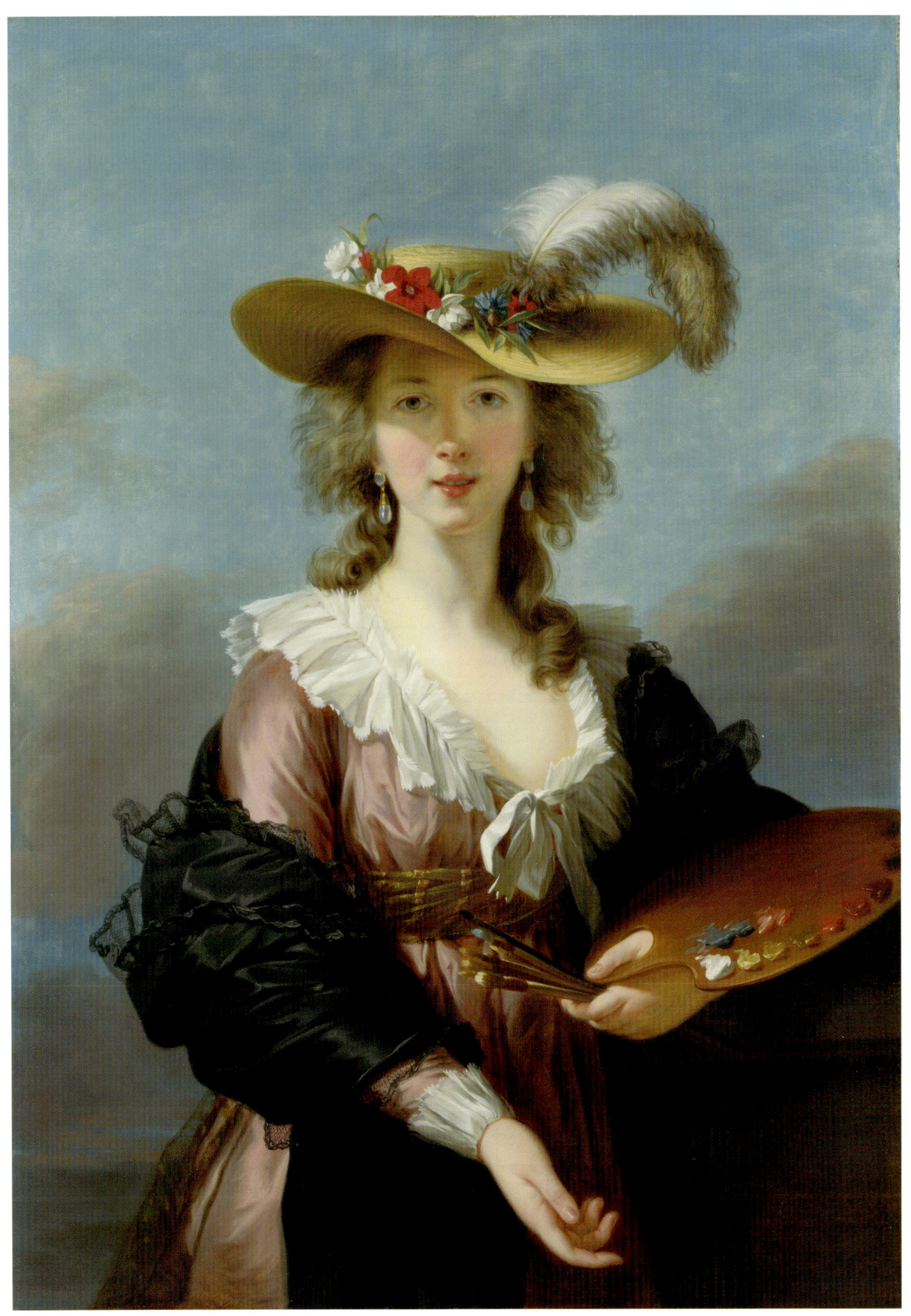

## 3. Alexander Roslin (1718–1793)

*Self Portrait* dated 1790

Oil on canvas, 103 × 81 cm

Galleria degli Uffizi, Florence (1890 n. 1673)

One of the most accomplished portraitists of his age, Alexander Roslin enjoyed a distinguished international career. Born in Sweden, he established himself as a painter of the Swedish aristocracy. His connections led to an invitation to the court of Brandenburg-Culmbach and in 1745 Roslin was appointed Court Painter at Bayreuth. Following a tour of Italy, he settled in Paris in 1752 and was nominated to the Académie Royale in 1753. Commissions from Gustav III, King of Sweden and Catherine II of Russia followed. His oeuvre includes portraits of many fellow artists, architects, painters and sculptors, notably his close friend François Boucher (1760; Château de Versailles), Joseph-Marie Vien (1757; Château de Versailles) and Claude-Joseph Vernet (1767; Nationalmuseum, Stockholm). He also painted over 20 self portraits.

This, one of the artist's last and finest self portraits, shows the formal image that Roslin wished to project as a court artist. Although he holds his palette and brushes in his hand, his fine silk clothes are hardly working attire: Roslin clearly delighted in depicting the fine details of the lace, embroidery and silk-covered buttons. The artist has portrayed himself above all as a courtier and turns to the viewer with a seigniorial air. The unfinished portrait on the easel shows his great royal patron King Gustav III, and around his neck Roslin wears the Swedish Royal Order of the Vasa. Roslin had been one of the first recipients of this distinction, which was instituted by Gustav III in 1772.

Roslin painted this portrait for the famous Medici collection of artists' self portraits now in the Uffizi, Florence. It was exhibited at the Paris Salon in 1791 and entered the Medici collection in June 1793.

The Italian inscription in the upper left of the picture reads 'Alexander Roslin, Swedish born 1718. Knight of the Royal Order of the Vasa. Painter to the King of France. Sketching the portrait of his sovereign the King of Sweden. Made in Paris, 1790'.[1] LO

**1** *'Alessandro Roslin, suezese nto 1718. Caval: re/del Real ordine di Vasa. Pittore del Re di/Francia. Sbozzando il Ritratto del Suo/ Soverano il Re di Suezia. Fato in Parigi, 1790.'*

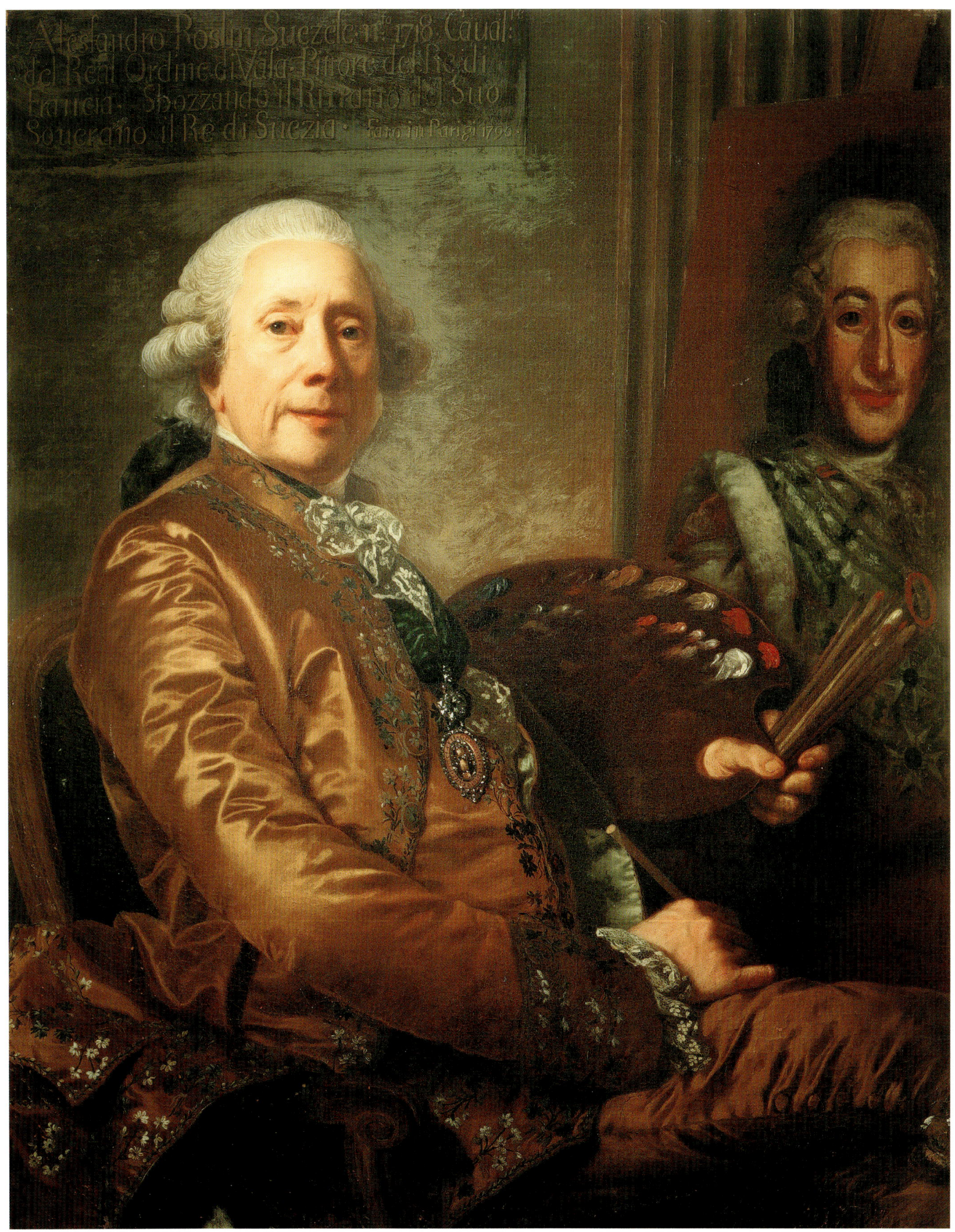
Alessandro Roslin Suezese n° 1718 Caual:
del Real Ordine di Vasa: Pittore del Re di
Francia: Sbozzando il Ritratto del Suo
Souerano il Re di Suezia. Fatto in Parigi

## 4. Christoffer Wilhelm Eckersberg (1783–1853)

*Portrait of Bertel Thorvaldsen* 1838

Oil on canvas, 89 × 73 cm

Ny Carlsberg Glyptotek, Copenhagen (MIN no. 880)

The Danish sculptor Bertel Thorvaldsen (about 1770–1844) was one of the most celebrated artists of his age. He spent most of his working life in Rome, executing works in a heroic Neoclassical style for patrons all over Europe. He ran a large studio in order to supply the great demand for his work. His success brought him substantial personal wealth, which he used to amass an important collection of art, now housed in the Thorvaldsen Museum, Copenhagen. His collection of contemporary paintings, including works by the Nazarenes, was the finest in nineteenth-century Rome.

As the first Danish artist to achieve international fame, Thorvaldsen became a central figure among the Scandinavian and German artists based in Rome, many of whom revered him as a hero. The young Danish artist Christoffer Wilhelm Eckersberg arrived in Rome in the summer of 1813, and during his stay lived in the same lodgings as Thorvaldsen. Eckersberg's letters and diaries indicate that the sculptor showed a genuine interest in his younger compatriot, while his own admiration for the older artist is clearly evident here. The portrait follows well-established conventions for displaying the sculptor's worldly achievements: Thorvaldsen is depicted wearing the robes of the Roman Academy of St Luke, where he was professor, with the decorations of the Danish and Neapolitan orders of chivalry on a ribbon around his neck. Behind the sculptor is a section of one of his most celebrated works, *The Alexander Frieze*, which he executed for the Quirinal Palace in 1812 in anticipation of Napoleon's visit to Rome. The detail shows Alexander entering Babylon; in a letter that Eckersberg wrote to his friend Johan Frederik Clemens he described it as 'Alexander's triumph, which is also Mr Thorvaldsen's triumph'. The portrait also suggests a Romantic sense of the nature of creative genius. The artist's relaxed pose and distant gaze seem deliberately to privilege not the trappings of worldly success, but the internal moment of artistic inspiration.

This portrait of a pre-eminent national figure exists in three versions. Eckersberg painted the first in 1814 during his stay with Thorvaldsen and sent it as a gift to the Royal Danish Academy of Fine Arts in Copenhagen, where Academy documents record that it was viewed 'with special pleasure'.[1] A replica dating from 1832 is in the Nationalmuseum in Stockholm; this, the third and final version, dates from 1838. LO

**1** Conisbee et al. 2003, no. 12, p. 81.

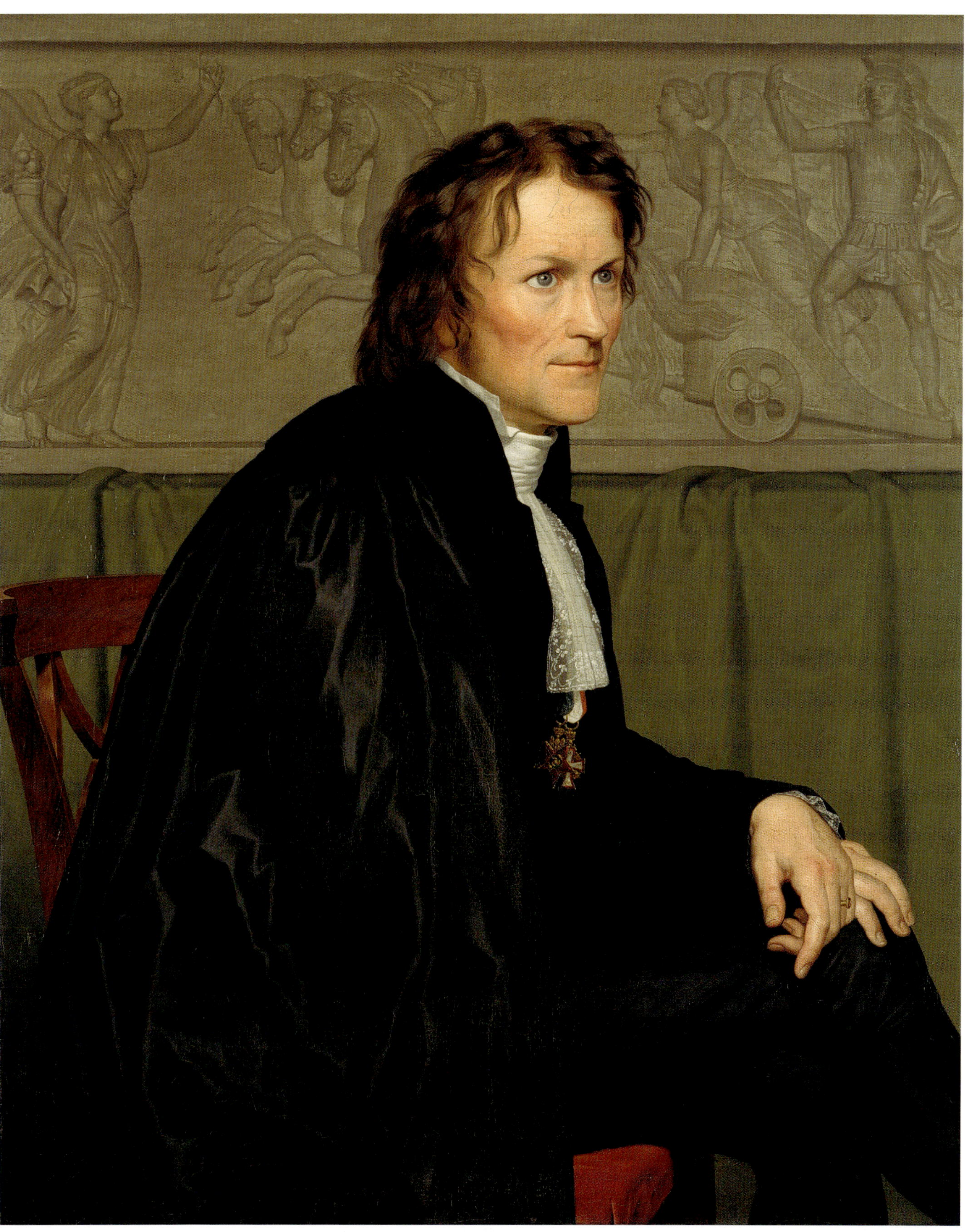

## 5. James Barry (1741–1806)

*Self Portrait* about 1780

Oil on paper, 42 × 34.4 cm

Victoria and Albert Museum, London (564-1870)

A history painter in the grand style, the Irish artist James Barry was elected to membership of the Royal Academy in London in 1773. His friends included the influential statesman and aesthetician Edmund Burke (who had paid for Barry's recent five-year study tour of Italy) and the founding President of the Royal Academy, Sir Joshua Reynolds, yet his career stands in sad contrast to that of his older contemporary.

Barry painted this self portrait around 1780, when he was engaged on his most celebrated work, the decoration of the Great Room of the Society for the Encouragement of Arts, Manufactures and Commerce in Robert and James Adam's prestigious new Adelphi development. Barry believed passionately in the role of history painting to improve civilisation and in 1777 had submitted a proposal for the decorative scheme to the Society. His subject was ambitious – encompassing, as his biographer Edward Fryer, wrote, 'no less than the complete history of the human mind in its various stages from barbarity to refinement'.[1] His series of six monumental canvases were described by Sir Ellis Waterhouse as 'the most considerable achievement in the true "grand style" by any British painter of the century'.[2] Although the pictures attracted critical acclaim, after six years of labour Barry received only £503.12*s*; Reynolds was at this time charging 200 guineas for a full-length portrait. At the outset of the project the Society had agreed to pay for Barry's materials and models, but no provision was made to pay the artist a living wage. The artist was forced to lead a very frugal existence, relying on profits from the printmaking that he worked on in the evenings.

The disillusionment and fatigue of those years are clearly apparent here: Barry appears defiant, challenging a hostile world, ' a driven and haunted individual struggling against the waking nightmare of his life'.[3] This self portrait serves to summarise the fundamentally untenable position of the history painter in eighteenth-century Britain. Although history painting was in theory esteemed as the highest form of art, the only genre that was readily patronised was portraiture.

In later years Barry increasingly cast himself as a persecuted genius. Quick to react when he thought he had been slighted or opposed, his paranoia led him into abusive tirades against his colleagues. He was expelled from the Royal Academy in 1799 and in his last years lived as a recluse. When his house was attacked by local vandals, he became more than ever convinced that there was a conspiracy against him, telling the poet Robert Southey that he would not go out in the evening because 'the Academicians would waylay him and murder him'.[4] The Irish lawyer William Henry Curran described a visit to his house in 1804:

> The area was bestrewn with … the many kinds of missiles, which the pious brats of the neighbourhood, had hurled against the unhallowed premises. A dead cat lay upon the projecting stone of the parlour window, immediately under a sort of appeal to the public, or a proclamation setting forth that a dark conspiracy existed for the wicked purpose of molesting the writer and injuring his reputation … This was in Barry's hand-writing, and occupied the place of one pane of glass. The rest of the framework was covered with … some of his own etchings, but turned upside down, of his great paintings at the Adelphi. LO

**1** *The Works of James Barry*, ed. E. Fryer, 2 vols (1809), vol. 1, p. 317, quoted in W.L. Pressly, 'Barry, James (1741–1806)', *ODNB*, 2004.

**2** Waterhouse 1953, p. 199.

**3** Pressly 1981, p. 195.

**4** *The Life and Correspondence of Robert Southey*, ed. C.C. Southey, 6 vols (1849–50), vol. 6, p. 54, quoted in W.L. Pressly, 'Barry, James (1741–1806)', *ODNB* 2004.

**5** W.H. Curran, *Sketches of the Irish Bar*, 2 (1855), pp. 171–2; quoted in Pressly, loc. cit. *ODNB* 2004.

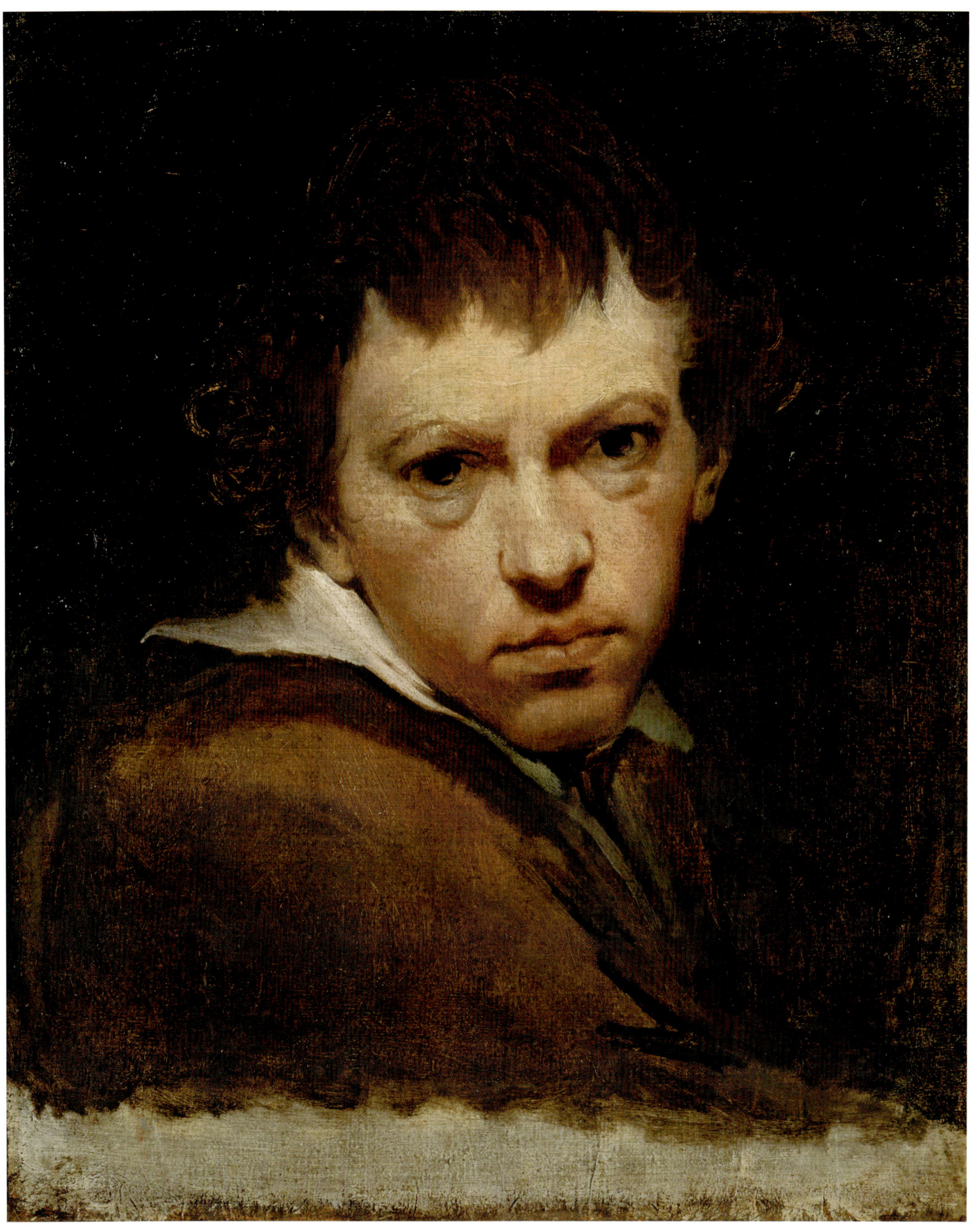

## 6. Henry Fuseli (1741–1825)

*Self Portrait Study* about 1780–90

Black and white chalk on paper, 27 × 19.4 cm

Victoria and Albert Museum, London (E.1028-1918)

Fuseli's intense self portrait drawing, made when he was in his forties, is devoid of references to his place within society or the tools of his trade. Instead, the portrait focuses attention on his internal resources: posed in the traditional attitude of Melancholy, a humour long associated with creativity, the artist subjects himself to intense scrutiny.

Fuseli's was an art of the imagination. Passionate about literature and mythology, he frequently drew his subjects from the *Iliad*, the *Odyssey*, the *Nibelungenlied*, Dante, Shakespeare and Milton. He explored the world of the unconscious in fantastic pictures described by the Romantic poet Samuel Taylor Coleridge as 'Convulsia & Tetanus upon innocent Canvas.'[1] 'One of the most unexplored regions of art are [*sic*] dreams', wrote Fuseli,[2] and his notorious painting *The Nightmare* (1781; Detroit Institute of Arts) caused a sensation when it was exhibited at the Royal Academy in 1782, Horace Walpole describing it as 'shockingly mad, madder than ever, quite mad.'[3]

Fuseli mixed with many of the influential thinkers of his age. His teachers in Zurich included Johann Jakob Bodmer and Johann Jakob Breitinger, whose ideas influenced the emerging *Sturm und Drang* movement, and he later associated with the movement's leading proponents, Johann Wolfgang von Goethe and the philosopher Johann Gottfried von Herder. He translated Winckelmann's *Reflections on the Painting and the Sculpture of the Greeks* (1765) and published *Remarks on the writings and conduct of JJ Rousseau* (1767) after meeting Rousseau in France. In London, where he spent most of his career, his circle included Mary Wollstonecraft, the advocate of women's rights, and the artists Sir Joshua Reynolds and William Blake. Fuseli's fiery personality and commanding intellect made him a central figure in the artistic and intellectual circles in which he moved. Herder likened his genius to 'a mountain torrent.'[4] Writing to Herder from Rome, where Fuseli spent the years 1770–8, one of his lifelong friends, the physiognomist Johann Caspar Lavater declared 'he is everything in extremes – always an original; His look is lightning, his word a thunderstorm.'[5] Fuseli shared Lavater's belief that the character of an individual was written in his features, making his self portrait a study in self-revelation.

Fuseli gained considerable public recognition. He was elected Royal Academician in 1790. In 1799 he was appointed Professor of Painting, and in 1804 he also became Keeper of the Royal Academy, the only individual ever to hold both these positions simultaneously. In 1816, at the recommendation of the sculptor Antonio Canova, he was elected a member of the first class of the Academy of St Luke in Rome. LO

**1** *The Notebooks of Samuel Taylor Coleridge*, ed. K. Coburn (1957), vol. 1, p. 954, quoted in D.H. Weinglass, 'Fuseli, Henry (1741–1825)', *ODNB* 2004.

**2** Aphorism 231 in Knowles 1831, vol. 3, p.145, quoted in Weinglass, loc. cit.

**3** W.T. Whitley, *Artists and their friends in England, 1700–1799*, vol. 2 (1928), p. 377, quoted in Weinglass, loc. cit.

**4** E.C. Mason, *The mind of Henry Fuseli* (1951), p. 69, quoted in Weinglass, loc. cit.

**5** Letter dated 4 November 1773, quoted in Schiff and Hofman 1975, p. 40.

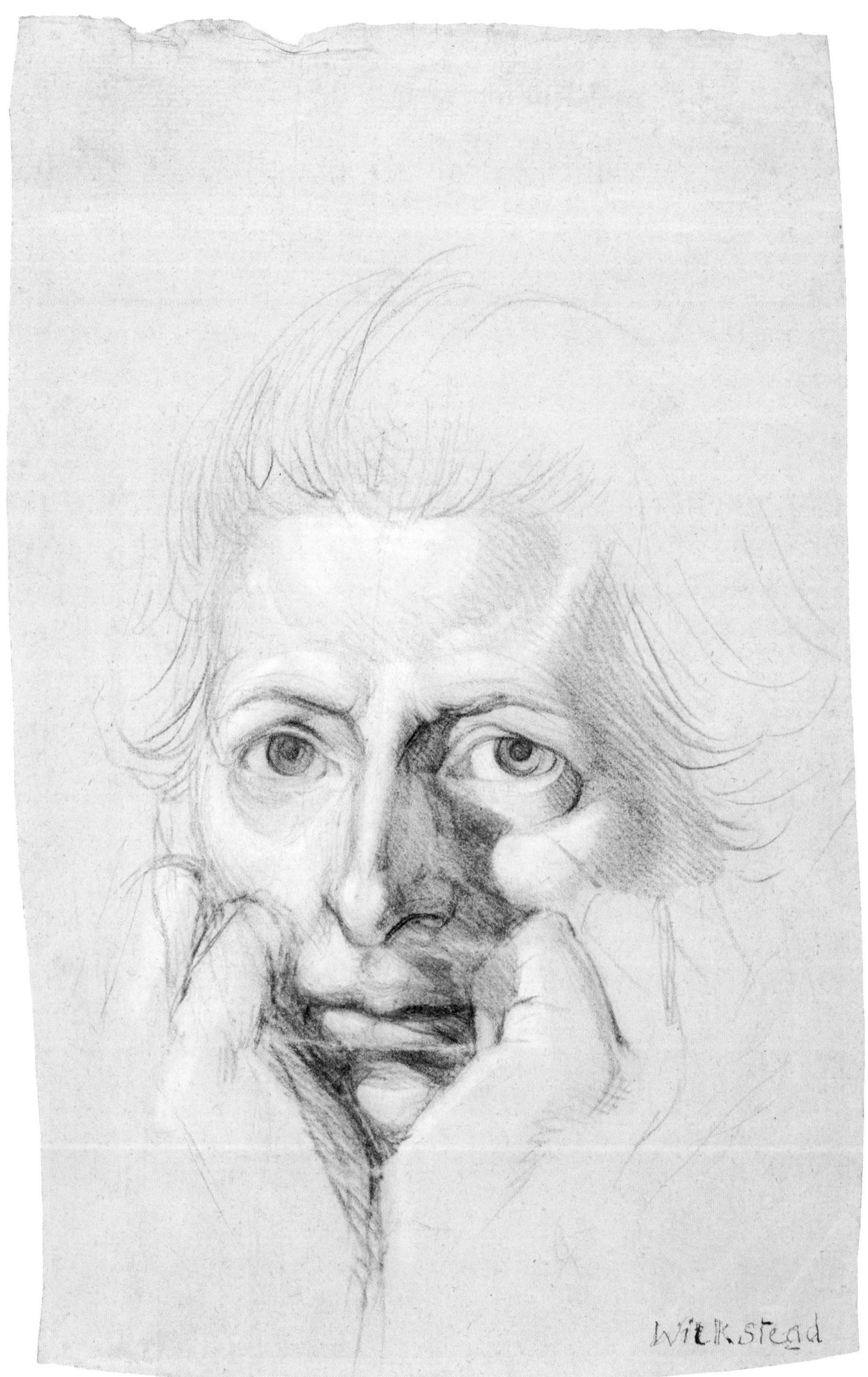

## 7. Alexandre Abel de Pujol (1785–1861)

*Self Portrait* 1806

Oil on canvas, 71.5 × 55.5 cm

Musée des Beaux-Arts, Valenciennes (P.46.1.293)

Alexandre Abel de Pujol's self portrait, in which he addresses the viewer with a gaze of exceptional expressive force, conveys a powerful sense of self-examining individuality and restless youth. The illegitimate son of Baron Alexandre de Pujol de Mortry, Provost of Valenciennes, Abel de Pujol was only permitted to use his father's name after 1811, when he won the prestigious Prix de Rome. Later he would sign his works 'Abel de Pujol', but this early portrait is simply signed 'AD Abel/1806'.

Abel de Pujol received his early training at the Académie de Valenciennes and the Ecole des Beaux-Arts in Paris, before entering the studio of Jacques-Louis David in 1804. At the end of 1805 he thought he would have to end his apprenticeship because of financial difficulties, but David was so impressed with his work that he let him continue free of charge. This self portrait has been described as giving the artist the 'uncanny appearance of a Romantic physically emerging out of his neo-classical background.'[1] The Neoclassical style had official sanction in France, where it was associated with the glorious images of Napoleon created by David and the sculptor Antonio Canova. Abel de Pujol referred to antique models in his own history paintings, and here adopts the theatrical effect of a toga and tousled hairstyle found in many Roman portrait busts.

The toga also had more revolutionary political associations, as the costume shared by the ancient Roman Republic and the democracy of Ancient Greece. In the late 1790s it was adopted as a form of dress by a breakaway group of an earlier generation of pupils from David's studio, nicknamed the 'Barbus' for their habit of growing beards. They believed that David, a leading member of the Jacobins in the early days of the French Revolution, had betrayed his revolutionary ideals by modifying his politics to suit the new Napoleonic regime. For them the toga was a sign of their wish to renew art and society by recreating the democratic ideal of Ancient Greece. It seems significant that Abel should have created this self portrait in the studio of David, one of the most important milieux for the re-evaluation of the role of the artist in society in turn-of-the-century Paris. It is also significant, given the importance of youth to the Romantic conception of the artist, that this work is exceptional in the artist's oeuvre: in his self portrait of 1812 he adopted a much more conventional image as an accepted member of the artistic establishment. LO

**1** Honour 1981, p. 247.

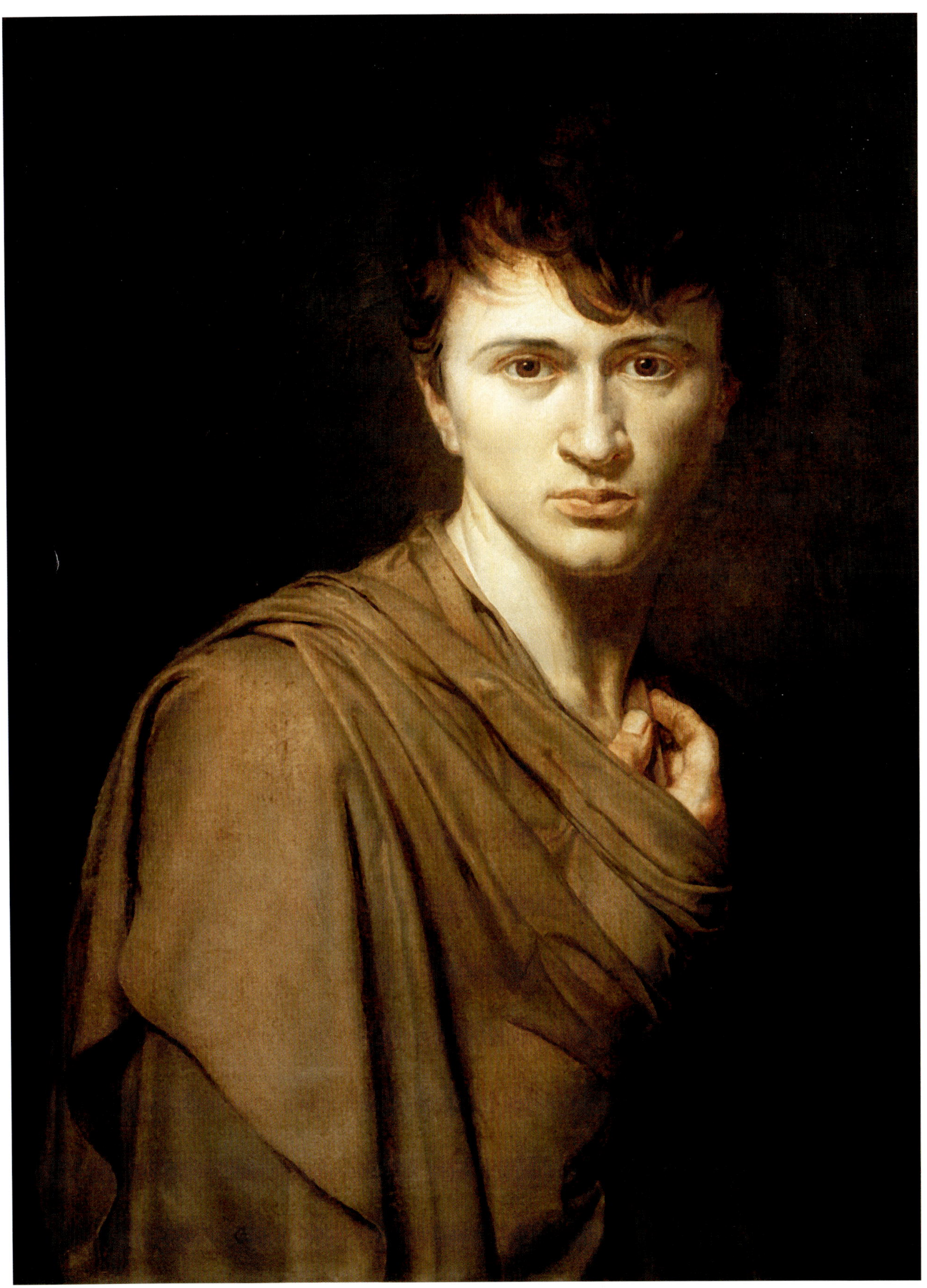

## 8. Philipp Otto Runge (1777–1810)

*Self Portrait at the Drawing Board* 1802

Chalk on paper, 55.2 × 43.3 cm

Hamburger Kunsthalle and Runge family, thanks to the generous support of the Kulturstiftung der Länder, the Hermann Reemtsma Stiftung and the Campeschen Historischen Kunststiftung, 2002 (1950-150)

While he was living in Dresden in 1801–2 Runge produced many self portraits in quick succession. In this drawing, the finest of the sequence, his tousled hair, Byronic open collar and wide-eyed gaze all contribute to a powerful evocation of the Romantic spirit by one of the most important figures of the movement.

In his life and art Runge demonstrated the Romantic independence of spirit that was to inspire a later generation. In 1798, at the age of 21, against the initial opposition of his family, he left his position as a clerk in his brother's Hamburg shipping firm and set out to become an artist. For Runge art was not a trade or a profession, but a vocation. He came from a committed Protestant family, and in his esoteric works attempted to represent the divine harmony that he found in nature. His circle of acquaintances included the artist Caspar David Friedrich, the Norwegian philosopher Henrik Steffens and the Romantic writers Friedrich Schlegel and Ludwig Tieck. Tieck introduced Runge to the writings of the Baroque mystic Jakob Boehme, whose ideas greatly influenced the young artist's developing thought.

Like many artists of his time, Runge felt the need for a new kind of art. In 1802, the year of this self portrait, he wrote of the end of history painting and the advent of a 'new landscape', which could evoke the moral order of the universe.[1] That year he started work on the first outline drawings for his great project *The Times of Day*. His ambition was to create a *Gesamtkunstwerk* (synthesis of the arts) on this theme, in which paintings would be combined with architecture, poetry and music to express the divine harmony evident in the natural cycles of day and night, the seasons, and human life. His idea of a work of art that appealed to many senses had a great influence on later nineteenth- and twentieth-century artists and thinkers. But Runge never lived to complete this work: he died at the age of 33 and his one major painting for the series, *Morning*, was dismembered after his death. This sense of an unfulfilled talent, given too short a time in the world, contributed to his Romantic myth. The poet Goethe, who had met Runge in Weimar in 1803, remarked shortly after his death:

> It is enough to drive one mad, beautiful and at the same time nonsensical … the poor devil couldn't stand the pace, he is gone already; there is no other solution: anyone who stands on the brink like that must either die or go mad; there is no salvation.[2] LO

**1** P.O. Runge (ed. D. Runge), *Hinterlassene Schriften*, Hamburg 1840–1 (reprinted Göttingen 1965), vol. I, pp. 6–7.

**2** Said to Sulpiz Boisserée in 1811; see E. Firmenich-Richartz, *Die Brüder Boisserée*, Jena 1916,vol. I, p. 130, quoted in Vaughan 1980, p. 52.

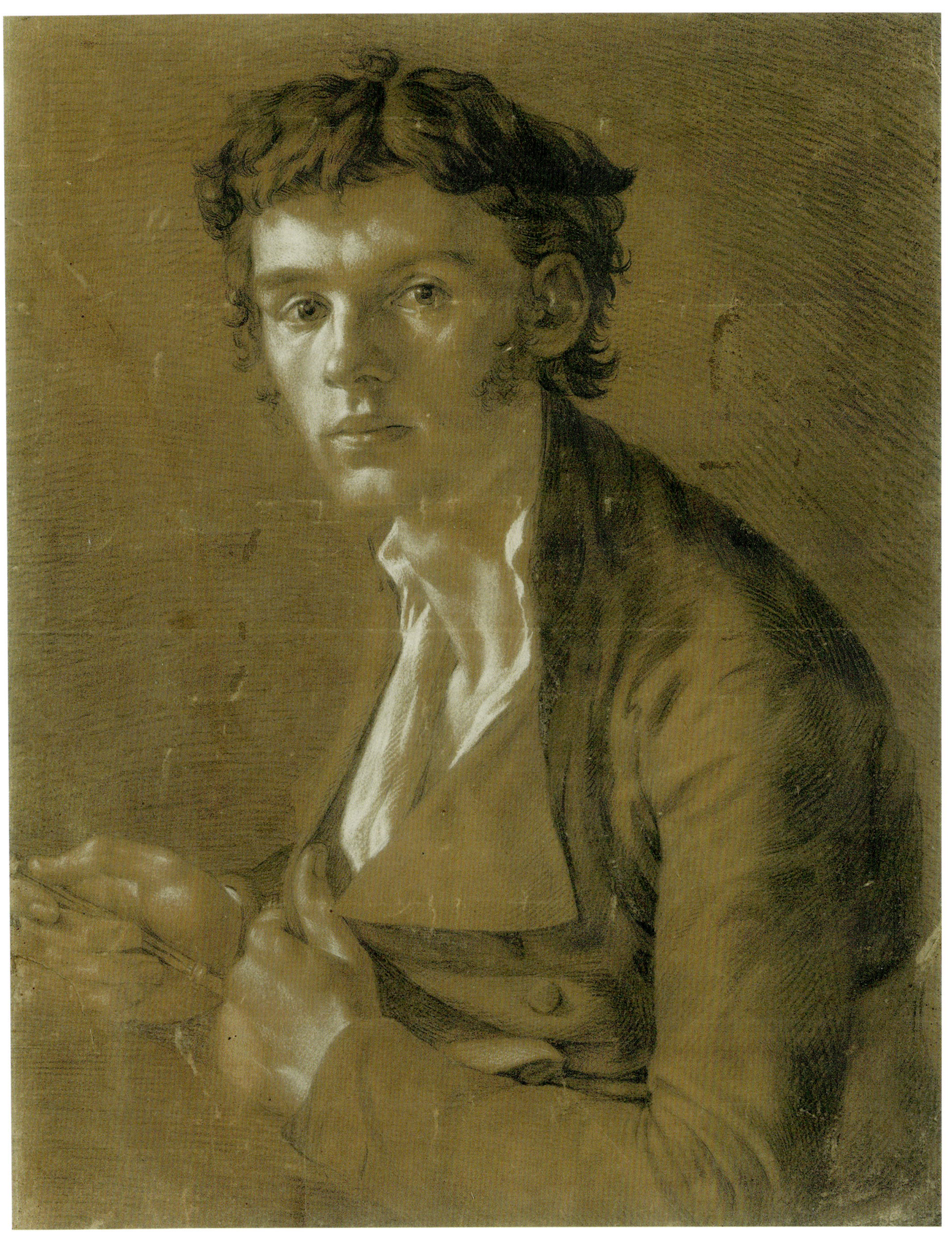

## 9. Georg Friedrich Kersting (1785–1847)

*Friedrich in his Studio* 1812

Oil on canvas, 53.5 × 41 cm

Nationalgalerie, Berlin (A I 931)

Caspar David Friedrich (1774–1840), together with Philipp Otto Runge, is regarded as one of the greatest artists of the German Romantic movement. A painter of atmospheric, symbolic landscapes, he believed passionately in the importance of an individual response to nature.

Friedrich placed great emphasis on artistic inspiration, instructing painters to 'close your bodily eye so that you may see your picture first with the spiritual eye. Then bring to the light of day that which you have seen in the darkness so that it may react upon others from the outside inwards.'[1] The Norwegian landscape painter Johann Christian Dahl, who moved into an apartment in Friedrich's house in 1823, recalled, 'Friedrich knew and felt quite clearly that one does not or cannot paint nature itself, but only one's own sensations, which must, nevertheless, be natural.'[2] Another of Friedrich's close friends, Carl Gustav Carus, described how the artist would wait in his studio – characteristically bare of all distractions – before starting a painting, until the image 'stood life-like in his mind's eye'. He would then immediately sketch it on the canvas, first in chalk and pencil, then more definitely in pen and ink, and then begin to paint.[3]

Kersting's portrait of Friedrich can almost be read as a manifesto of Friedrich's artistic philosophy. Its modesty of scale, the deliberate bareness of the studio, the fact that Kersting shows Friedrich not at work but contemplating the canvas, which we cannot see, and the unspecific nature of the view of cloud-filled sky beyond the window, all focus attention on the artist's creative process, emphasising the primacy of his internal world in the act of creation. It has been suggested that the light coming through the window to form a halo around the artist's head represents the divine aspect of his inspiration. Friedrich leans on the back of his chair, brushes and palette in hand. Significantly, the studio contains no allusions to Classical or Renaissance precedent.

Kersting met Friedrich after he moved to Dresden in 1808. They became close friends, going on a walking tour together through the Zittau Mountains and the Riesengebirge in July 1810. An earlier portrait by Kersting, *Caspar David Friedrich in his Studio* (Kunsthalle, Hamburg), was exhibited together with his *Gerhard von Kügelgen in his Studio* (Staatliche Kunsthalle, Karlsruhe) at the Dresden Kunstakademie in 1811, to great acclaim. Kersting continued to develop this genre that he made his own, epitomising the Romantic interest in the individual and his relationship with his environment. LO

**1** Vaughan 1980, p. 68.

**2** Op. cit. p. 66.

**3** C.G. Carus, *Lebenserinnerungen und Denkwürdigkeiten*, 1865–6, repr. 1968, p. 200, cited in Vaughan 1980, p. 68.

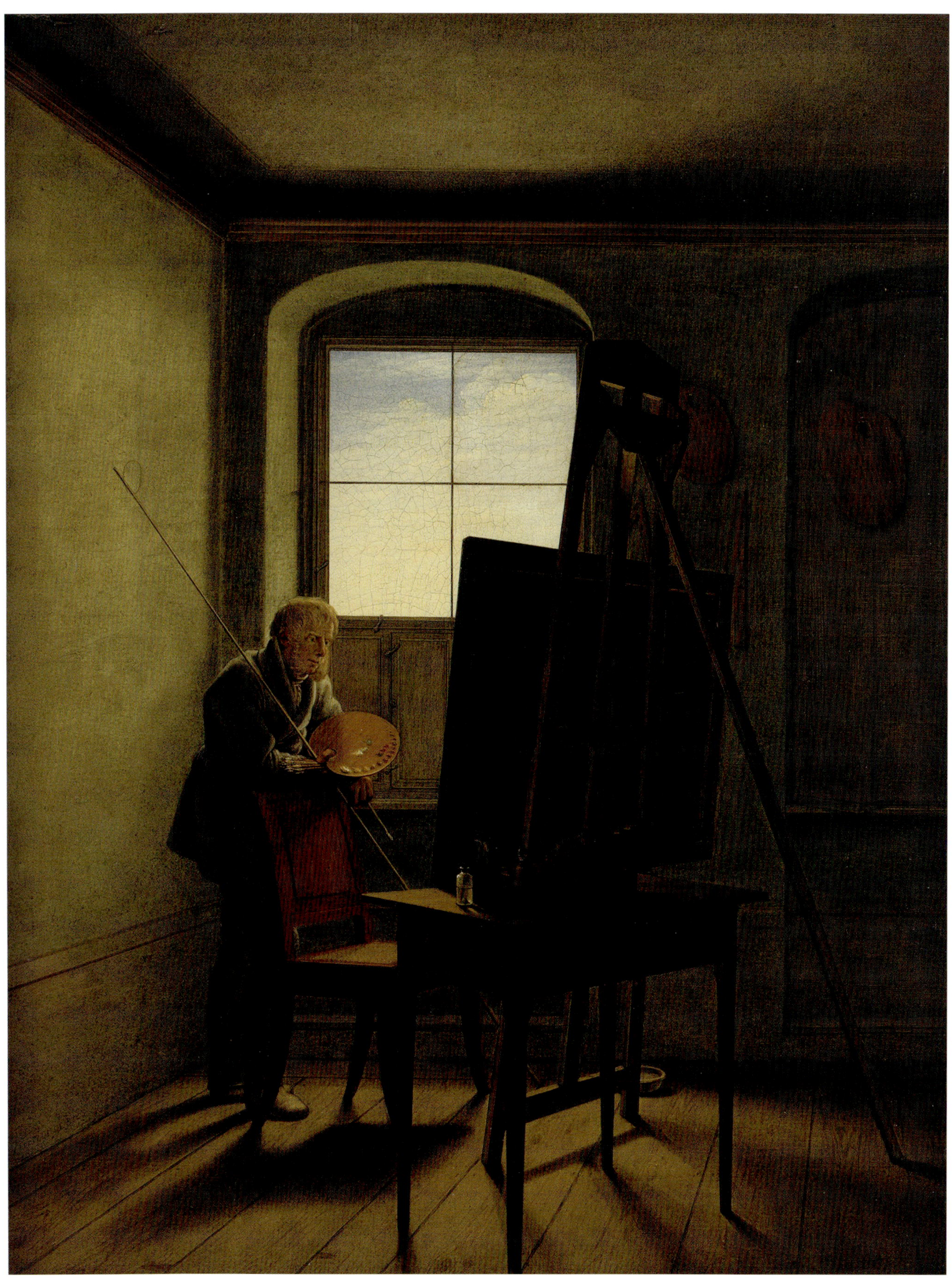

## 10. Friedrich Overbeck (1789–1869)

*Portrait of Franz Pforr* about 1810

Oil on canvas, 62 × 47 cm

Nationalgalerie, Berlin (A II 381)

In 1808 a group of six dissatisfied students[1] from the Vienna Academy began meeting regularly to discuss their work. They felt that the Academy training stifled the development of an artist's individual style. Inspired by a Romantic desire to create work that expressed their own genuine experience, they sought to match their life to their art, taking as their model the spiritual life and work of the early Italian and German masters, as represented in Romantic works such as Wilhelm Heinrich Wackenroder's *Confessions from the Heart of an Art Loving Friar* (1798). The group formed a movement, the Lukasbund (Brotherhood of Saint Luke), which expressed new Romantic ideals through a medieval revivalism.

Led by Friedrich Overbeck and Franz Pforr (1788–1812), the Lukasbund was formally established in 1809, one of the first of many artistic brotherhoods created during the nineteenth century. They took their name from the patron saint of painting, Saint Luke. In 1810 the brothers moved into the dilapidated monastery of Saint Isidoro, Rome, where their monastic lifestyle and devotion to spiritual art earned them the nickname 'Nazarenes'. 'Now we thus become monks,' wrote Overbeck to his father on 29 September 1810.[2] Taking their stylistic influences from early Italian and German art, the members of the Brotherhood consciously attempted to revive fifteenth-century life, replacing 'the model of the academic painter with the role of the monk-artist'.[3]

Most portraits made by the Nazarenes and their circle were intended as personal records of friendship. Describing his portrait of Pforr to Joseph Sutter on 10 October 1810, Overbeck wrote that he intended it to present his fellow leader 'in the situation in which he would feel happiest'.[4] Appropriately, the portrait recalls the Old German art that Pforr sought to emulate. Framed by a Gothic window, Pforr wears the Old German costume and long hairstyle adopted by the members of the Brotherhood; behind him is a woman, 'busy knitting and at the same time reading a holy book'. The white lilies beside her are an attribute of the Virgin Mary, and her presence suggests ideal piety and domesticity; she may also be intended to symbolise Pforr's own purity of soul.[5] The colour of Pforr's dress, red, indicates saintliness, according to a colour scheme established by Pforr and Overbeck.[6] The grapes around the frame allude to Christ's Passion, a sombre allusion emphasised by the presence of the skull mounted by a cross directly below the sitter: Pforr chose this device as his own personal emblem at the time of the foundation of the Brotherhood, no doubt intending it as 'a reflection of his own precarious hold on life'.[7] Pforr never enjoyed robust health and died in his early twenties, in 1812. Many details of this composition correspond to notes made by Pforr headed 'A Dream of the Future';[8] indeed, the whole structure of the picture, from arched frame to the view onto the sea, is a variation on the device of the Lukasbund seal designed by Overbeck the previous year,[9] which was intended to appear on the back of every picture completed by a member of the Brotherhood and approved by the group. LO

**1** Friedrich Overbeck, Franz Pforr, Joseph Sutter, Franz Hottinger, Ludwig Vogel and Joseph Wintergerst.
**2** Quoted in Frank 2001, p. 12.
**3** M.B. Frank, 'The Nazarene Gemeinschaft: Overbeck and Cornelius' in Morowitz and Vaughan 2000, pp. 48–66, p. 52.
**4** Overbeck letter to Joseph Sutter, 10 October 1810, quoted in Frank 2001, p. 13.
**5** Vaughan 1980, pp. 175–6; Frank 2001, p. 14.
**6** Overbeck, letter to his father, 30 July 1808 in Hasse 1887, p. 1191; Frank 2001, p. 14.
**7** Vaughan 1980, pp. 175–6.
**8** Published in Lehr 1924, pp. 293f.
**9** Forster-Hahn et al 2001, p. 82

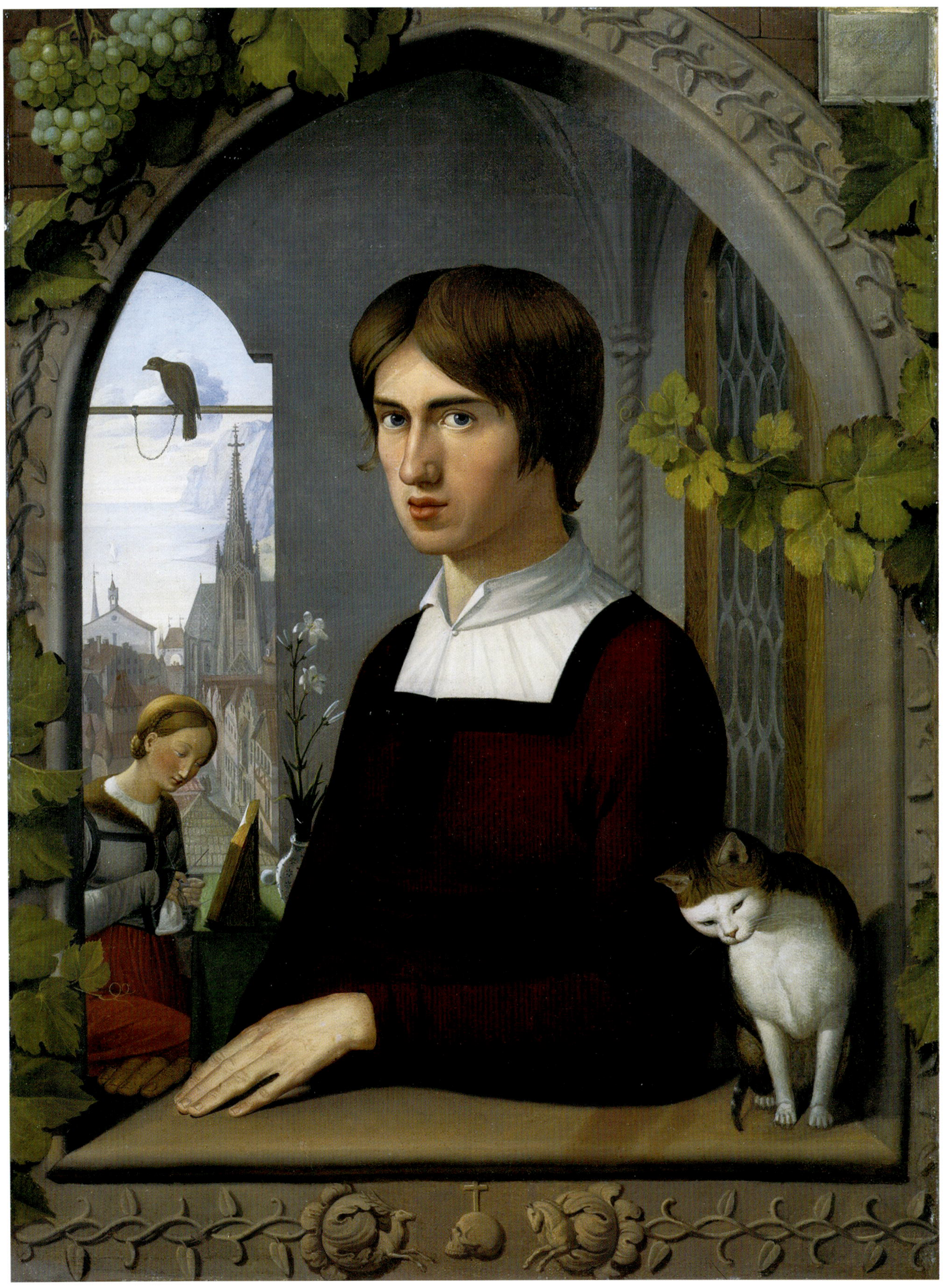

## 11. Samuel Amsler (1791–1849)
## after Carl Barth
## *Portrait of Carl Philipp Fohr* 1818

Engraving, 15 × 11.7 cm

The British Museum, London (1993-6-20-8)

Carl Philipp Fohr (1795–1818), although not an official member of the Brotherhood of Saint Luke, became part of the Nazarene circle in Rome after arriving in the city in 1816. His enthusiasm for historical German art and his devotion to his friends made him a popular figure amongst the colony of German artists living in Rome.

Many of the portraits made by members of the Brotherhood of Saint Luke and their circle are records of friendship. Fohr himself planned to make a large-scale work showing German artists gathered in one of their favourite meeting places in Rome, the Café Greco. Although he made a number of drawings for the project, featuring artists such as Friedrich Overbeck and his fellow Nazarene Peter Cornelius, he never completed the work.

In 1818, at the age of 22, Fohr drowned while bathing in the Tiber with Amsler, Barth and Johann Anton Ramboux. Barth had dived into a dangerous part of the river and rashly encouraged Fohr, a much weaker swimmer, to follow him; none of his friends had been able to rescue him. The tragic circumstances surrounding Fohr's early death led his friends to publish this portrait to raise funds for a monument to him. Fohr and Amsler had previously made portrait drawings of each other – Amsler's drawing of Fohr is in the Ashmolean Museum, Oxford – but Amsler chose to make this engraving after an 1817 drawing by Barth (Museum of Heidelberg) instead: Barth was too distressed to make the print himself. The resulting engraving is a testimony to the close friendship between the three men.

The print is noteworthy as one of the first attempts to revive the engraving technique of Albrecht Dürer, a hero for many German Romantic artists; even the monograms recall Dürer's own. Fohr wears the Old German costume and long hairstyle adopted by the Nazarenes and popular among patriotic student societies: he had been an active member of one such group in Heidelberg, the so-called Teutonen, before moving to Rome. LO

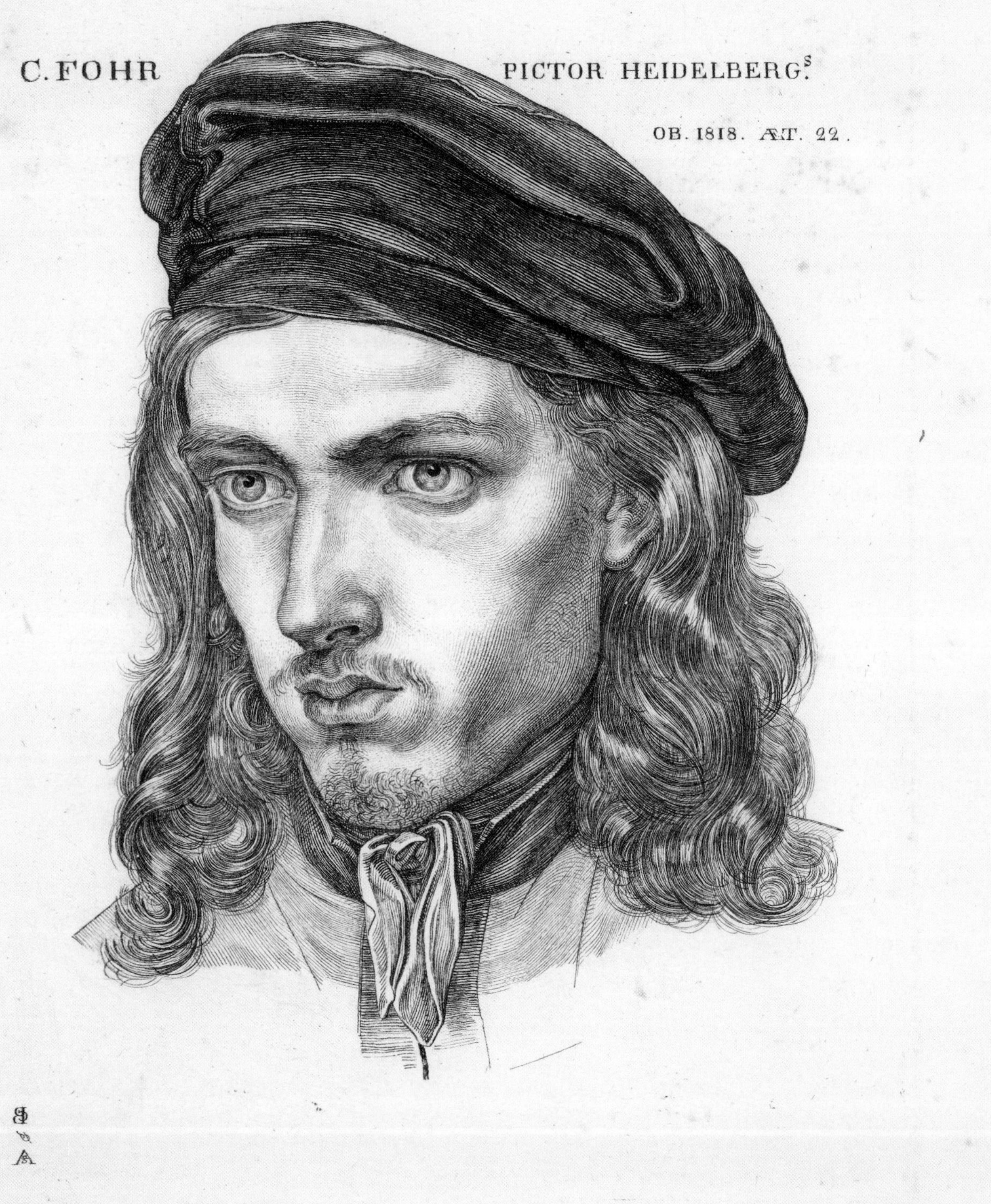
C. FOHR
PICTOR HEIDELBERG.S
OB. 1818. ÆT. 22.

## 12. Victor Emil Janssen (1807–1845)

*Self Portrait at the Easel* about 1828

Oil on paper, laid on canvas, 60 × 34.7 cm

Kunsthalle, Hamburg (2488)

Victor Emil Janssen's intensely personal self portrait has become an icon of German Romantic painting. The artist depicts himself at work in a room that is both his studio and living space, turning from his easel to look over his shoulder at his mirror image. The reflection of his open paintbox appears in the foreground, his bed behind him. Although he is engaged in the act of painting, his easel is cut from the picture plane. The focus of the picture is on the figure of the artist himself, seen from a close viewpoint and depicted in a three-quarter-length format that was unusual for this period. Stripped to the waist, the artist literally lays himself bare. Janssen almost certainly made this intimate self portrait as a private work: there is no evidence that it was exhibited during his lifetime. Painted on paper, and only later laid on canvas, it passed to his friend and fellow artist Friedrich Wasmann.[1]

Janssen was associated with the circle of artists of the Brotherhood of Saint Luke, known as the Nazarenes (see cats 10, 11). Born in Hamburg in 1807, he studied at the Munich Academy with Peter Cornelius, who became one of the leaders of the Brotherhood following the death of Franz Pforr. At the time when Janssen painted this self portrait he was in great demand as a model among fellow artists, who admired his good looks and physique. With his fine features, long nose, dark eyes and curly hair, he embodied the Nazarene ideal, the Old German type depicted by Albrecht Dürer in his own self portraits. Many commentators have remarked on the contrast between the idealised, athletic young man depicted by his contemporaries and the startling realism of Janssen's self-image here. His ribs are visible and his rounded back suggests that he was already in the early stages of the bone disease that was later to cause him terrible affliction. The violets and heather scattered in the foreground are traditional emblems of the transitory nature of life. The shirt knotted around his waist suggests a loincloth, bringing to mind images of Christ's Passion and of Christian martyrdom. It is not known whether Janssen was yet aware of his illness: it was only twelve years later, from about 1840, that he spoke of it with friends.[2] As his illness progressed he found it difficult to work and became increasingly depressed. On 10 July 1845 he was admitted to the Allgemeine Krankenhaus in Hamburg, where he died two months later. Janssen's illness and early death contributed to the myth that has grown up around this picture and enhanced its status as an icon of suffering creativity. LO

**1** Giesen 2001, p. 30.

**2** Op. cit. p. 19.

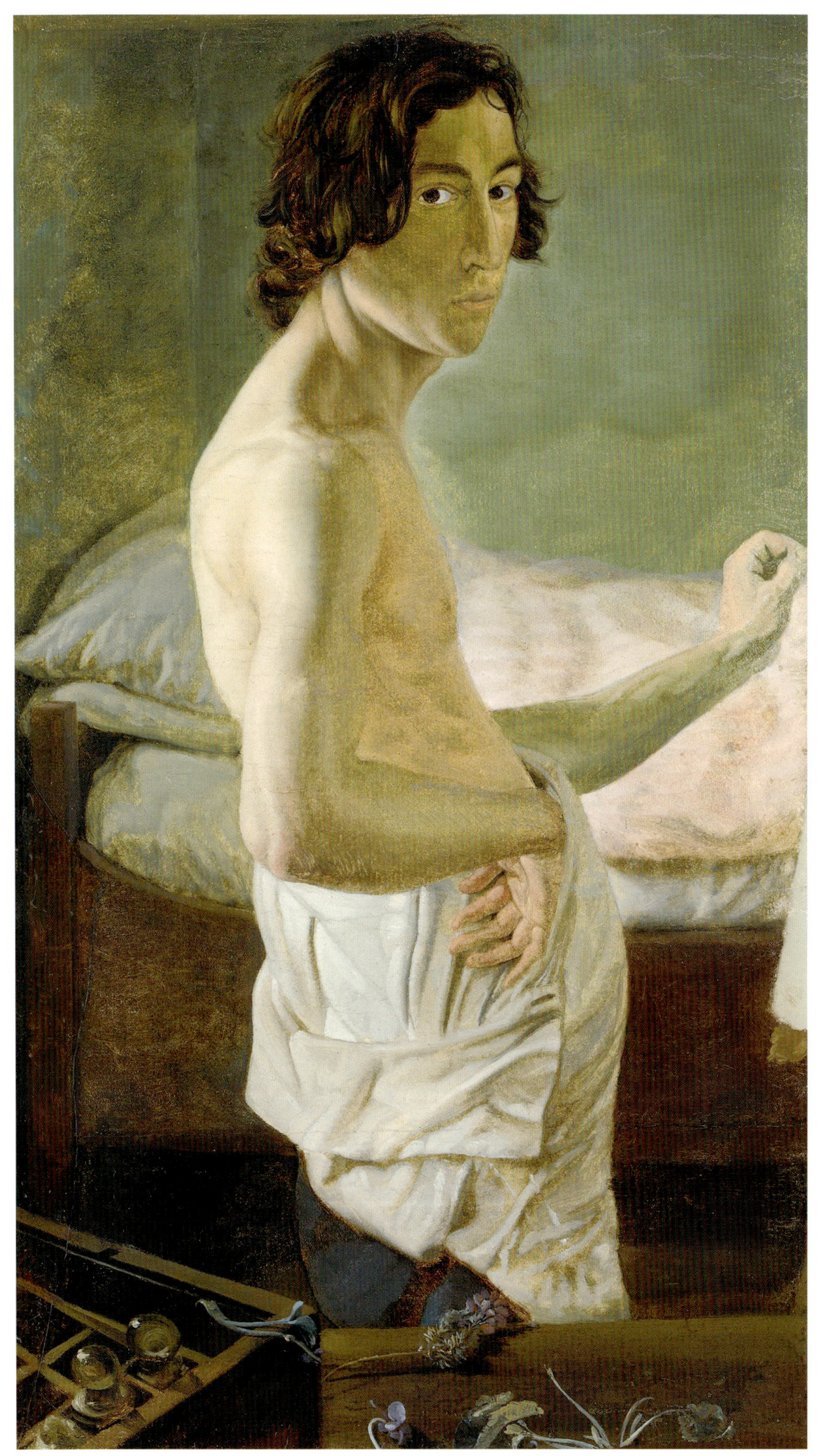

# Romantic Myths

Romantic ideas about the artist and his calling are reflected in many of the themes chosen by painters as subjects for their work. In particular they are evident in the predilection for scenes from the lives of artists and poets of the past, which helped to validate the Romantic myth. From the late eighteenth century there arose a fashion for deathbed scenes of great artists, especially of Leonardo da Vinci expiring in the arms of Francis I, a subject treated by Ingres in 1818 (cat. 13). The association of artists with royalty, of Titian with Charles V and Poussin with Louis XIII, for example, asserted to contemporary audiences the elevated status of the artist.

In the middle decades of the nineteenth century, painters tended to favour episodes focusing on the childhood of artists, in order to stress another key idea: the innateness of genius. Ever since Jean-Jacques Rousseau had urged that the natural instincts of children should be encouraged, youth had been associated with innocence and untainted vision. 'We must become children again to reach perfection', claimed Philipp Otto Runge.[1] Thus true genius came to be regarded as a divine gift, complete and self-sufficient from childhood. Vasari's tale of Giotto as a young shepherd discovered drawing his flocks (cats 14, 15) became a favourite with painters. In a fanciful transposition, Arthur Hughes depicted himself as a young poet in Renaissance garb, keenly alive to the beauties of nature (cat. 16).

The Romantic artist was haunted by the fear of the loss of youthful inspiration, through age and stale familiarity. He was haunted too by the spectre of early death. The child's vision was ill-suited to withstand the hardships of the artist's struggle for survival in an uncomprehending and hostile world, and heroes were found to exemplify this cult of the unfulfilled genius: André Chénier, Keats, and Shelley, who himself yearned to be absorbed into the infinite, 'and hear the sea Breathe o'er my dying brain its last monotony'.[2] Most famous of all these short-lived geniuses was the boy poet Thomas Chatterton, Wordsworth's 'marvellous boy' and the subject of Wallis's painting (cat. 21), who took his own life at the age of 17.

The genius of the artist condemned him, in the Romantic imagination, to loneliness and suffering, not only because of the struggles he experienced in realising his inner vision, but because he was destined to be rejected by the philistine public. 'The history of great men is always a martyrology', wrote the poet Heinrich Heine.[3] With the rise of a new, wealthy middle class, especially in England and France, the art market changed. The artist insisted on his need to express his own vision, irrespective of the preferences of the public, and an increasingly wide gulf emerged between the avant-garde painter and popular taste, leaving the artist feeling isolated and unappreciated.

The prevalence of this myth of the suffering artist encouraged the treatment of subjects that reflected and endorsed it. The myth of Orpheus, the bereaved poet who is destroyed by jealous bacchantes, was a favourite with Romantic and Symbolist painters, especially Gustave Moreau (cat. 20). The story of the Renaissance poet Tasso, who was condemned by his enemies to a madhouse, was made into a play by Goethe (*Torquato Tasso*) and later taken up by painters such as Delacroix (cat. 17). Believing himself to be unjustly neglected, Delacroix above all others chose to project the image of the suffering genius in paintings of artists and poets of the past, including Michelangelo (cat. 18), and Ovid exiled to the shores of the Black Sea (cat. 19). MW

**1** Philipp Otto Runge, *Hinterlassen Schriften*, 1840, I, p. 3.

**2** Percy Bysshe Shelley, *Stanzas written in Dejection, near Naples*, 1818.

**3** Heinrich Heine, *Religion and Philosophy in Germany* 1834, trans. J. Snodgrass, Boston 1959, p. 99.

## 13. Jean-Auguste-Dominique Ingres (1780–1867)

*The Death of Leonardo da Vinci* 1818

Oil on canvas, 40 × 50.5 cm

Petit Palais, Paris (P DUT 01165)

Scenes of the lives of great artists of the past became very popular in Europe in the first half of the nineteenth century, especially in France. They reflected the growing interest in the history of art, encouraged by an increasing number of public museums as well as by the proliferation of art books and periodicals. The choice of subject and manner of representation also frequently expressed contemporary ideas about the nature and role of artists. Here, Ingres illustrates the account of the death of Leonardo da Vinci from *The Lives of the Artists* (1568) by Giorgio Vasari, which was published in numerous editions in the late eighteenth and early nineteenth centuries:

> Finally, having grown old, he [Leonardo] remained ill many months … The king, who was wont often and lovingly to visit him, then came into the room; wherefore he, out of reverence, have raised himself to sit upon the bed, giving him an account of his sickness and the circumstances of it, showed withal how much he had offended God and mankind in not having worked at his art as he should have done. Thereupon he was seized by a paroxysm, the messenger of death; for which reason the king having risen and having taken his head, in order to assist him and show him favour, to the end that he might alleviate his pain, his spirit, which was divine, knowing that it could not have any greater honour, expired in the arms of the king, in the seventy-fifth year of his age.[1]

Similar tales of other artists being honoured by great patrons were frequently repeated: Charles V stooping to pick up Titian's brush, Emperor Maximilian ordering a nobleman to hold a ladder for Dürer while he painted, and Queen Cristina telling Guercino that she wished to touch the hand that had created so much beauty. Paintings illustrating such anecdotes were implicitly about the respect due to all artistic genius. It is significant that this king who visited Leonardo on his deathbed was Francis I of France. It was a source of great pride in France that Leonardo left Italy to live and work in France, and French art collectors and patrons would have been flattered by the implication that the French knew how to recognise a great artist. Ingres painted this picture as a pendant to a work showing another French monarch, *Henry IV Playing with his Children* (1817; Petit Palais, Paris). Both paintings entered the collection of the Comte de Blacas. LO

**1** Vasari 1996 edn, I, p. 639.

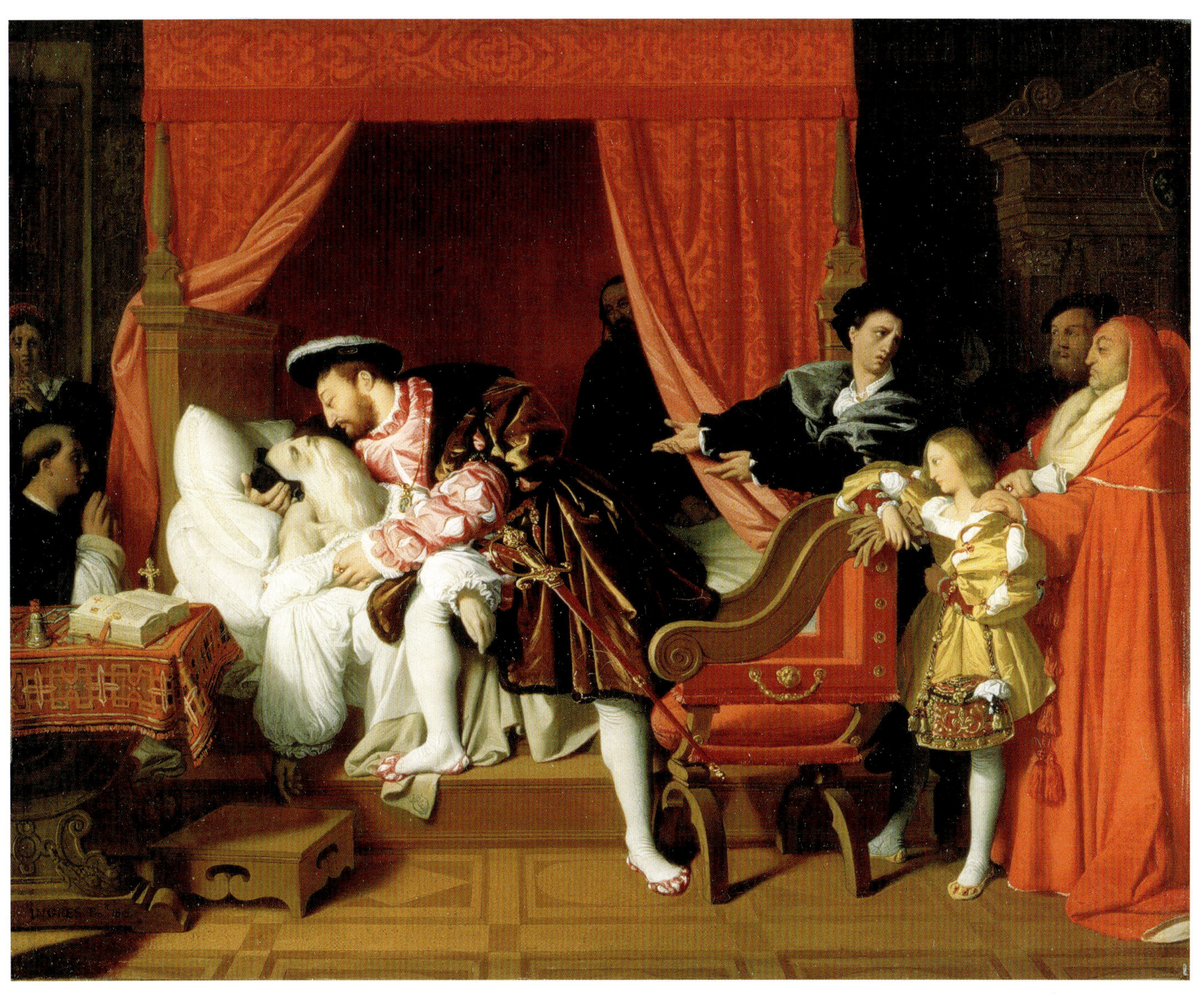

## 14. Pierre Henri Révoil (1776–1842)
*The Childhood of Giotto* 1840
Oil on canvas, 82 × 66 cm
Musée des Beaux Arts, Grenoble (MG 205)

## 15. Gustave Moreau (1826–1898)
*Giotto* about 1882
Watercolour on paper, 20.3 × 22.1 cm
Musée d'Orsay, conservé au département des arts graphiques du Musée du Louvre (RF 31174)

> When he had come to the age of ten [Giotto] showed in all his actions, though childish still, a vivacity and readiness of intelligence much out of the ordinary, which rendered him dear not only to his father but to all those also who knew him, both in the village and beyond. Now [his father] Bondone gave some sheep into his charge, and he, going about the holding, now in one part and now in another, to graze them, and impelled by a natural inclination to the art of design, was for ever drawing, on stones, on the ground, or on sand, something from nature, or in truth anything that came into his fancy. Wherefore Cimabue, going one day on some business of his own from Florence to Vespignano, found Giotto, while his sheep were browsing, portraying sheep from nature on a flat and polished slab, with a stone slightly pointed, without having learnt any method of doing this from others, but only from nature; whence Cimabue, standing fast all in a marvel, asked him if he wished to go to live with him.[1]

Giotto di Bondone was born in about 1266–7. Little is known of his early life and training, but the legend that he was discovered by the great Florentine artist Cimabue appears to have originated in an oral tradition that emerged in Florence in the century after Giotto's death. Documents published in 1999 suggest that Giotto may have been the son of a Florentine blacksmith rather than a peasant from the village of Vespignano.[2] The story of Cimabue discovering the shepherd boy Giotto is first found in Ghiberti's *Commentary on Art* (about 1450) and was later embellished by Vasari. The key features of the story are also found in biographies of several other artists: a young shepherd is sketching his animals when a connoisseur happens to pass by and recognises his extraordinary talent; the stranger arranges proper artistic training for the boy, who later emerges as a famous artist.[3] Vasari's famous account of the discovery of the young Giotto became a favourite subject among artists in the mid-nineteenth century. The tale of extraordinary natural talent bore witness to the idea that creative genius was an innate gift, an idea promoted by Romantic writers and artists. The image of the shepherd boy drawing his flocks also appealed to Romantic sentiments about the importance of returning to nature.

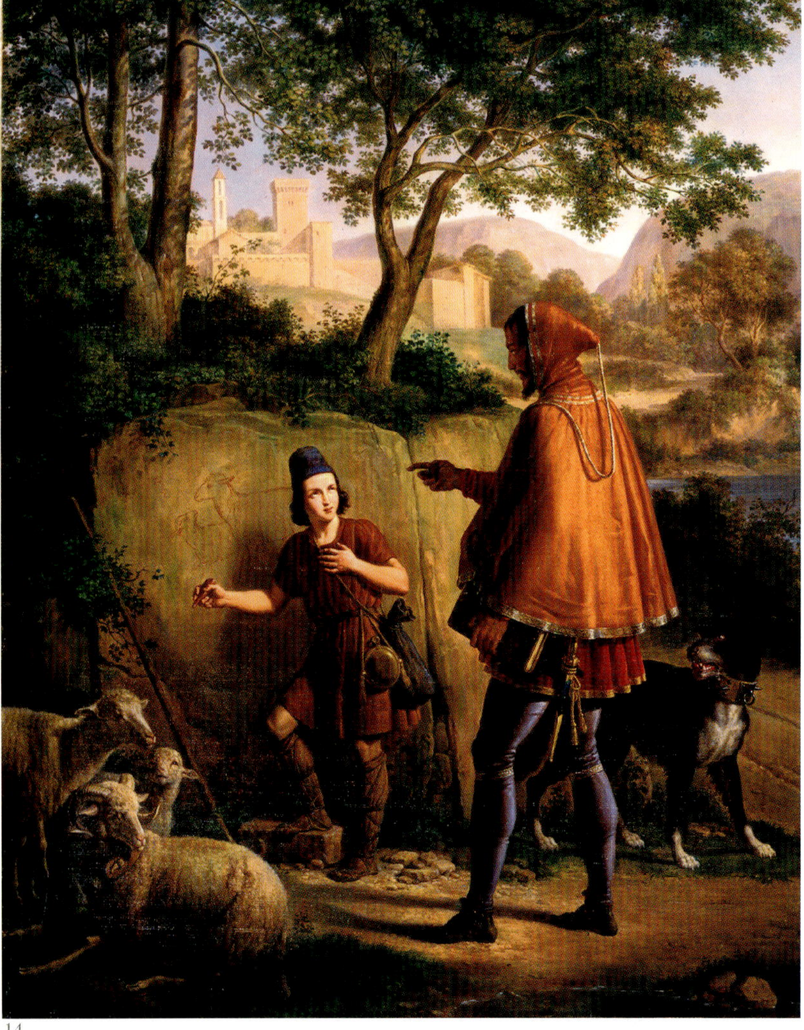
14

**1** Vasari 1996 edn, I, p. 97.
**2** Derbes and Sandona 2004, p. 3; Schwarz and Theis 1999, pp. 676–7.
**3** For further examples see Kris and Kurz 1979.

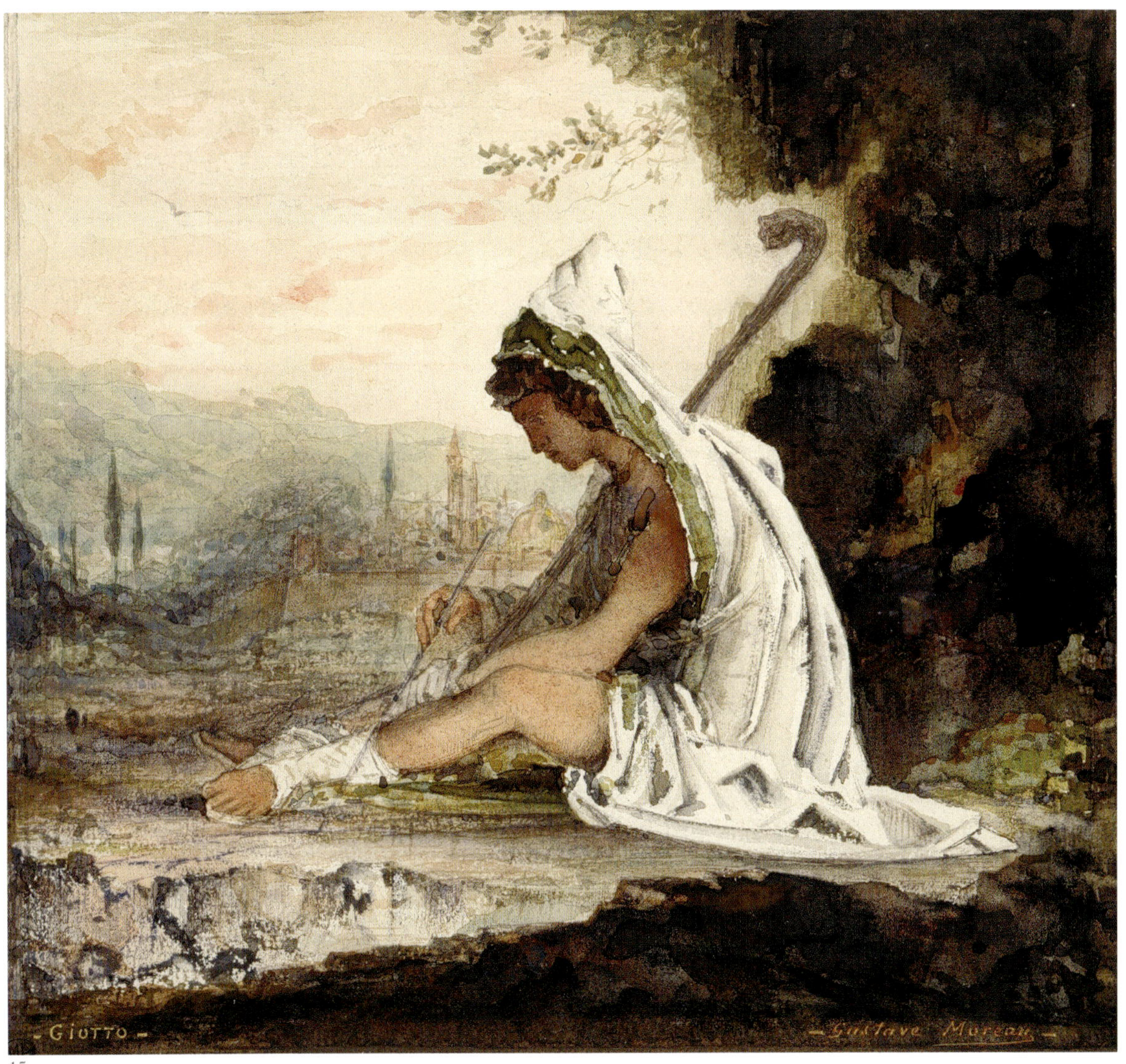


15

Pierre Henri Révoil was born in Lyons, where he trained at the Ecole de Dessin before entering the studio of Jacques-Louis David in Paris. In 1807 he returned to Lyons to take up a teaching post at the newly founded Ecole des Beaux-Arts. He was a leading exponent of the so-called 'Troubadour style' of painting that emerged with the vogue for medieval literature. Révoil showed a great concern for historical accuracy and built up his own collection of objects from the Middle Ages and Renaissance; he sold this 'cabinet de gothicités' to the Musée Royal in Paris in 1828. His painting exemplifies the Romantic nostalgia for the Middle Ages and the Gothic style that gave rise to the Nazarenes in Germany and the Pre-Raphaelites in England. The figure of Cimabue is a quotation from a fresco in the Spanish chapel of Santa Maria Novella in Florence.

John Ruskin, writing in 1854, drew a direct connection between the Giottesque movement of the fourteenth century and the Pre-Raphaelites of the nineteenth century, seeing them as 'literally links in one unbroken chain of feeling' because of what he perceived as their shared emphasis on the direct observation of nature.[4] Although Moreau's art was of a different kind, he too focuses on Giotto's response to nature, omitting the figure of Cimabue so that it is we as viewers who become the witnesses to Giotto's early artistic efforts. Moreau perhaps knew Lorenzo Ghiberti's account of the story, which describes the boy Giotto 'sitting on the ground drawing a sheep on a slab of stone'.[5] LO

**4** John Ruskin, *Giotto and his works at Padua* (1854); extract reprinted in Schneider 1974, pp. 53–6.

**5** Lorenzo Ghiberti, *Commentari* (about 1450); extract reprinted in Schneider 1974, pp. 39–40.

## 16. Arthur Hughes (1832–1915)

*The Young Poet (Portrait of the Artist)*

About 1849

Oil on canvas, 63.5 × 91.4 cm

City Museum and Art Gallery, Birmingham (1935 P38)

Arthur Hughes was born in London and showed such early artistic promise that in 1846, aged 14, he was allowed to enter the Government School of Design at Somerset House, where he studied with Alfred Stevens. The following year he won a scholarship to the Royal Academy Schools, where he enrolled on 17 December 1847. In 1849, aged just 17, he was awarded the Royal Academy silver medal for drawing from the antique and exhibited an oil painting at the Royal Academy Summer Exhibition. He became a follower of the Pre-Raphaelite Brotherhood after reading their journal, *The Germ*, which appeared in four issues in 1850.

Painted just before that, in 1849, this youthful self portrait reflects many Romantic notions about art. Reclining on a grassy bank in a costume reminiscent of the chivalric age, Hughes has the appearance of a medieval troubadour. The lilies in the foreground suggest the purity of youth, and the arrangement of the figure within an Arcadian setting echoes some of the ideas about youthful creativity and nature seen in images of Giotto's childhood (cats 14, 15). It is significant that the artist depicts himself as a 'poet', without any reference to his artist's tools. Poets, especially young poets, were amongst the greatest heroes of Romanticism: like artists, they were seen as visionaries whose works were engendered in thought and imagination. Furthermore, Hughes can hardly have been unaware of the young poet Thomas Chatterton who had died in 1770 aged 17 – exactly Hughes's age – and who would later be depicted in Henry Wallis's celebrated *Chatterton* (cat. 21). An oil sketch for the painting is also in the Birmingham City Museum and Art Gallery.

Hughes himself came to embody the Romantic myth that linked the production of great art with youth. He enjoyed great success in the 1850s but his reputation declined in his later years. William Michael Rossetti, writing in 1870, declared him 'one of those artists who reach, before youth has passed, to as high a point of development as they are destined for.'[1] LO

**1** W.M. Rossetti, *Portfolio* (1870), p. 114, quoted in S. Wildman, 'Hughes, Arthur (1832–1915)', *ODNB* 2004.

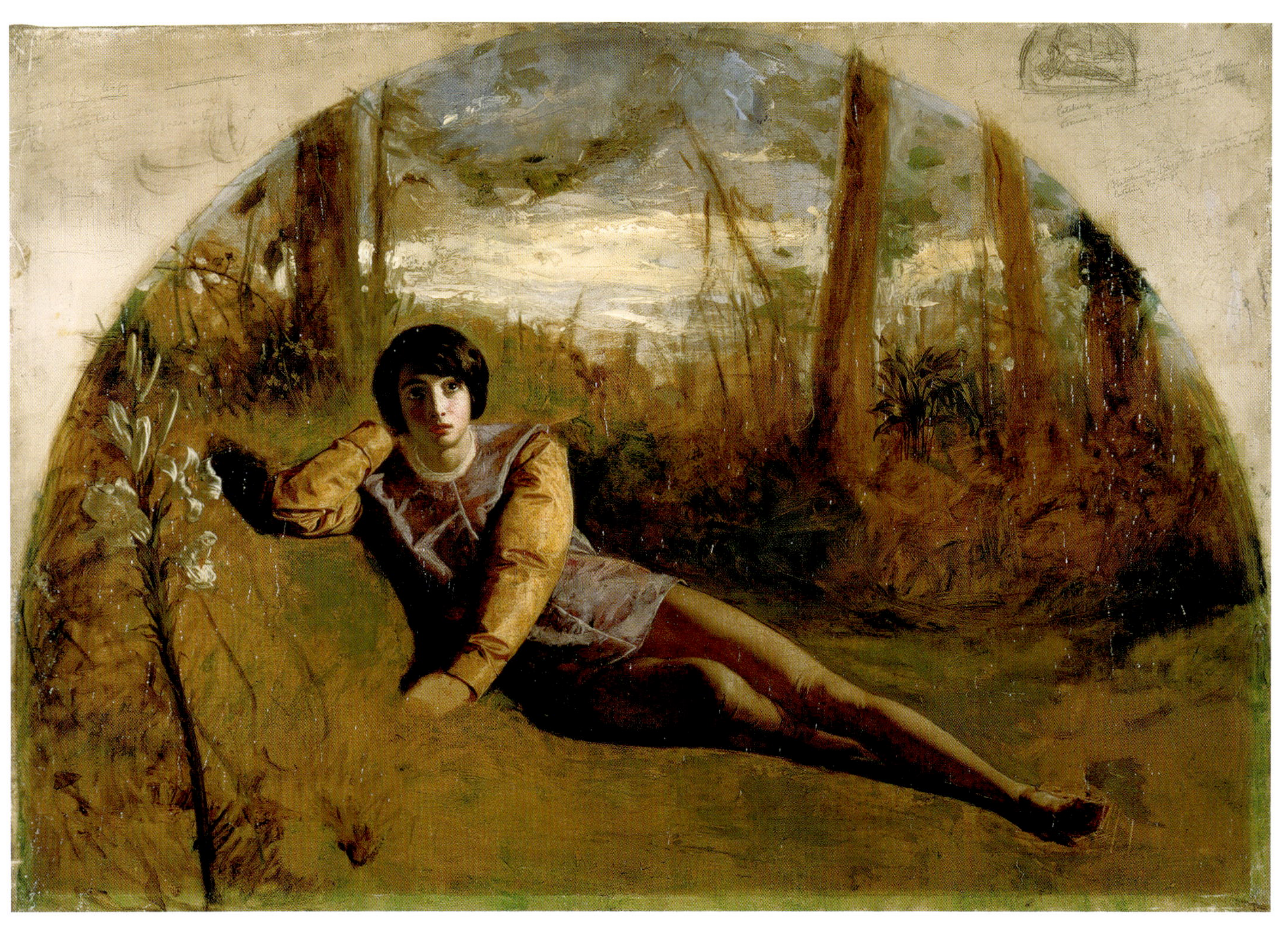

## 17. Ferdinand-Victor-Eugène Delacroix (1798–1863)

*Tasso in the Hospital of St Anne, Ferrara* 1824

Oil on canvas, 50 × 61.5 cm

Private Collection

## 18. Ferdinand-Victor-Eugène Delacroix

*Michelangelo in his Studio* 1849–50

Oil on canvas, 41 × 33.5 cm

Musée Fabre, Montpellier (868.1.40)

## 19. Ferdinand-Victor-Eugène Delacroix

*Ovid among the Scythians* 1859

Oil on canvas, 87.6 × 130.2 cm

The National Gallery, London (NG 6262)

Delacroix first made a note of his intention to paint 'Tasse à l'hôpital des fous' in about 1820 on the inside cover of a sketchbook (Musée du Louvre, Paris, RF 23357). The works of the poet Torquato Tasso had been read and illustrated by artists ever since they first appeared, but by the end of the eighteenth century there was a growing interest in the story of his life. Goethe's play *Torquato Tasso*, begun in the 1770s and completed in 1789, was translated into French in 1823. John Black published his two-volume *Life of Torquato Tasso* in 1810, and the poet was the subject of dramatic works by Byron and Shelley, and paintings by Fleury Richard, F.M. Granet and Louis Ducis, among others.

Tasso was confined in the hospital of St Anne for the insane on the orders of his patron, Alfonso d'Este, Duke of Ferrara, between 1579 and 1586. The myth that he was in fact completely sane and had been imprisoned because he was in love with Leonora d'Este, the Duke's sister, was already circulating by the end of the sixteenth century, and gathered momentum in the Romantic period (although discredited by Black in his scholarly biography). Byron's Tasso endures 'long years of outrage, calumny and wrong;/Imputed madness, prison'd solitude' for love of Leonora. Swiss writer Madame de Staël, introducing the French translation of Goethe's play, described Tasso as 'brave as his knights, in love, loved, persecuted, crowned and dying of grief while still young on the eve of his triumph, he is a superb example of all the splendours and all the misfortunes of great talent'.[1]

Delacroix shared the common Romantic view that Tasso was a persecuted genius unjustly accused of madness, and in this painting he shows the poet as a lone sane figure surrounded by uncomprehending lunatics. There is reason to believe that the painting is in some sense autobiographical: wounded by criticism of his work, Delacroix believed himself isolated and misunderstood. He returned to the theme of Tasso in a painting of 1839 (Oskar Reinhart Collection, Winterthur), showing the poet alone in his cell while onlookers from the outside world peer through the bars to look at the supposed lunatic; they do not recognise the great poet for what he is. This later painting inspired a sonnet by Baudelaire, 'Sur Le Tasse en prison d' Eugène Delacroix' (1844).

The theme of the solitary genius was one that preoccupied Delacroix through much of his career. In 1830 he wrote an essay on Michelangelo in which he portrayed the celebrated Renaissance master as a lonely genius, despised by the mediocre. The epigraph that Delacroix chose for the essay was Michelangelo's statement: 'I go my lonely way along paths which no man has made for me'. 'Think of the great Michelangelo', he wrote in his journal on 4 January 1824, '... seek solitude'. Two decades after his essay was published, he painted *Michelangelo in his Studio* (cat. 18) showing the artist deep in thought, seated at the feet of his statue of Moses and beside his Medici Madonna. The essay and the painting both reflect Delacroix's ideas about his

**1** *De l'Allemagne* (1813), Paris 1968, I, p. 338, quoted in Honour 1981, p. 264.

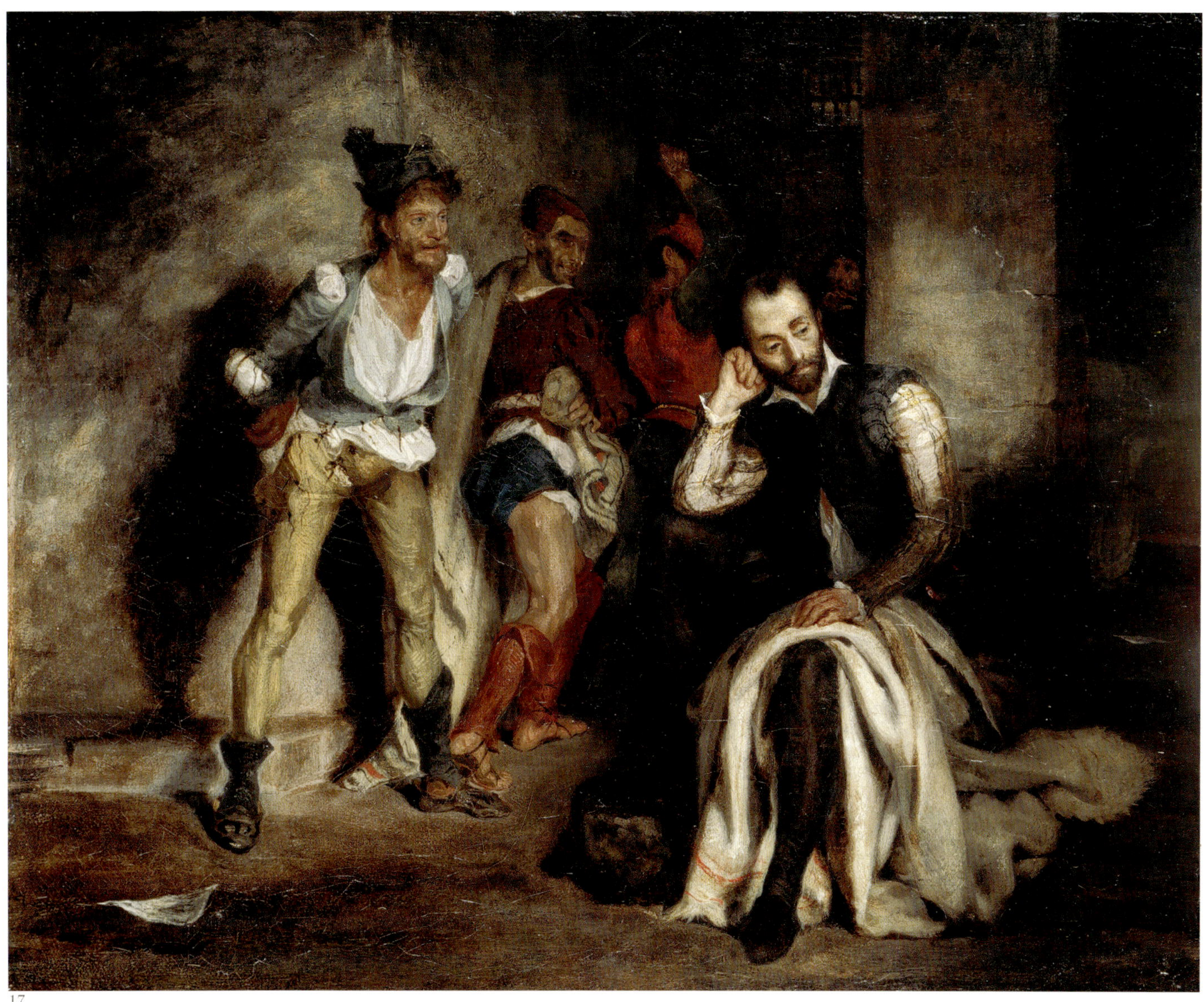

17

own work, and a sense that solitude is in some sense necessary for the creation of great art.

When Delacroix began his painting of *Ovid Among the Scythians* (cat. 19) in 1856, he was returning to a subject that he had included in his great decorative scheme for the ceiling of the library of the Chambre des Députés in the Palais Bourbon, Paris, completed in 1848, in which the subject had been executed by one of his assistants.[2] As another variation on the theme of the persecuted and lonely artist, Ovid held great interest for Delacroix: on 10 April 1849, in a list of possible subjects for easel paintings in his Journal, he had included 'the subject of Ovid in Exile in a larger composition'. The current painting was exhibited at the Salon in 1859.

The celebrated Roman poet Ovid, author of *Ars Amatoria* (*c.* 16 BC) and *Metamorphoses* (*c.* AD 7), was banished from Rome by Emperor Augustus in AD 8 for an unknown offence. He went into exile in Tomi, a village on the shores of the Black Sea in modern-day Romania, a region then inhabited by the Persian-speaking Scythians. Here he wrote his last works, *Tristia (Songs of Sadness)* and *Epistulae ex Ponto* (*Letters from the Black Sea*). His repeated petitions for pardon were in vain, and he died in exile in AD 17. Chateaubriand included Ovid's story in his prose poem *Les Martyrs* (1804), in which the hero Eudorus comes across Ovid's grave and laments the great poet's rejection by his own people, while 'less ungrateful … the wild peoples

**2** Johnson 1981–9, III, no. 334, p. 151; Sérullaz et al. 1998, no. 95.

of the banks of the Ister still remember the Orpheus who appeared in their forests.'[3]

Delacroix chose to illustrate the Scythian barbarians' treatment of Ovid after he landed on their shores. The poet, wearing a toga-like garment, reclines on the ground to the left of centre, apparently giving in to despair at his exile. Two men and a woman with an infant talk to him and offer him food. In the foreground, a man milks a mare, a detail of Scythian life derived from the classical writer Strabo,[4] while on the left a child with a dog stares at the stranger. Delacroix himself described the subject in the Salon catalogue thus: 'Ovid in exile among the Scythians. Some of them examine him with curiosity, others welcome him in their own way, offering him mare's milk, wild fruit etc.'

In this work Delacroix revisits the theme explored in his two earlier paintings of Tasso, of a poet condemned by his society. At the same time he was preoccupied by another great theme: the juxtaposition of civilisation and barbarism. There is a restorative quality to Ovid's encounter with the uncultivated Scythians here. Delacroix wrote the title of this painting in pencil opposite an undated section of his Journal describing the invigorating solitude of a man surrounded by uncivilised peoples: 'Setting for depicting the feeling of a heart and of a sick imagination, that of a man who after a worldly life, finds himself enslaved among the barbarians, or cast onto a desert island like Robinson Crusoe, forced to fall back on the strength of his body and his own industry – which restores to him natural feelings and calms his imagination.'[5]

This idea of the importance of a return to a state of nature for over-civilised man had been developed extensively by the philosopher Jean-Jacques Rousseau. Delacroix re-read Rousseau's works zealously and railed against the loss of unspoilt country-side to technological progress. This painting draws together the idea of the persecuted genius that Delacroix had depicted in his paintings of Tasso, with a sense of the importance of solitude, a theme touched on in his exploration of the life of Michelangelo. As Vincent Pomarède wrote: 'The content of this pivotal work thus represented, a few years before the artist's death,

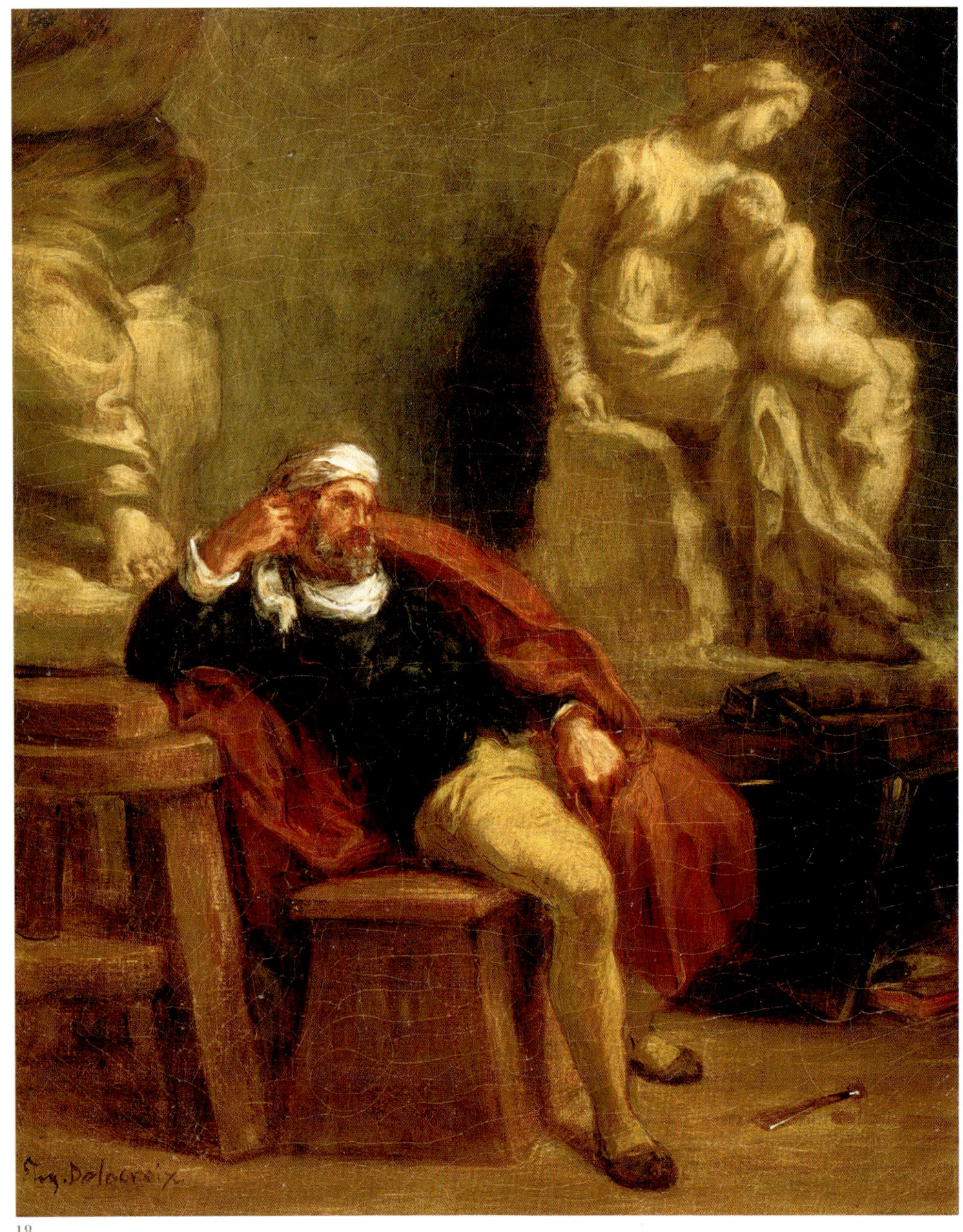


18

3 Cited by Charles Baudelaire in his review of Delacroix's work at the 1859 Salon, Baudelaire 1955, p. 258.

4 Davies and Gould 1970, p. 77.

5 Joubin 1950, III, p. 382, cited in Tinterow and Loyrette 1994, cat. 69.

6 Sérullaz et al. 1998, cat. 95.

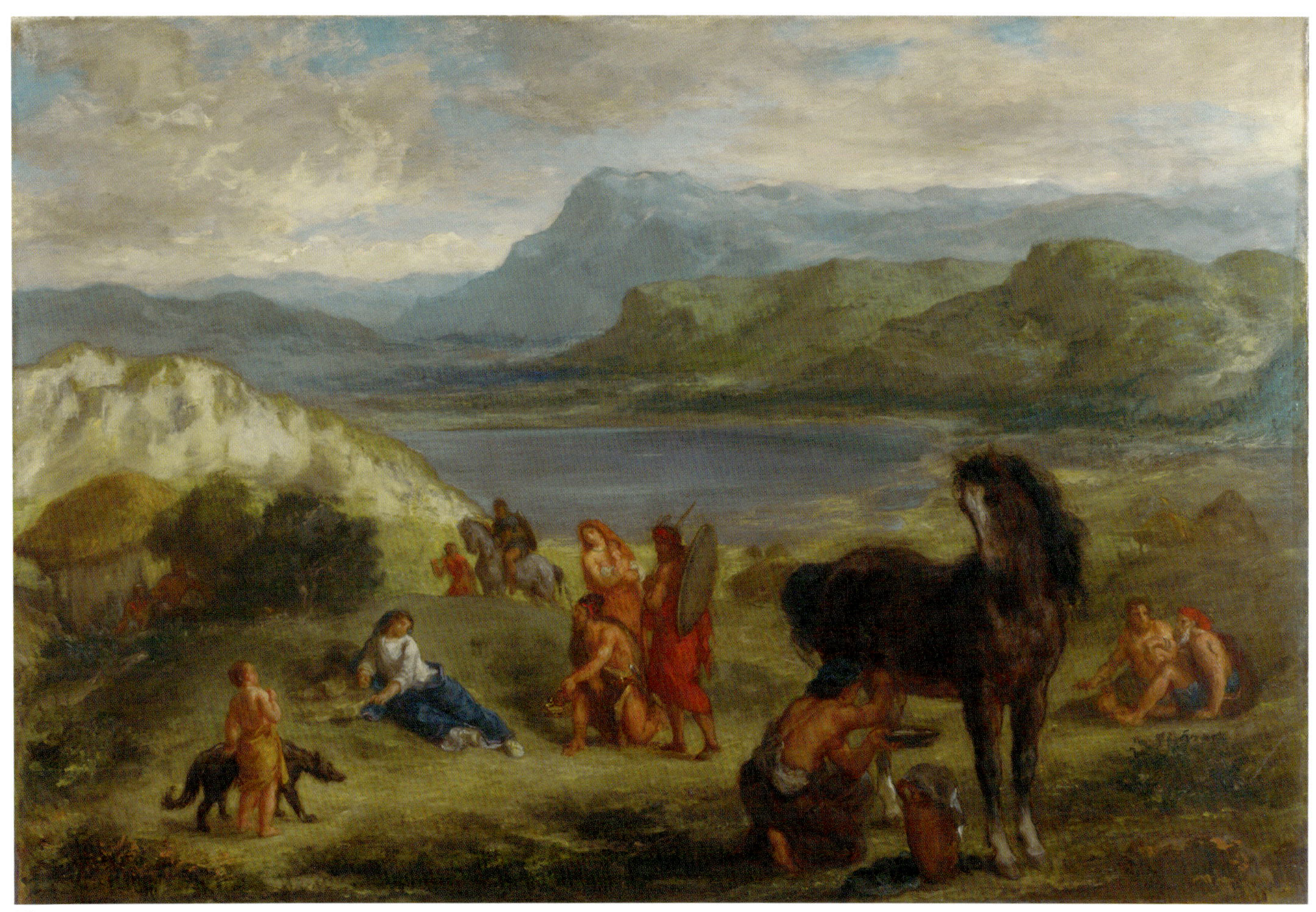

19

something of a summary of his philosophical and aesthetic convictions.'[6]

Delacroix exhibited several works at the 1859 Salon. Most of them were harshly criticised, but the response to *Ovid Among the Scythians* was more mixed. The landscape was admired by a number of critics, but Paul de Saint-Victor complained about the 'gigantic beast cluttering up the foreground' that looked as if it had been 'foaled by the Trojan horse';[7] Maxime Du Camp dismissed it as a 'spectacle of unpardonable decadence', advising the painter 'to return to the literary works that he loves and to the music for which he was certainly born'.[8] Baudelaire, clearly attracted to the theme of the exiled poet, wrote a moving piece about the work:

Look next upon the famous poet who taught the Art of Love; there he is, lying on the wild grass, with a soft sadness that is almost that of a woman. Will his noble friends in Rome be able to quell the emperor's spite? Will he one day know again the luxurious pleasures of that prodigious city? No: from this inglorious land the long and melancholy river of the Tristia will flow in vain; here he is to live and to die … All the delicacy and fertility of talent that Ovid possessed have passed into Delacroix's picture. And just as exile gave the poet that quality of sadness which he had hitherto lacked, so melancholy has clothed the painter's superabundant landscape with its own magical glaze.[9] LO

**7** Loc. cit.

**8** Maxime Du Camp, *Le Salon de 1859*, Paris 1859, p. 34, cited in Tinterow and Loyrette 1994, cat. 69.

**9** Baudelaire 1955 edn, p. 258.

## 20. Gustave Moreau (1826–1898)

### *Orpheus at the Tomb of Eurydice* 1890–1

Oil on canvas, 173 × 128 cm

Musée National Gustave Moreau, Paris (194)

The story of the legendary musician Orpheus was first recorded in Virgil's *Georgics* (30 BC) and Ovid's *Metamorphoses* (about AD 7), which recount the tale of Orpheus' loss of his beloved wife, Eurydice, who died from a poisonous snakebite. Orpheus followed her into the underworld, where he sang so beautifully of his love and sorrow that Pluto, god of the underworld, allowed him to reclaim his wife. All Orpheus had to do was lead her out to the light without looking back. Unable to resist, Orpheus turned to look at Eurydice. She died a second time and was lost to him forever. The tragic songs of the bereaved poet charmed the animals and the birds, and even the rocks and the trees. The Thracian women, however, were insulted by his vow never to love another woman, and tore Orpheus limb from limb. The river Hebrus received Orpheus' head and lyre and it is said that they went on singing and playing as they were carried downstream.

It is not surprising that the myth of Orpheus should have inspired countless artists and composers through the ages. It treats universal themes of love and loss and speaks of the power of love and art to overcome death. In the nineteenth century two aspects of the myth found particular resonance: the idea that great art could spring from tragedy, and the idea that the works of a persecuted artist could live on. For artists who felt themselves torn apart by critics, Orpheus' singing head was a powerful symbol of the immortality of their own art.

In 1866 Gustave Moreau submitted a painting to the Paris Salon showing the finding of Orpheus' head and lyre (Musée du Louvre, Paris). That same year Emile Lévy exhibited *The Death of Orpheus* (Musée d'Orsay, Paris). Returning to the theme 30 years later, Moreau painted this picture of Orpheus mourning at the tomb of Eurydice. Gluck's opera *Orfeo ed Euridice* (1762) opens with Orpheus mourning at Eurydice's grave: Moreau had almost certainly seen the opera, by one of his favourite composers, when it was revived in Paris in 1858. The present work may show Orpheus before or after his fateful journey to the underworld. Moreau painted it in response to the death in March 1890 of his own beloved Alexandrine Dureux, and described it thus:

> The divine singer is quiet for ever. The great voice of beings and things is extinguished. The poet has fallen prostrate at the foot of a tree with withered branches, moaning and sorrowful. The soul is alone, it has lost everything that was to it splendour, strength and sweetness, it weeps, giving way to inconsolable solitude. Silence is everywhere, the moon appears above the tomb and the sacred pool enclosed by walls. Only the drops of dew, falling from the flowers into the water, make their steady and unobtrusive sound, that sound full of melancholy and sweetness, the sound of life amid the silence of death.[1] LO

**1** Description from Moreau's manuscript inventory of the collection in the Musée Gustave Moreau, no. 194, cited in Mathieu 1976, p. 161.

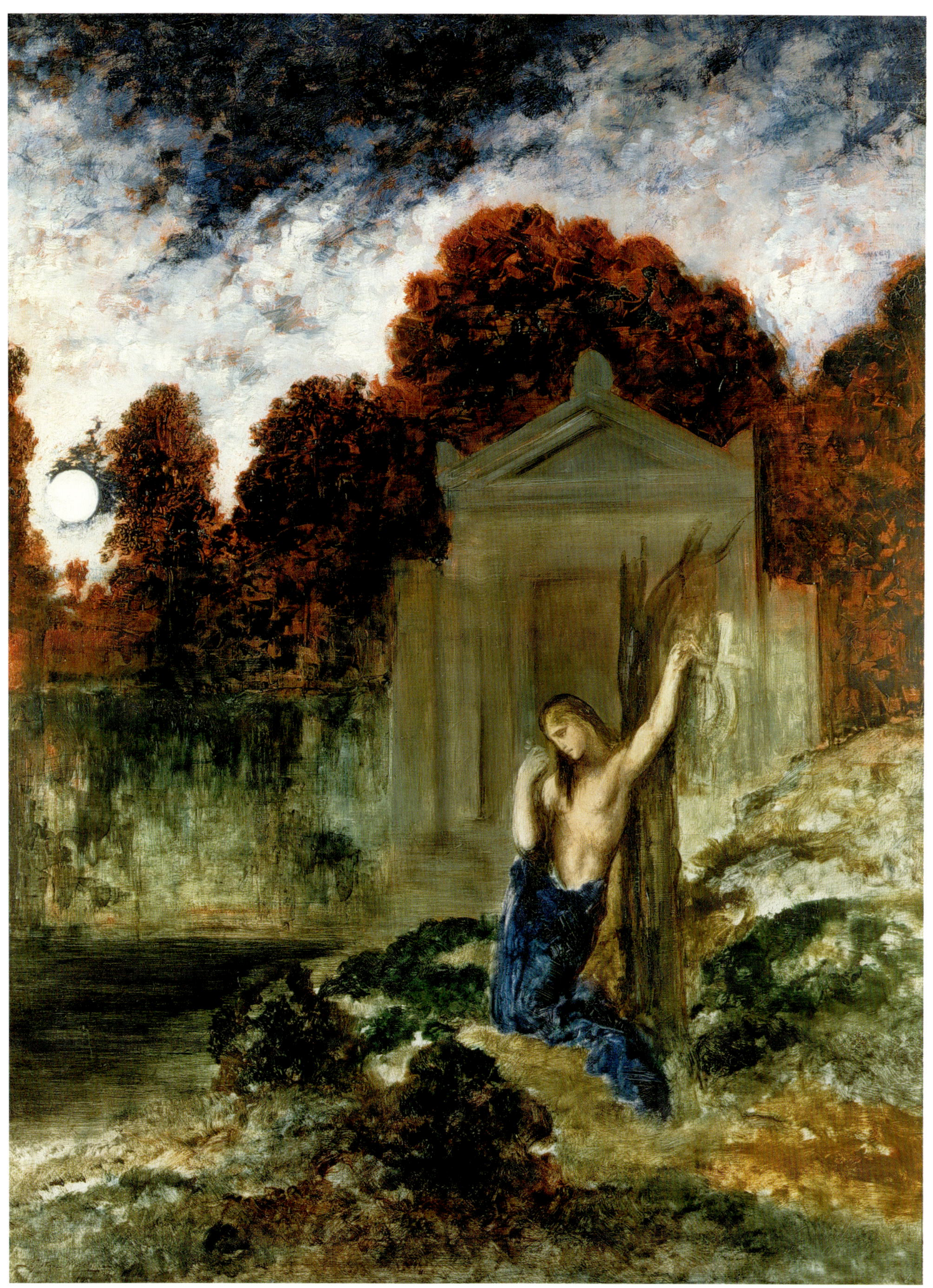

## 21. Henry Wallis (1830–1916)

*Chatterton* 1855–6

Oil on canvas, 62.2 × 93.3 cm

Tate Britain, London

Bequeathed by Charles Gent Clement, 1899 (NO1685)

> We Poets in our youth begin in gladness;
> But thereof come in the end despondency and madness.[1]

Thomas Chatterton (1752–1770) was a precociously talented poet, who as a boy produced what he claimed were medieval histories, plays and ballads, but which he himself had written and copied onto old parchment. His elaborate forgeries were detected by Horace Walpole when Chatterton sought his patronage in 1769. In 1770 Chatterton decided to seek his fortune in London, where he earned a meagre living contributing political satires, narratives and songs to many of the leading journals (including the *Middlesex Journal* seen here in Wallis's painting). In June 1770 he moved to a garret at 39 Brooke Street, Holborn. On the night of 24 August, aged 17, Chatterton died after swallowing arsenic. It is now thought that his death may have been the accidental result of mixing the medicine he was taking to treat venereal disease with opium – but it was universally assumed that it was suicide.[2] A powerful myth arose that cast Chatterton as the archetypal starving poet, an unrecognised genius, who had poisoned himself in despair.

Chatterton was a Romantic hero for young and struggling artists, his myth intimately connected with the birth of English Romanticism. One of Coleridge's first poems was *Monody on the death of Chatterton* (1791–4). In *Resolution and Independence* (1807), Wordsworth invoked 'Chatterton, the marvellous boy/the sleepless soul that perished in his pride', while Keats dedicated *Endymion* to his memory in 1818.

Wallis's *Chatterton* caused a sensation when it was exhibited at the Royal Academy in 1856. Ruskin described it as 'faultless and wonderful', exhorting the viewer to 'examine it well inch by inch: it is one of the pictures which intend and accomplish the entire placing before your eyes of an actual fact – and that a solemn one. Give it much time'.[3] In the words of the *Saturday Review*, within a few days of the opening of the exhibition, 'young Wallis found himself famous'.[4] The success of the painting was such that when it was exhibited at Manchester the following year, it had to be protected from the crowds by two policemen.

Wallis depicts Chatterton lying dead in his small attic room, the floor strewn with torn manuscripts and an empty phial near his hand. There has been much debate as to whether Wallis painted Chatterton's own garret at 39 Brooke Street: between 1855 and 1858 he himself lived in the same area of London, at 8 Gray's Inn Square. However, the exact address where Chatterton died seems only to have been positively identified in 1857: by 'lucky accident', as the antiquarian J.C. Hotton later expressed it, the view from Chatterton's room towards St Paul's Cathedral would have been as it appears in Wallis's picture.[5] But Wallis probably chose this view east towards the City of London to show the breaking dawn, and possibly also as a comment on the heartlessness of commerce.[6]

The painting contains many symbolic details: Chatterton's pride is conveyed by his fashionable clothes; the smoking candle and the fading rose both evoke the passing of time and the passing away of a spirit. When the painting was exhibited at the Royal Academy it was accompanied in the catalogue by two lines from Christopher Marlowe's *Dr Faustus* (about 1590), which were also inscribed on the frame: 'Cut is the branch that might have grown full straight/ And burnèd is Apollo's laurel bough.'

Two compositional sketches (Tate, London) were probably made from a studio model, but for the face of Chatterton (of whom no portrait existed) Wallis chose, appropriately, the struggling young poet George Meredith (1828–1909). LO

**1** W. Wordsworth, *Resolution and Independence* (1807).
**2** N. Groom, 'Chatterton, Thomas (1752–1770)', *ODNB* 2004.
**3** Cook and Wedderburn 1902–12, vol. 14, p. 60, quoted in Parris 1984, no. 75.
**4** *Saturday Review*, 17 May 1856, quoted in Parris 1984, no. 75.
**5** Parris 1984, no. 75.
**6** Wildman 1995, no. 39.

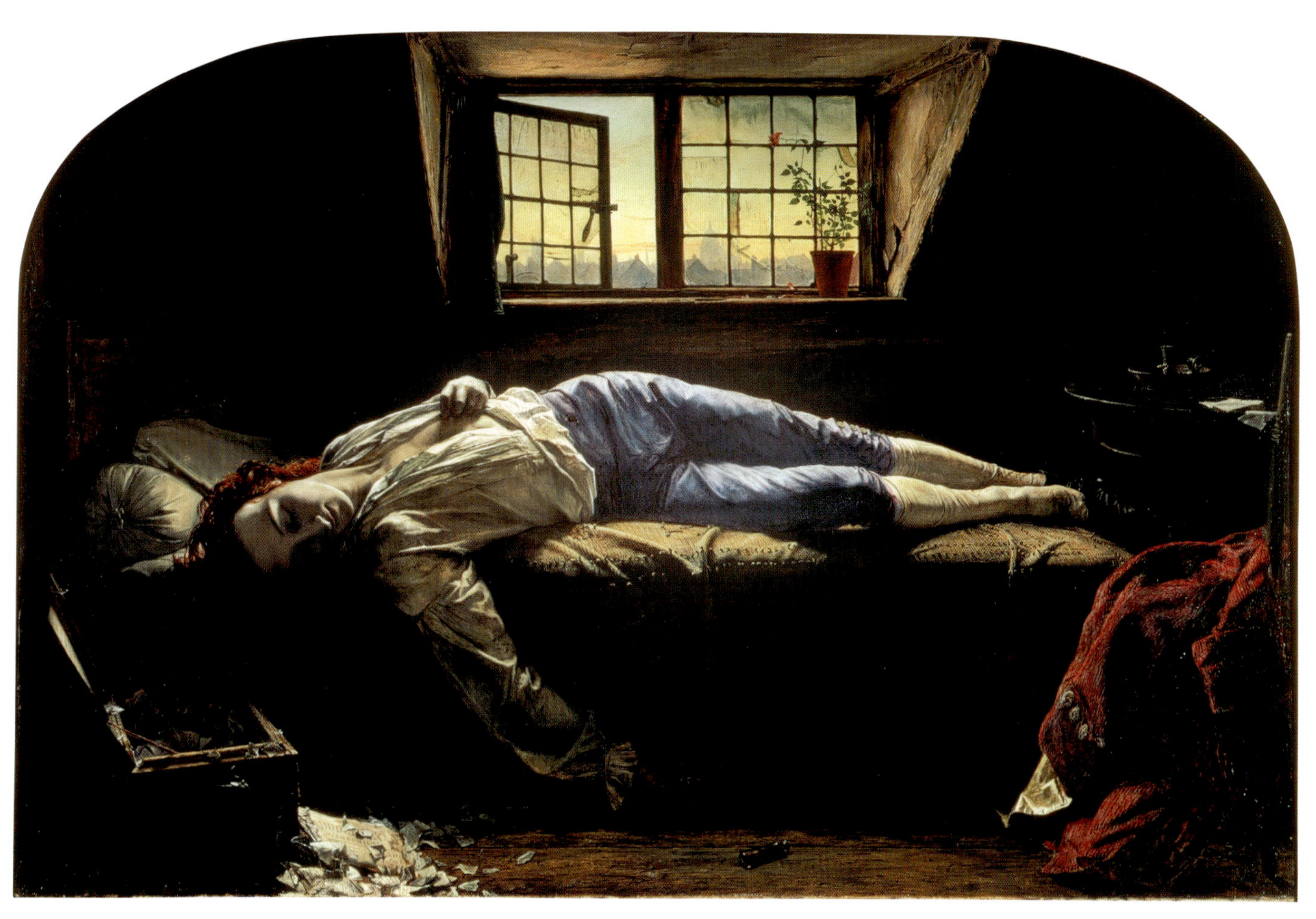

## 22. Leonardo Alenza y Nieto (1807–1845)

*Satire on Romantic Suicide* about 1839

Oil on canvas, 36.5 × 28.5 cm

Museo Romántico, Madrid (0032)

> With extended arms I looked down into the yawning abyss and cried 'Plunge!' … O Wilhelm, how willingly could I abandon my existence to ride the whirlwind or embrace the torrent: and then might not rapture perchance be the portion of this liberated soul.[1]

The Spanish painter and illustrator Leonardo Alenza is often described as the last follower of Goya. He was based in Madrid where he was one of a literary set, providing illustrations for Alain René Lesage's *Gil Blas* (1840), the poems of Francisco de Quevedo and the periodicals *Semanario Pintoresco* and *El Reflejo*. Madrid was an uncomfortable environment for liberal thinkers and artists under the oppressive regime of Ferdinand VII (1814–1833) and the Spanish Inquisition, and many related to the Romantic idea of the artist as persecuted hero.

Romantic notions about suicide were widespread in Europe. In England the tragic death of the young poet Thomas Chatterton acquired mythical status (cat. 21). The publication of Goethe's semi-autobiographical novel of 1774 concerning his hopeless love affair with Charlotte Buff, in which the young hero Werther, an amateur artist and poet, takes his own life, inspired numerous imitation novels and souvenirs.[2] *The Sorrows of the Young Werther* also prompted parodies such as W.M. Thackeray's burlesque 'Sorrows of Werther', published in *The Southern Literary Messenger* in 1853.

In the current work, one of a pair of canvases by the artist entitled *Satire on Romantic Suicide*, Alenza parodies the notion that a suffering poet's fame could be guaranteed by self-inflicted death. The paradigmatic tortured soul, here a poet, appears as a melodramatic figure, as he prepares to stab himself and plunge over the precipice. He leaves behind his papers, his sword, a skull symbolising his preoccupation with death, and – most significantly – his poet's laurel crown hung on a cross, in expectation that his dramatic death will bring him lasting fame. He joins two other figures, presumably also suicides, one hanging from a tree and the other lying in a pool of blood. The painting probably alludes to the contemporary political situation, but it also suggests the influence of Goya's *Caprichos* (1799), a series of prints satirising the follies of Spanish society. Alenza perhaps also had in mind the death of the 28-year-old Spanish satirist and liberal Mariano José de Larra, whose suicide in 1837 following a disastrous love-affair shocked Madrid. Alenza probably empathised with the figure of the troubled artist: following his own death, contemporaries remarked on his serious melancholy character, and although he achieved some fame, he died in poverty.[3] LO

**1** Johann Wolfgang von Goethe, *The Sorrows of the Young Werther* (1774), ed. E. Lane, London 1988.

**2** Goethe 1988 (edn), p. 9.

**3** 'La Nota de Mesonero sobre Alenza', *Nuevo Manual Histórico-Topográfico-Estadístico y Descripción de Madrid*, 1854, pp. 135–6; 'Don Leonardo Alenza', *Semanario Pintoresco Español*, 1848. Both obituaries reproduced in E. Lafuente Ferrari, *Antecedentes, Coincidencias e influencias del arte de Goya*, Madrid 1947, pp. 335–7.

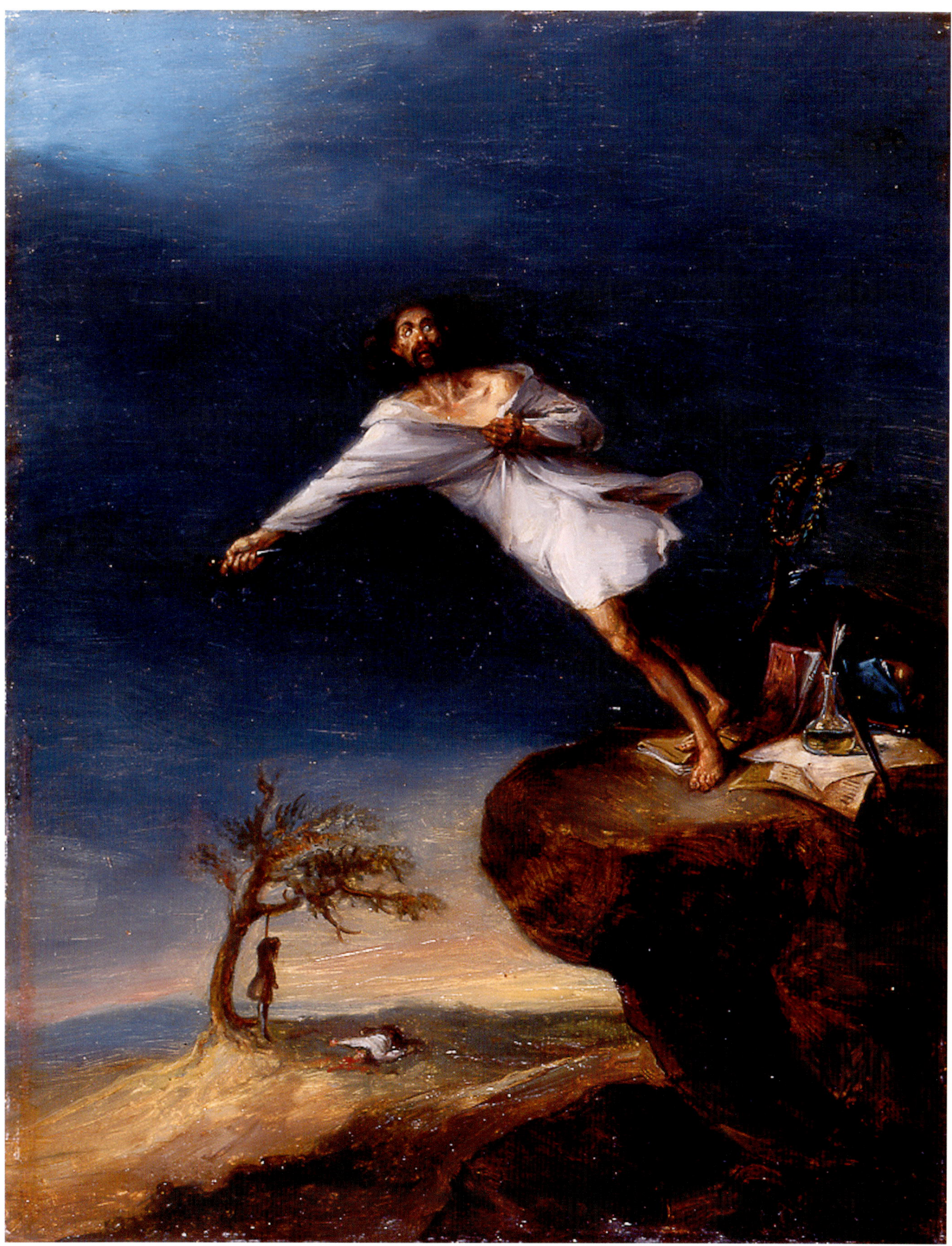

# Bohemia

Bohemia, bordered on the North by hope, work and gaiety, on the South by necessity and courage; on the West and East by Slander and the Hospital.[1]

The Romantic emphasis on the independence of the artist contributed to the emergence in the 1830s of the most characteristic and familiar of nineteenth-century artistic types, the bohemian – youthful, adventurous, eccentric and poor, living in defiance of society's conventions and rules. The first use of the term 'bohemian' – from the French for gypsy – to describe an artistic community appears to have been in an essay by the playwright Félix Pyat in 1834: 'The ordinary mania of young artists to wish to live outside their time, with other ideas and other customs, isolates them from the world, renders them strange and bizarre, puts them outside the law, banished from society; these are today's Bohemians.'[2]

An artistic bohemia emerged in the Paris of the 1830s and 1840s, in part because of the excessive numbers of artists there and the decline of state patronage under the July Monarchy, and was always inextricably linked to that city. The bohemian, who regarded himself as the enemy of the bourgeois, became associated with political radicalism, and art and politics were the chief topics of debate at the cafés where artists habitually met.

The bohemia of Paris was celebrated by Henri Murger in his *Scenes of Bohemian Life* (*Scènes de la vie de Bohème*), which first appeared in instalments from 1845. Murger's colourful, romanticised tales of hardship and enterprise, of love affairs and idealism chronicled a world he knew, and the artists, writers and musicians he wrote about had real-life counterparts. His tales clearly struck a chord of recognition and their enduring popularity was assured by their transformation into a sensationally successful musical play in 1849 (the source of Puccini's 1896 opera *La Bohème*) and by their publication in book form in 1851. The bohemian was also the subject of many a satirical print by artists such as Gavarni (cats 25, 26) and Daumier (cats 23, 24), which usually focused on his eccentric dress and his dire poverty. The humble stove in the studio or garret became a symbol in prints and paintings of the hardship suffered by struggling artists.

As Murger's stories appeared, the painter Gustave Courbet was developing his own identity as a bohemian. Although Courbet moved in the same circles as Murger, the aggressively independent, beer-drinking, vagabond style of bohemianism he invented was very different from the picturesque romanticism of Murger's tales. In *The Meeting* of 1854 (cat. 29), which depicts an encounter with his patron Alfred Bruyas on a country road, Courbet strikes an attitude which is self-assured and uncompromising. Over the following decades he was to use his art as a means to assert his independence and to attack both the art establishment and the government.

Courbet had a huge influence on younger painters, and the bohemia he represented endured too, in the artistic cafés of the Batignolles district of Paris in the 1870s and, in very different form, in the cabarets of turn-of-the-century Montmartre, where it became theatre for consumption by bourgeois pleasure-seekers. It gave rise to imitations elsewhere too, in Toorop's Brussels, in Munch's Christiana (modern-day Oslo), in Picasso's Barcelona, in Beckmann's Berlin, and in Greenwich Village, New York, in the 1940s – anywhere, in fact, where artistic communities were established to create art in defiance of bourgeois conventions and politics. AS/MW

**1** Théodore Barrière and Henri Murger, *Scènes de la vie de Bohème*, Paris 1849, p. 14.

**2** Félix Pyat, 'Les Artistes' in *Le nouveau tableau de Paris*, IV, Paris 1834, pp. 8–9, quoted in Brown 1985, p. 10.

### 23. Honoré-Victorin Daumier (1808–1879)
### *Wood is expensive and the arts aren't going well*

From *Le Charivari*, 6 May 1833

Lithograph, 19.8 × 22.2 cm

Bibliothèque Nationale, Paris (DC 180b res T3, L.D. 146)

### 24. Honoré-Victorin Daumier
### *A Frenchman painted by himself*
### No. 2 in the series *Scenes from Studios*

From *Le Charivari*, 29 March 1849

Lithograph, 23.1 × 21.6 cm

The British Museum, London (1918-5-11-215)

### 25. Gavarni (Guillaume Sulpice Chevalier) (1801–1866)
### No. 2 in the series *The Artists*

From *Le Charivari*, 24 May 1838

Lithograph, 19.6 × 15.9 cm

Bibliothèque Nationale, Paris (M337, dépot legal 1838.292)

### 26. Gavarni (Guillaume Sulpice Chevalier)
### No. 7 in the series *The Artists*

From *Le Charivari*, 23 June 1838

Lithograph, 20 × 15.6 cm

Bibliothèque Nationale, Paris (M337, dépot legal 1838.41)

### 27. Marie Alexandre Alophe (Menut) (1812–1883)
### *Glory and the Stockpot* 1858

Photograph, 20.9 × 16.6 cm

Bibliothèque Nationale, Paris (E0 68)

The emergence and definition of a self-conscious bohemian identity in the Paris of the 1830s and 1840s can be followed as much in the work of popular graphic artists as of writers. Indeed, it was the graphic artists working for the satirical papers that proliferated after 1830 who did much to establish the currency of the bohemian type, his appearance, attitude and iconography in the popular imagination even before he acquired his name. The influence of their images is indeed all pervasive in the bohemian tales of Murger and his contemporaries in the mid-1840s.[1] The artists of the popular press, chief among them Daumier, Gavarni, Monnier and Grandville, shared with writers a desire to dissect the manners of contemporary society. In his famous preface to the *Comédie Humaine* (1842–55) Balzac likened his attitude towards society to that of a zoologist cataloguing by genus and species; artists such as Daumier and Gavarni were acknowledged as his accomplices. As the Goncourt brothers later commented, the *Comédie Humaine* 'could as well be the title of Gavarni's comedy of the pencil as Balzac's of the pen'. Of course writers and graphic artists often worked together, collaborating both in the press and in the production of the hugely popular books that described Paris through its inhabitants, such as *Les Français peints par eux-mêmes* (1840–2) (which provided the title for Daumier's print here, cat. 24), *Le Diable à Paris* (1844) or *La Grande Ville* (1844), as well as the so-called *Physiologies* dedicated to the delineation of particular noteworthy Parisian types. It is hardly surprising in this climate that lithographers turned their discriminating gaze upon their own profession. Gavarni produced an entire series of 16 prints dedicated to *The Artists* (*Les Artistes* from 1838), while artists and their clients, connoisseurs and exhibition-goers recur as subjects throughout Daumier's career.

In Daumier's first print of the world of the artist made in 1833 *Wood is expensive* (*Le bois est cher*) (cat. 23),

**1** Most obviously, Gavarni's famous female types, the *Grisette* and *Lorette*, define Murger's Mimi and Musette: 'Les heroines de Murger sont des grisettes de Gavarni' (Adhémar 1954, p. 13).

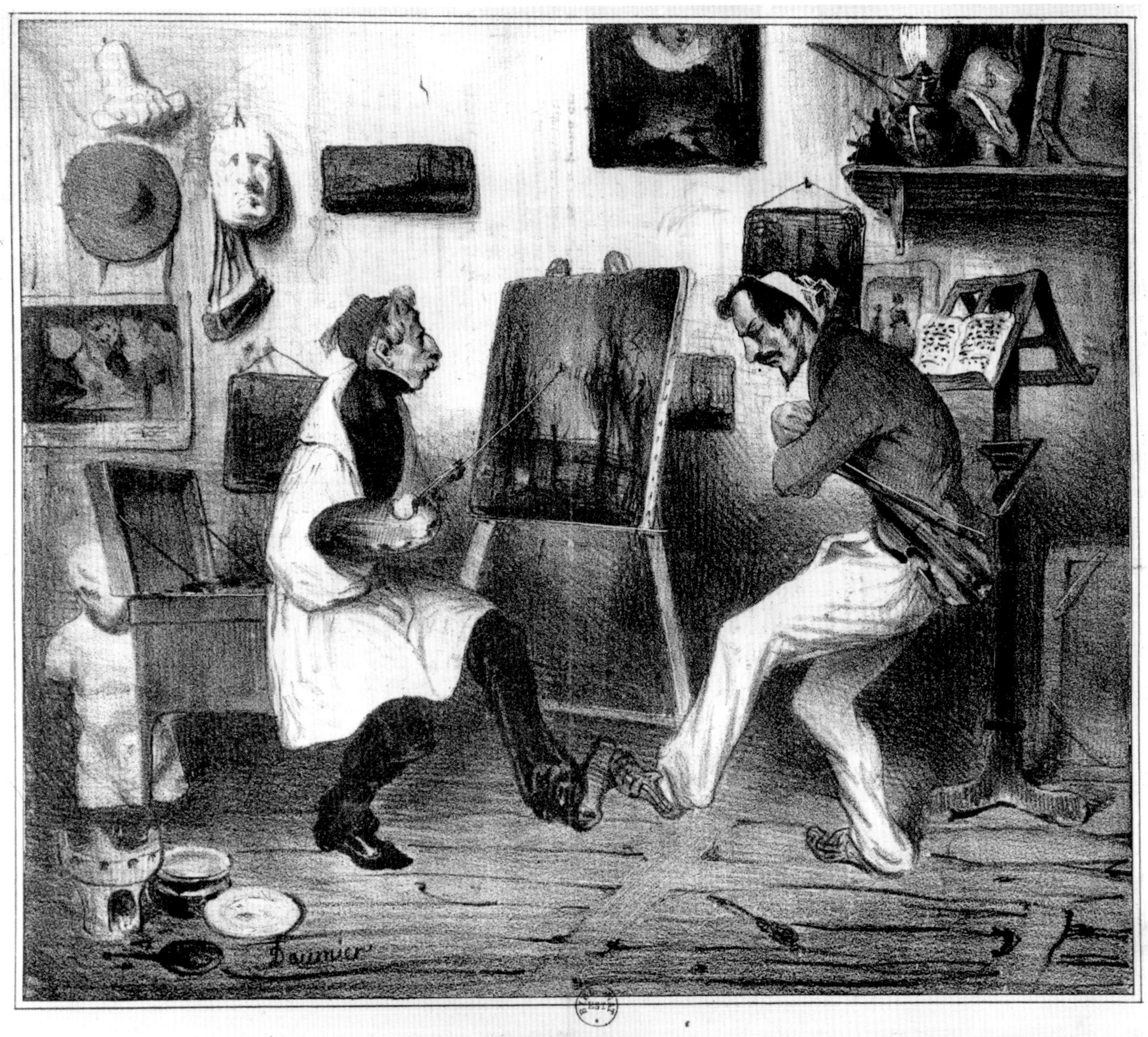


*Le bois est cher et les arts ne vont pas.*

23

the emphasis is on artistic poverty. Although many of the defining attributes of the bohemian are already in place – the bare-floored garret, the association of art and music, the humble cooking-stove and pot – its subject is hardship rather than the eccentricity or anti-bourgeois posturing of the bohemian. Indeed, Champfleury, together with Murger one of the original chroniclers of bohemia, later suggested the print was an almost documentary record of Daumier's circumstances: 'It's less satire than a sort of confiding in the public.'[2] This attitude has also led to the suggestion that the landscape painter is a portrait of his associate Paul Huet, although this seems untenable given that Huet was only 30 at the time.

In Gavarni's series *The Artists* a more clearly defined figure of the bohemian artist *avant la lettre* can be seen emerging. In the most masterful print of the series (cat. 26) an eccentrically dressed and wildly coiffured artist, hands stuffed in pockets and legs confidently apart stares, nonplussed, at the suited, bespectacled bourgeois awkwardly posing in front of him. The

**2** J.H. Champfleury, *Histoire de la caricature moderne*, Paris 1871, p. 103.

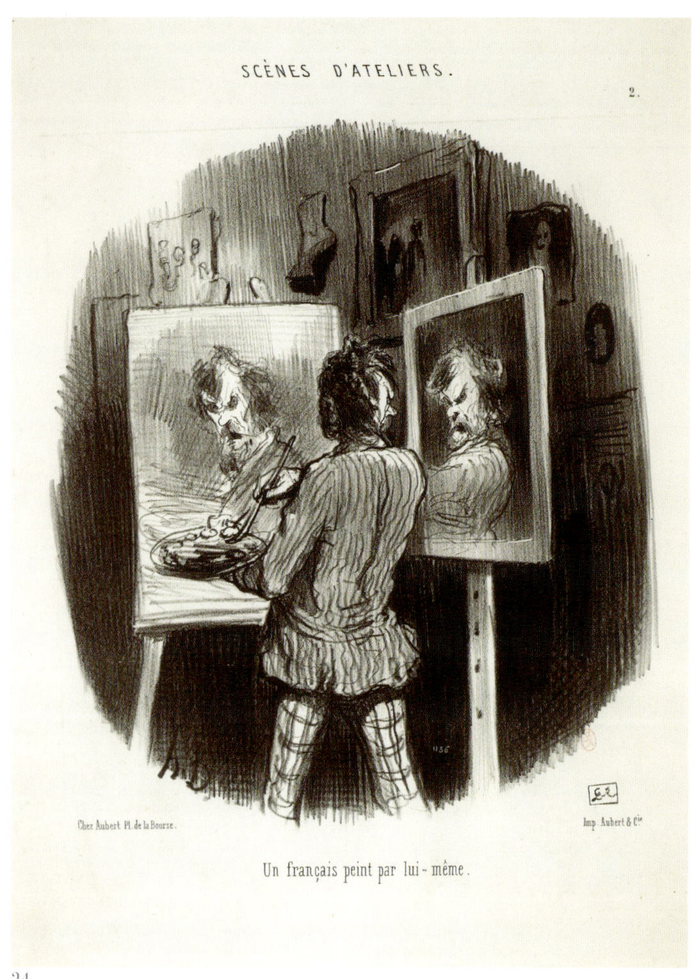


24

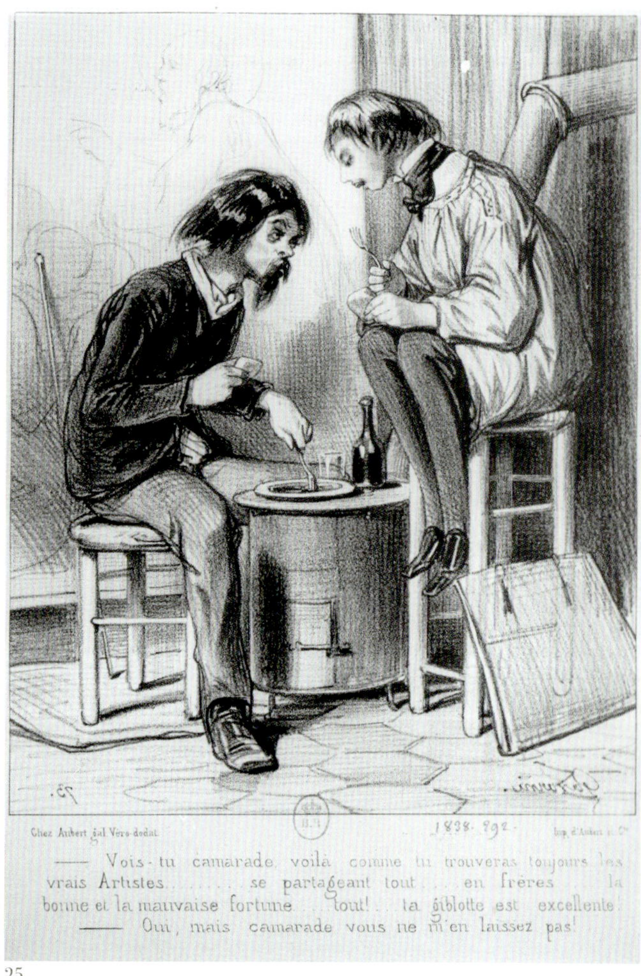


25

accompanying caption, 'Let's see! Do you find me alright like this?', though spoken by the sitter could with equal justification come from the painter. The confrontation of unconventional artist with his sworn enemy, the bourgeois, rendered piquant by their mutual dependence, was a central topos of the bohemian myth, but seldom conveyed with such economy of wit.

In the second print in the series (cat. 25) the camaraderie of the impoverished studio as well as its lack of ethics is encapsulated in a scene around the ubiquitous stove, where a long-haired and bearded painter, waxing eloquent on the brotherhood of artists, attempts to snaffle his young, and more conventionally dressed, companion's share of their meagre supper. The humble stove and meal as an attribute of the bohemian and his garret became a commonplace that was to be taken up by writers and painters. A number of Murger's bohemian stories revolve around stoves or fireplaces, upon which furniture is cheerfully tossed in moments of revelry – or on which, in more desperate straits, Murger's alter-ego, Rodolphe, dressed in a polar-bear costume, burns the manuscript of his play in order to warm himself. Indeed, with evident irony Murger makes Rodolphe's bourgeois uncle a manufacturer of stoves and in another scene has Rodolphe freezing in an apartment full of stoves, but with no fuel, forced to write a manual on 'The Perfect Chimney-Constructor'. Alophe's photographic tableau *Glory and the Stockpot (La Gloire et le Pot-au-feu)* (cat. 27) shows how conventional this association had become by the 1850s, the period in which Murger's tales were at their most popular. The photograph is the last in a series of twelve *Fantasies Photographiques*, a 'collection of subjects, tableaux, and scenes of Bohemian Life composed and executed in photography from nature by M. Alophe', produced and marketed in a manner entirely similar to the series

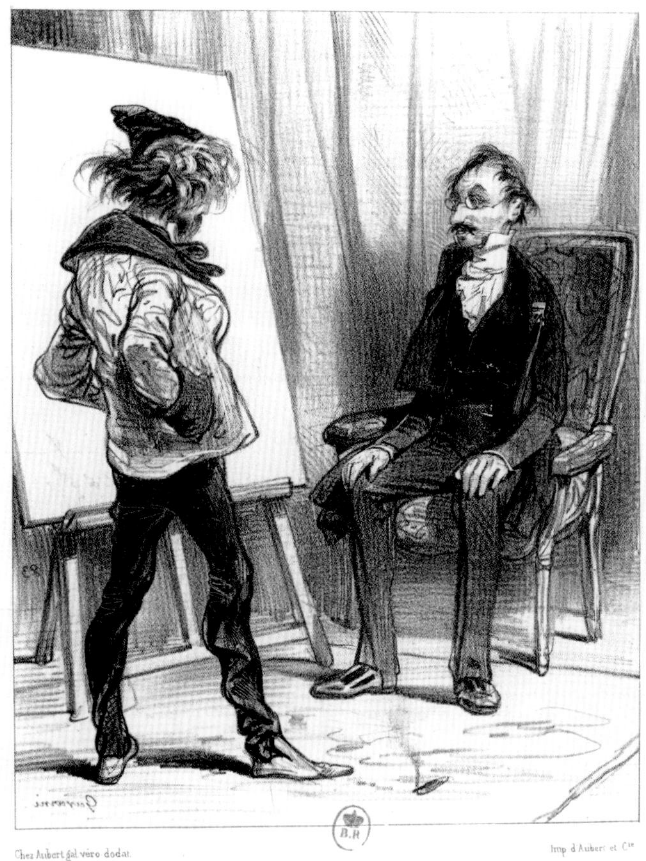


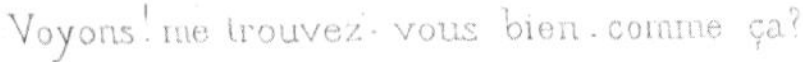


26

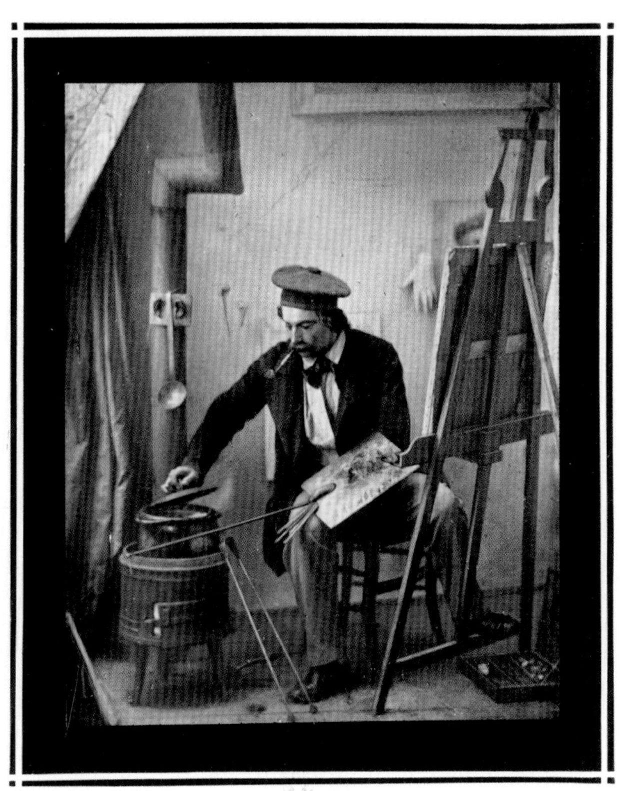


27

of lithographs by Daumier, Gavarni and others. Indeed, Alophe had trained as a painter: he was a one-time pupil of Delaroche, but achieved most success as a printmaker and portrait photographer. This is the only photograph in the series that explicitly shows an artist at work, although others clearly draw their inspiration from Murger's tales: the ninth scene, *La Séparation*, shows a bedridden, and, we assume, consumptive girl taking leave of her lover, on the model of Murger's Francine or Mimi. The humble meal of the *pot-au-feu* recalls both the prints of the 1830s and Tassaert's painting of 1845 (cat. 28), but here the image has been reduced to cliché and offers a cheerfully sanitised vision of artistic hardship.

The notion of bohemia's radicalism, beyond its enmity with the bourgeoisie, is seldom in evidence in popular representations of the artist in these decades. Many make stock jokes on the artist's trade: the uncomprehending confrontation between artist and bourgeois or peasant, the laughable gap between their creations and their circumstances, or more incidental episodes – such as visitors confusing artist's mannequins for real people.[3] But in Daumier's wonderfully animated *A Frenchman painted by himself* (*Un français peint par lui même*) (cat. 24), made in the aftermath of the 1848 Revolution, and given a title that invites an allegorical reading, Daumier caricatures not only the wild bohemian artist's self-regard but also his – assumed – revolutionary fervour. AS

**3** For a study of the recurring themes of artist caricatures see Wohlgemuth 1996.

## 28. Octave Tassaert (1800–1874)

*The Artist's Studio* 1845

Oil on canvas, 46 × 38 cm

Musée du Louvre, Paris (RF 2442), Département des Peintures, Ernest May Bequest. Held in usufruct until 1926.

This sombre little painting is remarkable in its pessimistic concentration on the enervating poverty of a young Parisian artist. It was painted in the same year as Murger published his first story of bohemian life in the newspaper *La Corsaire-Satan*, but it has no hint of the carefree eccentricity or brotherly solidarity that characterise Murger's stories, or the contemporary lithographs of Daumier and Gavarni. Tassaert's concentration on his subject's apparently hopeless isolation was not, however, unique – the same year also saw the publication of Champfleury's story *Chien-Callou*, centred on the solitary, short and tragic life of one of those 'unfortunate Bohemians who remain Bohemians all their lives', which explicitly contrasts the 'poetic garrets' of Romantic literature with the dark, dirty and lonely 'real garrets' of contemporary Paris.[1] Champfleury's protagonist cannot escape bohemia as he has not the talent, education or connections to do so; Tassaert's painting implies a similar predicament. The artist is not at work, his palette is clean and his easel leans uselessly behind him. He appears not even to have the wherewithal to paint: the peeled potato on the empty paintbox implies that he has had to put food before the materials of his trade. Slumped on the floor in the bare corner of his apparently unfurnished studio, he seems to lack even the energy to finish peeling his potato for the pot on the fire behind him. A pipe and tobacco pouch lie on the floor and a jug of water and hunk of bread sit on the mantelpiece.

Although bleak, Tassaert's painting appears sympathetic rather than satirical. Neither the dress nor hairstyle of the young artist are caricatured, although the significance of the red jacket, which appears to be a type of livery or uniform, is unclear. The print or drawing of a friar stuck to the back wall might even suggest a familiar Romantic parallel between the artistic and religious callings and their concomitant poverty. The 45-year-old Tassaert's sympathy for the young artist was perhaps born from his own situation in the mid-1840s when, following a period of moderate success in the previous decade, he was making a meagre living selling drawings to dealers and publishers while exhibiting paintings to little effect at the Salon. His situation seems to have worsened after the 1848 Revolution when he was visited by the director of the National Museums, Philippe Auguste Jeanron, in response to a plea for work, and found penniless and working in a dilapidated shed.[2] Ironically it was subjects of poverty that provided Tassaert's route back into public favour, particularly his painting, commissioned by the state after Jeanron's visit, of the *Unhappy Family* (1849; private collection) showing a destitute mother and daughter committing suicide. This picture's success at the 1850–1 Salon led to a number of works in a similar vein, which earned him the suitably bohemian nickname of the 'Correggio of the attic'. AS

**1** *Le Corsaire-Satan*, 5 October 1845, quoted in Seigel 1999, p. 43.

**2** Weisberg 1981, p. 158.

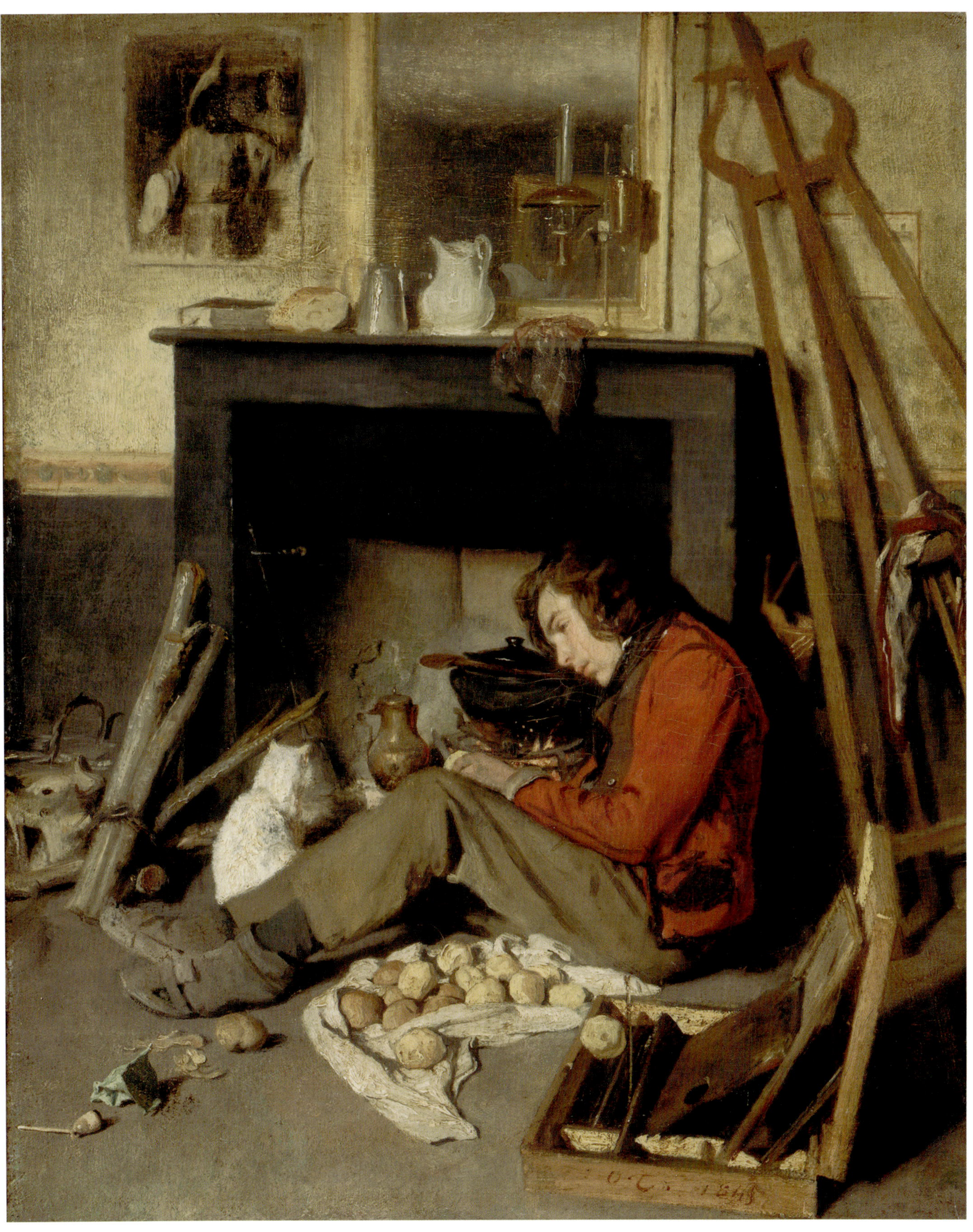

## 29. Jean-Désiré-Gustave Courbet (1819–1877)

*The Meeting ('Bonjour Monsieur Courbet!')* 1854

Oil on canvas, 132 × 150.5 cm

Musée Fabre, Montpellier (868.1.23)

No other artist associated himself with bohemia so explicitly and with such sureness of purpose as Courbet in the late 1840s and early 1850s, and none of his other works makes his bohemian persona as explicit and dramatic as *The Meeting*. It was painted in 1854 for his patron Alfred Bruyas, who appears, with his servant Calas and dog Breton, doffing his cap to greet the proud, confident figure of the independent 'vagabond' bohemian. Earlier that same year Courbet had written to Bruyas describing his many self portraits as 'the story of my life', adding: 'There remains one more of them for me to do, that is the man firm in his principles: the free man.'[1] *The Meeting* can be seen as this painting.

Courbet was associated with bohemia all his life, frequenting cafés in Paris from the Café Momus in the 1840s, where he met with the group made famous by Henri Murger, to the Alsatian beer hall, the Andler Keller, in the 1850s. Here he held court, a mesmerising, beery, laughing figure with rustic speech and the 'air of a jeering peasant'.[2] Courbet's much caricatured persona was, it seems, consciously assumed, even if sincerely held – in a letter to Bruyas of 1854 he speaks of his 'laughing mask'[3] – but he played the role of the bohemian with a purpose. There was certainly a political aspect to his persona: his bohemianism was a way of asserting his freedom and separation from convention, as well as from bourgeois Paris. This desire not only led to his periods of absence from the city, but also determined the particular form – vulgar and rustic – that his bohemianism took. In *The Meeting* he shows himself not in the beer halls of Paris but on the open road, less the bohemian of Murger's tales than the wandering gypsy.

For Courbet, art was inseparable from the development of an independent sense of self. In another letter to Bruyas he describes meeting the emperor's Superintendent of the Fine Arts and telling him that 'I was not only a painter but also a man, that I had become a painter, not to make art for art's sake but to achieve my own intellectual liberty'. His Realism, like Romanticism, had its roots in a consuming individualism and shared a similar insistence on sincerity and authenticity. But Courbet's persona had another equally powerful – if contradictory – impulse, and one to which he explicitly refers later in the same letter in which he proclaims himself a bohemian: 'It is a serious responsibility . . . first to provide the example of liberty and personality in art, and then afterwards to provide publicity to the art which I have undertaken.'[4] He clearly understood the importance of his bohemian persona for establishing himself – on his own terms – within the Parisian art world and market. He was perhaps the first artist to fully recognise and exploit the benefits of notoriety.[5]

*The Meeting* was certainly viewed by some critics as little more than self-advertisement when it was exhibited in the World Exhibition of 1855 – 'it must be of palpitating interest for him and his friends: I confess it means less to me'[6] – and the painting was swiftly dubbed 'Bonjour Monsieur Courbet!' or, by one commentator, 'Fortune Bowing to Genius'. The same critic went on to observe (not entirely accurately) that 'neither the master nor the valet cast their shadows on the ground; the shadow belongs to M. Courbet who alone can stop the rays of the sun'.[7] Bruyas was understandably unnerved by these reactions to the picture, for, ostensibly at least, and certainly for him, the image was intended to proclaim the common striving of patron and artist in pursuit of what Bruyas termed 'the Solution' to modern art.[8] Courbet certainly shared with Bruyas a belief in the redemptive, if not sacred place of art in society, but where Bruyas wished to assert his central, guiding role as patron towards this 'Solution', Courbet's equation of his Realist mission with the 'holy sacred cause . . . of Liberty and Independence' was perhaps bound to disappoint him.[9]

1 May 1854, *Lettres de Gustave Courbet à Alfred Bruyas*, ed. P. Borel, Geneva 1951, p. 20.

2 The description is from a police report of 1873, quoted in Clark 1973, p. 20.

3 Letter dated November 1854, quoted in Clark op. cit. p. 24.

4 Letter to Francis Wey (1850), quoted in Courthion 1950, p. 78.

5 In his letter to Bruyas of October 1853 Courbet claimed that it did not matter if those who flocked to see his paintings came as admirers or enemies as long as they paid.

6 Cited in Chang 1996, pp. 586–91, p. 586.

7 Edmond About, quoted in Courthion 1948/50, I, pp. 119–20.

8 On Bruyas's reaction to the exhibition of *The Meeting* see Chang 1996, esp. pp. 586, 590. See also S. Amic 'Bruyas versus Courbet: The Meeting' in *Bonjour Monsieur Courbet! The Bruyas Collection from the Musée Fabre, Montpellier*, ed. S. Lees, exh. cat., Williamstown and Paris 2004.

9 Letter to Alfred Bruyas (1855), *Lettres de Gustave Courbet à Alfred Bruyas*, ed. P. Borel, Geneva 1951, p. 89.

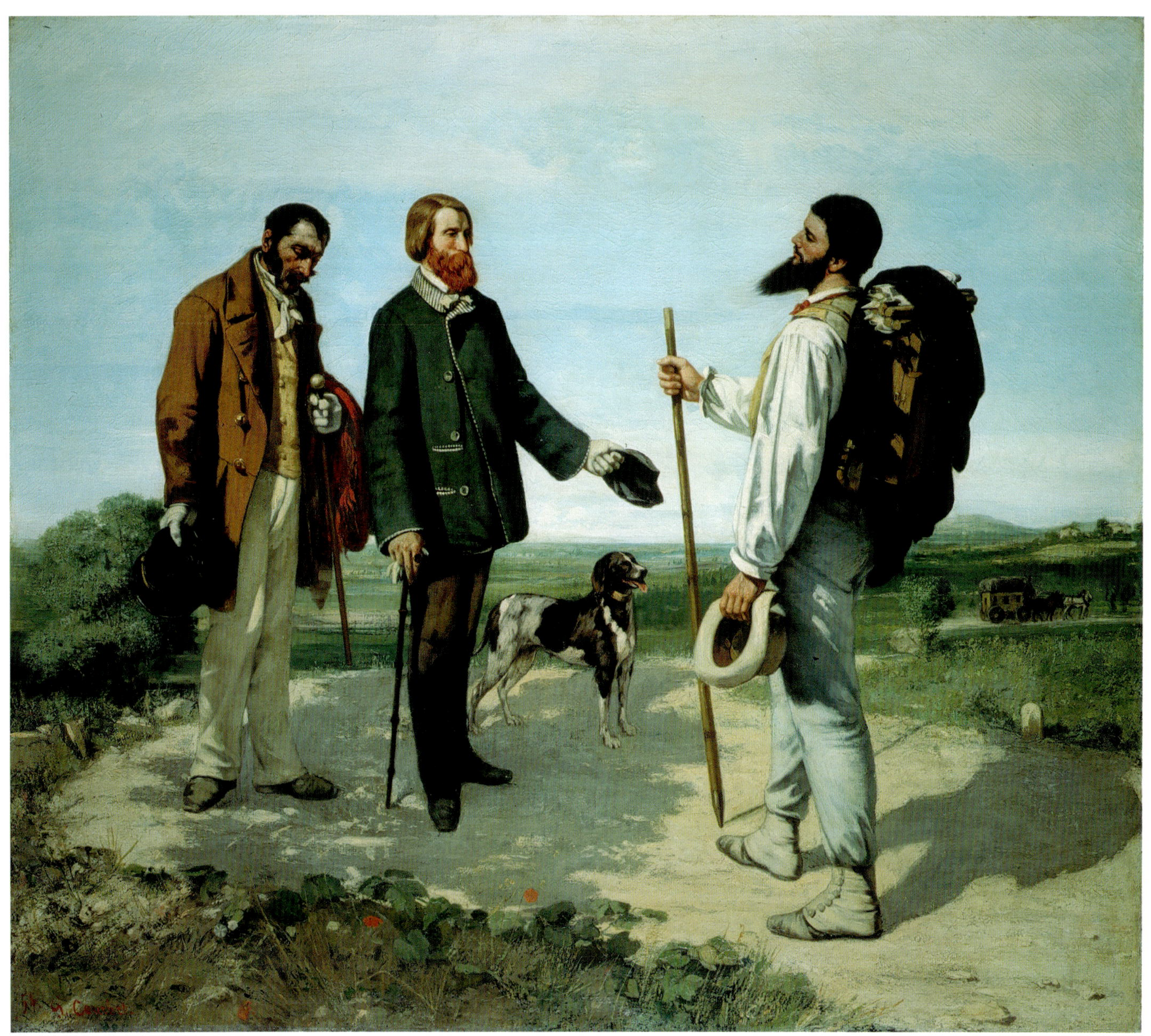

Courbet's liberty and independence are forcefully proclaimed here: his extravagantly jutting beard and dynamic striding pose, the tilt of his head, the distance he keeps from the pair that greets him, and even his size in relation to Bruyas and his servant, all suggest his unfettered confidence and freedom. The clarity of the figures' silhouettes against the blond landscape background – a crossroads outside Montpellier[10] – has a forceful simplicity that derives from popular graphic art. The composition is based on a scene from a popular printed broadside telling the story of the *Wandering Jew*.[11] Courbet's own appropriation of the role of the wandering Jew also deepens his bohemian persona: this popular myth – on which Courbet's friend Champfleury was to write a seminal study – cast the Jew as a symbol of the permanent outcast; but in many nineteenth-century reworkings of the myth, most notably Eugène Sue's *Le Juif Errant* (1844), he became a champion of the victims of contemporary society. AS

**10** The roads lead respectively to Sète and St-Jean-de-Védas at Lattes. Bordes 1985, p. 54.
**11** Nochlin 1967.

## 30. Thomas Couture (1815–1879)

*The Realist* 1865

Oil on canvas, 56 × 45 cm

National Gallery of Ireland, Dublin (NGI 4220)

It is ironic, in the light of this bitter little satire, that Thomas Couture's reputation today rests above all on his role as a teacher of Manet, as at least one of his other pupils believed that Manet was its subject.[1] That Couture should attack a fellow artist was entirely characteristic: he was renowned for his 'constant running-down of other artists greater than himself'.[2] But here his target is broader than any individual, although if anyone is intended it is surely Courbet rather than Manet. Couture's assault is on the Realist school, which he despised above all for what he saw as its confusion of reality with the sordid and the ugly. It was precisely his belief that Realism was 'merely a gross caricature of the coarsest things in nature'[3] that led him here to equate the realist with the bohemian – to draw an easy parallel between the poverty of the bohemian's garret with the baseness of his imagery. Couture himself gave a full account of his painting:

> I am depicting the interior of a studio of our time; it has nothing in common with the studios of earlier periods, in which you could see fragments of the finest antiquities: a head of Laocoön, the feet of the Gladiator, the Venus de Milo … But thanks to modern progress in matters of art … we have the most simple accoutrements … Laocoön has been replace by a cabbage, the feet of the Gladiator by a candlestick covered with tallow or by a shoe. As for the painter, he is a studious artist, fervent, a visionary of the new religion. He copies what? It's quite simple – a pig's head – and as a base what does he choose? That's less simple: the head of Olympian Jupiter.[4]

Couture's rapt young artist – ignoring the Classical head he sits on – is dressed in the characteristic broad-brimmed hat and smock of the archetypal bohemian, while dispersed around him are many of his familiar accoutrements: a tobacco jar and row of pipes are on the shelf below the pig's head, a conspicuous bottle and glass sit in the foreground, while behind him a staff and umbrella are propped beneath the hanging knapsack of the wandering landscape painter, suggested too by the battered (solitary) boot. In viewing the artist from behind the picture recalls paintings by Chardin of young artists at their drawing boards copying from the antique; the painter's lost profile also allows Couture to draw a visual parallel between his physiognomy and the fleshy snout of the pig – emblem of ignorance and vulgarity.

Of course the final irony of the painting is that in his depiction of the vulgar paraphernalia of a bohemian garret, and perhaps above all in the depiction of the pig's head itself, Couture, despite himself, reveals his own considerable strengths as a realist.[5] AS

**1** Boime 1980, p. 333.
**2** John La Farge cited in Rewald 1978, p. 24.
**3** T. Couture, from manuscript note quoted in Boime 1980, p. 334.
**4** From Couture, *Méthode et entretiens d'atelier*, Paris 1867, pp. 155–6, cited in Boime op. cit. p. 331.
**5** In the 1880 retrospective exhibition a Couture sketch for the pig's head led G. Geoffroy to suggest in *La Justice* that Couture was indeed a frustrated Realist (see Boime op. cit. p. 335).

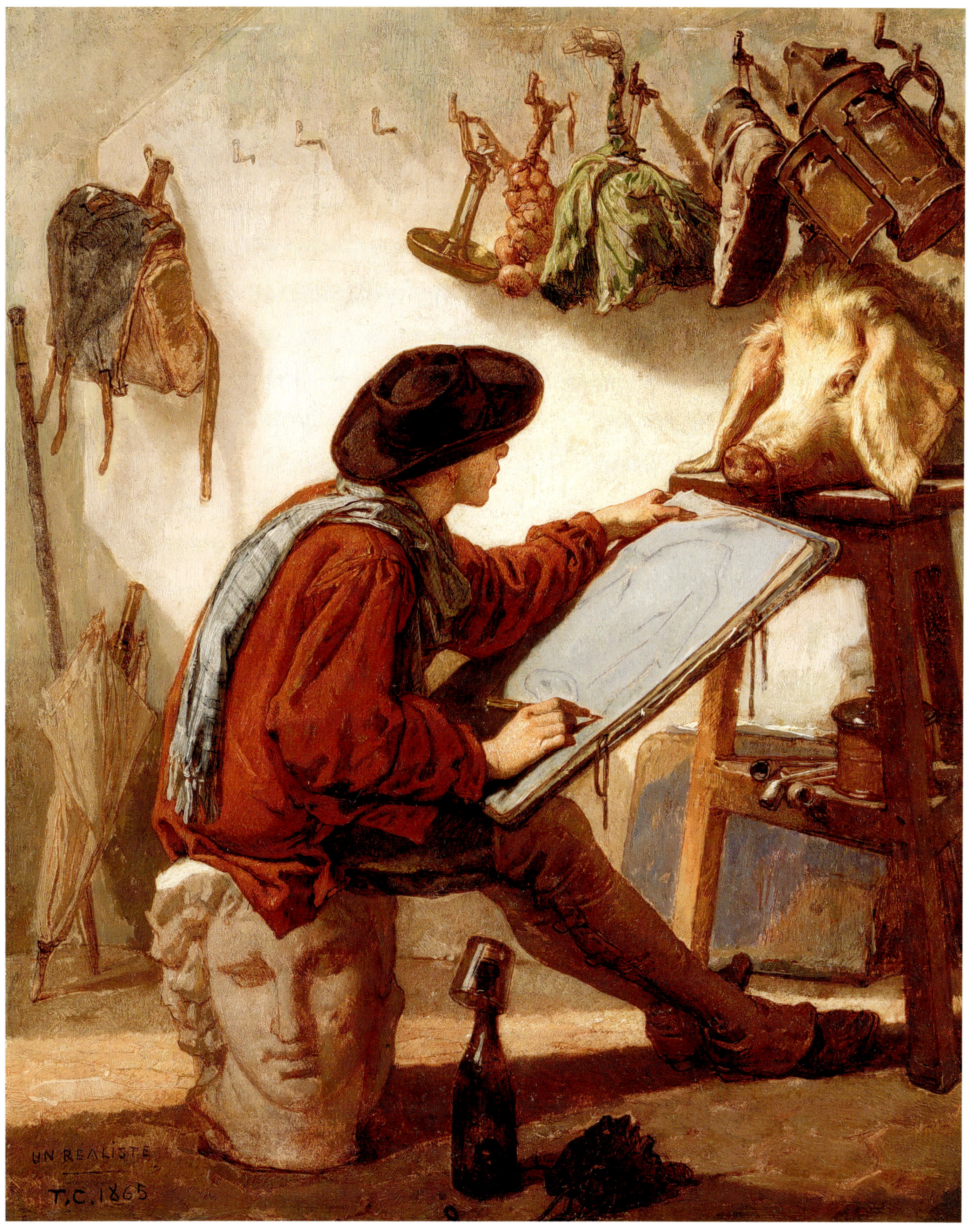
UN REALISTE
T.C. 1865

## 31. Pierre-Auguste Renoir (1841–1919)

### *The Inn of Mère Antony* 1866

Oil on canvas, 194 × 131 cm

Nationalmuseum, Stockholm (NM 2544)

> Le Cabaret de Mère Anthony [*sic*] is one of my paintings of which I have kept a most pleasant memory. It's not that I find this canvas particularly exciting, but it reminds me so strongly of the good *mère* Anthony [*sic*] and her inn in Marlotte, a real village inn! I took as the subject of my study the common room, which also served as the dining room. The old woman in the head scarf is *mère* Anthony [*sic*] in the flesh; the superb girl serving drinks is the waitress Nana. The white poodle is Toto, who had a wooden leg. I had a few of my friends, including Sisley and Le Coeur, pose around the table.[1]

So Renoir later recalled the circumstances surrounding the painting of this early work. But this seemingly casual scene of post-prandial discussion is less innocently charming than Renoir's reminiscence might suggest. Elsewhere Renoir self-deprecatingly referred to the picture as his '*grande tartine*' – slang for an (overlong) tirade or harangue: the painting, made in the aftermath of his rejection by the Salon Jury of 1866,[2] appears to have been conceived as a deliberate statement of radical allegiances. The explicitly bohemian scene is, indeed, presided over by Henri Murger himself, who lived in Marlotte from 1855 until his death in 1861 and whose prominent caricature on the rear wall was Renoir's own: 'As for the motifs that form the background of my painting, I borrowed them from the subjects painted right on the walls; they were the unpretentious, but often very successful, handiwork of the regular customers. I myself drew the Murger silhouette, which I reproduced in my canvas at the top left.'[3] The passage implies (as one would suspect) that the positioning of this caricature was carefully considered; indeed, Murger turns his eyes towards the group of after-dinner debaters, while his identity is underlined by the accompanying verse from the hit musical version of his *Scenes of Bohemian Life*.[4]

Renoir places his protagonists in an explicitly bohemian setting, the painting positioning him within the orbit of Courbet and Manet, his fellow *refusés* of the Salon of 1866. It recalls Courbet's famous *After Dinner at Ornans*, while the prominent newspaper around which the diners' conversation seems to centre is *L'Evénement*, the paper which, in the months preceding Renoir's painting, had published Zola's attacks on the 1866 Salon jury and his defence of the rejected Manet ('M. Manet's place in the Louvre is marked out, like that of Courbet, like that of any artist of original and strong temperament').[5]

The identity of the three men around the table has been the subject of much debate, but the seated figure in the hat is certainly Sisley, while the standing man about to roll a cigarette is the painter Jules Le Coeur, with whom Renoir was staying. The clean-shaven figure at the table may have been a Dutch artist friend of Le Coeur's.[6] Renoir depicts this bohemian scene sympathetically; however, the fact that Le Coeur, despite his worker's smock, was independently wealthy, with houses in Normandy and Paris as well as Marlotte, suggests the self-conscious artificiality of the pose.

By the 1860s, drawn in part by Murger himself, the villages of Fontainebleau were attracting all sorts of sightseers, including Napoleon III and the Empress Eugénie, who came to indulge in a bit of vicarious weekend bohemianism. Establishments such as Mère Antony's were, according to the Goncourts, host to 'the bourgeois, the city gent, the eager holiday maker on a budget, the curious desiring to observe that strange creature, the artist, to watch him eat, to see his customs in his natural surroundings, his habits and his unguarded slovenliness.'[7] Such an audience might well have been sympathetic to Renoir's painting and, indeed, the work was apparently first displayed in the room it depicts: an exhibition which, Renoir remembered, 'seemed like glory already.'[8] AS

**1** A. Vollard, *Auguste Renoir*, Paris 1920, pp. 40–41, trans. in Tinterow and Loyrette 1994, p. 452.

**2** On the dating of the picture to the early summer of 1866 see D. Cooper, 'Renoir, Lise and the Le Coeur Family: A Study of Renoir's Early Development', *Burlington Magazine* CI (1959), pp. 163–71, 322–8, p. 164–7.

**3** Vollard op. cit., p. 41.

**4** 'Musette qui n'est plus elle / Disait que je n'étais plus moi', first identified by T. Reff (1975, p. 42).

**5** E. Zola, 'Mon Salon', *L'Evénement*, 27 April – 20 May 1866, quoted in Rewald 1955, p. 124. At the same time, and with similar intent, Cézanne painted his father reading *L'Evénement* in the portrait now in the National Gallery of Art, Washington DC.

**6** A 1905 reference to the painting suggests that the third man was called Bos, the name of two Leiden artists of the period; see Bailey 1997, p. 97.

**7** Goncourt, *Manette Salomon* (1867), p. 246. While preparing their novel the Goncourts had visited Marlotte and described the Inn of Mère Antony as a hovel for 'low-life painters' (*bas peintres*). *Goncourt Journal* (1956 edn), vol. 6, p. 101, trans. in Tinterow and Loyrette 1994, p. 452.

**8** A. Vollard. 'La Jeunesse de Renoir', *La Renaissance de l'Art Français et des Industries de Luxe* (May 1918), pp. 16–24, p. 23, quoted in Bailey 1997, p. 97.

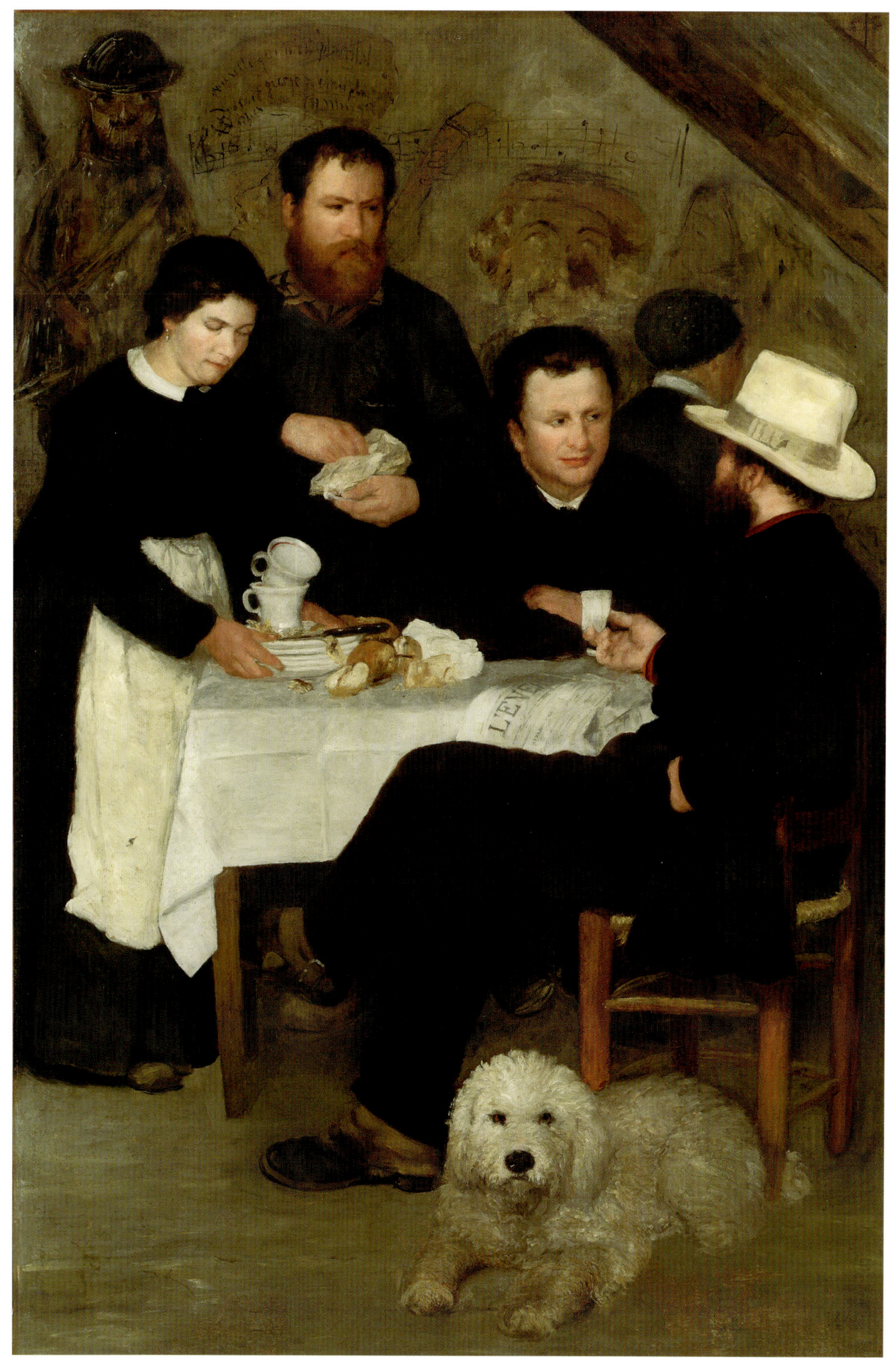
L'EVE

## 32. Paul Cézanne (1839–1906)

*The Stove in the Studio* probably 1865–70

Oil on canvas, 41 × 30 cm

The National Gallery, London (NG 6509). Acquired from the estate of Mrs Helen Chester Beatty under the acceptance-in-lieu procedure, 1992

## 33. Ferdinand-Victor-Eugène Delacroix (1798–1863)

*Corner of the Studio, the Stove* about 1830

Oil on canvas, 51 × 44 cm

Musée du Louvre, Paris, Département des Peintures, Don de la Société des Amis du Louvre, 1913 (RF 2058)

The association of the stove and *pot-au-feu* with the bohemian garret was well established, and – as with Alophe's photographic tableau (cat. 27) – bordered on cliché by the time Cézanne came to paint his powerful little painting in the latter part of the 1860s. But, although by this time bohemianism was under increasing attack as the tired pose of the unfulfilled, Cézanne, like Renoir, still saw in the bohemian persona a means of proclaiming a particular and combative artistic identity. Where Renoir characteristically appealed to the sociability and solidarity of the bohemian café, Cézanne's stove suggests the embattled isolation of the garret. During the 1860s Cézanne divided his time between his native Aix and Paris. While in the city, like Courbet before him, he seems to have deliberately played the crude countryman in dress and speech. In 1866 he was apparently 'wonderful … with his scarce and extremely long hair and his revolutionary beard'.[1] Cézanne's self-consciously bohemian theatricality was at odds with other members of the avant-garde, particularly Manet, whose refined bourgeois exterior Cézanne despised and ridiculed: 'I do not shake your hand, Monsieur Manet', Monet later recalled him saying; 'I have not washed for a week'[2].

Cézanne's painting of his stove (cat. 32), although explicitly bohemian, suggests less bluster than isolation and struggle, a sense that, for his friend Zola at least, also lay behind his aggressive exterior: 'He swore, used filthy words, wallowed in mud, with the cold rage of a tender and exquisite soul who doubts himself and dreams of being dirty'.[3] Here the squat black stove, glowing red, with its pile of spent ashes beneath and framed by the back of the canvas behind, seems a fitting emblem of the struggling, passionate artist. It is surely not entirely fanciful to find suggestive the echo between the French word for stove (*poêle*) and Cézanne's own name (Paul).[4] Romantic in spirit and painted with a confidence that combines discipline with vigour, the picture seems to marry perfectly the twin currents of the Realist and Romantic that characterise Cézanne's works in the 1860s, and which met in the figure of the bohemian.

It is possible that Cézanne had a particular Romantic model in mind when choosing to paint his stove. He may have known the painting of a stove in the corner of a studio (cat. 33), which was exhibited in the large Delacroix exhibition of 1885. This is a suggestion that has been made before – indeed, the two pictures have been brought together in the past, compared for the first time by Bernard Dorival in 1948.[5] Cézanne was preoccupied by Delacroix in the 1860s, copying his paintings and also identifying with his Romantic persona as a figure of fierce artistic independence. In the mid-1860s he made a small vigorous portrait drawing of Delacroix based on his self portrait (Musée Calvet, Avignon). The painting of the stove in the corner of the studio bears a false Delacroix signature: the attribution has been disputed and the painting has also been ascribed to Charles-Emile de Champmartin (1797–1883).[6] The addition of Delacroix's signature to the painting perhaps suggests a retrospective desire to associate the archetypal Romantic painter with what had become an emblem of artistic struggle; but it would not have so evidently held these associations in 1830.

Cézanne's painting itself came to contribute to the envisioning of an artistic bohemia in one more important way. It was owned by Zola, presumably a gift from the painter, and its presence can be felt in many

**1** Letter from Fortuné Marion to Heinrich Morstatt, 1866, quoted in Rewald 1986.
**2** Quoted in Rewald 1955, p.200.
**3** Zola, notes for *L'Oeuvre*, quoted in Rewald 1986, p. 62.
**4** This suggestion, made among many much more fanciful others, is found in Geist 1988, pp. 11–13.
**5** B. Dorival, *Cézanne*, Paris 1948, p. 176.
**6** Johnson 1981–9, vol. 1, p. 242.
**7** E. Zola, *The Masterpiece* (1886), trans. T. Walton, Oxford 1999, p. 17.

of the descriptions of artists' studios in *The Masterpiece* (*L'Oeuvre*), Zola's anti-bohemian novel of the 1880s which described the artistic milieu of the 1860s and led to his rupture with Cézanne. Early in the novel a description of the studio of Claude Lantier – the central figure of the novel based on aspects of both Manet and Cézanne – includes a stove with the ashes from the previous winter still lying beside it;[7] the painting itself seems to appear in an entirely unflattering light later in the novel. It is painted by the most uncouth, ill-educated and incompetent of the artists of the novel: Chaîne is described as 'silently copying onto a diminutive canvas the rusty old studio stove'; he mixes his colours roughly, like a workman making mortar and his stove, 'with its perspective completely askew', was 'lifeless and the colour of mud'.[8] AS

**8** E. Zola, op. cit. pp. 68–9.

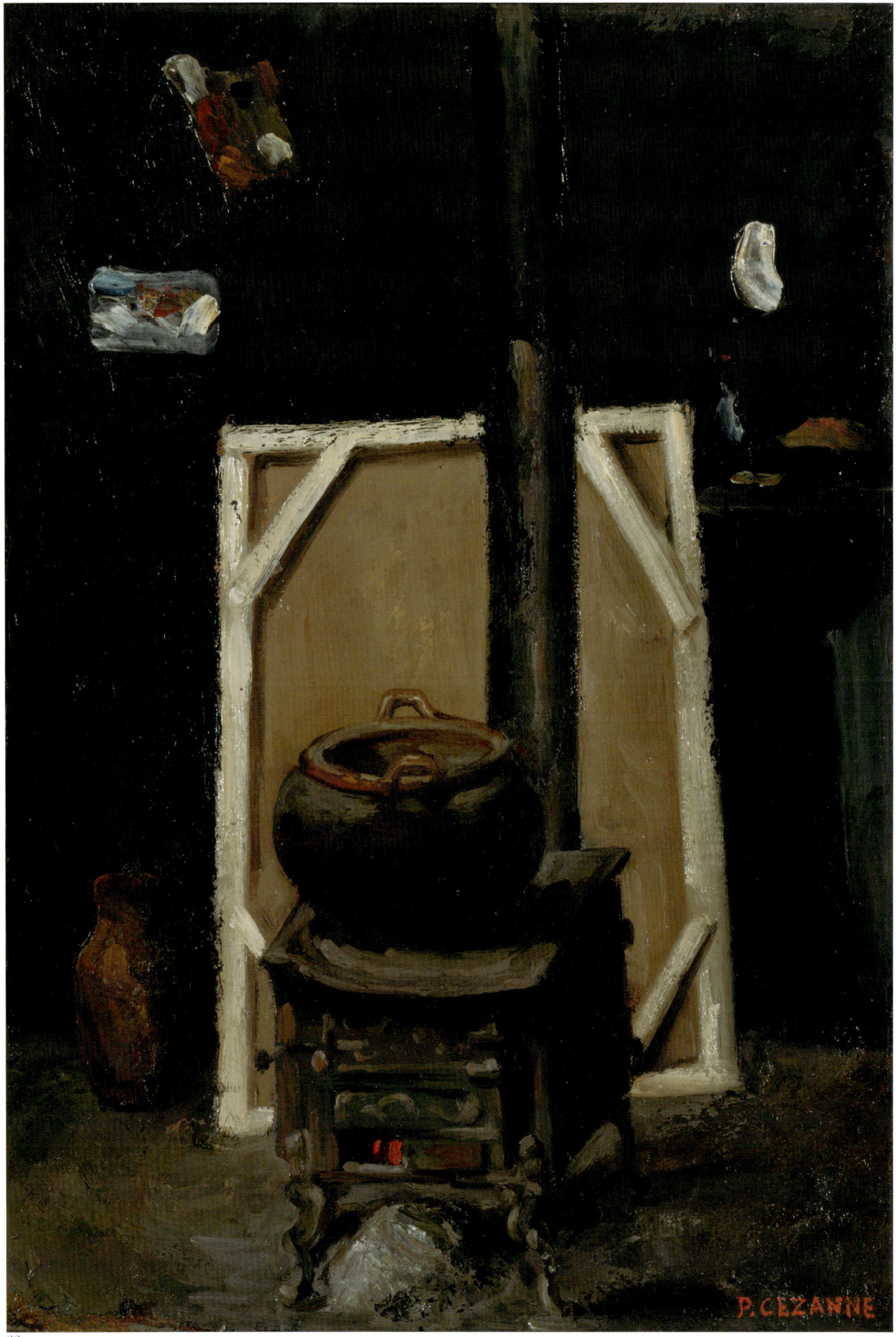
P. CEZANNE

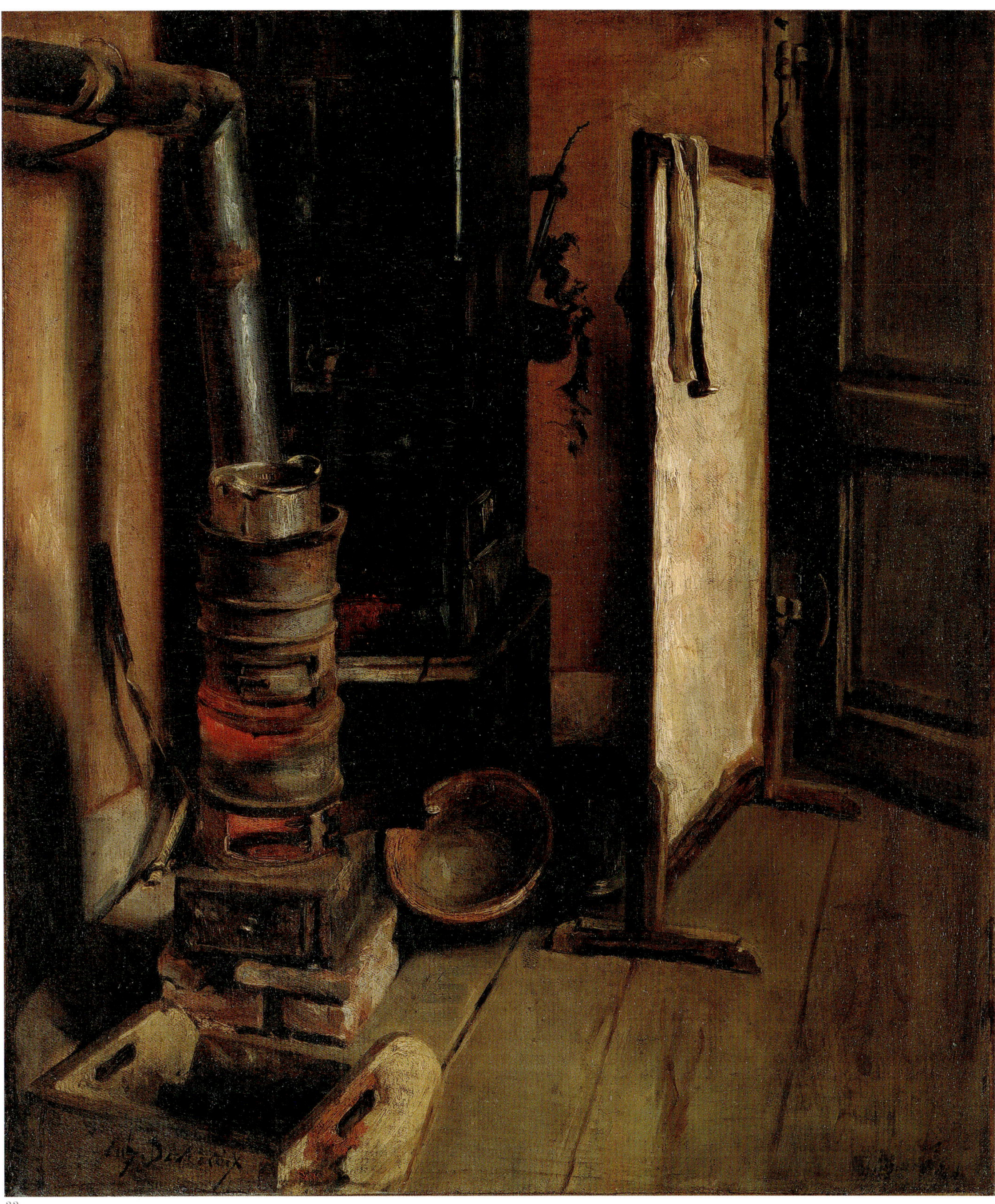

33

## 34. Camille Pissarro (1830–1903)

*Portrait of Cézanne* 1874

Oil on canvas, 73 × 59.7 cm

Graff Diamonds Ltd, on long-term loan to the National Gallery, London

Pissarro's affectionate and witty portrait of Cézanne was painted towards the end of the two-year period during which the two artists were working closely together in Pontoise, a small town to the north of Paris: Cézanne had joined Pissarro there in 1872. This was a period of immense importance to Cézanne's development as a painter; he later described Pissarro as a father to him.[1] Pissarro's portrait was a private painting, one of the very few portraits he painted not of a family member, and it remained in his studio until the end of his life.[2] Nonetheless, it seems to provide a considered – if mildly subversive – summary of Cézanne's artistic personality.

The painting appears to be a conscious and playful parody of Manet's portrait of Cézanne's childhood friend Emile Zola of 1868 (Musée d'Orsay, Paris; fig. 19), which shows the elegantly dressed author surrounded by objects and images that define his tastes and enthusiasms. Here, in contrast to Zola's refinement, Cézanne is shown in shabby cap and coat, with a thick, shaggy beard and 'large black eyes', which Pissarro's son Lucien later recalled 'rolled in their orbits when he was excited'.[3] The pictures that surround Zola in Manet's portrait include Japanese prints and copies of works by Velázquez and Manet; Pissarro surrounds Cézanne with images that are both rustic and popular.[4] At bottom right is a painting by Pissarro himself of the main street in Pontoise, explicitly linking and locating the two men. Most conspicuous, at top right is a coloured print of Courbet, who appears to toast Cézanne with a glass of beer. The intended parallel between Cézanne's unconventional rusticity and Courbet's similar front is evident; more profoundly, Pissarro seems to have regarded both men as exemplars of artistic independence and originality. The caricature of Courbet by Léonce Petit was first published in *Le Hanneton* in 1867, when it was accompanied by an article heralding Courbet as a martyr to reactionary France and a champion of independence. Much later, in a letter of 1898, Pissarro was again to link the two artists as models of individuality and originality.[5]

The print on the left of the portrait, from the front page of the newspaper *L'Eclipse*, shows the altogether different – if not opposing – figure of Adolphe Thiers. Thiers was the bourgeois statesman responsible for leading the 1871 suppression of the Paris Commune in which Courbet had played a famously active role. It has been suggested that the page of *L'Eclipse* serves principally as an example of an anti-establishment satirical paper; it is certainly true that the image of Thiers is far less recognisable than that of Courbet. It might also be possible that the left-wing Pissarro's inclusion of the statesman here slyly implies that Cézanne's radical bohemian persona, though modelled on Courbet's, did not extend to the political sphere – although largely reticent on political matters, he appears to have held essentially conservative views. If this suggests an element of caricature in Pissarro's depiction of his friend, its emphasis on the painter's fiercely independent individuality was of profound importance to both artists. Pissarro later recalled how in this their period of closest collaboration each learned from the other, but that, although they set up easels side by side, they each 'held on to the only thing that counts, his [individual] "sensation"'.[6] AS

**1** 'Ce fût un père pour moi … et quelque chose comme le bon Dieu', quoted in Reff 1967, p. 627.
**2** See Rewald 1963, p. 41 for a photograph of the portrait in Pissarro's studio.
**3** Lucien Pissarro, undated letter to his brother Paul, quoted Meadmore 1962, pp. 25–6.
**4** The works around Cézanne and their significance are discussed most fully in Reff 1967.
**5** Letter to Lucien, 7 March 1898: Pissarro, *Lettres à son fils Lucien*, ed. J. Rewald, Paris 1950, pp. 450–1: 'J'ai vu des paysages de Courbet dernièrement. C'est autrement mieux [que Legros] et bien à lui, Courbet! Et Cézanne, tout en ayant du caractère, cela empêche-t-il qu'il soit lui?'
**6** Letter to Lucien, 22 November 1895, op. cit. pp. 390–1.

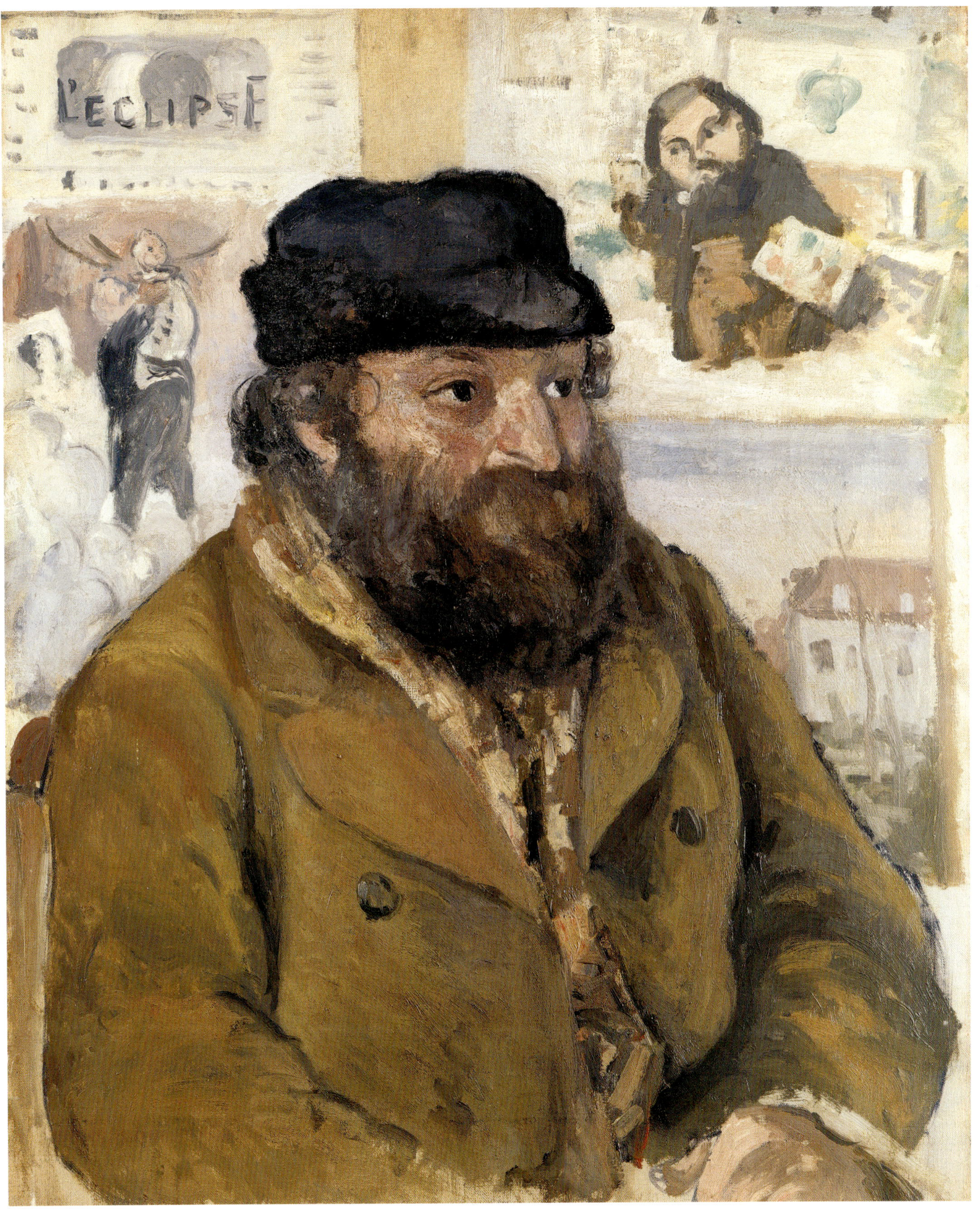
L'ECLIPSE

## 35. Edouard Manet (1832–1883)

*The Artist (Marcellin Desboutin)* 1875

Oil on canvas, 192 × 128 cm

Museu de Arte de São Paulo Assis Chateaubriand, São Paulo, Brazil (77.1958)

## 36. Hilaire-Germain-Edgar Degas (1834–1917)

*Desboutin engraving with Vicomte Lepic* about 1876

Oil on canvas, 72.1 × 81 cm

Musée des Beaux-Arts Jules Chéret, Nice

Oeuvre des collections nationales déposées par le musée d'Orsay, 1956 (RF 2209)

Manet's decision to depict *The Artist* as the crumpled, bohemian figure of Marcellin Desboutin (1823–1902) was both surprising and provocative. This explicit alliance with bohemianism was an unlikely act by the refined and elegant Manet, whom Cézanne had antagonised in the previous decade through his own aggressive bohemianism. In retrospect Manet came to see the portrait as epitomising 'an entire era', although he claimed his intention had merely been to paint 'the most extraordinary type of a particular district'.[1] That the sometime playwright, poet, painter and printmaker Desboutin was an 'extraordinary type' was undoubtedly true, but his brand of bohemianism was very different from the combative rustic model of Courbet or Cézanne.

Born into a wealthy family in Cérilly in central France, Desboutin had studied briefly in the Parisian studios of the sculptor Antoine Etex and the painter Thomas Couture before travelling to Italy where a combination of profligacy and speculation had led to his financial ruin. He returned to Paris in 1872, about to turn 50 and forced for the first time to work for a living. Working from a shabby studio in the Batignolles district, he found some success as a painter and more notably as a printmaker. At the same time he made his appearance in the cafés frequented by the artists of the Batignolles district: first the café Guerbois and then, in a move he apparently instigated, the Nouvelle Athènes. When Manet first saw Desboutin he apparently mistook him for a travelling musician, but soon recognised him as someone with a similar background, manners and attitudes – if not deportment – to himself. 'Père Desboutin' soon established himself as a central member of the group of artists and writers, including most of the emerging Impressionists, who met in the café and smoked, drank and 'aestheticised till two o'clock in the morning'.[2] Desboutin became a fixture, with his own special seat in the café and his pipes in a rack on the wall behind him.[3]

While Manet was evidently struck from the first by Desboutin, his decision to depict him on such a large scale – in the last of his full-length, sombre-toned 'philosophers' influenced by Velázquez[4] – was surely also a deliberate statement of allegiance to the artists of the 'New Painting' who congregated at the Nouvelle Athènes.

The picture was painted in the summer of 1875,[5] when Manet's relations with the emerging Impressionists were both close and problematic. The previous year had seen the first of the self-mounted Impressionist exhibitions in which Manet had – despite Degas's pleading – refused to exhibit, preferring to fight for recognition at the official Salon. Manet was nonetheless almost universally seen as the guiding figure of the emerging movement, and his portrait of Desboutin can be seen as a means of further proclaiming this position. That the Impressionists – despite their almost universal disdain for self-dramatisation – were associated in the popular imagination with bohemianism is certain. The elder artist Adolphe-Félix Cals (1810–1880), participating in the first Impressionist exhibition, referred to his young fellow-exhibitors as 'bohemians'; critics did so too, often characterising them in ways very similar to Manet's portrait. One writer in the *Echo Universel* suggested the organisers of the second exhibition of 1876 should replace the doorman with 'some brother or friend with a long beard and a pipe in his mouth',[6] while a satire in *Le Charivari* dramatised the initiation of a young artist into the Impressionist circle who is finally welcomed with the words: 'you are accepted … here is your pipe'.[7] The pipe was

1 A. Proust quoted in Cachin et al. 1983 p.170.

2 G. Moore, *Confessions* (1928 edn), p. 85.

3 'Two marble tables were pushed together for our use. Marcellin Desboutin had his immutable place on the moleskin banquette with its back against the partition separating us from the interior of the establishment; and Manet, Degas, Armand Silvestre … took their places next to him or on chairs, depending on their times of arrival. In fact with the tacit agreement of everyone, Desboutin was a sort of presiding officer for our meetings. No one could have been as skilful as that excellent man at directing the talk and keeping it on a level of cordiality', Rivière 1935, p. 91.

4 See Rouart and Wildenstein 1975, nos 99, 100, 106 and 137.

5 A letter from Desboutin of 15 May to Mme de Nittis describes the recent arrival of Crouton, the large water-hound, a gift from Degas, which appears in the painting. He sold the painting in September to Hubert Debrousse. Pickvance 1996, p. 232.

6 A. Baignieres, *L'Echo Universel*, 13 April 1876, quoted in Herbert 1986, p. 54.

7 L. Leroy, *Le Charivari*, 15 April 1876, quoted in Herbert 1986, p. 90.

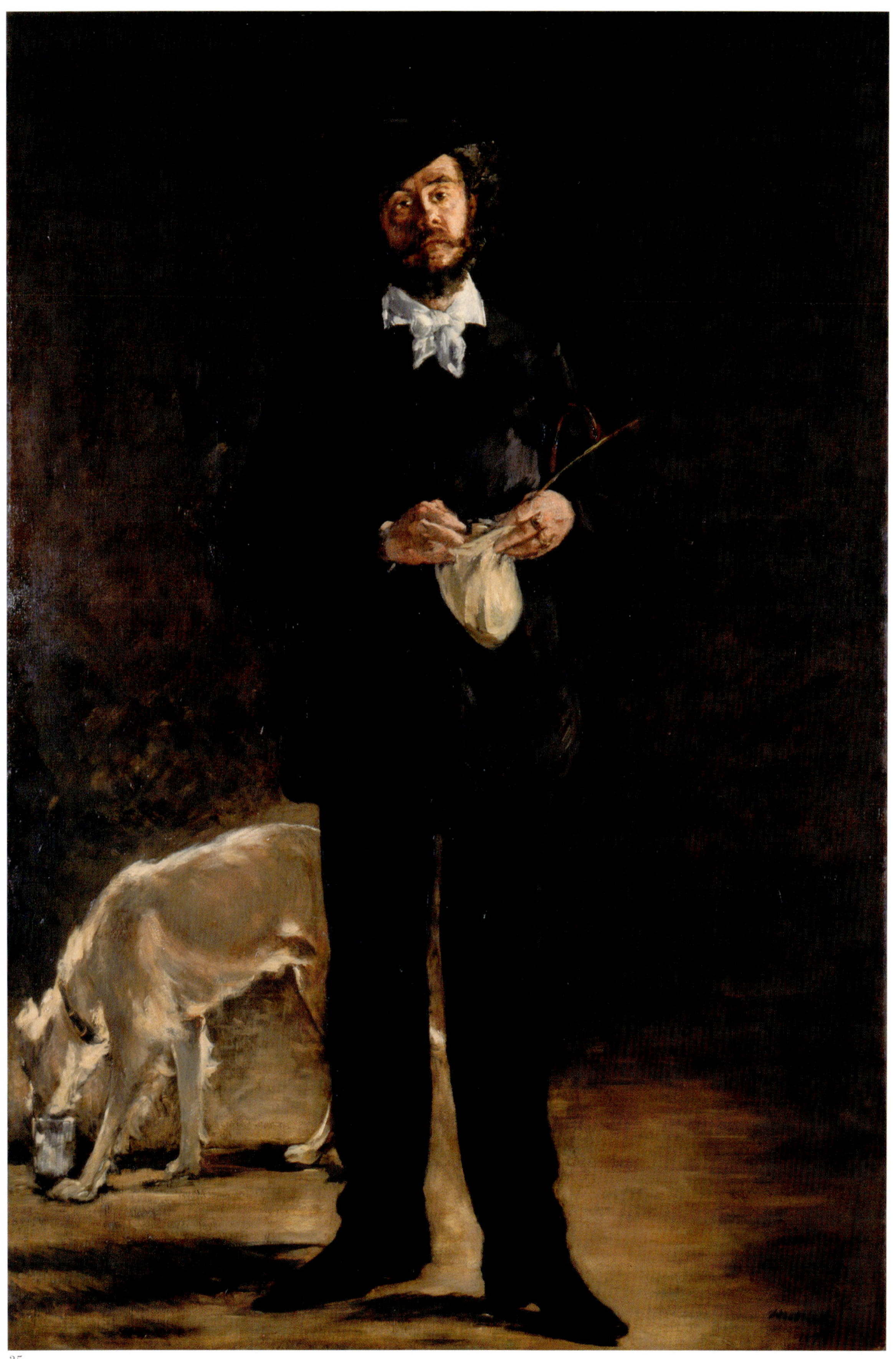

35

indeed one of the recurring attributes of the bohemian, most famously in Courbet's self portrait (fig. 9), but Manet's decision to show Desboutin with his pipe rather than palette or brushes may also have had its impetus from Desboutin himself. According to one anecdote told of the artist, he saw his pipe as 'the main tool of my trade'; it is an almost invariable presence in his own self portraits.

Desboutin's attitude towards his own bohemianism was ambivalent. In a letter of 1875, after the refusal of all but one of his submissions to the Salon, he complained that his failure was 'once again the result of the eccentric life, outside of every social convention, within which I have closed myself up in my artist's individuality for years. It makes me I know impossible, and often very shocking to the milieu of respectable people living a regular sociable life.' But against this was his evident exploitation of his colourful persona in his self portraits, nowhere more effectively than in his masterpiece of 1879 (Musée Départemental de Moulins), whose title, *Man with Pipe* (*L'homme à la pipe*), makes explicit reference to Courbet.

The idea that Manet conceived this portrait specifically as 'The *Impressionist* Artist' is perhaps supported by his plans for its exhibition. It was one of the two works that he submitted to the Salon of 1876, due to open in May just as the second Impressionist exhibition – at which Desboutin himself exhibited prominently – drew to a close. Shockingly for Manet, both pictures were refused and he was forced to exhibit them himself in his studio – a *salon d'un refusé* as one wag had it. He opened his own private exhibition in the middle of April, sending out invitations with the motto '*Faire vrai et Laissez dire*', a fortnight after the opening of the Impressionist exhibition and before the Salon. Critics made much of his absence from both: Castagnary claimed that his portrait of Desboutin 'would have been one of the most powerful canvases of the Salon',[8] while another critic, less favourably, asked: 'But why hasn't he favoured the exhibition of his brothers and friends the Impressionists with these two paintings? Why keep himself apart? It's ungrateful behaviour. What an impact the presence of M. Manet could give to that club of the charlatans of painting.'[9]

Shortly after Manet completed his portrait of Desboutin, Degas began planning his own famous painting of the artist sitting in the Nouvelle Athènes together with the actress Ellen Andrée; which is now popularly known as *L'Absinthe* (1876; Musée d'Orsay, Paris). Degas was closer to Desboutin than Manet – indeed, the dog in Manet's painting had been a gift from him – but *L'Absinthe* is less a portrait than a depiction of particular modern types in a manner that recalls Gavarni's prints, of which Degas was an avid collector. Desboutin is nonetheless instantly recognisable as a quintessentially bohemian figure, his pipe once again prominent. At the same time Degas was also working on *La Place de la Concorde* (1876; Hermitage Museum, St Petersburg), a painting similar in spirit, if not in subject, in which he depicted another friend and artist, Vicomte Jules Lepic, another painter and printmaker who exhibited with the Impressionists.[10] Like *L'Absinthe*, the painting hovers between portraiture and the delineation of a particular urban type, in this case the *flâneur*, the other principal persona of the Parisian artist. Neither painting hints at the role of either Desboutin or Lepic as artists, but their connection in Degas's mind as two types of the contemporary artist is suggested by his intense, unfinished portrait of the two men together in the studio (cat. 36).

This portrait, Degas's only picture of artists at work, brings both men together in extraordinary proximity, almost as if their two heads belong to a single body. Both are recognisable from the earlier paintings. Indeed Desboutin, his pipe still in place, presents exactly the same profile and dress as in the earlier painting, suggesting that both derive from the same drawn study; only the hat is, slightly awkwardly, adjusted. Lepic, in contrast, is painted from a different angle and the greater finish of his features perhaps suggests that Degas painted directly from the model. Degas's combination of his two artists friends whom he had recently characterised in such very different, and unflattering, ways is certainly suggestive. It might be read as proclaiming art as a common cause transcending or uniting different artistic personas, or perhaps as an apology to his two friends for his previous treatment of them.

Degas shows the two men as artists, or more particularly printmakers, utterly absorbed by their unseen subject. He also carefully distinguishes the innovative

**8** Cachin et al. 1983, p. 370.
**9** Quoted in Tabarant 1947, p. 285.
**10** Studies for both paintings are found within a few pages of each other in Degas's 26th notebook (p. 96). See Reff 1976b.

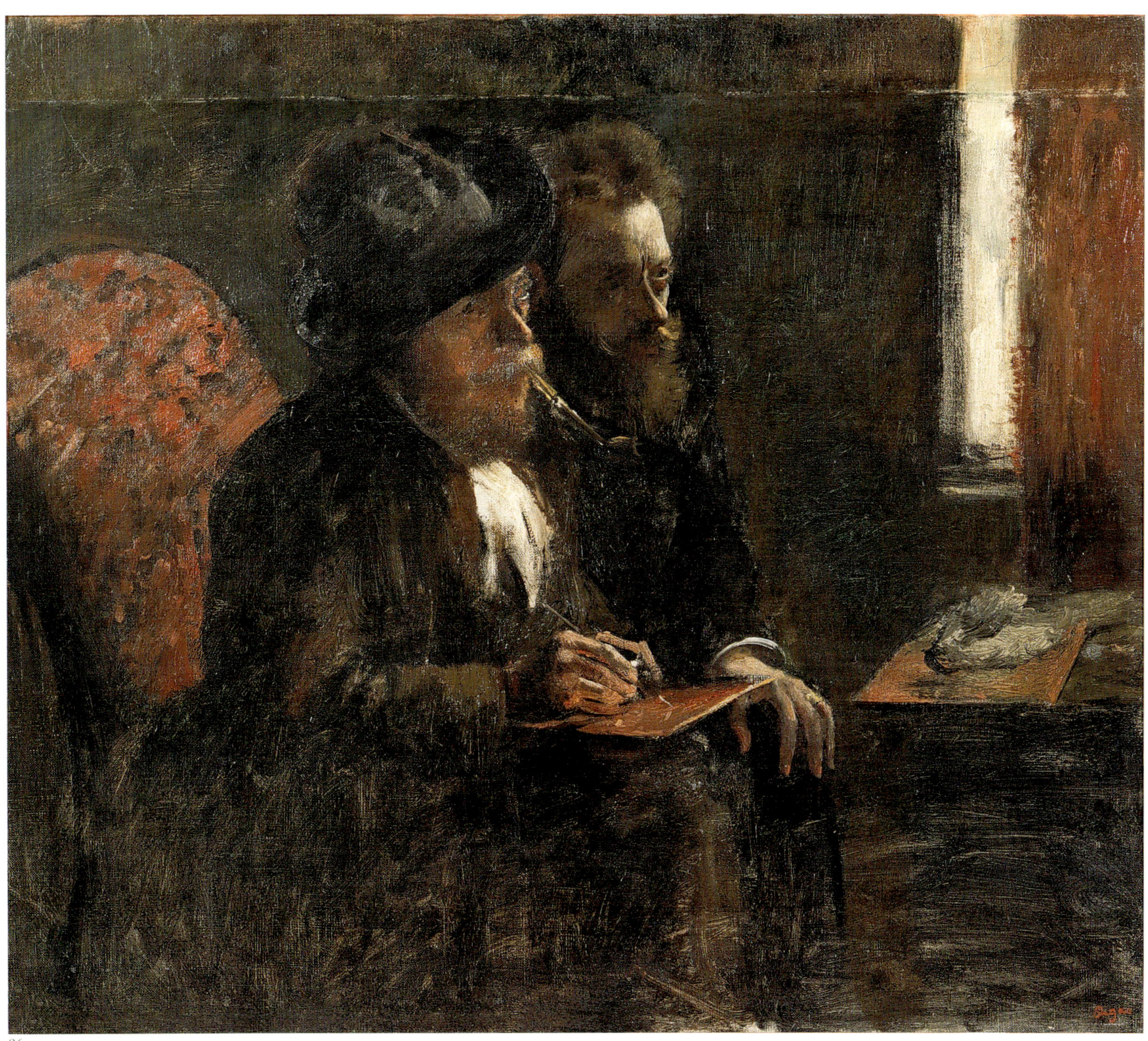

36

practices of the two men. Desboutin was admired above all for his drypoints, which he made with extraordinary freedom, swiftly scratching his designs directly onto the plate. Lepic was, for Degas, a more important innovator, developing what he called his 'mobile etchings' in which he would manipulate the ink once on the plate with a rag to produce widely different effects from the same plate. This in turn led to the invention – or rediscovery – of the monotype.[11] In the portrait Desboutin works on his plate with his needle while Lepic's plate and rag sit on the table in front of him. The whole might almost be an illustration of the passage on printmaking by Duranty, a fellow frequenter of the Nouvelle Athènes, written in support of the Impressionists' 1876 exhibition:

> … almost everything is new or wants to be free. Even printmaking … one [Desboutin] takes up the drypoint again and using it like a pencil, attacks the plate directly and traces the work at a single stroke … another [Lepic] varies each etched plate, brightens, makes it mysterious, literally paints it by means of the ingenious handling of ink at the moment of painting.[12] AS

**11** Desboutin describes Degas's obsession in a letter of 17 July 1876: 'Degas … is no longer a friend, a man, an artist! He is a zinc or copper plate blanched with printer's ink, and plate and man are flattened together by his printing press whose mechanism has swallowed him completely…' quoted in Buchanan 1997, pp. 32–121.

**12** Herbert 1986, p. 79

## 37. Jan Toorop (1858–1928)

*Self Portrait in Studio* 1883

Oil on canvas, 50 × 36 cm

Van Gogh Museum, Amsterdam (s 388 M/1989)

In Toorop's wonderfully assertive self portrait he plays the bohemian to the hilt. The painting assembles a virtual catalogue of bohemian attributes: the simple jacket with turned-up collar, the battered wide-brimmed hat casting the sitter's eyes into shadow, the extravagant pipe and the cheerful disarray of the studio with its books, broken plates and cracked stove all proclaim his youthfully unabashed bohemianism. The painting was made the year after Toorop's arrival in Brussels at the age of 24, where he threw himself wholeheartedly into the ambit of the vibrant Belgian avant-garde.

Toorop was born in Java in the Dutch East Indies. He was sent back to be schooled in the Netherlands at the age of 11, before studying for a time at the National Academy of Arts in Amsterdam. As an artist he was to prove himself extraordinarily susceptible to outside influences and in the 1880s alone he was to adopt styles that veered from the Realist to Pointillist, before creating the Symbolist works with which he is most closely associated from the 1890s. At the time of this self portrait he was closely involved with the group of independent and progressive artists, among them Ensor and Theo van Rysselberghe, who were to found the group 'Les XX' the following year. One of the chief spokesmen of the group, the lawyer Edmond Picard, had from 1881 been preaching a doctrine of artistic independence outlined in his paper, *L'Art Moderne*. For Picard the familiar enemies of the artist were the bourgeoisie, the press, the Salon and Academy: 'No more Greeks and Romans … Enough old rubbish, enough carnival, we need realistic art, where convention is banished. We need sincere feelings, human passions, things plumbed to the bottom of hearts that throb. And finally, we need life. Down with masks and long live nature.'[1] He called for a new socialist and realist art, and for artists to have the freedom to express themselves unconstrained by all conventions or rules. Toorop embraced these ideas wholeheartedly, sympathising with the anarcho-socialism of his friend, the Belgian critic Jules Destrée, and travelling to paint workers in the Belgian countryside. By 1884 he was seen as one of the most radical and left wing of Les XX.[2]

The depiction of his aggressively bohemian persona in this self portrait was clearly intended to suggest Toorop's oppositional attitudes, both artistic and political. Painted with a meticulousness that he was soon to abandon for a rough use of the palette knife derived from Courbet, one of Picard's heroes, Toorop here harks back to the earlier artist's bohemian self portraits. AS

**1** *L'Art Moderne*, 23 March 1884.

**2** According to H. Vigoureux in *L'Etudiant* (1884), cited in Block 1984, p. 33.

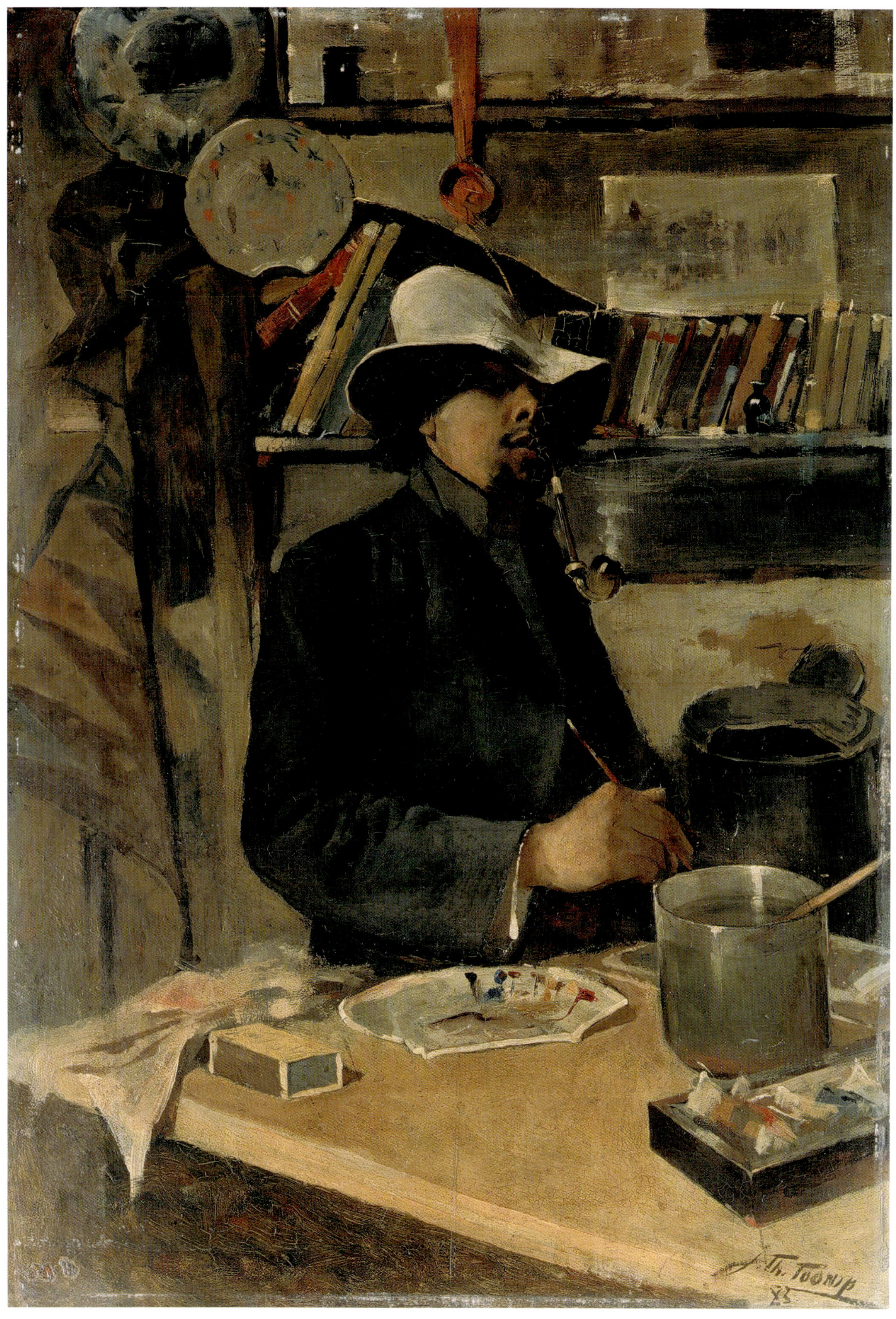

## 38. Hermann-Paul (Georges Hermann René Paul) (1864–1940) Poster for the *Salon des Cent* 1895

Colour lithograph on paper, 65.4 × 50 cm

Victoria and Albert Museum, London (E.2686–1962)

There could be few more telling demonstrations of the fact that by the century's end the bohemian idea had become a seductive promotional tool than this colourful and witty poster. This caricature of flamboyant unconventionality, all puckered lips and floppy bow tie, is in fact an advertisement for an exhibition of works by precisely the young avant-garde that it gently satirises. Here is none of the danger or confrontational radicalism of Courbet's bohemianism of half a century earlier: its proclamation of artistic eccentricity is both unexceptional and entirely unthreatening.

The poster was for the seventh 'Salon des Cent' exhibition held at the offices of the magazine *La Plume* on rue Bonaparte, Paris, in December 1894 and January 1895. An earlier poster for the same exhibition by F.A. Cazal had shown the quintessential bohemian poet Verlaine and the dandyish Jean Moreas as visitors. *La Plume* was a bi-monthly artistic and literary magazine founded by the energetic and charismatic 26-year-old Léon Deschamps in 1889. The journal was explicitly dedicated to youthful experiment, as it proclaimed at the beginning of 1891 it was 'open to all talents but especially to youth. Free from favour towards any school, this review lets everyone express ALL their thoughts: FOR ART! This is its unique motto'.[1]

Although the idea of an exhibition organised by the journal had first been mooted within its pages in early 1892 it was not until January two years later that the first of the 'Salons des Cent' opened on the rue Bonaparte. The shows combined many artists and all media; the name derived from the fiction that the exhibitions were to showcase the work of a hundred privileged artists, although in fact there was not the space to exhibit anything like this number. Six month-long group exhibitions were held each year, interspersed with shows dedicated to individual artists or particular media, and each was advertised with specially commissioned posters. Here, too, the emphasis was on experiment and the encouragement of young artists. Although some posters were designed by the established names of the avant-garde such as Toulouse-Lautrec and Pierre Bonnard, others were solicited from younger artists and accompanied by articles to promote them in the magazine.

By 1895 Hermann-Paul was an established member of the group of adventurous graphic artists around Toulouse-Lautrec and the Nabis. He published his first colour lithograph in 1891, the same year as Toulouse-Lautrec's, and throughout the 1890s his works were published in various journals including, from 1894, two of the most important and influential: the *Courier français* and *Le Rire*. Although this poster has been described as a self portrait it bears little relationship to Hermann-Paul's surviving self portrait of 1891–3, which shows him dark-haired and soberly dressed.[2] AS

**1** *La Plume*, no. 41, 1 January 1891, quoted in Van Deputte 1994, p. 12.

**2** Reproduced in Cate and Boyer 1985, p. 112.

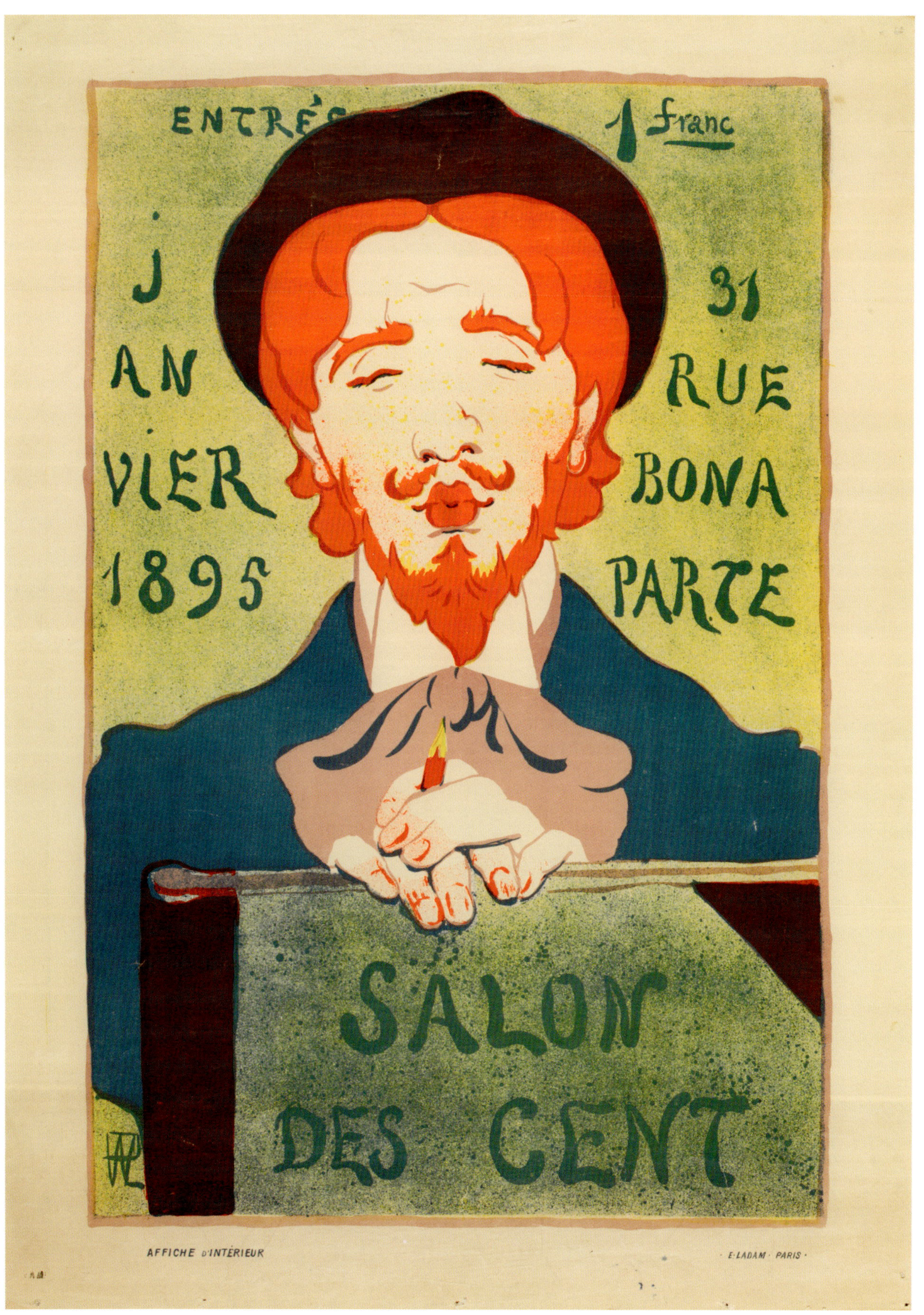
ENTRÉE
1 franc
J
AN
VIER
1895
31
RUE
BONA
PARTE
SALON
DES CENT
AFFICHE D'INTÉRIEUR
E. LADAM · PARIS

## 39. Pablo Picasso (1881–1973)

*Portrait of Angel Fernández de Soto* 1903

Oil on canvas, 69.5 × 55.2 cm

The Sir Andrew Lloyd Webber Art Foundation, London

Picasso's Blue Period, which lasted from late 1902 to early 1904, was dominated by the theme of the outcast and social outsider;[1] in this portrait of his friend Angel de Soto he addresses the subject of the bohemian dandy with sardonic wit and a degree of cruelty. Picasso had met de Soto in Barcelona in 1899 and the two had 'raised hell together'[2] in the nightspots and brothels of the city. 'Slender and elegant … and almost always surrounded by women',[3] De Soto was one of the circle of aspiring artists and writers who frequented the famous café Els Quatre Gats, self-consciously modelled by its founders on the Parisian cabarets of Montmartre.

By 1903 the 22-year-old Picasso had been dividing his time between Barcelona and Paris for three years. He had arrived back in Barcelona in January to share a studio with De Soto, as he had done the year before. But his patience with his surroundings and his friends seems to have been wearing thin. The previous year he had written to Max Jacob in Paris, full of disdain for the '*artistas*' of Barcelona: 'It's very funny … they write very bad books and they paint idiotic pictures. That's life. That's how it is …'[4]; now he found himself driven to distraction by De Soto's laziness. De Soto's pose as an artistic bohemian was scarcely matched by any serious application as ân artist. Picasso recalled him as an 'amusing wastrel';[5] by the time of this portrait he was earning a meagre living as the employee of a spice merchant by day and returning to fill the studio with friends by night, disturbing Picasso at the very moment when he liked best to work. Exasperated, Picasso moved out towards the end of the year, before moving to Paris permanently in 1905.[6]

In this deceptively simple portrait Picasso seems to tread a line between accepting and ridiculing the melancholic yet pugnacious pose of the bohemian dandy. He depicts De Soto elegantly dressed at a café table, with the bohemian attributes of pipe and glass. In a pose of studied (and slightly awkward) nonchalance his left arm rests on the back of his invisible seat, while he regards the viewer with a look that is a curious mix of defiance and anxiety. Picasso treats his friend's face with caricatural exaggeration, emphasising his jutting chin, twisted mouth and jug-ear, which are instantly recognisable in his other pictures of De Soto (e.g. *De Soto with a Whore*, 1902–3, Museu Picasso, Barcelona). One heavy-lidded eye stares coolly out of the painting while the other drifts off to suggest a more pensive mood, a feeling reinforced by the thickly painted swirl of smoke which seems to render visible the sitter's clouded thoughts. AS

**1** See Weiss 1997.
**2** Quoted in Richardson 1991, p. 116.
**3** Josep Palau i Fabre, *Picasso y els seus amics catalans*, Barcelona 1971, p. 56, quoted in Asleson et al. 2003, p. 288.
**4** McCully 1981, p. 38.
**5** Richardson 1991, p. 115.
**6** Op. cit. p. 291.

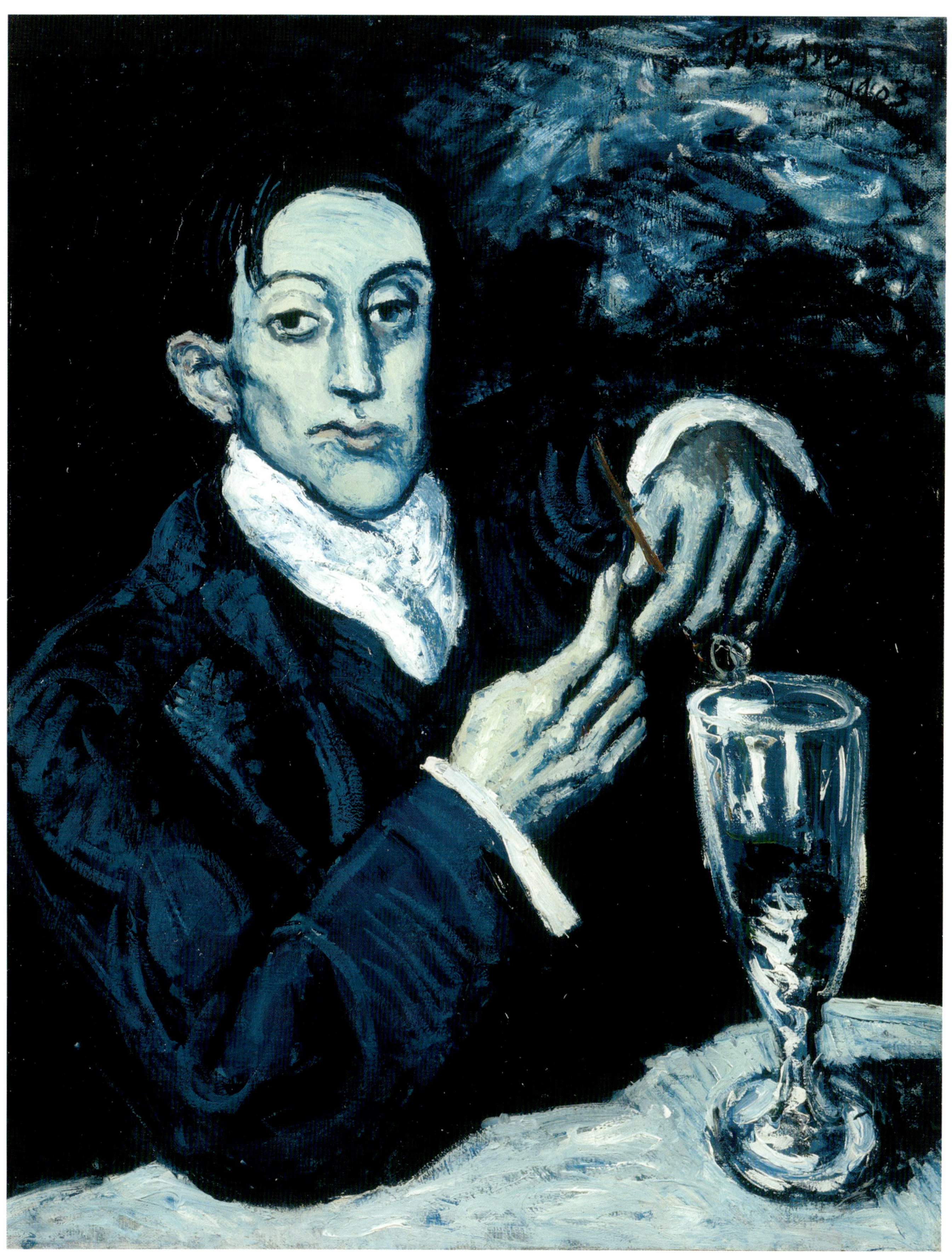

# The Dandy and Flâneur

Just as bohemianism was adopted by artists as a means to express their rejection of the values of bourgeois society, so too was dandyism. Despite their evident differences the two often came together: Murger, the chronicler of bohemia, occasionally dressed in dandified styles; Baudelaire, responsible above all others for claiming dandyism as a pose for the artist and poet was, in Théophile Gautier's famous description, 'a dandy lost in bohemia'.[1] In the face of the prevailing nineteenth-century virtues of equality, industry and utility, the dandy proclaimed his superiority through his aristocratic manner, his immaculate dress and his contempt for vulgarity.

Although dandyism had its origins in Regency England, it was imported into post-Napoleonic France as part of a pervasive Anglomania, and there developed as a pose of political protest and defiance against the bourgeois monarchy of Louis Philippe. Balzac, noting the erosion of class barriers, called in 1830 for a new aristocracy of artists and intellectuals to assert its social and moral supremacy through the elegance of their manners. In his influential biography of Beau Brummell of 1845, Jules Barbey d'Aurevilly presented the most famous of all regency dandies as 'a great artist ... only his art was not some special one exercised at a particular time. It was his very life.'[2] Dandyism, Barbey claimed, was a heroic achievement founded on an exalted individuality, supported by an acid wit and a lofty detachment.

It was Charles Baudelaire, however, who gave the definitive account of the dandy in his influential essay, *The Painter of Modern Life*, in which he used the term to describe a new kind of aristocrat whose superiority depended not upon birth but upon the cultivation of a personal originality and a dedicated opposition to triviality and vulgarity. Baudelaire's definition of dandyism as 'a kind of cult of the self' and 'the last spark of heroism amid decadence'[3] had a profound effect on younger artists such as Tissot (cat. 43), Whistler (cats 44, 45) and Beardsley (cats 46–48), as well as on writers like the Goncourt brothers, who adopted a pose of sartorial elegance and aristocratic disdain as an expression of the cult of art for art's sake which they pursued. In their rejection of the vulgarity of modern life, they celebrated artifice, cultivating a purely aesthetic pleasure in the refined beauties of Japanese art and French art of the eighteenth century.

In his essay Baudelaire also celebrates the artist-*flâneur*, the man of the world who takes pleasure in mingling with the crowd and observing the spectacle of the modern city. The *flâneur* shares the aristocratic reserve and refined sensibility of the dandy, but not his impassivity. 'The dandy aspires to insensitivity, and it is in this that Monsieur G. [Constantin Guys, Baudelaire's 'painter of modern life'], dominated as he is by an insatiable passion – for seeing and feeling – parts company decisively with dandyism.'[4] While the dandy stands aloof from the vulgar crowd, the painter of modern life immerses himself in it with the joyful curiosity of the child and the convalescent. Edouard Manet cannot have been untouched by his description of the artist-*flâneur* in pursuit of the beauty of modern life. In his portrait by Fantin-Latour (cat. 40) he appears stylishly dressed for the boulevard. His painting *Music in the Tuileries Gardens* (cat. 41), which includes Baudelaire's portrait as well as his own, captures the fashionable Parisian crowd – an 'immense reservoir of electrical energy' – that Baudelaire evokes in his prose. AS/MW

**1** Quoted in Moers 1960, p. 273.
**2** Barbey d'Aurevilly, *Du dandysme et de Georges Brummell* (1887), p. 59, *Oeuvres de Jules Barbey d'Aurevilly*, Paris 1878–89.
**3** Baudelaire 1964 edn, pp. 27–8.
**4** Op. cit. p. 9

## 40. Ignace-Henri-Théodore Fantin-Latour (1836–1904)

*Portrait of Manet* 1867

Oil on canvas, 117.5 × 90 cm

The Art Institute of Chicago

The Stickney Fund (1905.207)

## 41. Edouard Manet (1832–1883)

*Music in the Tuileries Gardens* 1862

Oil on canvas, 76.2 × 118.1 cm

The National Gallery, London (NG 3260)

When Fantin-Latour's portrait of Manet was exhibited at the Salon of 1867, an anonymous critic reacted with a mixture of admiration for the painting and astonishment at the refined and well-dressed figure it depicted:

> Monsieur Fantin-La Tour is showing a highly distinguished portrait of ... Monsieur Manet ... the creator of *Olympia*. So there we have it! This correct, well gloved, well-dressed young man, whom one would take to be a member of the race-course set, is in fact the painter of the black cat, whose fame spread on a wave of laughter, and whom one would have imagined looking like a long-haired art student, wearing peaked russet-coloured hats and smoking death's head pipes.[1]

The passage demonstrates both the passions aroused by Manet as an almost mythical figure of artistic rebellion and the expectation that his oppositional stance be reflected in a recognisably Romantic, bohemian persona. The surprise of Fantin's portrait – also expressed by other critics – was that this inveterate shocker of the bourgeoisie should be shown to have 'such a *gentlemanly* appearance'.[2]

The effect was surely calculated by Fantin. Certainly the portrait, with its conspicuous dedication, was a proclamation of allegiance to his slightly older contemporary. By 1867 Manet had established himself in the public mind as the most prominent and controversial figure of the '*jeune école*'. In the year that Fantin exhibited his portrait in the Salon, Manet had himself refused to submit works to either the Salon or the Exposition Universelle held in Paris that same year. Instead – in an adversarial act, emulating Courbet – he had mounted a one-man retrospective of 50 of his paintings in a specially built pavilion to coincide with the exhibition. On the walls of the Salon, Manet was represented by Fantin's portrait alone.

Fantin painted Manet as he found him, but his elegant dress and bourgeois exterior were less neutral than was recognised by the Salon critic: the son of a prominent magistrate, Manet could and did count himself among the aristocratic bourgeoisie of the Second Empire. Socially he undoubtedly upheld his position within this sphere, but as an artist he deliberately placed himself beyond its pale. Manet, no less than Courbet, cast himself as an artist-outsider, but he did so in the guise of both *flâneur* and dandy, whose opposition to bourgeois values was intellectual, a question of attitude rather than dress. Where, for the bourgeois, the bohemian cast himself as the opposing army, the *flâneur* was the spy or fifth-columnist.[3]

Fantin shows Manet with hat, gloves and cane, dressed for the boulevards of the city rather than its drawing rooms; it was in the public spaces of the city that Baudelaire's *flâneur* operated, as described in *The Painter of Modern Life* (1863):

> The crowd is his element, as the air is that of birds and water of fishes ... For the perfect flâneur, for the passionate spectator, it is an immense joy to set up house in the heart of the multitude, amid the ebb and flow of movement, in the midst of the fugitive and the infinite. To be away from home and yet to feel oneself everywhere at home; to see the world, to be at the centre of the world, and yet to remain hidden from the world – such are a few of the slightest pleasures of those independent, passionate, impartial natures which the tongue can but clumsily define.[4]

**1** Quoted in Druick and Hoog 1983, pp. 199–200.
**2** A letter from Edwin Edwards in London to Fantin-Latour (July 1867) reported that the critic of the *Saturday Review* in England had been similarly 'astonished'. Quoted in Druick and Hoog op. cit. p. 200.
**3** The related simile most often used for the *flâneur* was that of the detective or policeman: see A. Bazin, *L'Epoque sans noms, esquisses de Paris 1830–33*, quoted in Herbert 1988, pp. 33–4.
**4** Baudelaire 1964 edn, p. 9; c.f. Walter Benjamin's famous formulation: 'The street became a dwelling for the *flâneur*, he is as much at home among the façades of houses as a citizen is in his four walls ... The walls are the desks against which he presses his notebooks; news stands are his libraries and the terraces of cafés are the balconies from which he looks down on his household after his work is done' (*Charles Baudelaire: A Lyric Poet in the Era of High Capitalism*, trans. H. Zohn, London 1973, p. 37).

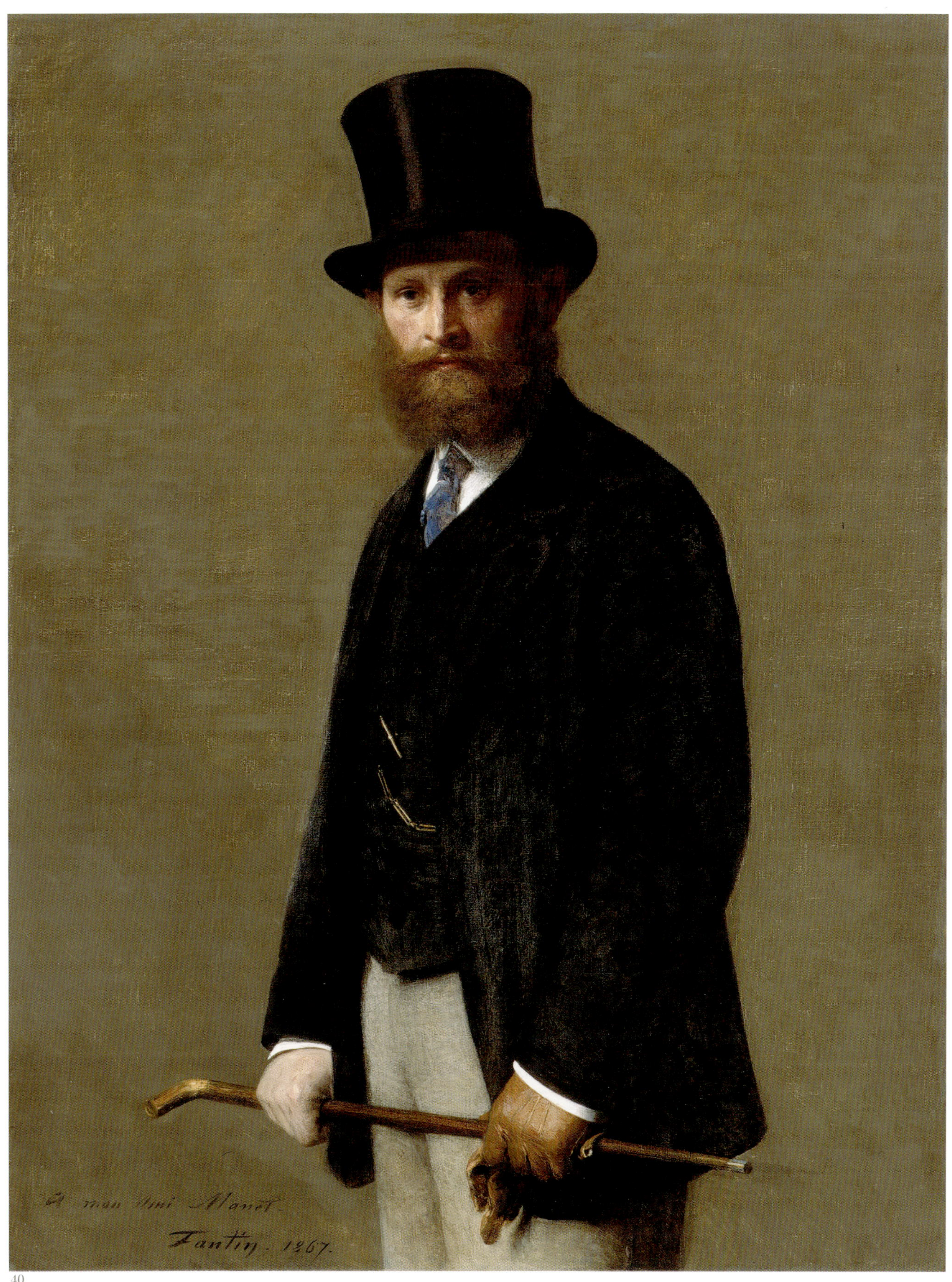


40

In the early 1880s Manet was to paint his friend and biographer Antonin Proust in almost identical guise, and it is Proust who provides one of the most forceful accounts of Manet as a passionate spectator – with evident debts to Baudelaire: 'With Manet the eye played such a big role that Paris has never known a flâneur like him, nor a flâneur strolling more usefully.'[5] Proust also provides the most detailed account of the genesis of Manet's first painting of modern life, made five years before Fantin's portrait, *Music in the Tuileries Gardens* (cat. 41). According to Proust, Manet's painting grew from almost daily visits to the Tuileries Gardens with Baudelaire. There Manet would make 'studies in the open air under the trees, after the children at play and the groups of nursemaids resting in chairs' before retiring to the Café Tortoni on the boulevard Italiens, where a group of friends and fellow artists 'would complement him on his studies which they passed from hand to hand.'[6] The account suggests that the development of the painting was almost a group enterprise, with Baudelaire at Manet's shoulder and the results of his labours discussed round the café table. As much is also suggested by Manet's inclusion in the painting of portraits of many of the artists, critics and writers who comprised his circle, most notably Baudelaire himself, but also Albert de Balleroy (with whom Manet had shared a studio until 1859), the poet and critic Zacharie Astruc, Théophile Gautier, Manet's brother Eugène, Fantin-Latour and others.

There is no doubt that *Music in the Tuileries Gardens* is profoundly informed by Baudelaire's ideas as expressed in *The Painter of Modern Life*. He had written his essay from 1859–60 and was looking for a publisher for the piece at the time when he was accompanying Manet to the Tuileries, where concerts were held twice a week for the 'worldly and elegant crowd' that Manet depicts.[7] Baudelaire's belief in the significance of contemporary fashion to create the characteristic beauty of an era finds expression in Manet's exploitation of contemporary dress, which can almost be said to provide the subject of this painting. This emphasis on the present, the artificial and transitory that was so important to Baudelaire, also informs the startling manner in which Manet's picture was painted. Its daring sketchiness and wilful lack of focus (the central part of the painting – a seated woman beneath a veil – is almost illegible) together mimic the effect of a roving eye flitting from group to group within a crowd, as well as providing an equivalent in paint to the rapid caricature-style sketches of Constantin Guys which are the ostensible subject of Baudelaire's essay.

Perhaps most telling of all is Manet's own position within this crowd: wearing a top hat, he appears at the extreme left – only just in the painting – and behind the more conspicuous figure of his monocled friend Albert de Balleroy. Inconspicuous, anonymous, both part of the crowd yet detached from it, it is hard to envisage a neater encapsulation of the persona of the artist-*flâneur* than this. Baudelaire's essay plays upon the contradictory impulses of absorption by the crowd and removal from it: 'He is an "I" with an insatiable appetite for the "non-I"', both absorbing and being absorbed by the crowd. He has the dandy's detachment but combined with a passionate involvement in the crowd, a fascination for 'seeing and feeling'. Manet's self portrait and its positioning in *Music in the Tuileries Gardens* gives visual form to this paradoxical position: he casts himself explicitly as Baudelaire's painter of modern life, just as Fantin-Latour was to do five years later. AS

**5** A. Proust, *Edouard Manet: Souvenirs*, Paris 1913, p. 29.

**6** Loc. cit.

**7** T. Duret, quoted in Wilson 1983, p. 14.

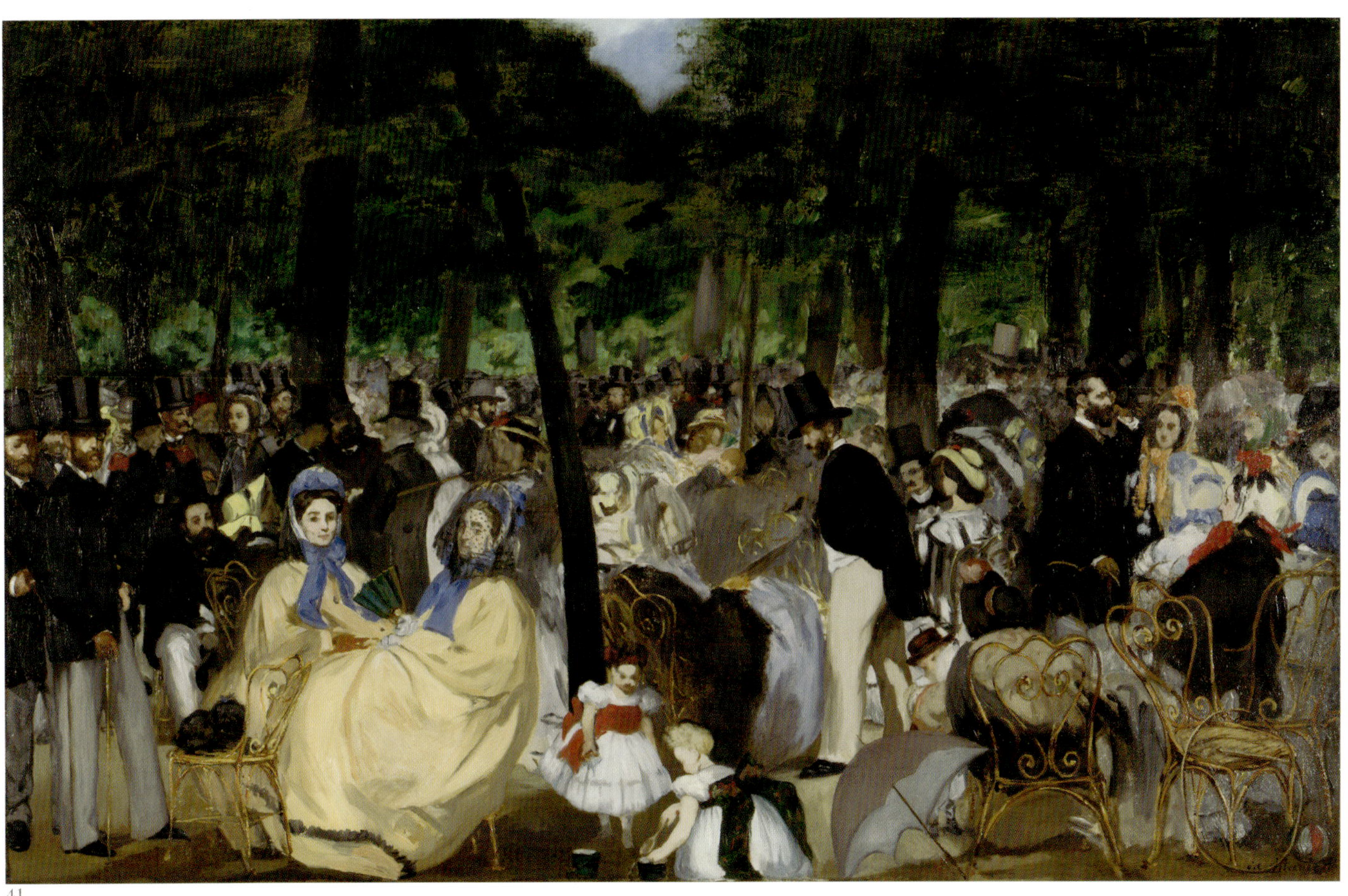

41

## 42. Edouard Manet (1832–1883)

*George Moore at the Nouvelle Athènes* 1879

Oil on canvas, 65.4 × 81.3 cm

The Metropolitan Museum of Art, New York

Gift of Mrs Ralph J. Hines, 1955 (55.193)

> I did not go to either Oxford or Cambridge, but I went to the 'Nouvelle Athènes' ... He who would know anything of my life must know something of the academy of the fine arts. Not the official stupidity you read of in the daily papers, but the real French academy, the *café*.[1]

The Irish poet, critic and novelist George Moore (1852–1933) had arrived in Paris in 1873 intending to become a painter; by the time he pushed open the glass door of the Nouvelle Athènes he had abandoned painting for literature. His discovery of the café and his encounters there with Manet and Degas were among the most important events of his life, endlessly recalled and mythologised. Moore was to claim that '... those years and our home, for [the Nouvelle Athènes] was our home, live only in a few pictures and a few pages of prose'.[2] That the pages of prose are now countless is in no small measure thanks to Moore himself.

The young Moore cut a deliberately eccentric figure. Théodore Duret, a chronicler of the Impressionists, remembered him as 'a golden haired fop, an aesthete before the days of Wilde ... none of us thought anything of him as a writer, but he was very welcome wherever he went, for his manners were amusing and his French very funny. He tried to shock and astonish people'.[3] According to Moore's own description, which in its excesses has the air of an intentional parody, his apartment in the rue de la Tour des Dames was bedecked with Turkish couches, censers, church candlesticks, palms, an altar, a Buddhist temple, a bust of Shelley and statue of Apollo, and housed a pet python fed on live guinea pigs.[4]

Moore set out for the Nouvelle Athènes, on the advice of Stéphane Mallarmé, with the express intention of meeting Manet; the artist seems in turn to have been immediately drawn to the young Irishman's eccentric appearance – he was later to describe him as having the 'air of a crushed yellow egg'.[5] In one of his many descriptions of his meeting with Manet, Moore described the genesis of the portrait:

> On several occasions shyness had compelled me to abandon my determination to speak to him. But once he had spoken I entered eagerly into conversation, and next day I went to his studio ... Being a fresh-complexioned, fair-haired young man, the type most suitable to Manet's palette, he at once asked me to sit. His first intention was to paint me in a café; he had met me in a café, and he thought he could realise his impression of me in the first surrounding he had seen me in.[6]

The account suggests that Manet saw in Moore a particular type of café habitué, and that the impulse to paint him may have been akin to that which led him to paint Marcellin Desboutin four years earlier (cat. 35). But Manet's plan was never realised: although he was to make a striking pastel portrait of the 'dandy of the Batignolles',[7] the first painting that Manet made of Moore was abandoned and destroyed. This oil sketch reveals the first stages of another, clearly related picture, whose rapid, almost casual strokes convey with extraordinary immediacy the eager chronicler of the Nouvelle Athènes. AS

**1** G. Moore, *Confessions of a Young Man* (1888), rev. edn London 1928, p. 85.
**2** Op. cit.
**3** Quoted in Hone 1936, p. 71.
**4** Moore 1928 edn, p. 47.
**5** 'Est-ce ma faute à moi si Moore a l'air d'un jaune oeuf écrasé et si sa binette n'est pas d'ensemble?' Manet to Antonin Proust, discussing the pastel portrait of Moore, 1897, pp. 306–7, quoted in Cachin et al. 1983, p. 427.
**6** G. Moore, *Modern Painting*, London 1893 pp. 30–1.
**7** According to J.E. Blanche (*Portrait of a Life*, London 1937, pp. 136–7) the epithet was given to Moore in response to Manet's pastel portrait exhibited in 1880.

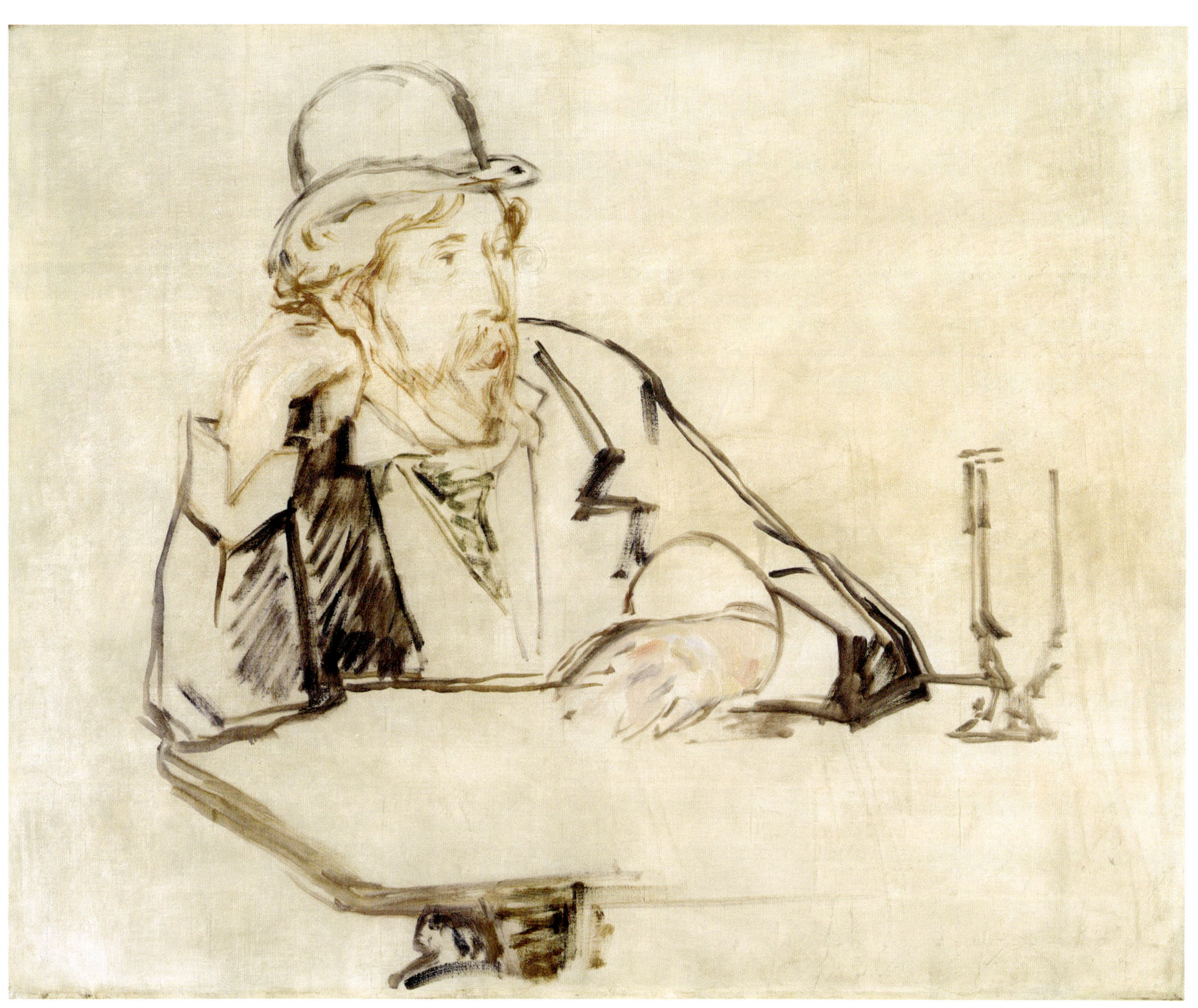

## 43. Edgar Degas (1834–1917)

*James-Jacques-Joseph Tissot (1836–1902)*

1867–8

Oil on canvas, 151.4 × 111.8 cm

The Metropolitan Museum of Art, New York

Rogers Fund, 1939 (39.161)

Degas's rich and subtle portrait of his friend and fellow painter Tissot reveals him as the dandy he was. He is dressed immaculately and sprawls sideways in his chair, one arm hooked over its back, the other leaning on the table behind him. The garb of the *flâneur*, his hat and cape, sit behind him while he casually holds his cane at a rakish angle. But although seemingly languorous, he is hardly comfortable: his body is twisted towards us and his feet are tucked under the chair in a pose that is at once languid and awkward, conveying the effort behind such studied effortlessness.

Both pose and dress suggest that Tissot is just passing through and may leave at any moment. None of the pictures ranged on the walls and easels around him is by Tissot: all were apparently assembled by Degas with deliberate intent. Most obviously, they reveal Tissot's interests and influences. The small portrait in an elaborate gold frame on the back wall is Cranach's portrait of Frederick the Wise, which hung in the Louvre (where it is today), and perhaps reflects Tissot's enthusiasm for Early German art. The Japanese scene above, seemingly a Western transcription of a Japanese model, might similarly indicate Tissot's advanced taste in Japanese art.[1] He was one of the earliest collectors of Japanese art and his own studio, in the grand house he was building for himself in the boulevard de l'Impératrice in Paris at the time of his portrait, was to be decorated *à la Japonaise*.[2] But although the works can be read in this way, they also suggest a more particular understanding that directly relates to Tissot's persona as the artist-*flâneur* and to Baudelaire's *Painter of Modern Life*.

In his call for a painter of modern life Baudelaire argued that beauty and hence art comprised both an eternal and a transient, ephemeral element. He associated the latter with 'modernity', and so the painter of modern life 'makes it his business to extract from fashion whatever element it may contain of poetry within history, to distil the eternal from the transitory'.[3] In Degas's portrait the artfully arranged pictures seem to contrast the modern with the foreign and historical, to similar purpose. Two of the paintings show contemporary subjects: on the easel to the right is a picnic scene, while on the table to the left women in fashionable dress sit beneath trees in a manner that recalls Manet's *Music in the Tuileries Gardens* (cat. 41). The corner of this painting overlaps the frame of the oriental scene which similarly shows women in their own fashions within a park-like landscape. In the same way the picnic scene sits in front of a painting of figures in a landscape – perhaps the finding of Moses – apparently based on a sixteenth- or seventeenth-century Venetian prototype. If the juxtapositions seem suggestive, more telling still are the evident visual echoes between the Cranach portrait of Frederick the Wise, with his dark hat and drooping moustache, and the figure of Tissot himself. Together the trio of Japanese, Venetian and Early German paintings provide an elegant summary of influences shared by Tissot and Degas, and each historical picture seems paired with its 'modern' equivalent – the final pairing being between the Cranach and Degas's portrait itself. If such a reading is justified, Degas's portrait becomes almost a manifesto for the portraiture of modern life and a depiction of the figure who, for Baudelaire at least, was its most heroic member, the artist-*flâneur* – the painter of modern life. AS

**1** The paintings within the portrait were first discussed in detail in Reff 1976a, pp. 101–10.

**2** The Japanese studio was described by Champfleury in *La Vie Parisienne* (21 November 1869). Tissot's taste for Japan led to him being appointed, from March to October 1868, as *gwa-gaku*, or drawing master, to Prince Akitake, the younger brother of the last Tokuwaga shogun, then in Paris as titular head of the Japanese Imperial Commission to the Exposition Universelle of 1867.

**3** Baudelaire 1964a edn, p. 12.

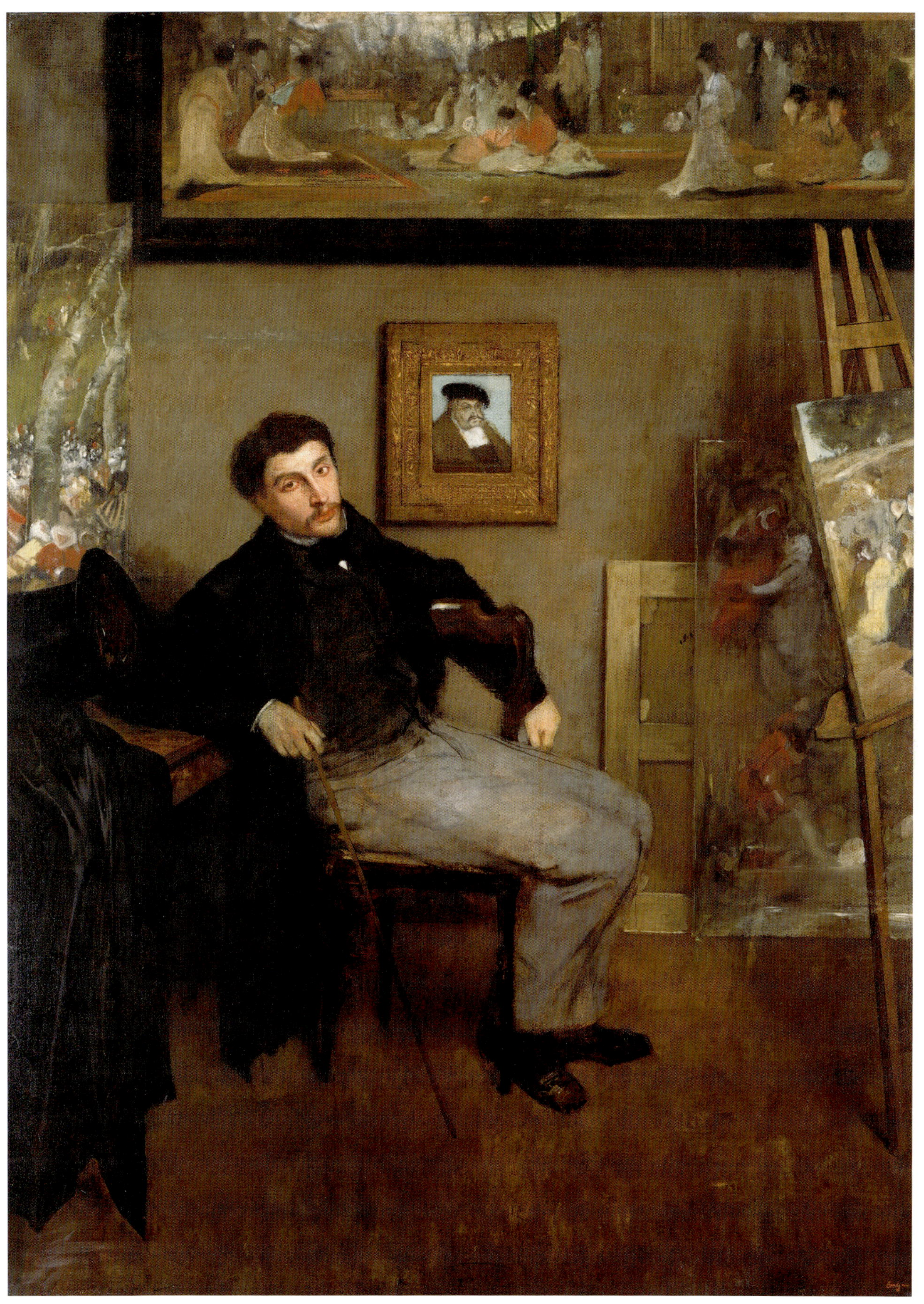

## 44. James Abbott McNeill Whistler (1834–1903)

*The Artist's Studio* 1865

Oil on millboard, 62.2 × 46.3 cm

Dublin City Gallery, The Hugh Lane (2655)

## 45. Sir John Bernard Partridge (1861–1945)

*Portrait of Whistler* about 1889

Watercolour on paper, 26.4 × 13.7 cm

The National Portrait Gallery, London (NPG 3541)

On 16 August 1865 Whistler wrote to Fantin-Latour describing a painting he was planning for the following year's Salon. Whistler had recently appeared in two of Fantin's group portraits which brought together avant-garde painters and writers, his *Homage to Delacroix* (1864; Musée d'Orsay, Paris), exhibited the previous year, and *The Toast* (destroyed), shown a few months earlier. Both of Fantin's works were explicit statements of artistic allegiances and beliefs, and Whistler appears to have been thinking along similar lines:

> I've just done a study which is jolly good – it shows the interior of my studio – porcelain and everything! There's you and [Albert] Moore, the white girl, sitting on a sofa and *la Japonaise* walking around! In short an apotheosis of everything that could scandalise the Academicians, the chosen colours are charming, me in light grey – Jo's white dress – the flesh-coloured dress of *la Japonaise* (seen from behind) you and Moore in black – the wall of the studio grey – it's upright and will be nearly ten feet high by six or seven feet wide.'[1]

Whistler never completed this ambitious painting, but the oil sketch here is one of two that evidently relate to it.[2] The sketches reveal a painting which, while inspired by Fantin, more evidently recalls Velázquez's *Las Meninas* (1656; Museo del Prado, Madrid) with which it shares its proposed scale and many of its details, including the poised brush, the mirror on the back wall and the manner in which Whistler addresses the viewer. Neither sketch includes the figures of Fantin-Latour and Albert Moore, who together with Whistler comprised the self-styled 'Société des Trois', nor is there any obvious place for them.[3] In every other respect – including their proportions – the sketches accord fairly accurately with the painting that Whistler describes.

Whistler's intention to scandalise the Academy, and by extension the bourgeois public, was characteristic and, according to the critic Théodore Duret, an attitude inherited from Courbet, whose own *The Studio: A Real Allegory* (1854–5; Musée d'Orsay, Paris) was yet another precedent for Whistler's painting.[4] Less obvious perhaps is how a collection of blue and white porcelain and four figures were going to shock anyone. By including '*la Japonaise*' and 'the white girl' (Jo Hiffernan) Whistler was making sly reference to two of his earlier works, *La Princesse du pays de la porcelaine* (1864; Freer Gallery of Art, Smithsonian Institution, Washington DC), recently exhibited at the 1865 Salon,[5] and his notorious *White Girl* of 1862 (Tate, London), which – together with Manet's *Le Déjeuner sur l'herbe* (1863; Musée d'Orsay, Paris) – had been the *succés de scandale* of the 1863 Salon des Refusés.

The conspicuous porcelain and the proposed inclusion of Moore and Fantin would, in their turn, have made the painting a clear proclamation of Whistler's developing aestheticism. At precisely this time he was re-examining his ideas about painting, inspired above all by both oriental art and Albert Moore's subjectless studies of classically draped women. Rejecting the Realism of Courbet, Whistler was reaching towards an entirely aesthetic subjectless art which, as he later articulated, 'should stand alone, and appeal to the artistic sense of eye or ear, without confounding this with emotions entirely foreign to it, as devotion, pity, love patriotism'.[6] The importance of his advanced taste in Chinese and Japanese porcelain painting in his developing ideas was paramount. He was a passionate collector and, according to his mother, believed the paintings on porcelain to be 'the finest speciments [*sic*] of Art … You will not

**1** Letter to Fantin-Latour, 16 Aug 1865, quoted in McLaren Young et al. 1980, p. 37.

**2** The other is in Chicago and the relation between the two is problematic. According to Hugh Lane the Dublin version was the source for the Chicago version. Conversely, Pennell tells the story of Whistler repudiating the Dublin picture in 1890 before later signing a declaration that it was indeed by him. See McLaren Young et al. 1980, pp. 36–7.

**3** Moore replaced Alphonse Legros as the third member of the Société des Trois in 1865.

**4** Elizabeth Robins Pennell Journal, 10 February 1904, cited in Merrill 1998, p. 44.

**5** Whistler referred to the painting as '*la Japonaise*' in other letters to Fantin, e.g. March 1865, quoted in McLaren Young et al. 1980, p. 26.

**6** Whistler, 'The Red Rag', *World* 22 (May 1878), reprinted in J.A.M. Whistler, *The Gentle Art of Making Enemies*, London and New York 1890, pp. 126–8.

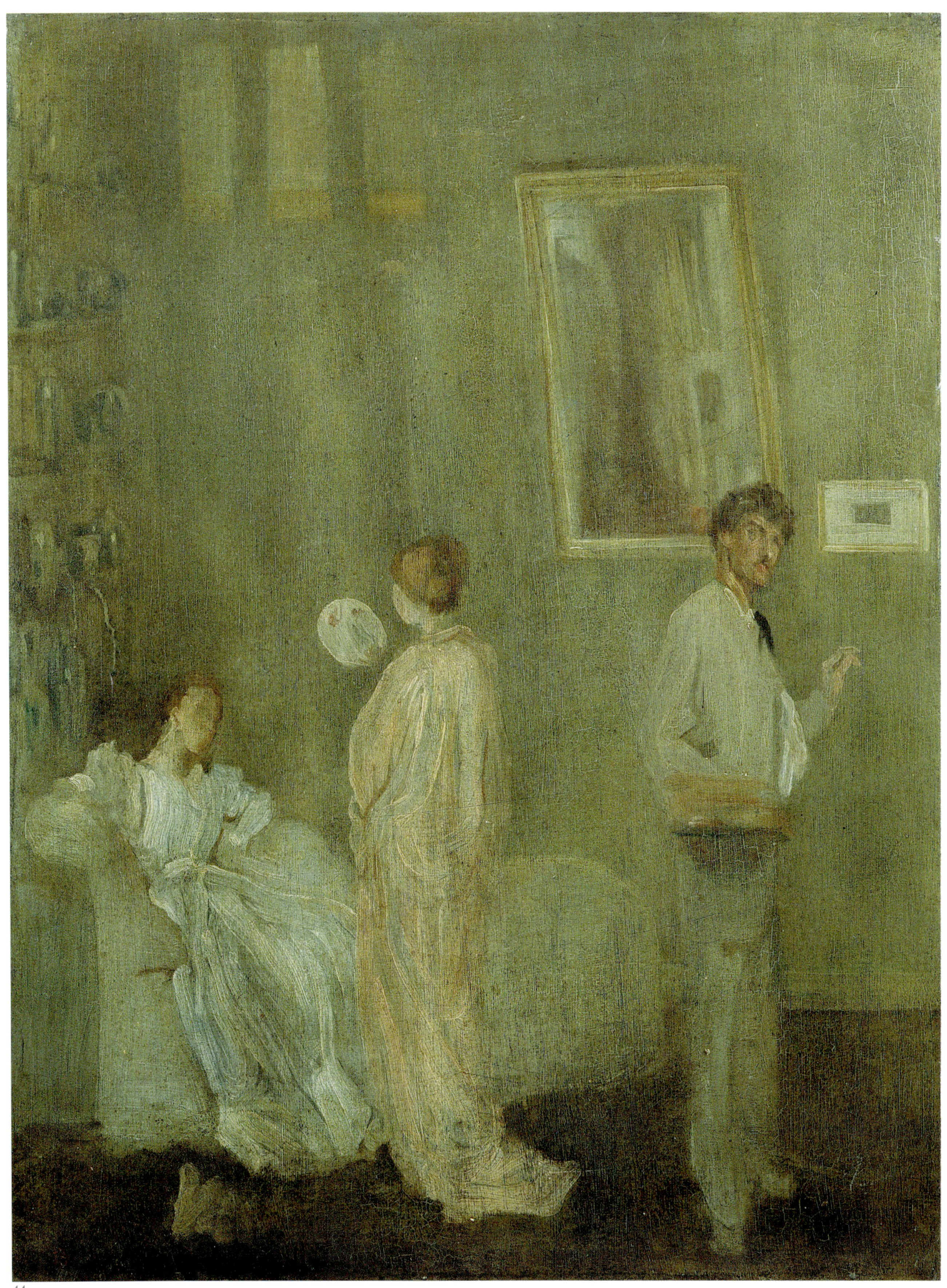
44

wonder that Jemies inspirations should be (under such influences) of the same cast'.[7]

We do not know whether the absence of Moore and Fantin in the sketches reflects an earlier or later idea for the composition, but it is characteristic of Whistler that, unlike Fantin in his group portraits, he assumes the prominent role within his own painting. Whistler was a consummate self-publicist and cultivated his personal style as a promotional tool. Always deeply dress-conscious – as a young man his mother had despaired of his tailors' bills – Whistler developed his dandified persona, with his monocle, famous tuft of white hair and acid epigrammatic wit, as public spectacle. It was a pose through which he could proclaim his aestheticism, just as he did with his personal emblem of the beautiful yet unproductive butterfly. Through his manner he drew attention to himself while paradoxically expressing his disdain for the very public he courted. The sensational but professionally catastrophic Whistler versus Ruskin libel trial of 1878 and Whistler's famous 'Ten O'Clock' lecture of 1885 – at which, after dinner in Piccadilly, he explained his aesthetic creed to a theatre 'crowded with literature and fashion' – made Whistler one of the most notorious if dubious figures of the London art world. Whistler's dandyism had none of the reserve advocated by Baudelaire: all who met him spoke of his extraordinary vitality and vivacity, and journalists reported breathlessly on his carefully staged Sunday breakfasts, as they were expected to do: 'One must see the impeccable artist, with supreme dandyism, monocle in his eye, more correct in his dress than Lord Brummell, occupied, in part of his studio reserved for culinary preparation, in … grilling a slice of salmon.'[8] Bernard Partridge, who was to become the principal caricaturist on *Punch* in 1891, was not the only caricaturist in the 1880s to find Whistler an irresistible figure. AS

**7** Letter from Anna McNeill Whistler to James H. Gamble, 10–11 February 1864, quoted in Merrill 1998, p. 51.

**8** *L'Art Moderne* (August 1885), quoted in MacDonald et al. 2003, p. 10.

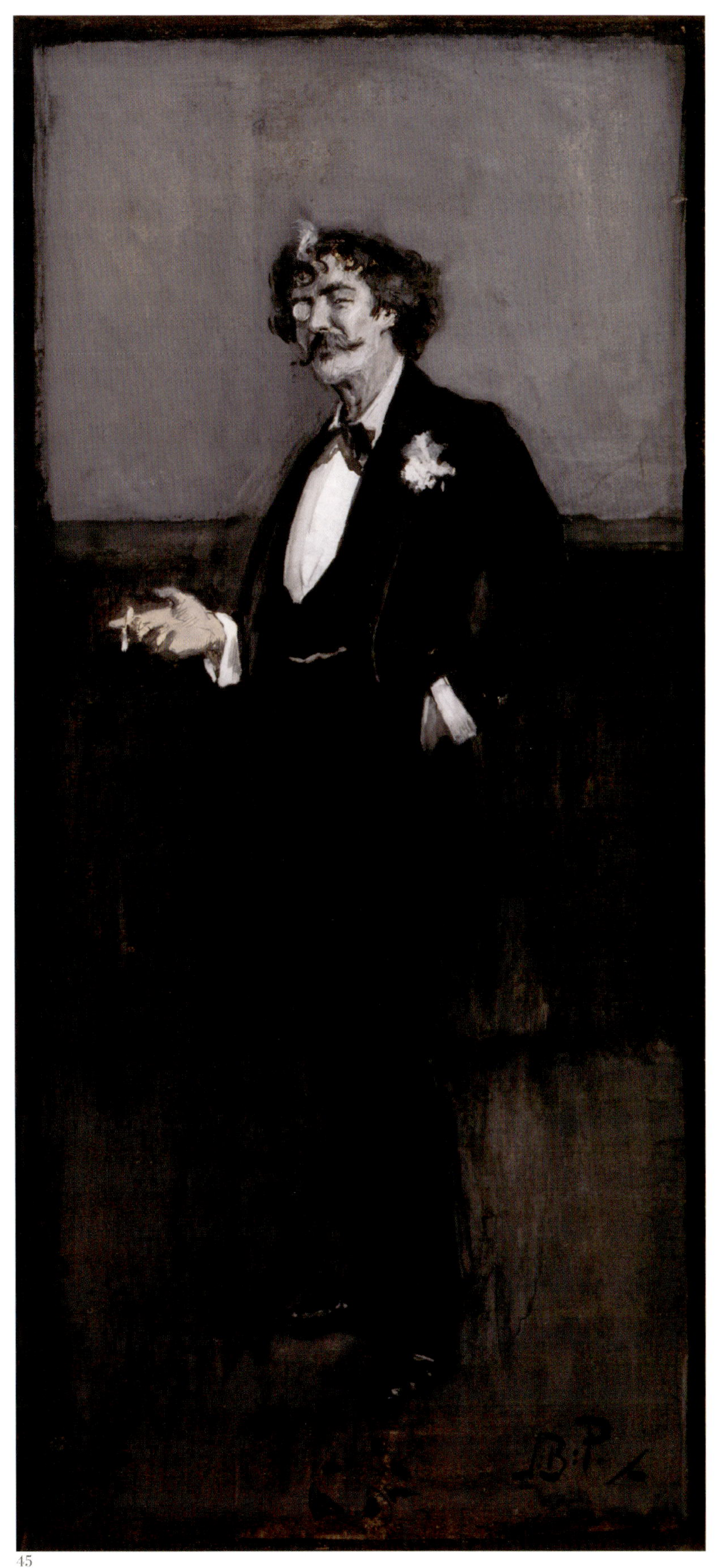

45

## 46. Jacques-Emile Blanche (1861–1942)
*Portrait of Aubrey Beardsley* 1895

Oil on canvas, 90.2 × 71.8 cm

The National Portrait Gallery, London (NPG 1991)

## 47. Max Beerbohm (1872–1956)
*Caricature Portrait of Aubrey Beardsley*

about 1894

Pen and ink, 29.5 × 18.4 cm

Victoria and Albert Museum, London (E.1379-1931)

## 48. Aubrey Beardsley (1872–1898)
*Portrait of Himself in Bed* 1894

Pen and ink, 16.5 × 10.4

Victoria and Albert Museum, London (E.429-1899)

Aubrey Beardsley's scrupulous dandyism was deliberately and successfully provocative. Throughout his startlingly brief career, which spanned little more than five years before his death from tuberculosis aged just 25, it was his extraordinary individuality and persona that fascinated as much as his work. To his contemporaries it was Beardsley who best distilled the 'essence of the decadent *fin de siècle*'; it was his 'irrepressible personality' that was seen as 'dominating everything'. Max Beerbohm was the first to describe the late 1890s as 'The Beardsley Period', but the term was widely used.[1]

In his dress Beardsley resorted not to Wildean flamboyance but to Baudelairian discipline and restraint. In Beerbohm's phrase he sought the 'supreme effect through means the least extravagant' – a phrase that might, with equal justification, be applied to his art.[2] Always meticulously clean, he dressed in either black or, as described by Arthur Symons and shown in Blanche's portrait (cat. 46) in his 'dandiacal uniform of grey coat, grey waistcoat, grey trousers, grey suede gloves, grey soft felt hat, and grey tie knotted wide and loose in the approved French manner: a small triumph of underplayed affectation.'[3] Blanche, aware of Beardsley's immersion in the eighteenth century also emphasised this affinity by exaggerating his two moles, which take on the appearance of the beauty patches of a Regency beau.

Max Beerbohm, similarly youthful, prodigious and dandified, caricatured his friend's attenuated angularity and his 'face like a silver hatchet'[4] several times, with the example here (cat. 47) apparently the earliest. In his appreciation of Beardsley written after his death, Beerbohm wrote of his dandyism in language that directly recalls Baudelaire's *flâneur*: 'He always seemed rather remote … a kind of independent spectator … no man ever saw more.'[5] More surprisingly, Beardsley himself, in his first press interview, claimed that the only label he would accept for himself was that of a 'Realist', insisting that 'I represent things as I see them.'[6] Such a claim was almost certainly mischievous and although Beardsley's dandyism shared with the refined elegance of the Parisian *flâneur* its source in Baudelaire's writings, it had a very different emphasis. Of central importance for Beardsley and his fellow decadents was the artificiality and unnaturalness of the dandy's persona. Baudelaire had proclaimed the superiority of the artificial over the natural, and the cult of artifice was developed to even greater heights in the character of Des Esseintes in J.K. Huysmann's hugely influential *A Rebours* (1884, usually translated as *Against Nature*) – 'The Breviary of Decadence'.[7] In Huysmann's short novel Des Esseintes retreats from the world and nature to indulge his senses in an atmosphere of perverse and heady artificiality. Beardsley, who bore a physical resemblance to Huysmann's description of 'a young man … with hollow cheeks, steel blue eyes, a thin yet aquiline nose, and dry tapering hands', clearly modelled aspects of his persona on Des Esseintes, even following his lead in interior design by painting the walls of his Cambridge Street house

**1** *Studio* 1, p. 84.
**2** M. Beerbohm, 'Dandies and Dandies' in *The works of Max Beerbohm*, New York and London 1896, p. 2.
**3** A. Symons, 'Aubrey Beardsley' in *Studies in Seven Arts*, vol. 9 of *The Collected Works of Arthur Symons* (9 vols), London 1924, p. 92.
**4** The phrase is Oscar Wilde's, quoted in M. Sturgis, *Aubrey Beardsley: A Biography*, London 1998, p. 160.
**5** M. Beerbohm, 'Aubrey Beardsley', *Idler* 13 no. 4 (May 1898), p. 546.
**6** *To-Day* 12.5, 1894, p. 28–9.
**7** The phrase is Arthur Symons's, quoted in S. Weintraub, *Aubrey Beardsley: Imp of the Perverse*, University Park and London 1976.

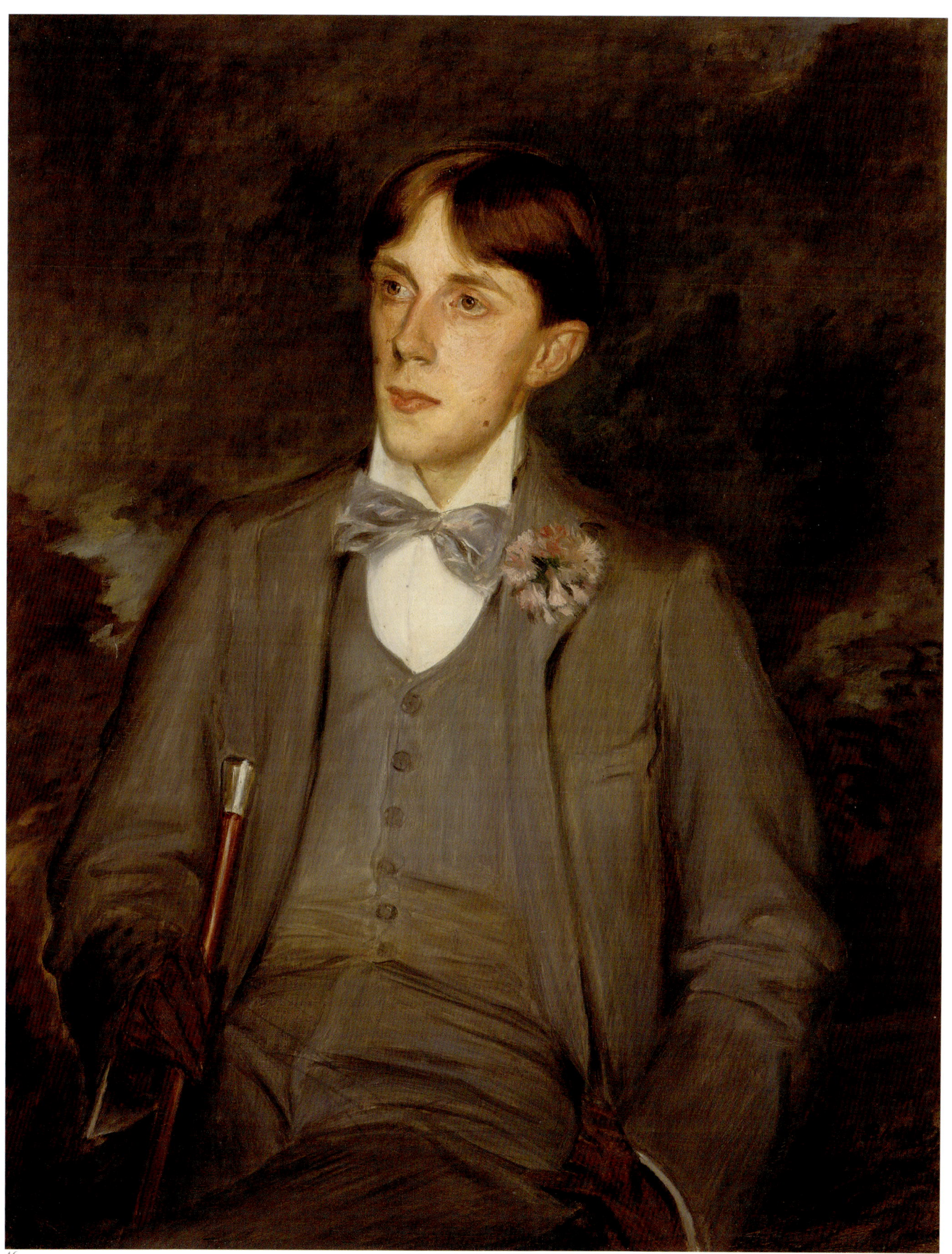

46

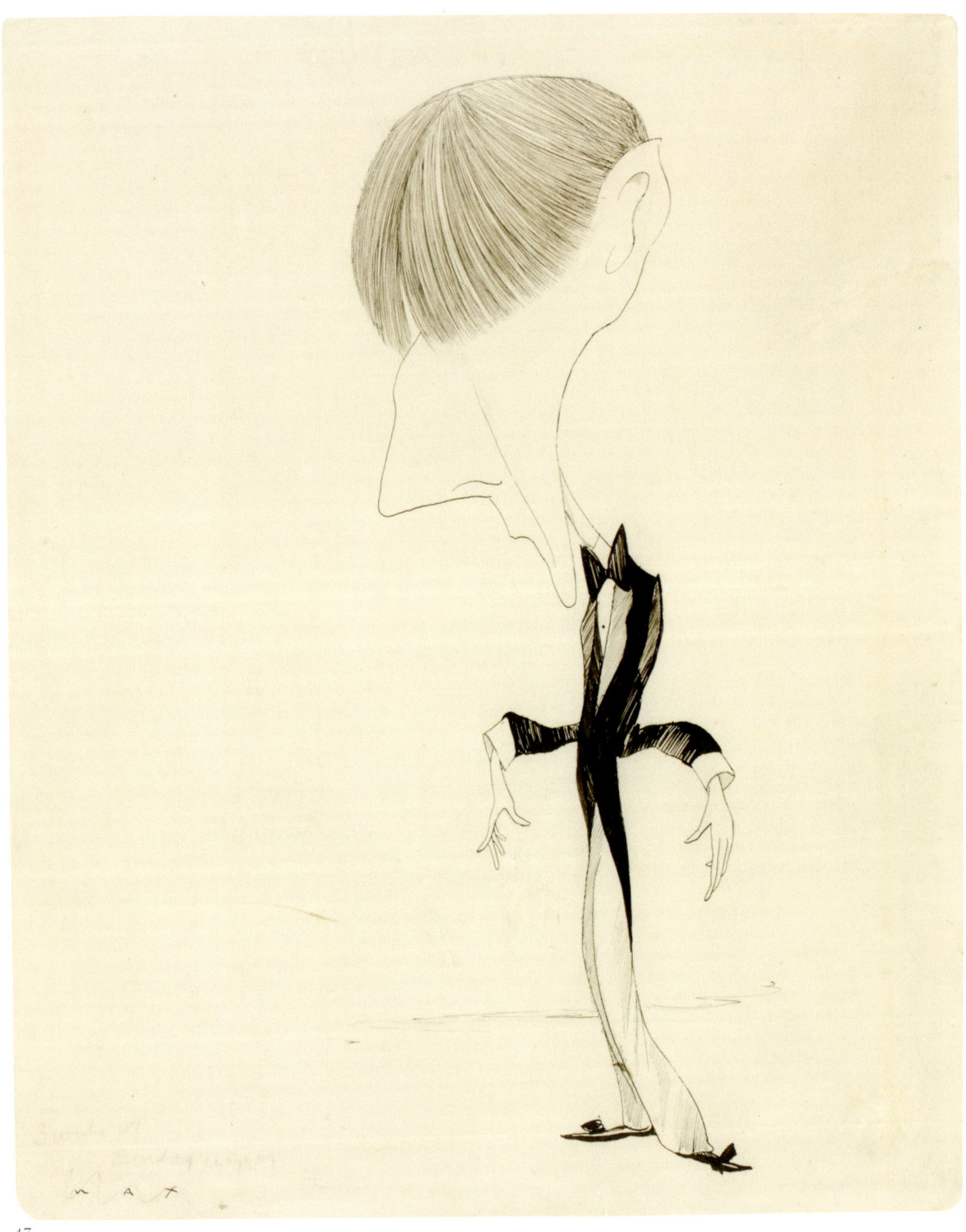


47

orange. His dress deliberately made no concessions to practicality or utility: he refused to wear a coat when cold and appeared with gloves and cane even on Dieppe beach. In one much reported *bon mot* he blamed a cold on his having gone out without a tassel on his cane. On another occasion, in a characteristic piece of calculated theatre, Beardsley invited Ada Leverson to come early to a dinner party to help him 'scent the flowers' by spraying them with opopanax and frangipani. The serious position behind these playful poses was a confrontational stance against the bourgeois norms of Victorian society. In an age that championed utility, practicality and efficiency, Beardsley's dandyism, and that of his fellow decadents, with its wilful emphasis on the useless, the unproductive and the artificial was calculated, in concert with his art, to outrage and antagonise.

In his self portrait of 1894, made for the third illustrated quarterly, the *Yellow Book*, Beardsley shows

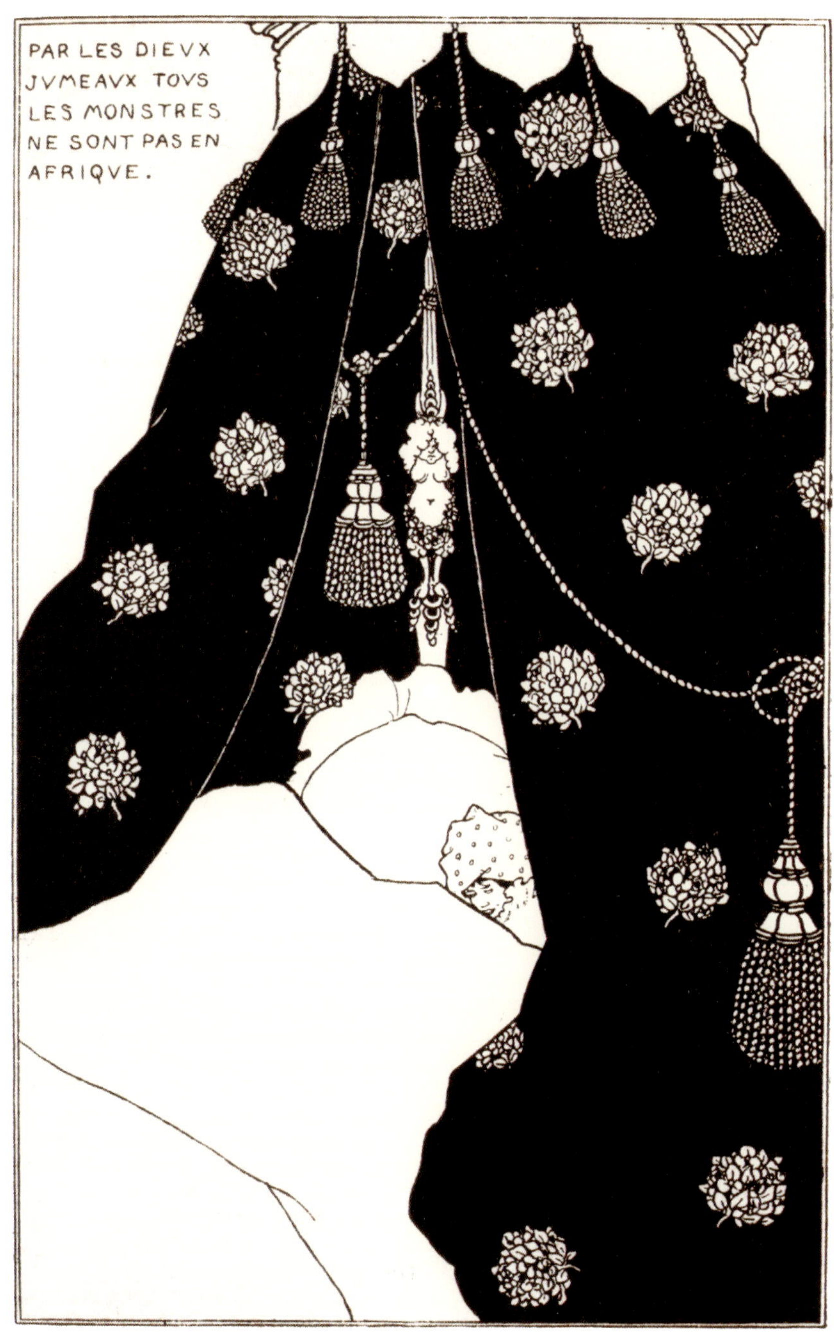


48

himself, or rather hides himself, as a homunculus swamped by a night-cap and huge canopied bed, with a large-breasted satyress on its bed-post (cat. 48). The accompanying inscription is both abstruse and perverse: 'By the twin gods, not all the monsters are in Africa.' The work was met with understandable incomprehension, with critics resorting to bad puns in their confusion. The critic of the *Artist* complained that Beardsley had abandoned the 'wall-poster for the four poster', while *Punch* labelled the picture 'Portrait of the artist in Bed-Lam'. Beardsley clearly meant to confuse, but in depicting himself as both child and invalid, while also proclaiming himself monstrous, he plays upon the perversity of his artistic persona of which his dandyism was a part. As Beardsley's contemporary Charlie Mariller noted, 'It was part of his pose to baffle the world. He did it in his exterior manner as in his work.'[8] AS

**8** Quoted in S. Calloway, *Aubrey Beardsley*, London 1998, p. 83.

## 49. Lovis Corinth (1858–1925)
## *The Painter Otto Eckmann* 1897

Oil on canvas, 110 × 55 cm

Kunsthalle, Hamburg (1640)

Otto Eckmann (1865–1902) was one of the leading figures in the Art Nouveau or *Jugendstil* movement in Germany; in this portrait by his friend Lovis Corinth he seems, with eyes glowing, to be cast as the movement's high priest.[1] His painter's smock, worn over an impeccable suit and white collar, takes on the appearance of a priestly vestment, while his angular hands, with their extravagantly tapering fingers, brandish a flower as if participating in some aesthetic rite. Corinth, whose characteristic style is usually more bullish, here wittily adopts many stylistic elements, such as linear elongation, derived from *Jugendstil*. The flower held by Eckmann, together with the floral wallpaper against which he stands, proclaim a principal source of his artistic inspiration: his use of decorative plant forms.

1897, the year of Corinth's portrait, was an important one for Eckmann, bringing a number of important commissions and culminating in his appointment as the Instructor of Decorative Painting at the Kunstgewerbeschule in Berlin in the autumn, after the portrait was painted. Eckmann had trained as a painter, enrolling in the Munich Academy in 1885; but although he established a reputation with his Symbolist paintings in the early 1890s, he abandoned painting completely in 1894 and auctioned off all his works with the words 'may we never meet again'.[2] From then on he concentrated exclusively on applied art, producing a wealth of designs in a deliberately wide variety of media, from metalwork to ceramics, women's fashions to Japanese-influenced woodblock prints and including his famous *Five Swans* tapestry (1897) that remains one of the iconic works of *Jugendstil*.

Eckmann's self-conscious abandonment of painting for decorative art was characteristic of a movement that sought to collapse the hierarchy dividing fine from applied art. In common with the earlier aesthetic movement in England, *Jugendstil* sought to introduce all aspects of life with the aesthetic, calling for '*originality of invention*' and … the '*perfect artistic and technical execution* of those objects as fulfil the *requirements of our modern life*'.[3] That artists who championed the aesthetic in all aspects of life should use their own outward appearance as a means to promote their ideas is hardly surprising, and explains the popularity of dandified fashions among the proponents of *Jugendstil* and Art Nouveau, reflected here in Eckmann's elegantly waxed moustache. AS

**1** Inscribed 'Otto Eckmann aged 32 painted by Lovis Corinth 1897'.
**2** In letter to auctioneer quoted in Hiesinger 1988, p. 49.
**3** From the programme published to coincide with the first *Jugendstil* exhibition at the Munich Glaspalast, 1897. Hiesinger 1988, p. 12.

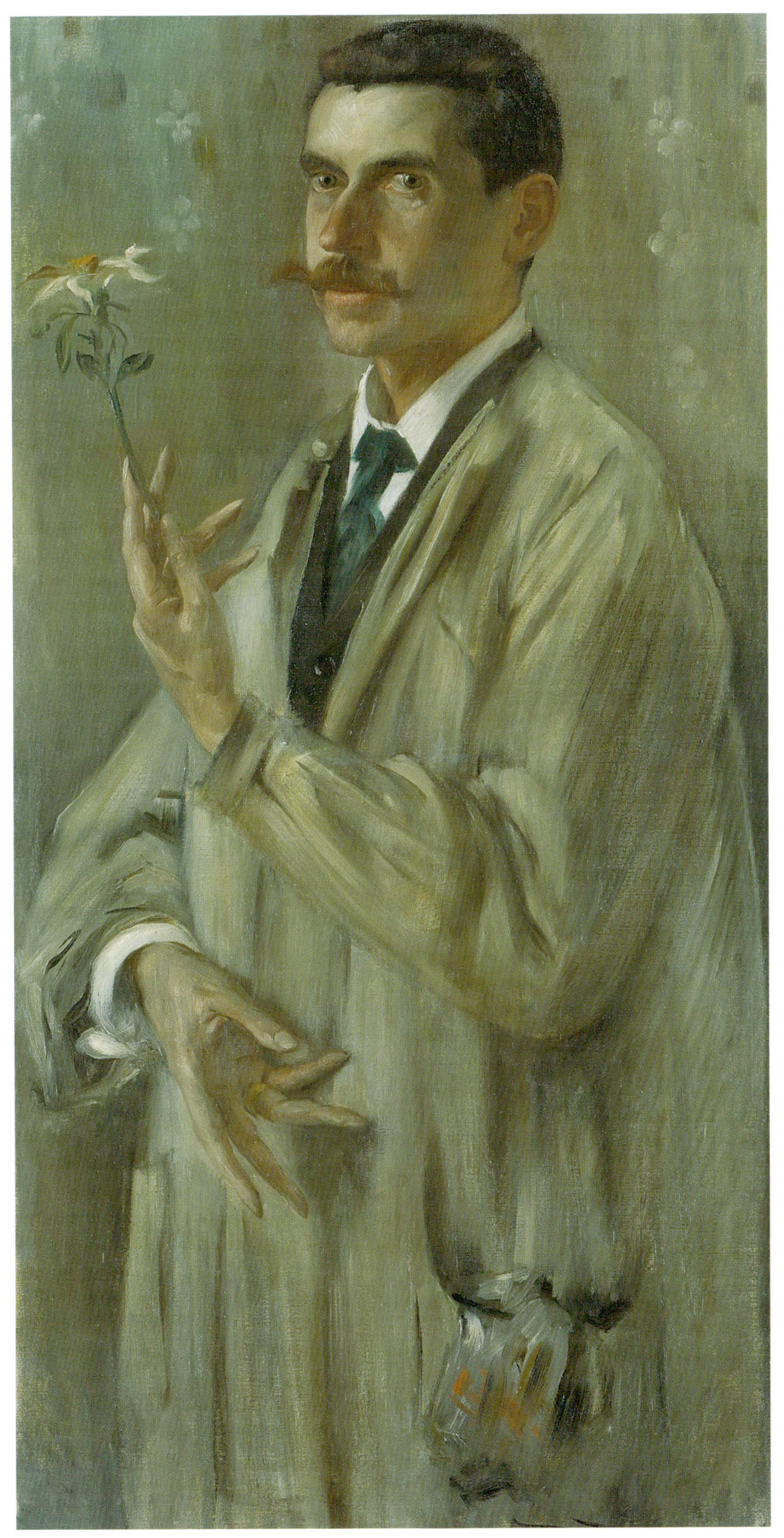

# Priest, Seer, Martyr, Christ

> I believe in a Last Judgement at which all those who in this world have dared to traffic with sublime and chaste art, all those who have sullied and degraded it by the baseness of their sentiments, by their vile lust for material enjoyment, will be condemned to terrible punishments. I believe on the other hand, that the faithful disciples of great art will be glorified and that, enveloped in a celestial tissue of rays, of perfumes, of melodious sounds, they will return to lose themselves forever in the bosom of the divine source of all Harmony.[1]

One of the chief characteristics of Romantic art, and one inspired by German philosophical ideas, was a rejection of the material world in the belief that a higher reality could be discovered only by an inner vision. This notion of an invisible, ideal world beyond the senses found expression in the paintings of Caspar David Friedrich and his contemporaries Philipp Otto Runge and the Nazarenes. It underpinned the landscape painting of the Barbizon artists, Théodore Rousseau and Jean-François Millet, for whom visible nature was the outer manifestation of God's presence. And this spiritual reality beneath appearances, the divine in nature, could only be perceived and expressed by a specially gifted artist, a visionary or seer, like the prophet of biblical times.

This concept of the artist as one of the elect was revived with increased fervour in the 1880s, when it was widely felt that the naturalism that had dominated painting over the previous decades had neglected the inner life. According to Symbolist writers and artists, contemporary bourgeois culture was decadent because it had been blinded by materialism and sapped of its spiritual force. It was the role of the artist to replace corrupt, utilitarian values and to reveal a spiritual truth, and he was to do so by perceiving and exploiting what Baudelaire had termed 'correspondences', the hidden relations between the material world and the spiritual realm. The grasping of eternal 'radiant truths' was, for Symbolist thinkers, an intuitive and emotional process, based upon the development of what the writer Albert Aurier, the early champion of both Van Gogh and Gauguin, called the 'eyes of the spirit'. The identification of the artist as seer was pervasive; it is evident, for example, in the striking, frontal self portraits of the Italian painter Segantini (cat. 60) and the Swiss Hodler (cat. 61). The notion of the artist as one of an elect brotherhood of visionaries led to the formation of the Nabi group of painters, whose name derived from the Arabic and Hebrew for 'prophet'. The impetus for the group came when Gauguin encouraged Paul Sérusier to paint in an abstracted visual language, as an equivalent for his inner sensation. The painters that gathered round Sérusier, among them Maurice Denis, Paul Ranson, Vuillard and Bonnard, adopted a similar bold, flat style, and, heavily influenced by the fashionable revival of the occult and esoteric cults, created an exclusive identity for themselves, based on arcane rituals and language.

However, the sense that they were swimming against the tide, and the hurt and disappointment that accompanied criticism of their work, led many artists to assume another, related identity – that of the martyr and Christ figure. They believed that in following his higher calling, the inspired artist, like the Christian martyr of former times, was destined to be hounded and oppressed by a philistine world. It was his fate, as a secular martyr, to suffer for his art. This explains why Delacroix, an unbeliever himself, chose to paint so many scenes of religious martyrdom (cat. 50) and of Christ's Passion. Gauguin identified himself with Christ in his *Agony in the Garden* (cat. 51), and Van Gogh, driven by a sense of his sacred mission, came to the point in moments of mental instability of believing himself a Christ or God. By the end of the century this identification becomes almost commonplace with writers and artists. The Belgian painter James Ensor was obsessed by an overwhelming sense of persecution, and, like his contemporary Edvard Munch, depicted himself as the crucified Christ, mocked by his enemies (cats 58, 59). The isolation and rejection which many felt they unjustly suffered encouraged such paranoia, and led some to mental illness and even suicide. Since his death, Van Gogh has become the archetype of the suffering, misunderstood artist, compelled to take his own life. AS/MW

**1** Paul Sérusier, 1889, written on the walls of an inn in Brittany where he was staying with Paul Gauguin. See Rewald 1978, p. 255.

## 50. Ferdinand-Victor-Eugène Delacroix

(1798–1863)

*Saint Stephen borne away by his Disciples*

1862

Oil on canvas, 46.7 × 38 cm

The Trustees of the Barber Institute of Fine Arts, University of Birmingham (62.1)

In his later years Delacroix came to exemplify the myth of the artist in many aspects of his life. Despite notable state commissions, he still felt that his gifts as an artist went unappreciated. Not until 1857, at his seventh attempt, was he elected to the Institut de France, and in 1859, after the criticisms of his submissions to the Salon exhibition, he resolved never to exhibit there again. Disgusted with the vulgarity of modern society, he turned his back on what he considered a hostile and philistine world, and devoted himself exclusively to his art. Unmarried, dogged by ill health, and with only his devoted housekeeper as his companion, he led a solitary existence, bitterly regretting the past. Through renunciation and resignation he sought peace of mind: as he expressed in his Journal, 'Conclusion, to remain in solitude, without undergoing other trials, since the ultimate goal is to be at last at peace, even if this should mean a kind of self-annihilation.'[1]

During these late years, religious painting assumed an ever-greater importance for Delacroix. Religious subjects had featured in his work since his youth but became more frequent after his *Death of Sardanapalus* (1827–8; Musée du Louvre, Paris) provoked outrage, with its depiction of a sadistic oriental potentate massacring his concubines. Wishing to convince his critics that he was a serious artist following in the tradition of the great masters, Delacroix thereafter increasingly adopted conventional subjects from history and the Bible. But among his late works are many small canvases and pastels, like this *Saint Stephen*, which he painted for himself for purely private reasons.

It was not faith that drew Delacroix to religious subjects. His writings reveal a man who, while moved by the ritual and music of the church, was tormented by doubt and sometimes succumbed to moods of bleak despair. The religious subjects he chose to depict all had a particular personal resonance: in his own words, 'religious subjects, among all the kinds of attraction they offer, have that of leaving complete freedom to the imagination, so that each person can give expression to his own personal sentiment.'[2] Delacroix's is a religion of 'universal anguish', as Baudelaire observed.[3] He was drawn to scenes of doubt and suffering, to Christ's Passion and to the martyrdom of saints at the hands of a vicious and unenlightened crowd, subjects in which he saw mirrored his own fate as an artist. And he focused on two elements, both of significance to him: the grief of the bereaved mourners and the impassivity of the victim.

Both these elements are evident in this depiction of the martyrdom of Saint Stephen, the last of three versions of the subject that Delacroix painted, in which the pallid, limp body of the saint is carried away by his grief-stricken followers. The story of Saint Stephen, a deacon of the early church who was accused of blasphemy and stoned to death outside Jerusalem in about AD 35, is told in chapters 6 to 8 of the Acts of the Apostles. Delacroix depicts the final moment of the account: 'And devout men carried Stephen to his burial, and made great lamentation over him' (Acts 8: 2). This last version, painted the year before the artist's death, differs significantly from his first, larger treatment painted in 1853 (Musée des Beaux-Arts, Arras). He changed the poses of the figures, perhaps in response to press criticism of the distortions of the martyr's body in the earlier painting, basing the revised group on Titian's *Entombment* (1523–6) in the Louvre. But most telling is the introduction of a mournful landscape and sunset sky behind the figures acting as a foil to the central group and emphasising the grief conveyed by their bowed postures and vivid draperies. Two figures turn back in anxiety, their agitation imbuing the whole scene with a sense of existential foreboding. As in *Ovid among the*

**1** *Journal d'Eugène Delacroix*, 2 May 1855 (Joubin 1950).
**2** Letter to Constant Dutilleux, 5 October 1850, (Joubin 1935–8).
**3** C. Baudelaire, 'The Salon of 1846', in Baudelaire 1964b, p. 61.

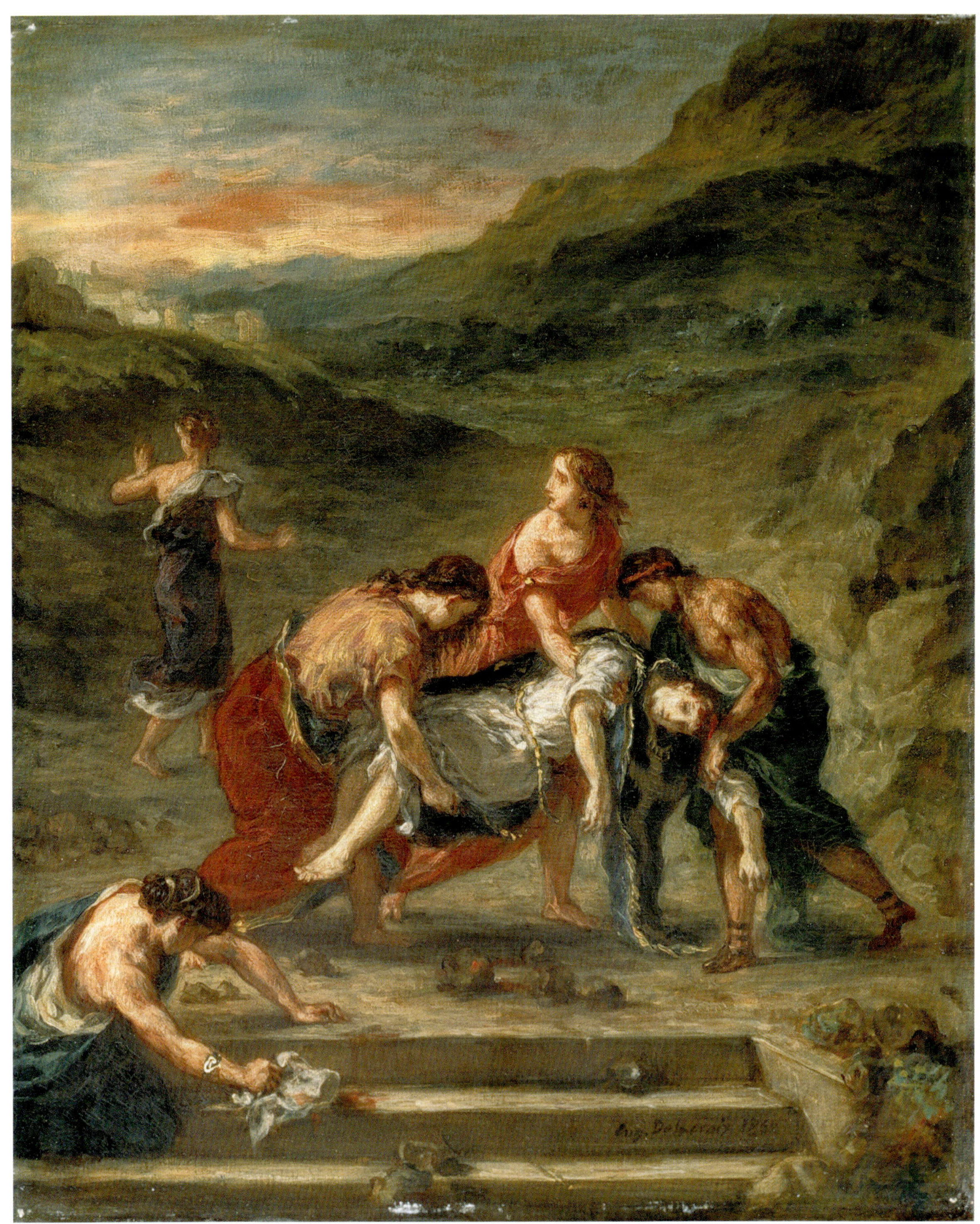

*Scythians* (cat. 19), the empty landscape isolates the actors in their tragedy and heightens their vulnerability.

The ashen-faced saint compares closely with the figure of Christ in Delacroix's paintings of *The Lamentation* (1847–8; Museum of Fine Arts, Boston) and *The Entombment* (1858–9; National Museum of Western Art, Tokyo), and in his depictions of Christ on the Sea of Galilee (fig. 13) – and, indeed, with the reclining Sardanapalus in his painting of 1827. Both in sleep and in death, these quiescent victims embody that inclination towards renunciation and impassivity expressed by Delacroix in his writings. MW

### 51. Paul Gauguin (1848–1903)
*Agony in the Garden* 1889
Oil on canvas, 73 × 92 cm
Norton Museum of Art, West Palm Beach, Florida.
Gift of Elizabeth C. Norton (46.5)

### 52. Paul Gauguin
*Bonjour Monsieur Gauguin* 1889
Oil on canvas laid down on panel
74.9 × 54.8 cm
Hammer Museum, Armand Hammer Collection, Los Angeles. Gift of the Armand Hammer Foundation (AH. 90.31)

### 53. Vincent van Gogh (1853–1890)
*Pietà after Delacroix* 1889
Oil on canvas, 73 × 60.5 cm
Van Gogh Museum (Vincent van Gogh Foundation), Amsterdam (s 168 V/1962)

In the summer of 1889 Paul Gauguin depicted himself for the first time – but not the last – as the suffering Christ: in *Agony in the Garden* (cat. 51) the figure of Christ is unmistakably a self portrait. He is shown bent, with eyes lowered, in the Garden of Gethsemane on the eve of the Crucifixion. Aware of his fate and abandoned by his disciples he is, in Gauguin's words, 'in a setting as sad as his soul.'[1] This was a painting that evidently meant a great deal to Gauguin. On its completion he wrote to the artist Emile Schuffenecker declaring it 'my best thing',[2] and he continued to see it as one of his most significant works. Eighteen months later, in an interview engineered to publicise the sale of his works at the Hôtel Drouot in Paris, Gauguin stationed himself in front of the painting to explain: 'There I have painted my own portrait … But it also represents the crushing of an ideal, and a pain that is both divine and human. Jesus is totally abandoned …'[3] Of the paintings he left on deposit with the dealers Boussod and Valadon when he left for Tahiti that same year, this was the one to which he gave the highest value, and on his return in 1893 the painting was one of the few French pictures he exhibited with his new Tahitian works.

Gauguin's decision to paint himself in the guise of Christ reveals a startling and significant development in his sense both of himself and of the mission and fate of the creative artist. Almost exactly a year earlier he had painted the self portrait known as *Les Misérables* (fig. 11) which he had sent to Van Gogh in anticipation of his joining him in Arles, and in which he took on the role of suffering outcast. *Agony in the Garden* is clearly reminiscent of the earlier self-portrait, yet the similarities between the two paintings only heighten their differences. Where in the earlier self portrait Gauguin, though an outcast, is defiant and powerful, fixing the viewer with a stare of red-eyed intensity, the figure of Christ is spent and defeated. But if the 'volcanic flames' of creativity are absent from the latter painting, the identification with Christ suggests far greater claims for the figure of the artist.

In identifying himself with Christ, Gauguin was responding to Symbolist ideas. The previous year, shortly before painting *Les Misérables*, he had written to his friend Claude-Emile Schuffenecker linking his new anti-naturalist, abstracted art to divine creation. What was new for Gauguin in *Agony in the Garden* was combining the notion of Christ as artist with that of the artist as suffering martyr, an elision that he may have encountered in contemporary Symbolist literature. Albert Aurier's poem *L'Oeuvre Maudit* of the same year describes artists as 'the accursed … of the tribe of Christ and Homer / knowing what it is to be spat upon, knowing crucifixion.'[4] It was also an identification that became central to Gauguin's energetic self-mythologising. In 1890 he wrote to Emile Bernard proclaiming: 'Yes we are destined (we searching thinking artists) to perish under the blows of the world.'[5] Later still, in his Journals, he was to write in even more heightened tones: 'You spend yourself, you spend yourself

**1** J. Huret 1891, cited in Brettell et al. 1988, p. 161.
**2** Letter to Schuffenecker, late August 1889 quoted in Brettell et al. 1988, p. 161.
**3** Huret, op. cit. note 1, p. 161.
**4** Poems of Albert Aurier, 1888 and 1889, in Albert Aurier, *Oeuvres posthumes*, ed. R. de Gourmont, Paris 1893.
**5** Malingue 1949, p. 193.

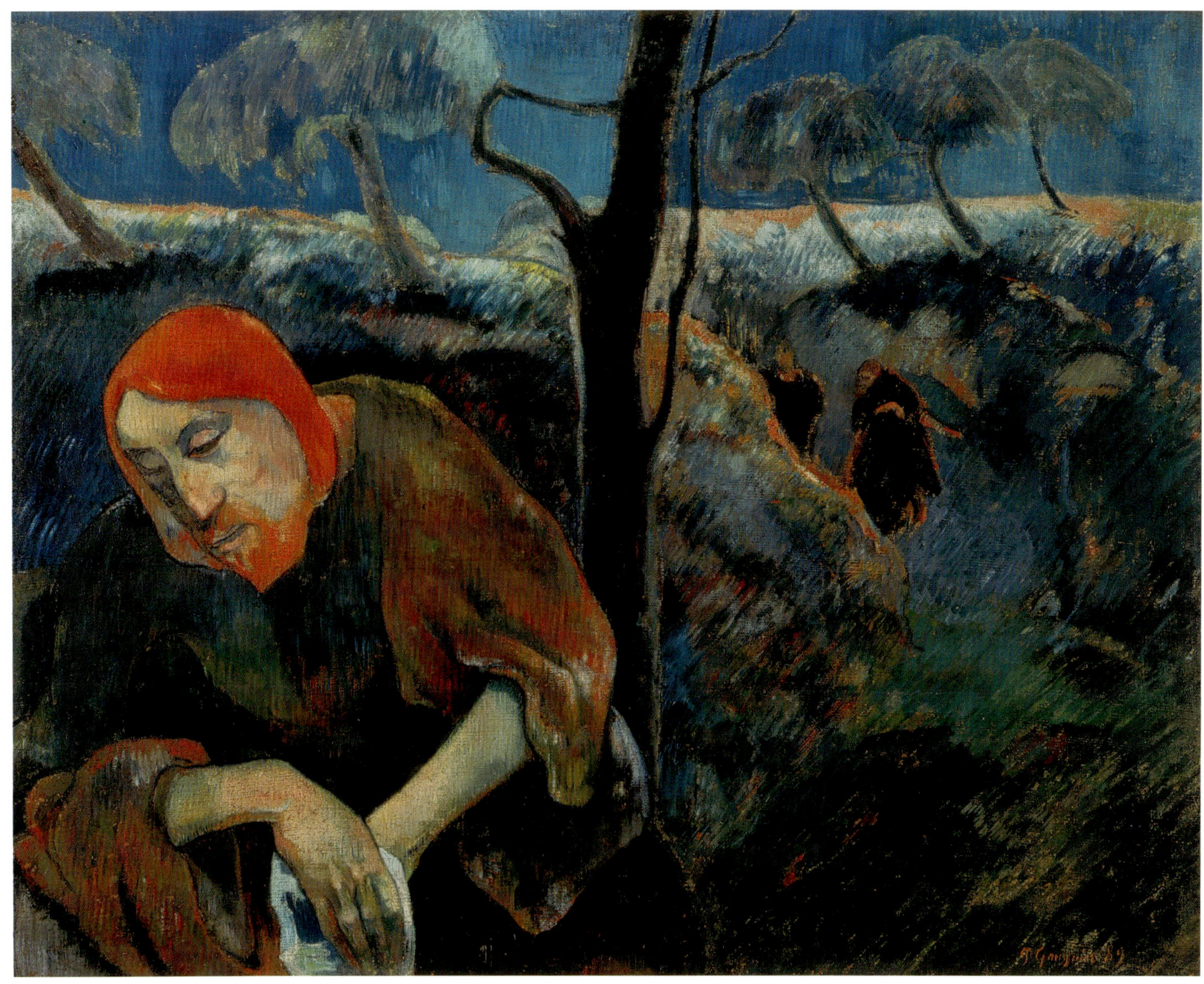

51

again; things only have value if you suffer ... You climb your Calvary laughing – legs shaking under the weight of the cross – having arrived you grit your teeth and then smiling again you avenge yourself – you spend again.'[6]

Gauguin's decision to paint himself as the abandoned Christ in the summer of 1889 has been linked to his disappointment at the reception of the exhibition of the 'Impressionist and Synthetist Group' at Volpini's Café des Arts, Paris, in June, which also marked his estrangement from Pissarro and the Impressionist painters. Certainly he saw himself, and was cast by others, as the leader of a new vanguard. Equally, his hurt at what he saw as the show's critical mauling ran deep: as late as November he was still smarting, writing to Bernard that 'of all my struggles this year, nothing remains save the jeers of Paris; even here I can hear them, and I am so discouraged that I no longer dare to paint ... let them look carefully at my recent paintings ... and they will see how much there is in them of resigned suffering.'[7]

But if current circumstances explain aspects of Gauguin's painting, the more profound influence had come from his two-month period of collaboration with Van Gogh in Arles the previous year (23 October to 23 December 1888). Van Gogh's vision of a 'Studio of the South' had been driven by an ideal of a spiritualised discipleship of painters, in which, moreover, he had cast Gauguin as the head, 'the abbot' of his envisaged brotherhood. Gauguin was evidently intrigued by Van Gogh's mythic and spiritual understanding of the

**6** Gauguin, *Avant et après*, quoted in Margolis Maurer 1998, p. 188.

**7** Letter to Bernard, November 1889, Malingue 1949, letter XCII.

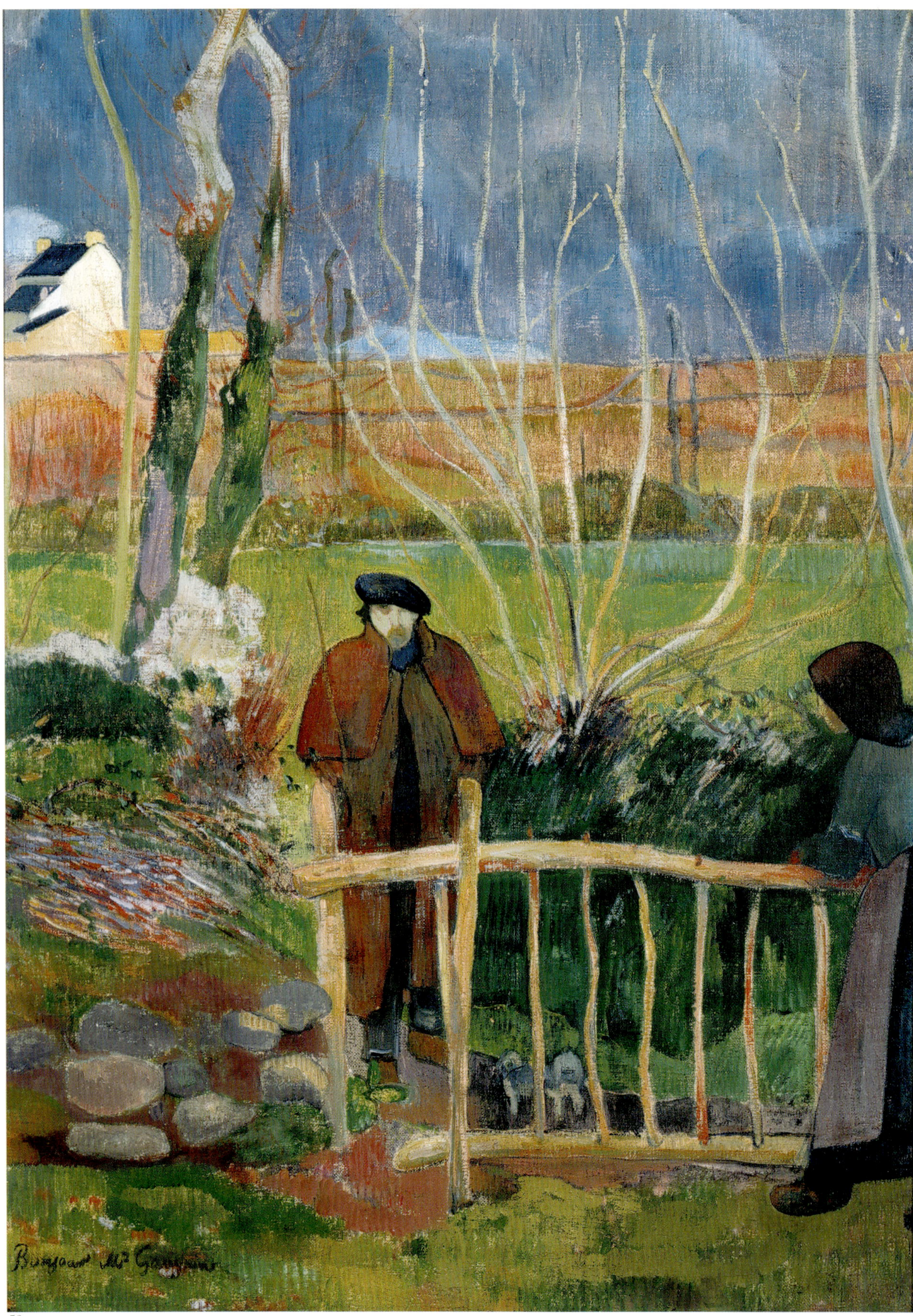
Bonjour Mr Gauguin

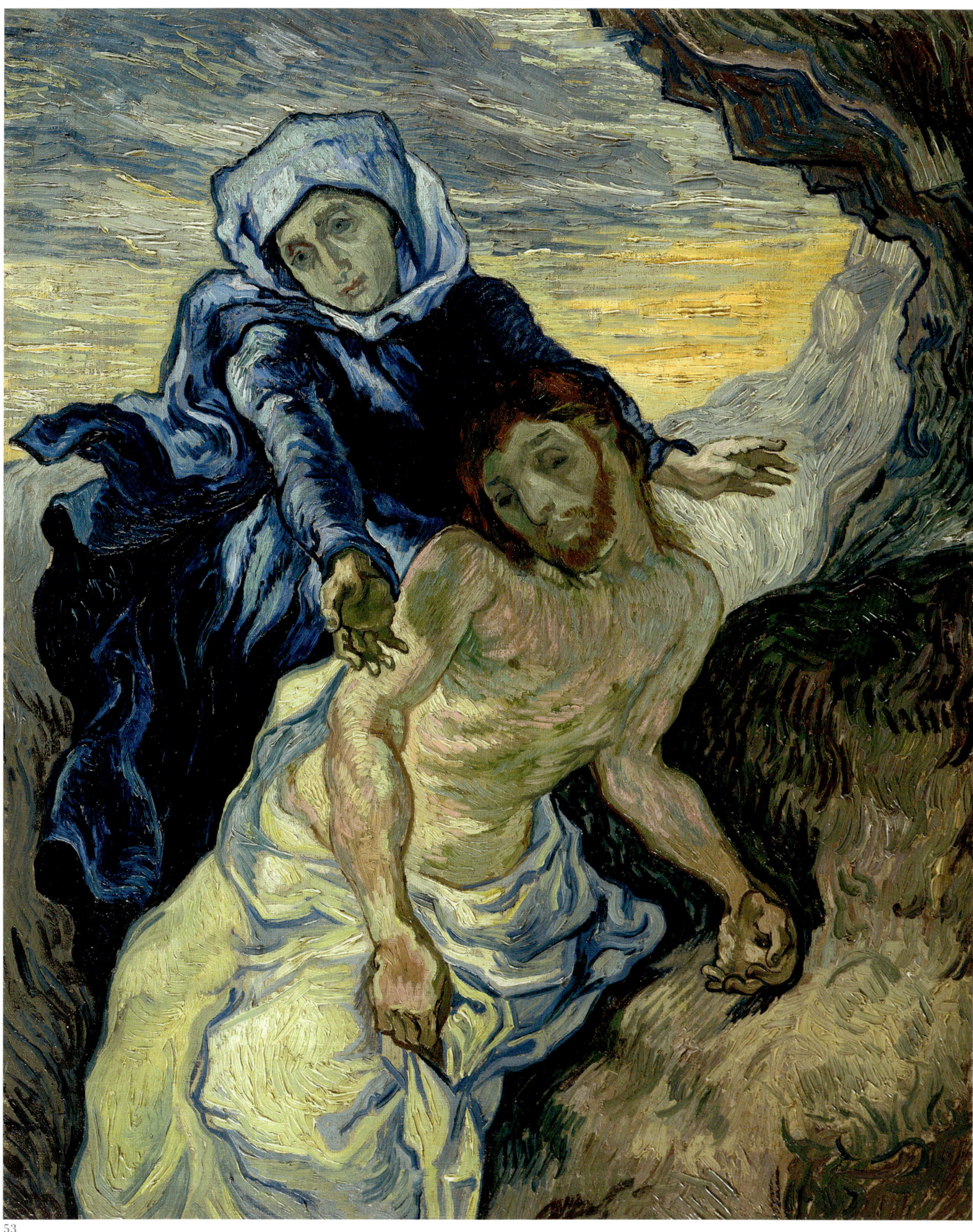

53

artist's mission, and stimulated by the position that he was assigned within it. In the aftermath of the bloody and violent breakdown of their collaboration – with Van Gogh's mental collapse and the severing of part of his ear, and Gauguin's flight – Gauguin, in a series of self-images, revealed a new, aggrandised and spiritualised persona bearing the imprint of his Arles experience and conversations with Van Gogh.

In *Bonjour Monsieur Gauguin*, painted later in the summer of 1889 and probably reprised the same year in the smaller version shown here (cat. 52), Gauguin deliberately recalls and subverts Courbet's *The Meeting* (cat. 29) that he and Van Gogh had seen together at the Musée Fabre in Montpellier in mid-December 1888, shortly before the 'Studio of the South' unravelled. The visit to Montpellier had led to discussions that Van Gogh described to his brother Theo as 'terribly electric'; although his letter does not mention Courbet's painting, its depiction of the wandering, vagabond artist evidently lay behind their discussion of a portrait, then attributed to Rembrandt, in the Louvre of a young man holding a staff.[8] 'I said to Gauguin that I myself saw in it a certain family or racial resemblance to Delacroix or to Gauguin as well. I do not know why, but I have always called this portrait "The Traveller" or "The Man Who Comes from Afar".'[9] The title clearly appealed to Gauguin, who both adopted it and, using Van Gogh's language, drew out its mythic implications. But if Gauguin's painting is dependent on Van Gogh's casting of him as the artist pilgrim, its mood, matching Gauguin's in 1889, is altogether more pessimistic. There are no followers here and in the place of Courbet's deferential patron he is greeted by a peasant woman, faceless beneath her black headscarf. In contrast to Courbet's striding confidence, Gauguin and his dog walk uncertainly beneath a glowering autumnal sky, towards a shut gate.

The irony is that, objectively at least, it was Van Gogh rather than Gauguin who in 1889 had most cause to depict himself as the abandoned martyr or solitary pilgrim. When he was working in Brittany Gauguin was surrounded by fellow painters. In contrast, Van Gogh was indeed alone, subject to intermittent breakdowns: he was first in Arles and then, from 8 May, in nearby the St-Rémy asylum. That Gauguin, whether consciously or not, abrogated Van Gogh's suffering for himself is certainly suggested by his self portraits. Most strikingly, his first self image after leaving Arles was a ceramic head, eyes closed and streaming with blood-like streaks – but without ears. Similarly, the red hair of Gauguin's Christ, while deliberately non-naturalistic and evoking the extremity of Christ's Passion, also carries with it associations of Van Gogh.

Before Gauguin's arrival in Arles in the autumn of 1888, Van Gogh had himself twice attempted what he described as an 'important canvas' of Christ in Gethsemane.[10] On both occasions he had abandoned the project, scraping the paint from the canvas, insisting: 'I cannot or rather I will not paint any more without models; but I have the thing in my head with the colours, a starry night, the figure of Christ in blue, all the strongest blues, and the angel blended citron yellow. And every shade of violet, from a blood-red purple to ashen in the landscape.'[11] The abandoned painting would certainly have been the subject of discussion between the two artists, and Van Gogh's investment in the subject may have been one of the reasons that Gauguin wrote to him on completing his own picture, including a sketch and suggesting it as something 'which would suit you, I believe. It is a Christ in the garden of olives. Blue sky, green twilight, trees all bent over in a purple mass, violet earth and Christ wrapped in dark ochre vermilion hair. This canvas is fated to be misunderstood, so I shall keep it for a long time.'[12] Van Gogh, far from liking the picture, was horrified and unnerved by it. To add to his unease, at the same time he received a photograph of a painting by Emile Bernard of the same subject.

The reasons for Van Gogh's disquiet were manifold and on several different levels. In the surviving letter to Theo on these paintings, his strongest criticisms relate to their divorce from reality: he complains that 'nothing [is] really observed' and that Bernard's picture looked as if he had 'never seen an olive tree'. 'Our duty is thinking not dreaming', he added; '… I was astonished at their letting themselves go like that'. For Van Gogh a spiritual art needed to derive its force from nature, and it was through its expressive interpretation that the artist could arrive at language to supersede that of the Bible. In a later letter to Bernard he describes two of his pictures of

**8** *Jeune homme au baton*, Louvre, Paris, now attributed to Studio of Rembrandt.
**9** Letter to Theo, 17–18 December 1888, Van Gogh 2000 edn, no. 564.
**10** Letter to Bernard, 4 October 1888, op. cit. no. B19.
**11** Letter to Theo, 22 September 1888, op. cit. no. 540.
**12** D. Cooper (ed.), *Paul Gauguin: 45 Lettres à Vincent, Théo et Jo van Gogh*, The Hague 1983, no. 37.2.

the garden of the St-Rémy asylum, centred upon a large blasted tree – 'a sombre giant' – its trunk sawn off after being struck by lightning: 'I am telling you about these two canvases … to remind you that one can try to give an impression of anguish without aiming straight at the Garden of Gethsemane.'[13]

The strength of Van Gogh's reaction to the two paintings suggests other motives for his response. Both paintings clearly challenged him, recalling his own failed attempts to depict the same subject. Gauguin, in casting himself as Christ, was also adopting a role for the artist which Van Gogh viewed with deep ambivalence: his mental breakdowns had had extreme religious overtones. Bernard, relaying Gauguin's account of events of 1888, described how 'my dear friend came to the point of believing himself a Christ, a God', and Van Gogh's subsequent reverses had been accompanied by what he himself described as 'sickly religious aberrations'. As a young man destined for the ministry, Van Gogh's self-identification with Christ, as consoler and comforter, had been a driving force and it lay behind his spiritual ideal of a consoling art founded upon nature. Gauguin in his painting not only took on Christ's persona, he also presented Christ not as a figure of consolation, but of despair. In his letters, and indeed his self portraits, written and painted in the aftermath of his attacks, Van Gogh deliberately distanced himself from the role of martyr. 'It is very probable that I will have to suffer a great deal yet', he wrote to his sister Wil, 'and to tell the honest truth, this does not suit me at all, for under no circumstances do I long for a martyr's career.' Van Gogh not only saw the identification with Christ as a threat to his sanity, but its interpretation by Gauguin ran counter to all Van Gogh's desire for an art of consolation and hope, founded on nature. 'Of course with me', he wrote in the letter responding to Gauguin's painting, 'there is no question of doing anything from the Bible.'[14]

Of course Van Gogh had in fact depicted a biblical subject only two months earlier. In early September, recovering from his breakdown of July and unable to go outside, he groped back towards work by painting two self portraits and a series of painted interpretations of prints that he owned. One of these, after a painting of the Pietà by Delacroix, had been damaged during his last attack, so his painting was in essence also an act of restoration. The choice of Delacroix for a model was not surprising but, in the light of Van Gogh's later criticism of Gauguin's painting, illuminating. For Van Gogh, Delacroix alone after Rembrandt had succeeded in investing his biblical narratives with the force of contemporary reality, because his figures were real, recognisable people. Van Gogh conveyed this sense in his letter to his sister describing his own painting:

> The exhausted corpse lies on the ground in the entrance of a cave … It is evening after a thunderstorm, and that forlorn figure in the blue clothes – the loose clothes are agitated by the wind – is sharply outlined against a sky in which the violet clouds with golden edges are floating. She too stretches out her empty arms before her in a large gesture of despair, and one sees the good sturdy hands of a working woman … And the face of the dead man is in shadow – but the pale head of the woman stands out clearly against a cloud – a contrast which causes those two heads to seem like one sombre-hued flower and one pale flower, arranged in such a way as mutally to intensify the effect.[15]

Van Gogh spoke of the prints he painted as posing to him like models, and he derived strength and comfort from the sense of dialogue with his artistic forbears and heroes that the process gave him. If the act of making the painting was itself a consoling and therapeutic one for Van Gogh, in giving the figure of Christ his own red hair and beard he seems to have tentatively sidled up to the identification with Christ that Gauguin publicly proclaimed. The contrasts remain stark: Christ in Van Gogh's painting is 'exhausted' rather than suffering, and awaits resurrection rather than crucifixion. If the scene is of sorrow, it is not of pain, and the hope of regeneration is conveyed in the extraordinary streaked yellow sky – a colour that for Van Gogh suggested hope and friendship – whose tones suffuse the whole painting. AS

**13** Letter to Theo, 17 November 1889, Van Gogh 2000 edn, no. 614; letter to Bernard, about 20 November 1889, op. cit. no. B21.

**14** Letter to Wil, 20 December 1889, op. cit. no. W18; letter to Theo, 17 November 1889, op. cit. no. 614

**15** Letter to Wil, 19 September 1889, op. cit. no. W14.

### 54. Paul Sérusier (1863–1927)
*Portrait of Paul Ranson in Nabi Robes* 1890
Oil on canvas, 61 × 46.5 cm
Musée d'Orsay, Paris (RF 2004-8)

### 55. Georges Lacombe (1868–1916)
*Portrait of Paul Sérusier, Le Nabi à la barbe rutilante* 1894
Tempera on canvas, 73.5 × 50 cm
Musée départmental Maurice Denis, Le Prieuré, Saint-Germain-en-Laye (PMD 989.8.1)

### 56. Emile Bernard (1868–1941)
*Portrait of Verkade* 1893
Oil on canvas, 50 × 30.5 cm
Musée départmental Maurice Denis, Le Prieuré, Saint-Germain-en-Laye (PMD 996.1.1)

> I dream of a brotherhood of pure souls, reserved for artists whose love of good and beauty will lead them to express in their works and life this indefinable character which I call Nabi.[1]

No group of late nineteenth-century artists gave more concrete expression to the idea of the artist as a member of an elect brotherhood of visionaries than the Nabis. Their name – a secret to all but initiates – was coined by the Symbolist poet Henri Cazalis and derived from the Arabic and Hebrew words for 'prophets'.[2] It was given to the closely knit group of young artists – students at the Académie Julian and the Ecole des Beaux-Arts in Paris, and a number of them old school friends – by Paul Sérusier in 1889. As Maurice Denis, the youngest member of the group and its most important theorist and chronicler, recalled: 'He gave us a name which, with respect to the studios, made us initiates, a sort of secret society with mystical tendencies, habitually in a state of prophetic fervour.'[3] The impetus for the group's foundation had come from Sérusier's visit to Pont Aven in Brittany in 1888, where, under Gauguin's guidance, he had painted a small landscape of the nearby Bois d'Amour: '"What colour do you see that tree?" Gauguin had asked "Is it green? Then use green, the finest on your palette. And that shadow? It's blue, if anything? Don't be afraid to paint it as blue as you possibly can".'[4] The resulting painting, far more unconventional than anything Gauguin himself was painting, pointed the way towards a new simplified, abstracted visual language. 'And so we realised', Denis was to write, 'that every work of art was a transposition ... the impassioned equivalent of a sensation experienced.'[5] The work assumed mythic qualities among the Nabis, who dubbed it 'The Talisman' (Musée d'Orsay, Paris).

The Nabis, who included Pierre Bonnard, Gabriel Ibels, Maurice Denis, Edouard Vuillard, Jan Verkade and Ker-Xavier Roussel, revelled in their sect-like exclusivity. Members were given nicknames: the red-bearded Sérusier, seen as the group's leader, became the '*Nabi à la barbe rutilante*', Verkade the '*Nabi obéliscal*' because of his height. Heavily influenced by the fashionable revival of the occult and esoteric cults, they peppered their correspondence with obscure language, dating letters according to their own system ('Day of Venus, one hour before the setting of Helios', for example). Letters were signed with the initials E.T.P.M.V.E.M.P ('*en ta paume mon verbe et ma pensée*' – 'in your palm my word and my thought'), whose sense depended upon the belief of esoteric philosophy and palmistry that the palm offered a physical manifestation of the soul. The group met weekly, first in a café in the passage Brady, Paris, which they dubbed '*L'Os-à-moelle*' after the marrowbone tied to the key of the lavatory, before moving their meetings to Paul Ranson's studio on

1 Paul Sérusier, quoted in M. Denis, 'Paul Sérusier, sa vie, son oeuvre', Sérusier 1942 edn, pp. 47–8.
2 According to Ernest Renan in his 'Discours et conférences de Judaïsme, race et religion' (*Oeuvres complètes*, vol. 1, Paris 1883, p. 929), the Hebrew 'nabis' were not strictly prophets but were those 'whom one consulted when, for example, one had lost a donkey or wished to know a secret. They were sorcerers. But the nabis of Israel were something else as well: they were the creators of a pure religion.'
3 M. Denis, 'L'époque de symbolisme', *Gazette des Beaux-Arts*, March 1934, p. 17.
4 Fréches and Tarrasse 1990, pp. 12–13.
5 M. Denis, *Theories*, Paris 1920, p. 167.

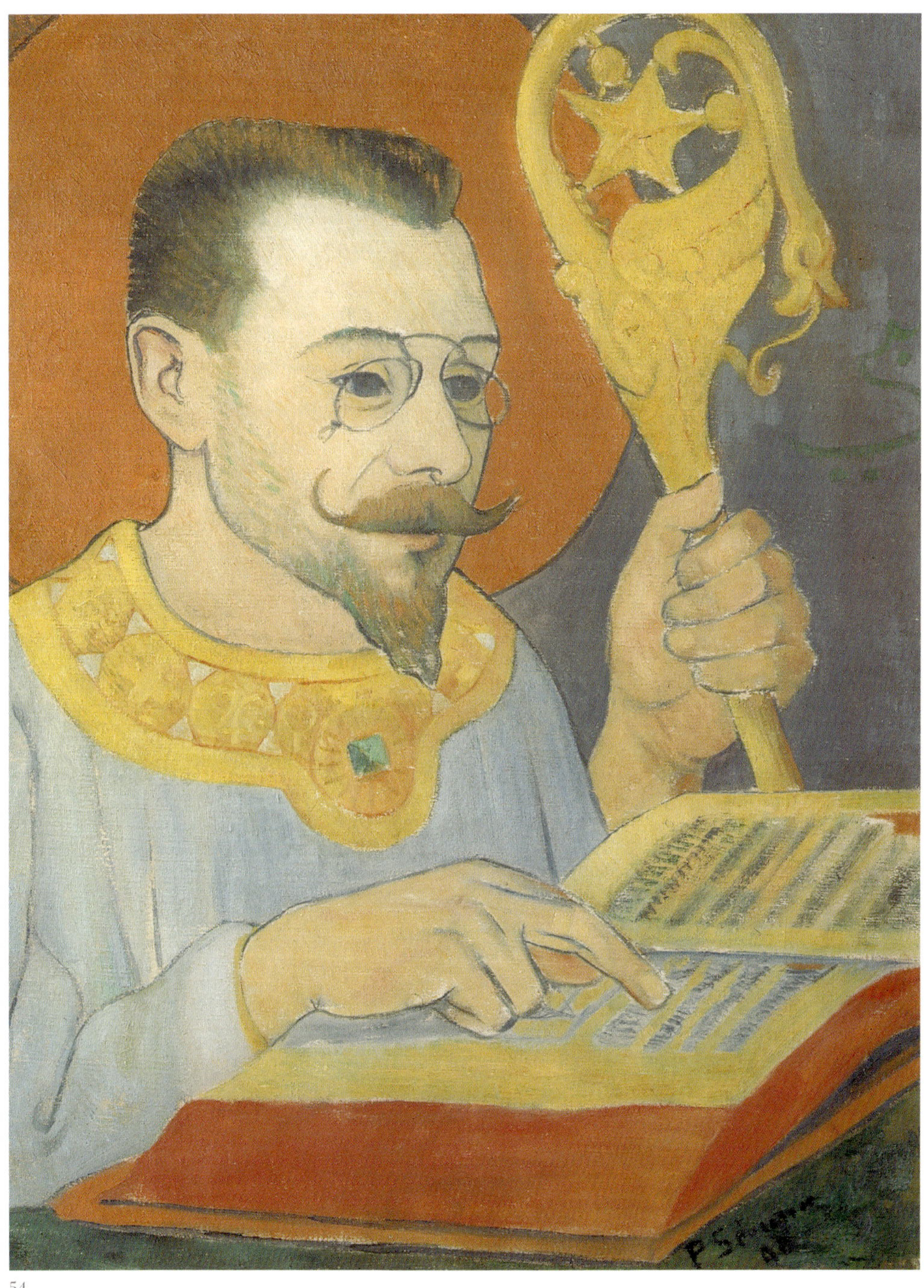
54

the boulevard Montparnasse. Ranson was the oldest member of the group, and married. His studio became the group's 'Temple' and his wife, France, *'La Lumière du Temple'* although her role appears to have been limited to laying on beer and tobacco.

The atmosphere of arcane Nabi ritualism is wonderfully conveyed in Sérusier's portrait of Ranson (cat. 54). Of all the members of the group Sérusier and Ranson were the most intrigued by and involved in esoteric religion – in astrology, black magic, alchemy and theosophy – and its influence can be traced in every aspect of the portrait. Ranson is shown as a bishop or abbot, clasping a crosier and apparently reading an illuminated manuscript. His robes and gold, emerald-studded collar are almost certainly an invention: apart from an isolated mention of Séguin and Ibels wearing oriental dress to a gathering at the Os-à-moelle there is no suggestion that the Nabis

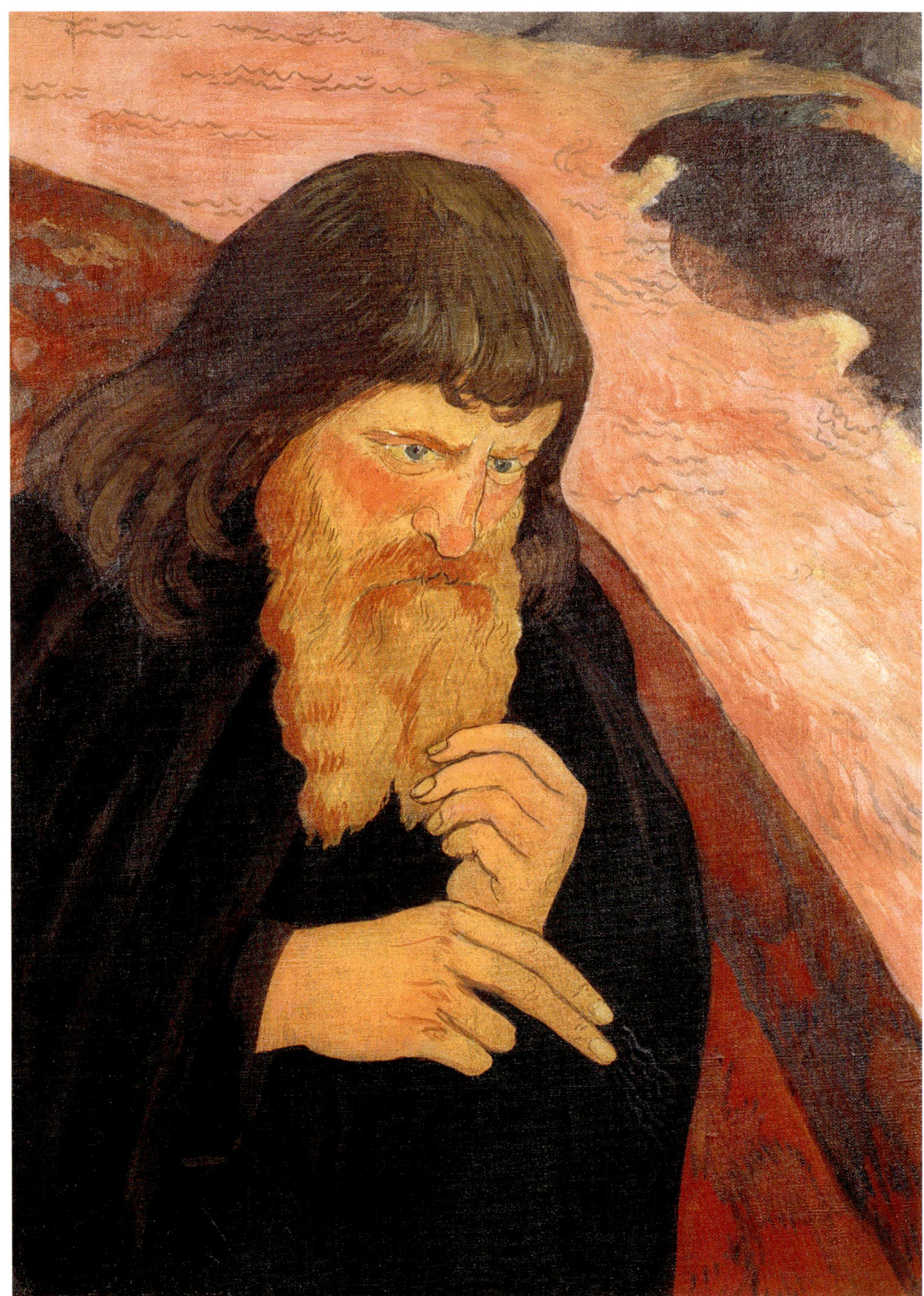

55

indulged in fancy dress. According to Ranson's wife the crosier did actually exist, passed from hand to hand as people spoke at Nabi gatherings, a suggestion that was later dismissed as a romantic fiction by her son.[6] Real or not, its combination of snake, five-pointed star and circles carries a host of potential mystical significances.[7] Sérusier gives Ranson an orange halo which, for Edouard Schuré in his theosophical book *Les Grands Initiés* (1889), of which both Ranson and Sérusier had copies, was a symbol of prophetic illumination.

Sérusier himself is depicted in the role of seer or prophet in George Lacombe's portrait (cat. 55). Lacombe had met Sérusier in 1892 and was ushered into the group the same year, after Sérusier had decorated his Versailles studio. Primarily a sculptor – and given the title of '*Nabi sculpteur*' – Lacombe took painting

**6** See Boyle-Turner 1980.

**7** For suggestions of the possible symbolic significance of the various motifs of the painting see Boyle-Turner op. cit. pp. 39–41 and Fréches and Tarrasse 1993, no. 107, pp. 252–3.

**8** See for example Congeval: 'The miracle, in fact, is that *despite* the burden of the group's ritualism, its members became, with only a few exceptions, such great artists' (G. Congeval, 'The Path to the Avant Garde' in Solana et al. 2004, p. 82. With the exception of Denis and Vuillard the Nabis were all from middle-class families who encouraged them in their artistic professions.

lessons from Sérusier, learning how to both mix and use the tempera medium with which he painted his portrait. Sérusier is shown in black robes as the '*Nabi à la barbe rutilante*', his bright, fiery beard and reddened cheeks suggesting creative passion, and echoed in colour and form by the swirling river behind. Although deliberately and characteristically ambiguous in its spatial construction, Sérusier seems to be on a boat, carried on the red river which his gesture of blessing might be read as calming.

The evident theatricality of Lacombe's portrait and the incongruity of Ranson's priestly garb with his pince-nez and carefully waxed moustache suggest a playful, ironic aspect to both the image and the group's mystic pretensions. Certainly discussions of the Nabis often view their ritualism with a degree of suspicion, casting it as adolescent role-play or a peculiarly middle-class stance of rebellion.[8] The suspicion was shared by critics at the time: 'Who is showing us a new conception of life? – After Mr Gauguin, a precursor(!), people are talking of Mr Sérusier, Mr Vuillard, Mr Emile Bernard, Mr Verkade, and Symbolism triumphs. What a joke! The much vaunted mysticism is nothing but a sham, the last resort of faithless times.'[9] Equally, it is often difficult to reconcile the esoteric theorising of Sérusier and Ranson with the small, decorative interiors painted by, for example, Vuillard and Bonnard. But despite the Nabis heterogeneity, it would be a mistake to underestimate the mutual support that the group offered, or the seriousness of its adherence to Symbolist theory in helping its members reach towards a new expressive, simplified visual language.

The seriousness of the group's spiritual preoccupations, which included discussions with the Dominican priests of the rue Fauborg St Honoré, is also borne out by the history of some of its members. Jan Verkade, a Dutchman who arrived in Paris in early 1891, came to believe that art's value depended upon religious conviction, which in turn led to his conversion to Catholicism in 1892, and later joined the abbey of Beuron in southern Germany as an oblate artist. Bernard's striking portrait of the young Verkade (cat. 56) was made

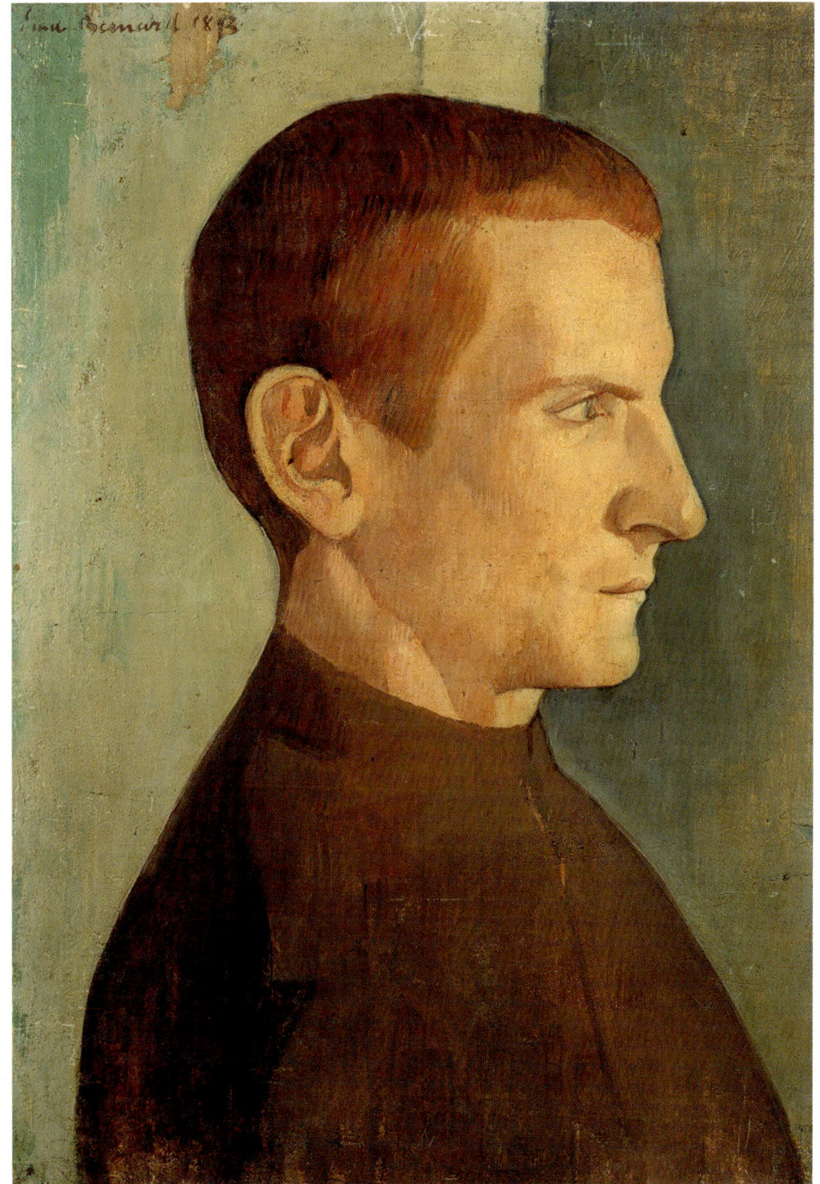


56

when both artists were in Florence in 1893. Verkade, with his friend Mogens Ballin, was staying in the Franciscan monastery in Fiesole above Florence. Verkade later recalled 'The poor man of Assissi became our spiritual father … It is in truth his marvellous life and example which initiated us into Christianity.' Bernard, visiting Florence for the first time – and himself on the path to a rigorous Catholicism, was overwhelmed by the artists of the early Renaissance: their influence permeates his crisp profile portrait of Verkade. With its brightly lit forehead, the priest-like tunic and the intensity of the sitter's forward gaze, the portrait conveys with a wonderful economy of means Verkade's spiritual purpose. AS

**9** M. Charles, 'Apologie pour la peinture' in *Mercure de France* no. 42 (June 1893), p.153, quoted in Solana et al. 2004, pp. 83–4.

## 57. Emile Bernard (1868–1941)

*Vision, Symbolic Portrait of Emile Bernard* 1891

Oil on canvas, 81 × 60.3 cm

Courtesy Galérie Cazeau-Béraudière, Paris

Bernard's extraordinary self portrait is quite unlike almost anything else he painted. The previous year he had depicted himself soberly dressed and tidily coiffured in front of a partially seen painting of monumental nudes with which he had decorated his studio.[1] Here the nudes have come to life; dishevelled and pale, the artist stands before a red vision of figures grouped around the glowing face of Christ. The picture was painted in 1891, a year of turmoil and deepening crisis for the young Bernard. The previous year had seen his mounting doubts about his capacity as an artist and in early 1891 he broke acrimoniously and irrevocably with Gauguin, until then his most important artistic collaborator and support. Although Bernard was later to give slightly contradictory accounts of the split, its cause was almost certainly the way in which he saw Gauguin claiming to be, and being proclaimed by others, as 'the chief of the symbolist school of painting'.[2] Early in the year a number of articles had appeared to publicise the sale of Gauguin's paintings at the Hôtel Drouot, Paris. Bernard had scarcely been mentioned in any of them, and not at all in the most important of them, Albert Aurier's 'Symbolisme en Peinture: Paul Gauguin'. No one had credited him with what he, rightly, saw as his crucial innovations of 1888 that had contributed to the new 'Symbolist' non-natural vocabulary of line and colour. In an episode which starkly reveals the importance of claims of originality for avant-garde reputations, Bernard felt himself being written out of history. Throughout his life he was to expend much energy writing himself back into it: 'It was always I', he was later to write of his time with Gauguin in Brittany, 'who showed myself to be the most audacious and greatest innovator.'[3]

At the same time Bernard was being drawn back to the Catholic church. He had treated religious subjects in his work from 1889 – including the *Christ in the Garden of Olives* that had so angered Van Gogh (see cats 51–53) – but it was in 1891 that he appears to have seriously embraced a faith, happy to be described as a devout, practising Catholic and signing himself for the first time 'Vostre frair en J. Christus. Bernard'.[4]

Bernard's self portrait is an uncharacteristically literal response, both defiant and anxious, to his situation. He presents himself explicitly as a Symbolist painter, his idealised vision rendered behind him. It is hard not to see the image as a direct response to his feeling that his crucial role in the birth of Symbolist painting was being ignored. Even the bright red of his vision can be read as a reminiscence of the red ground of Gauguin's *Vision after the Sermon* (1888; National Gallery of Scotland, Edinburgh), the signature painting of Aurier's article, which Gauguin had used to suggest the visionary nature of his scene. At the same time Bernard gives his ideal image a determinedly Christian slant: the nude figures of a new Eden collect around the floating face of Christ. The image of Christ, full face and wearing a crown of thorns, derives from the 'Veronica', an image not wrought by human hands but miraculously imprinted on a cloth at the Passion, and so a potent if literal symbol of an ideal Christian art. But if the painting is a proclamation of Bernard's status it appears undercut by the pale, equivocal figure of Bernard himself, addressing the viewer with an anxious sideways stare that seems to speak of his uncertainty in his position. AS

**1** Musée des Beaux-Arts, Brest.
**2** E. Bernard, 'L'Aventure de ma vie', intro. to Gauguin 1954, pp. 45–6. In his *Souvenirs inédits* (1939) Bernard wrote that the break had been due to Gauguin exhibiting alone at the Hôtel Drouot.
**3** 'L'Aventure de ma vie', loc. cit.
**4** Cited in Stevens 1990, p. 213.

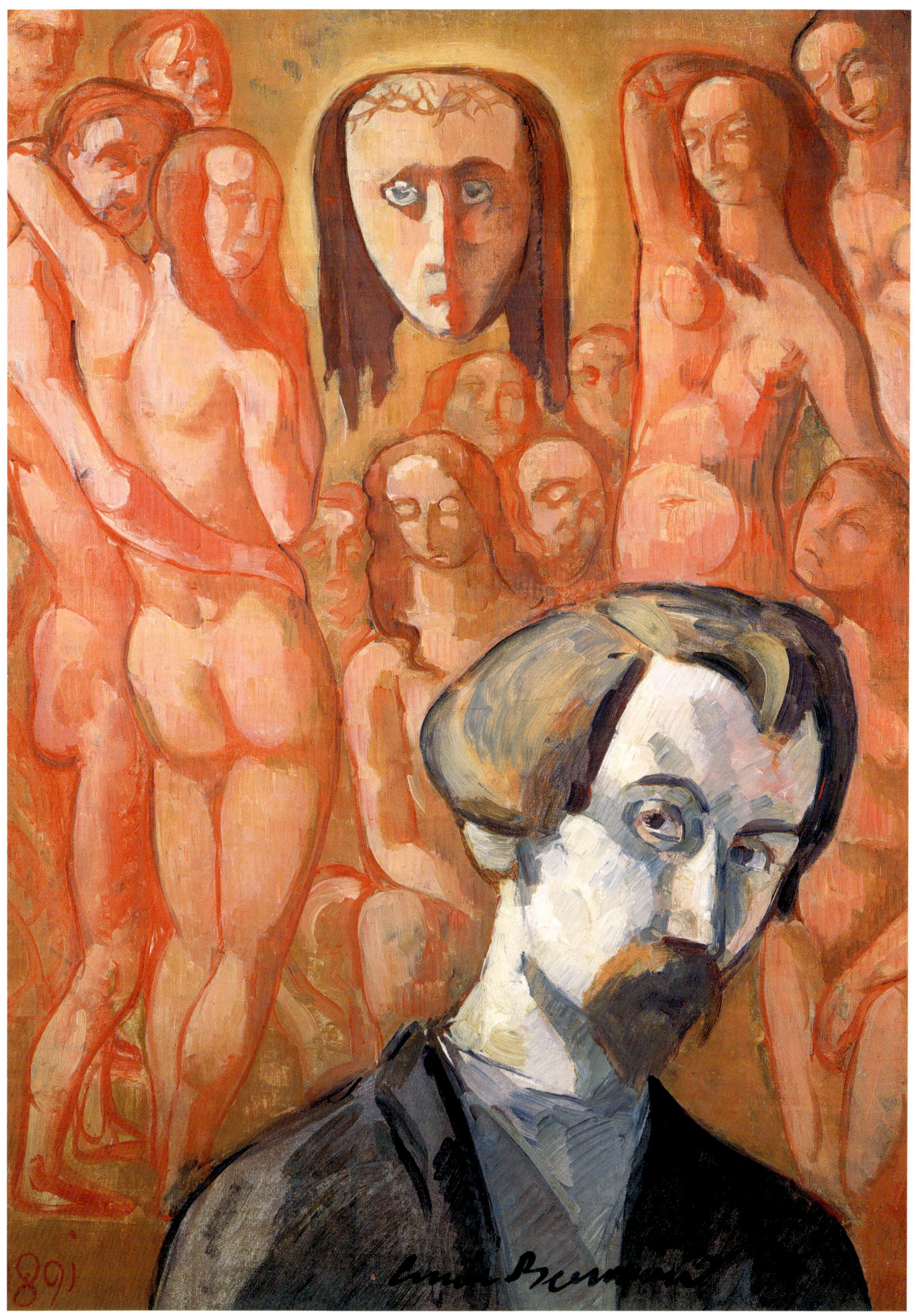

## 58. James Ensor (1860–1949)

*Christ Tormented by Demons* 1895

Etching on paper, 17.2 × 23.5 cm

The British Museum, London (1972-9-16-5)

## 59. James Ensor

*The Artist surrounded by Evil Spirits*

1898

Proof of poster advertising an exhibition of Ensor's works at the Salon des Cent, Paris

Colour lithograph, 53.3 × 37.2 cm

Victoria and Albert Museum, London (E.297-1947)

No artist carried his identification with Christ further, nor made it more explicit in his works, than the Belgian James Ensor. In a prolonged series of images from the mid-1880s onwards, Ensor cast himself repeatedly in the role of Christ – crucified, mocked, unrecognised and suffering.

Ensor first turned to scenes of Christ's life in 1885–6 in a series of large-scale drawings which he referred to as 'visions', and gave these the title *Haloes of Christ*, or the *Sensitivities of Light*.[1] These important works represented scenes from the life of Christ but, as their title suggests, were driven by Ensor's preoccupation with light, which they show emanating from the figure of Christ and eating into the surrounding forms. In 1882 Ensor had described an advanced kind of vision – accessible only to the artist – in which 'the artist discerns the subtleties and manifold effects of the light, its planes and gravitational fields. These progressive investigations alter primitive vision, undermining the line and rendering it subordinate. Such vision will not be widely understood.'[2] The belief that his art was destined to be misinterpreted, and that this was indeed a mark of its worth, ran deep with Ensor. It was as the misunderstood prophet of Truth and what he termed 'modern light' that he was to cast himself as Christ. In the earliest of his *Haloes* drawings Ensor depicts himself in the crowd mocking Christ, but in his next drawing, *Christ's Entry into Jerusalem*, he gives Christ his own features, as he does in the subsequent Crucifixion scene drawn in 1886 and reprised in 1895, in the etching shown here (cat. 58).

The Crucifixion drawing is unusual within the series of *Haloes*, as the light streams not from the figure of Christ but from Heaven, carrying a trumpet-blowing angel and flying skeleton on its rays. Ensor gave each of his drawings a subtitle describing the particular emotional effect of the light, labelling the Crucifixion *Sad and Broken, Satan and The Legions of Hell Tormenting Christ on the Cross*. In the drawing – much more markedly than in the subsequent print – Christ's head and body are in shadow as the light streams on to the ground in front of him, where Bosch-like demons crawl from an open tomb. Behind the cross and embracing Christ are the skeletons that were to become a central motif in Ensor's iconography but were here used for the first time. His prominent signature on the open tomb perhaps alludes to resurrection, possibly reflecting Ensor's hope and belief that his genius would be recognised in the future.

Ensor's identification with Christ, which extended to writing '*Moi*' with a capital letter, rested upon his Romantic sense of himself as the misunderstood and solitary genius. The demons and figures who assail him are cast – often recognisably – as the critics who attacked him, the ignorant public or the Belgian avant-garde whom he saw as failing to recognise or support him. In a drawing made in 1886[3] the Crucified Ensor-Christ (identified by the label 'ENSOR' where one would expect to find 'INRI') is pierced by a spear labelled 'Fetis', the name of a respected and influential critic. One of the bystanders has 'xx' on his back, a marked reference to 'Les XX', the group of Belgian avant-garde artists to which Ensor belonged and with whom he exhibited. Fetis appeared again in the *Ecce Homo* of 1891 (private collection), brandishing a scourge and gripping the rope around the neck of the Christ-Ensor, who is flanked on the other side by the critic Max Sulzberger.

It is scarcely surprising given such images that others were willing to cast Ensor in similar roles: 'He

**1** See G. Ollinger-Zinque, 'Le Christ-Ensor ou l'identification au Christ dans l'oeuvre d'Ensor' in Burollet and Schoonbaert 1990, pp. 27–34. The series in the order in which they were produced is: *Jesus Shown to the People* (1885; private collection); *Christ's Entry into Jerusalem* (1885; Ghent Museum voor Schone Kunsten); *The Ascension of Christ* (1885) and *The Descent from the Cross* (1886; both private collections); *The Adoration of the Shepherds* and *Satan and the Legions of Hell tormenting Christ on the Cross* (both 1886; Musées Royaux des Beaux-Arts de Belgique, Brussels).

**2** Ensor, *Mes Ecrits*, Liège 1974, p. 50.

**3** *Calvary* or *Ensor on the Cross* 1886, Imelda Delvaux collection, Belgium.

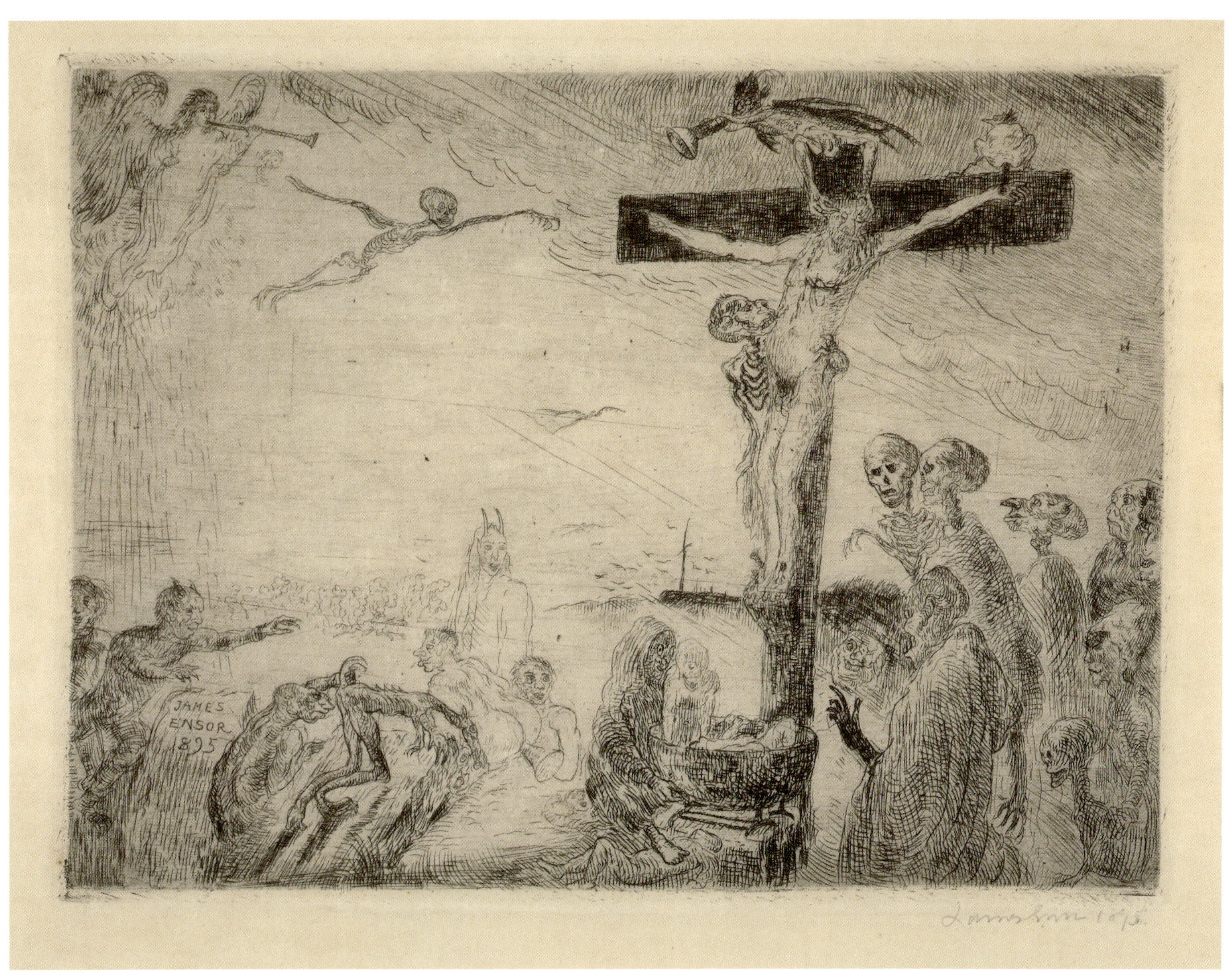


58

was tall, pale-skinned, sharp-eyed and had a wild moustache', wrote Eugène Demolder in 1892; 'As for his mentality, he was *misunderstood,* and remains so to this day. He's one of those people who are so outrageously original that from time to time the mob comes howling after their paintings, like a pack of scrawny dogs barking at some strange star.'[4] Ensor's imagery encouraged such responses, nowhere more obviously and publicly than in the poster he designed for the exhibition of his etchings held at the Salon des Cent in Paris in December 1898. For this he re-worked a drawing of 1888 which he had called *Démons me turlupinant* (*Demons teasing me*) recalling his use of the same verb (*turlupiner*) in describing his treatment by critics.[5] That Ensor should publicise himself as alone and tormented by demons was characteristic, but the most significant change he made between drawing and poster seems, like the open tomb in *Christ Tormented by Demons*, to suggest cause for hope. A crowing cock hovers above Ensor's head in a halo of light casting its rays upon him. This has been read as a reference to what Ensor saw as his growing fame and recognition in France, marked by the Salon des Cent exhibition.[6] The show was to be accompanied by a special edition of *La Plume*, the journal that had organised it, dedicated to Ensor and including a series of glowing articles about him. Ensor's hopes were, however, to be disappointed: although the exhibition attracted a degree of press attention, it was a commercial disaster and Ensor sold only one of the 55 works on show. AS

**4** Eugène Demolder, *James Ensor*, Brussels 1892, pp. 5–6, quoted in G. Ollinger-Zinque, 'Me and my circle' in *James Ensor* 1999, pp. 14–23, p. 16.

**5** 'Tous les critiques me turlupinent' ('all the critics tease me'), *Les Ecrits de James Ensor*, Brussels 1944, p. 117.

**6** Dominique Morel, 'James Ensor et la plume: histoire et fortune critique de la première exposition personelle d'Ensor à Paris (1898–99)', *Gazette des Beaux Arts* 118 no. 1474 (November 1991), pp. 205–12.

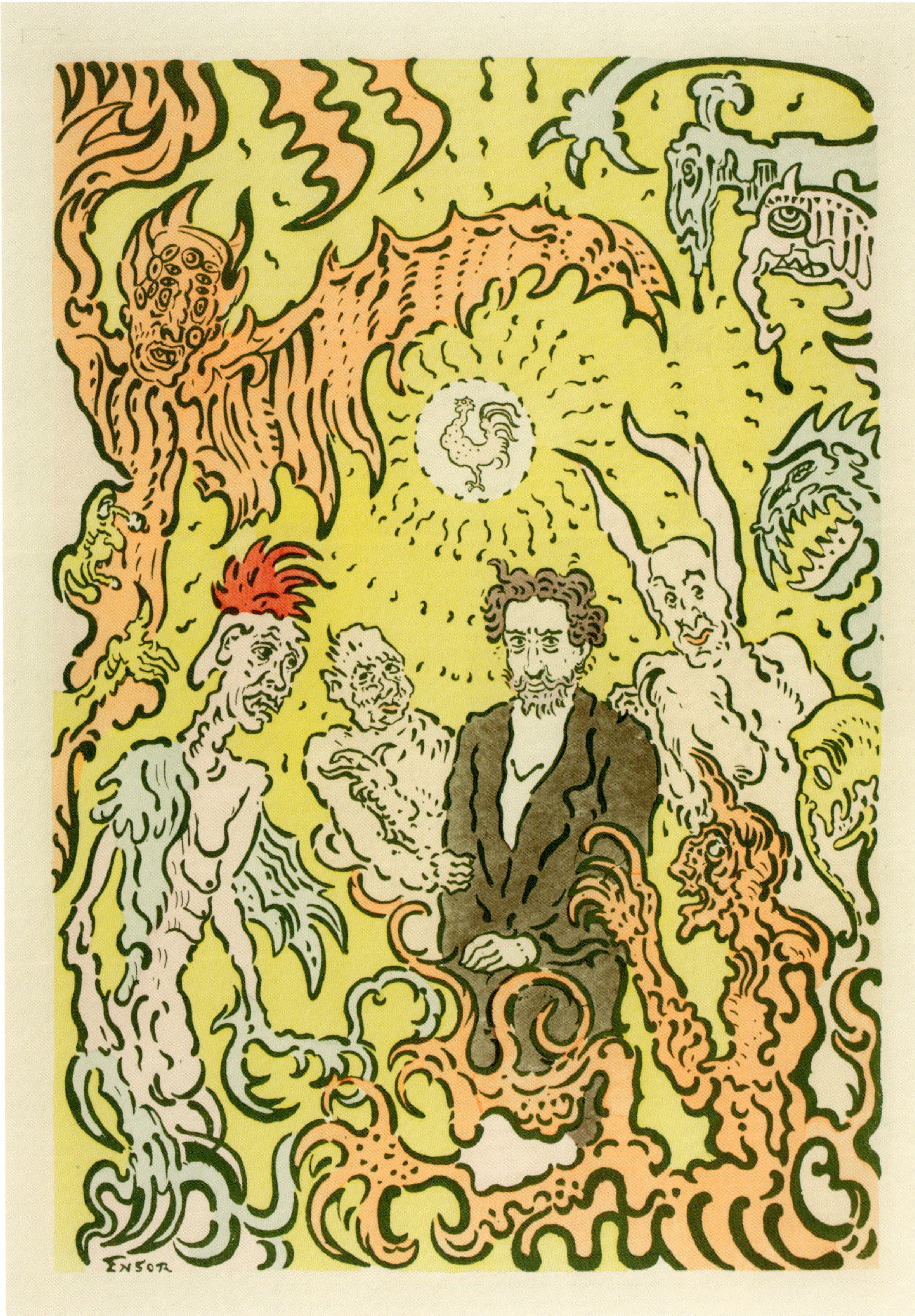
ENSOR

## 60. Giovanni Segantini (1858–1899)
*Self Portrait* 1895

Charcoal on canvas, 59 × 50 cm

Segantini Museum, St Moritz

## 61. Ferdinand Hodler (1853–1918)
*Self Portrait* 1900

Oil on canvas, 41.5 × 29 cm

Staatsgalerie, Stuttgart (1193)

Where Gauguin and Ensor's self-identification with Christ depended upon their adoption of the role of suffering martyr, these two remarkable self portraits offer a more assertive if not triumphant figure of the artist-Christ. Bearded and addressing the viewer full-face, Segantini and Hodler's portraits derive from the so-called 'Veronica' image of Christ. The Veronica (or Vera Icon, meaning True Image) was perhaps the most important of the miraculous images of Christ 'not made by human hands' in medieval Europe. Believed to have been imprinted upon a cloth with which Saint Veronica wiped Christ's face during the Passion, it established a 'type' for Christ's true portrait. The most famous earlier response to the Veronica by an artist remains Dürer's extraordinary self portrait of 1500, now in Munich, and it was almost certainly this famous precedent that provided the direct inspiration for Hodler and Segantini. Dürer's precise intentions in casting himself as Christ have been the subject of much speculation. As well as suggesting his pious imitation of Christ, the self portrait also seems to proclaim his role as a creator, perhaps equating the truth of his own portrait with the miraculous true likeness of Christ.

The intentions of both Segantini and Hodler in presenting themselves in this way seem equally multifaceted. Segantini's drawing on canvas is the most sophisticated of a number of similar self-images he made in the 1890s.[1] He had first depicted himself as a Christ figure, over a decade earlier, in a series of drawings based upon Mantegna's *Lamentation over the Dead Christ* (about 1490; Pinacoteca di Brera, Milan) in which he gave the foreshortened figure of the dead Christ his own features. But if these images suggest a familiar Romantic preoccupation with martyrdom, his portraits of the 1890s are far more assertive and heroic. Part Christ, part prophet – the twists of hair on his temples recalling the horns with which Moses is traditionally depicted – Segantini shows himself against the Alpine mountains which were the principal inspiration and subject of his art. The mountains add a further layer to the picture's meaning, casting him as the solitary prophet in the wilderness. They also subtly undermine the hieratic symmetry of the image, the mountain peaks on the right balanced, on the left, by the rise in Segantini's coat collar.

Hodler's self portrait of five years later is, if anything, even more direct and aggressive than Segantini's. Full-face against a neutral background, this is even more explicitly a response to Dürer's self portrait and, like the earlier picture, was painted in the first year of a new century. By 1900 Hodler's reputation as one of the principal figures of European Symbolism seemed assured. That same year he had received a gold medal at the Exposition Universelle in Paris and become a member of the Vienna and Berlin Secessions, while also triumphantly completing his huge and controversial frescoes, including the *Retreat of the Swiss Troops near Marignano* for the new National Museum in Zurich. But if the portrait suggests a degree of assertive triumphalism in its allusion to images of Christ, it also reflects Hodler's conception of the mission or role of the artist. In his essay 'The Mission of the Artist', first published in 1897, Hodler spoke in familiar Symbolist language: it was the artist's role to 'extract the eternal element from nature',[2] and his ability to do so lay in his elevated character: 'There is no true work of art that is not born in the mind and the heart [of the artist]. It is there that we find the higher vision'.[3] In the same article he developed his theories of 'parallelism', the symbolic and expressive power of repetitive rhythm and symmetry. Hodler explicitly linked his theory of 'parallelism' to the symmetry of the human figure, which he deliberately emphasises in his self portrait. With his intense gaze and glowing heightened forehead, Hodler casts himself as a Christ-like figure, both visionary and creator. AS

**1** For a discussion of Segantini's earlier self portrait see J. Albrecht, 'Giovanni Segantinis *Selbstbildnis* von 1895: Selbstbefragung und Selbstinszenierung' in Stutzer 2004, pp. 112–30.

**2** Hodler, 'La mission de l'artiste', first published in French in *La Liberté de Fribourg* (18 March 1897), printed in Brüschweiler and Magnaguagno 1983, French edn, p. 272.

**3** 'Il n'y a de véritable oeuvre d'art que celle qui germe dans la pensée et dans le coeur. C'est là la vision supérieure', op. cit.

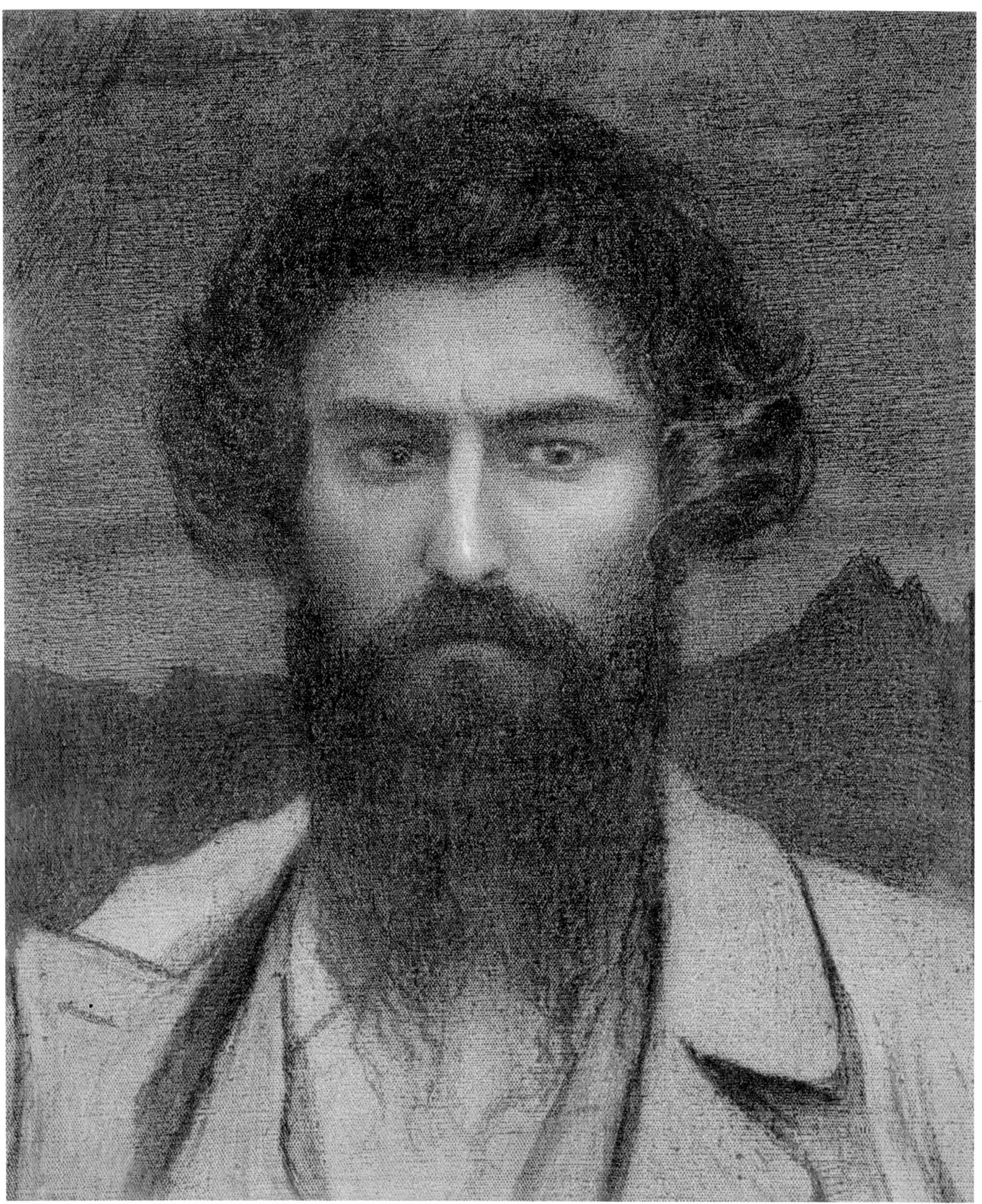

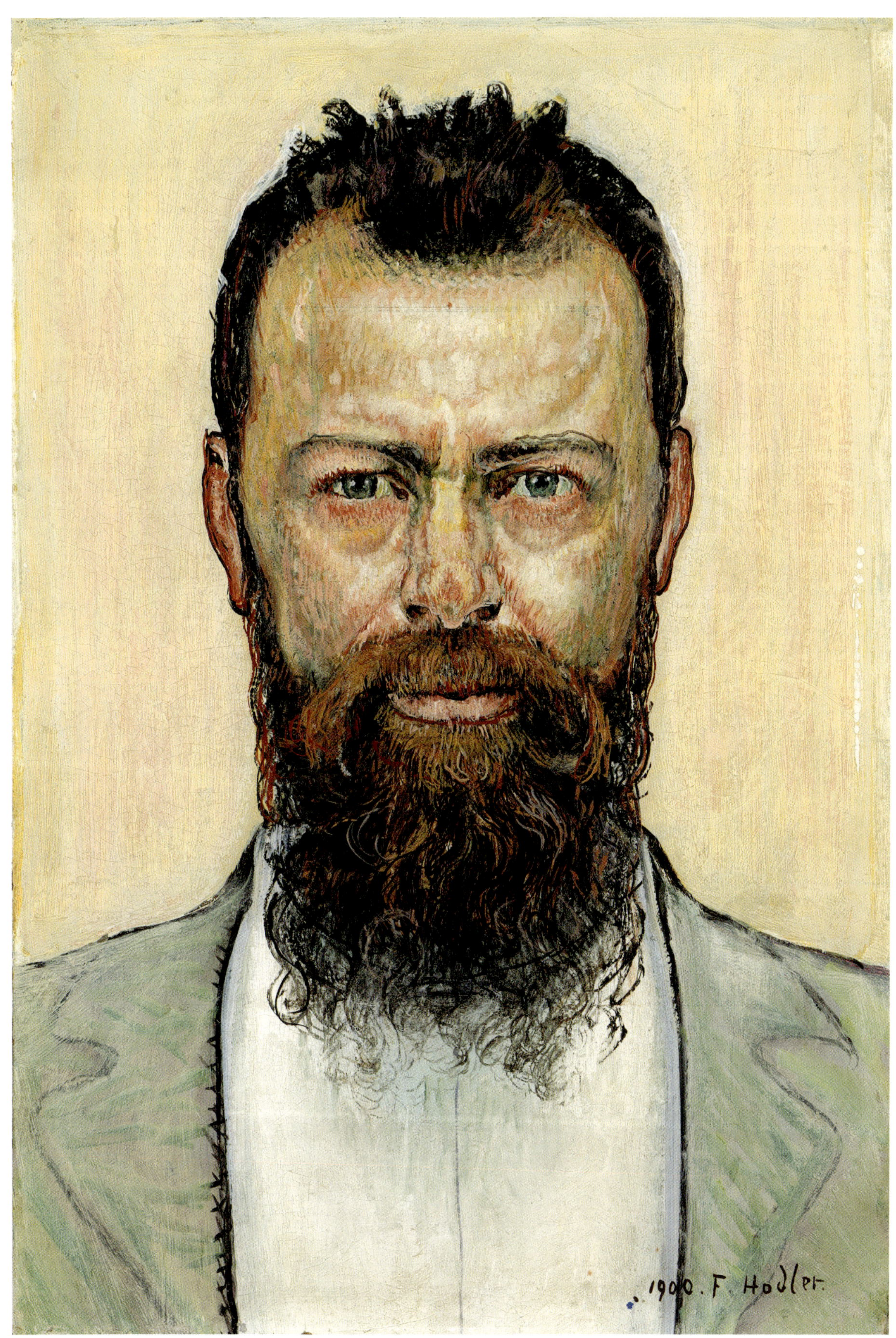
1900. F. Hodler

## 62. Richard Gerstl (1883–1908)

*Self Portrait against a Blue Background*
1904–5
Oil on canvas, 159 × 109 cm
Leopold Museum, Vienna (637)

## 63. Egon Schiele (1890–1918)

*The Poet* 1911
Oil on canvas, 80.5 × 80 cm
Leopold Museum, Vienna (450)

## 64. Oskar Kokoschka (1886–1980)

*Self Portrait* 1910
Colour lithograph, 70.7 × 47.3 cm
Poster for *Der Sturm*
Victoria and Albert Museum, London (Circ. 19-1964)

The figure of the suffering, Christ-like artist developed by Gauguin and the Symbolists and embodied in the developing myth of Van Gogh perhaps found its most heightened expression in the self portraits of Egon Schiele and the Austrian Expressionists in the early years of the twentieth century. Artists such as Schiele, Gerstl and Kokoschka shared with Symbolists the desire to penetrate beyond external appearances, and a sense of the sacredness of the artist's mission: 'I am glad there are so few who can recognise art', Schiele wrote to his uncle in 1911; 'That is constant proof of its divine nature.'[1] This divine, true art had at its source the inner emotional life of the artist, which in turn came to be the principal, if not the only, subject of their art. Nothing demonstrates the break between Gustav Klimt and his young Expressionist successors more clearly than their contrasting attitudes towards self portraiture. Klimt had famously never painted a self portrait, proclaiming that 'I am not interested in myself as the "subject of a picture"'.[2] For Schiele and Gerstl and – to a lesser extent – Kokoschka, 'myself' was the principal and most potent subject of a picture. It was only by probing his own psyche, by laying himself bare, that the artist could effectively penetrate beneath his appearance.

Richard Gerstl's extraordinary self portrait against a blue background makes explicit the Christ-like role of the artist as martyr, but perhaps even more powerfully suggests his role as redeemer. The symmetrically posed body recalls hieratic representations of Christ, as do his naked torso and the white cloth tied around his waist. Arms at his side, Gerstl confronts the viewer with a stare that combines immediacy and directness with a sense of remoteness. This sense of inaccessibility is heightened both by the otherworldly brightness of his torso and the glowing blue aura around his head and body. It is an image which recalls the Christ of the Passion, stripped to the waist, but more insistently suggests the Risen or Transfigured Christ. The Jewish Gerstl painted this self portrait when he was in his early twenties; he was to paint many self portraits throughout his brief career, casting himself in a variety of roles, including what has been claimed as the first painted naked self portrait since Dürer's famous drawing of about 1506.[3] Gerstl committed suicide at the age of only 25, after the collapse of his affair with Mathilde, the wife of his friend the composer Arnold Schoenberg. That he did so in front of his studio mirror – tying a noose around his neck and stabbing himself with a butcher's knife – is telling.

Gerstl's brief life, the fact that he destroyed many of his works and neither exhibited nor sold them during his lifetime, makes it difficult to judge his influence. But even if there was no direct link between the two artists, it is certain that Gerstl's preoccupation with simultaneously probing and posturing self-representation was taken up by Egon Schiele. Schiele painted and drew himself relentlessly throughout his career and, in a remarkable and unprecedented series of drawn and painted self-images from 1910–12, stripped himself bare both literally and metaphorically, appearing naked and emaciated in a stream of poses and guises (see cat.

**1** Letter to L. Czihaczek, quoted in Kallir 1990, p. 117.
**2** 'Was ich bin und was ich will …', quoted in K.A. Schröder, 'Not Blind to the World: Notes on Gustav Klimt and Egon Schiele' in Schröder and Szeemann 1989, p. 19.
**3** *Nude Self Portrait*, 1908, Rudolf Leopold Collection.

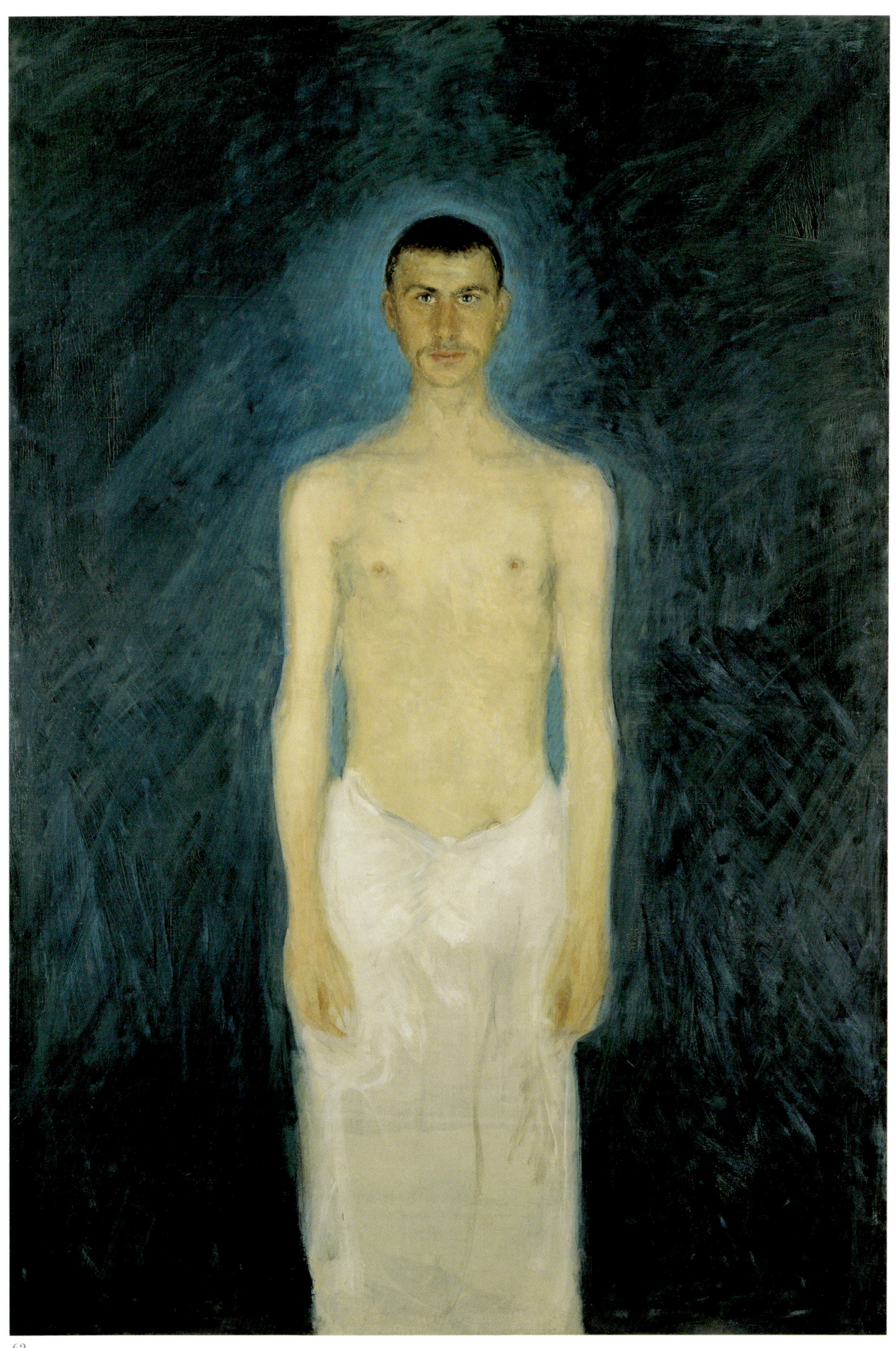

62

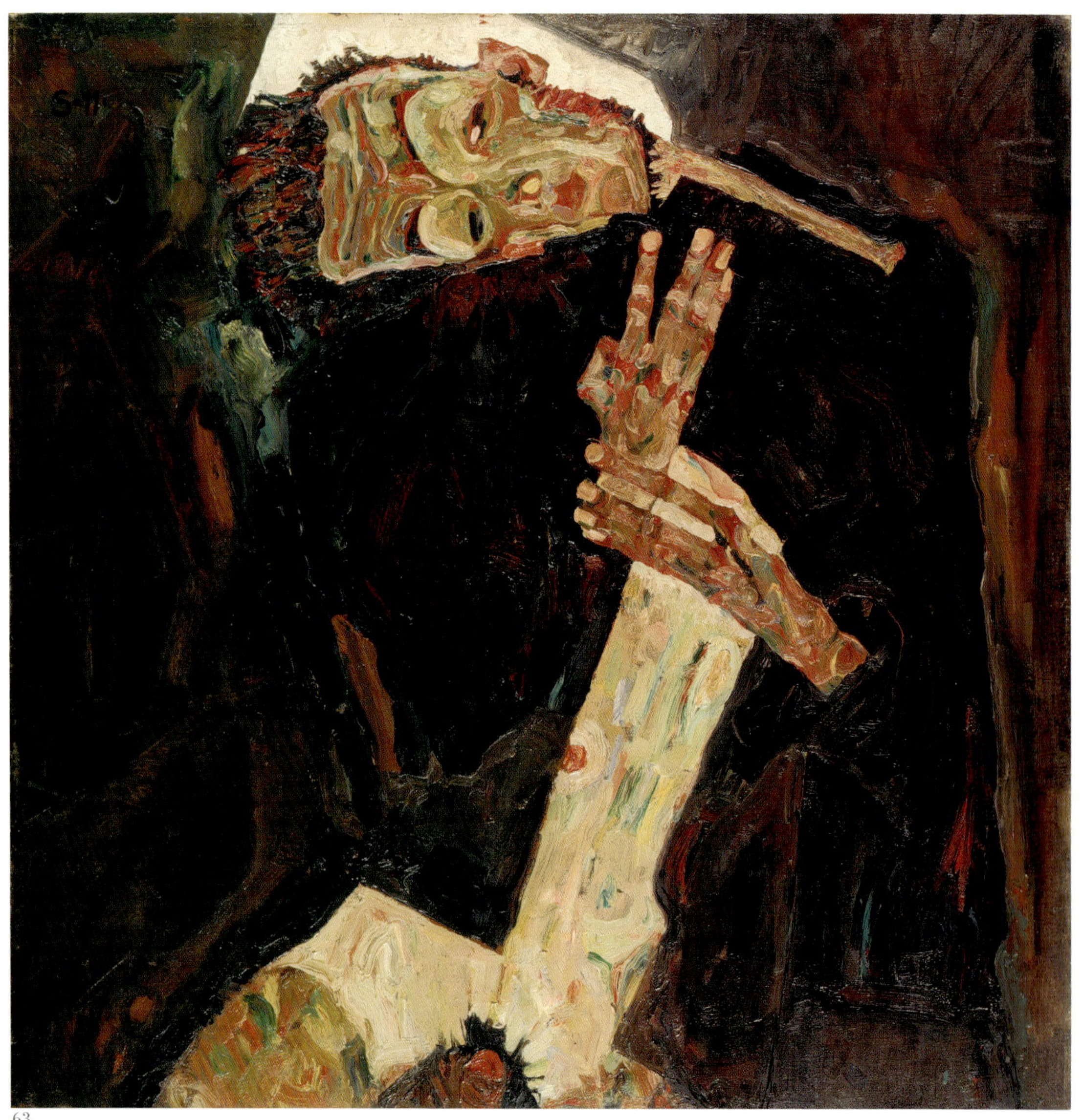

63

71). Viewed as a series, Schiele's self portraits appear both self-revelatory and self-dramatising, treading a precarious line between frank and merciless scrutiny and artificial posturing.

In *The Poet* the title makes explicit the artist's adoption of a role.[4] 1911 seems to have seen a brief moment of literary engagement on Schiele's part, with his introduction to the works of Rimbaud, Rilke and Nietzsche, and the same year saw him giving his works poetic titles, to emphasise their allegorical significance. The 'poet' of this painting is the '*poet maudit*' or accursed poet exemplified by Rimbaud and Verlaine, but here given Schiele's features. Naked from the waist down, his shirt open to reveal his stomach and navel, Schiele presses his bony hands to his chest. In a device he used elsewhere to suggest suffering or even death, his head appears pressed onto his shoulder by the top of the canvas. Around his head a halo proclaims – as in Gerstl's painting – the sacredness of the artist's mission. The suggestion of nudity is characteristic of Schiele's adolescent narcissism, but also exploits associations of nudity with suffering, ultimately derived from imagery of the suffering Christ and saints.

This association is made even more explicitly and aggressively by Oskar Kokoschka in his poster for the Berlin periodical *Der Sturm*. In contrast to the essentially retiring figures of Gerstl and Schiele, Kokoschka deliberately cultivated a theatrical persona as social outcast. He

**4** The title was Schiele's own and is written on the stretcher of the canvas.

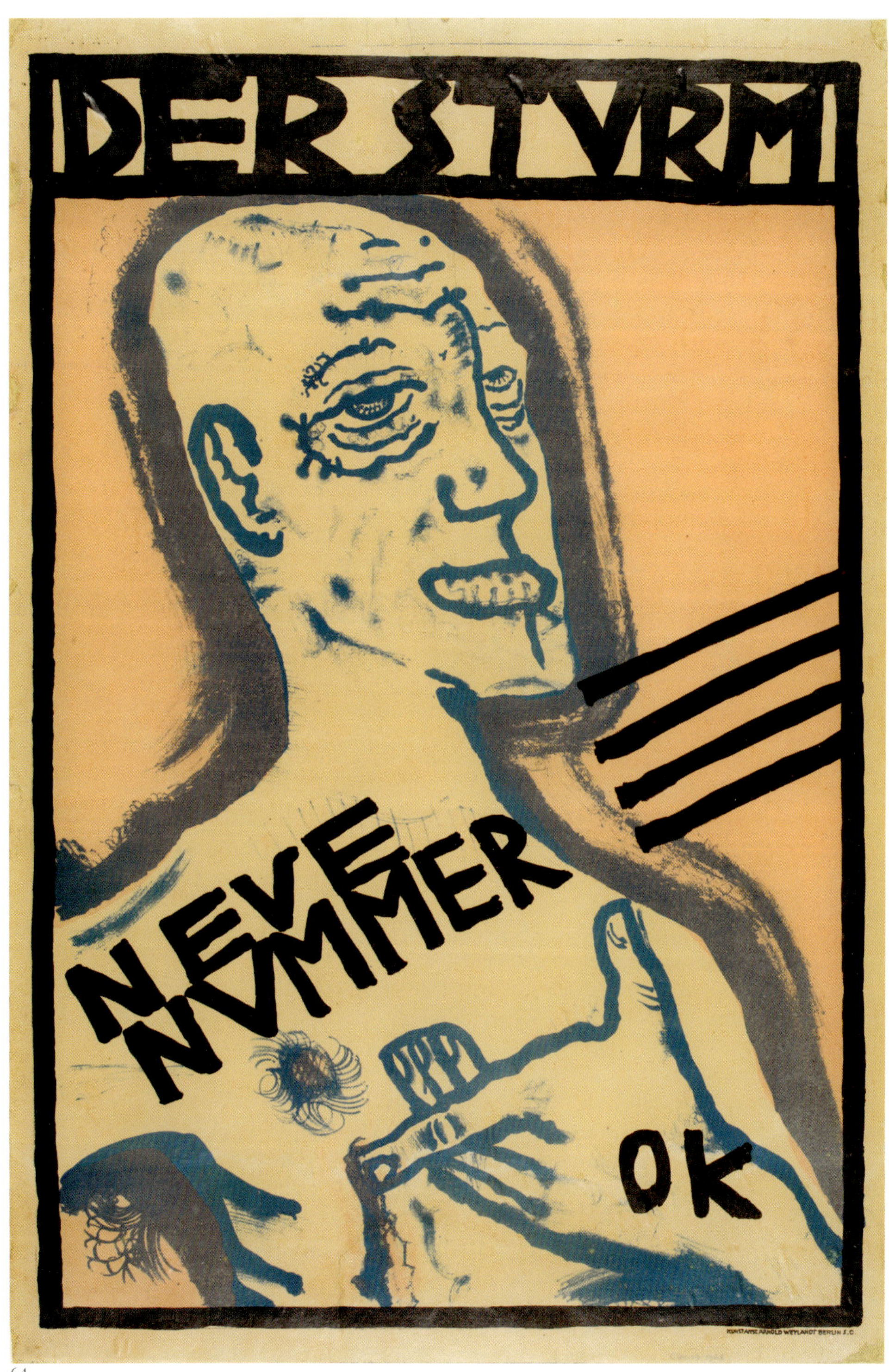


64

shaved his head like a convict and proclaimed himself, in his appearance as much as his art, as beyond the pale of bourgeois society. In this brutal and deliberately primitive image the shaven-headed and grimacing artist points to a wound in his side. The wound makes direct reference to Christ, but Kokoschka's probing finger can be read as either making the wound or else as exploring it, suggesting that it is precisely in the exploitation and examination of suffering that the source of art lies. In this interpretation suffering becomes not only the lot of the struggling artist, but an essential prerequisite for, and source of, his creativity. AS

# Creativity and Sexuality

It is conspicuous that among the ranks of nineteenth-century artistic rebels and martyrs there were virtually no women. Not that there was an absence of women artists: despite institutional and professional barriers, their numbers grew steadily through the century. But while men could adopt a rebellious stance and still enjoy a high reputation as an artist, it was virtually impossible for women to assume the identities that male artists had taken on to express their rejection of the norms of bourgeois society. To embrace bohemianism or any other outward show of rebellion would have placed a woman artist irrevocably outside respectable society. The only women in Bohemia were the already socially and morally suspect models and mistresses.

But another, more invidious reason for the exclusion of women was the prevailing association of inspiration, genius and creativity with men. Male artists were allowed to rebel against bourgeois society and live unconventional lives as the privilege of the genius that was their exclusive preserve. While Romanticism championed sensitivity and intuition over reason, it only praised such 'feminine' qualities as they were found in male creators, when driven by masculine intellect and energy. As the Goncourts asserted in an infamous epigram, 'there are no women of genius, the women of genius are men'.[1] In the last decades of the nineteenth century, the maleness of genius was asserted ever more forcefully, partly in response to the emergence of a new class of woman seeking independence and education rather than marriage and a home. In 1903, in his highly successful book *Sex and Character*, Otto Weininger stated: 'The man of genius possesses, like everything else, the complete female in himself; but woman herself is only part of the Universe, and the part can never be the whole; femaleness can never include genius.'[2]

This key idea was reinforced by the male artist through the association of creativity with his sexual drive. The sculptor Rodin represented Balzac, who himself equated his creativity with his sexual prowess, as a sturdy, powerfully muscled figure grasping his erect penis (cat. 65). Lovis Corinth in his self portraits presents himself as a vigorous, Dionysian hero, reflecting the ideal of the *Übermensch* (superman) of Nietzsche, who characterised the artist as exclusively male, his creativity stemming from instinctual forces deep within him.

Within this world of male artistic genius, woman is cast in a variety of supporting roles. While Corinth brandishes the tools of his trade like weapons, his submissive wife inspires and consoles (cat. 67). She is the enabling muse. But the muse can become a torment, as in Jacek Malczewski's extraordinary *The Inspiration of the Painter* (cat. 68), and woman can destroy. This is the role of the *femme fatale*, dear to Symbolist painters and poets. As harpy, vampire, sphinx or siren, she is the personification of devouring female voluptuousness. While the artist aspires to a transcendent spiritual realm, she, like Moreau's *Siren* (cat. 69), is of the earth – or of the swamp – and is driven by base, primeval urges. The sexual drive is held to be creative in man but never in woman. In this context, Paula Modersohn-Becker's self portrait (cat. 72) is a brave challenge to notions of male genius. Like her male counterparts she chooses to represent her artistic creativity through her sexuality. She shows herself half-naked, like the tormented Christ, and pregnant, a symbol of her explicitly female creativity. AS/MW

**1** Quoted approvingly by Cesare Lombroso in *The Man of Genius* 1863, trans. London 1891, p. 138.
**2** Otto Weininger, *Sex and Character*, 1903, trans. London 1906, p. 189.

## 65. Auguste Rodin (1840–1917)
### *Balzac Study* 1896

Plaster, 95.5 × 42 × 36.5 cm

Musée Rodin, Paris (S. 178)

## 66. Auguste Rodin
### *The Sculptor and his Muse* 1895–7

Stone, 66 × 58.3 × 53 cm

Musée Rodin, Paris (S. 1020)

Sexuality was for Rodin straightforwardly connected to creativity. He saw eroticism as a vital dimension of life – indeed, the source of life – an urgent creative impulse. Rodin, whose sexual voraciousness acquired him the nickname of the 'sultan of Meudon', linked his notion of artistic inspiration to sexual passion more than once in his letters: 'I have spied on myself in my moments of passions, of the intoxication of love, and I have studied them for my art.'[1] It is a connection that he also made explicit in his art.

Nowhere is the equation of creativity with male sexual energy more uncompromising than in his study for his statue of Balzac made in 1896 (cat. 65). In the light of this model, Rodin's first recorded comments on being awarded the commission for a statue of the great novelist to be set up in the square of the Palais Royale are revealing. When asked by a journalist in 1891 for his thoughts on the writer and his statue, he replied: 'Balzac is before everything a creator and this is the idea that I would wish to make understood in my statue … As of now I would want to execute a figure standing rather than seated.'[2] From the start of the project Rodin was driven by the idea of Balzac as the heroic vigorous creator and the idea sustained him throughout the entire tortuous process of the sculpture's gestation. Six years later, as the work neared completion, it was still paramount: 'I have sought to express the character, the power of the great novelist to the exclusion of all other aspects of his work. The severity of my project is destined to glorify not a man of the mind, but a man of genius.'[3]

Rodin's first solution, the extraordinary statue of a naked Balzac, arms folded, striding and strident, depicted as a fighter or wrestler, was rejected by the commissioners in 1893. Returning to the statue three years later, Rodin made the small headless model here. Its creation was later recalled by Moorhardt: 'A sturdy, squat, powerfully muscled model came to pose for Rodin. Of course he posed nude. He stood with his [right] foot a half step in front. But this first sketch did not yet give any idea of the magnificent swing of the head.'[4] What Moorhardt failed to mention is that Rodin showed the model grasping his erect penis. The detail is hardly incidental: it is also entirely appropriate for both sculptor and subject. Rodin, who thoroughly researched the author before commencing his statue, must have been aware of Balzac's own equation of his sexual prowess with his creative powers. According to the Goncourts' Journal, 'Sperm for [Balzac] … was an emission of pure cerebral substance, a sort of filtering out and loss, through the penis of a work of art.'[5]

According to Moorhardt, Rodin made six copies of the model and draped each with a cloth to arrive at the final form of the statue. In the final version, although the subject's hands now pull his dressing gown around him, his erection is still apparent. It is also perhaps implied in Rodin's description of the completed statue made to Paul Gsell in 1907: 'Balzac truly heroic who does not stop to rest for a moment … who is transported by passion, whose body is made frenetic and violent and who does not heed the warnings of his diseased heart from which he will soon die.'[6]

If Rodin showed Balzac as priapically independent, in a number of other works focusing upon the notion of artistic inspiration he invokes the figure of the female muse as inspiring and engendering the creative impulse. This, too, is an idea found in his writings. 'A gentle woman is the mighty intermediary between God and us artists', he wrote to Helene von Nostitz; 'Through her we express a thousand-fold that which is in us … Is there not great joy in imagination and is it not as advantage of man that he created the muse, the powerful awakener, like the Beatrice of Dante? Everyone has in his life a force which

1 Frisch and Shipley 1939, pp. 356–7.
2 Rodin in *Le Matin* (9 December 1891), quoted in Elsen 2003, p. 353.
3 From undated clipping from *Éclair* in Balzac file at the Musée Rodin, cited in Elsen op. cit. p. 384.
4 Moorhardt 1934, p. 467, cited in 'Monument to Balzac', Elsen op. cit.
5 Goncourt 1989 edn, vol. 1, pp. 639–40 (30 March 1875).
6 Gsell 1984 trans.

watches over him.'[7] Later, and in less measured tones he spoke of 'Feminine charm which crushes our destiny, mysterious feminine power that retards the thinker, the worker, and the artist, while at the same time it inspires them – a compensation for those who play with fire!'[8] This ambivalence in the relationship of artist and muse is conveyed with considerable power in his group *The Sculptor and his Muse* (cat. 66), whose title (given to the work by Rodin for his exhibition of 1900) invites us to read it as both a self portrait and a representation of artistic inspiration.[9] The muse both crushes and inspires the seated sculptor: she stands awkwardly on his lap, one leg pulled up behind her,[10] her hair enveloping his head in a manner that recalls Munch's *Vampire* (cat. 70), as she (perhaps) whispers into his ear and (certainly) reaches towards his groin. The sculptor, a muscular seated figure whose pose recalls Rodin's *Thinker*, reveals a face which seems tormented, his eyes closed and hand covering his mouth as if to suppress a scream. If the work unambiguously proclaims an eroticised reading of the creative inspiration, it also places the artist as the powerless (and voiceless) victim of the consuming muse. AS

**7** Helene von Nostitz, *Dialogues with Rodin*, New York 1931, pp. 75–6.
**8** Cladel 1917, p. 176.
**9** The stone group was executed by François Pompon (1855–1933) in about 1895 and remodelled in both 1907 and 1908, see *Rodin en 1900: L'exposition de l'Alma*, exh. cat., Musee du Luxembourg, Paris 2001, no. 70, p. 194.
**10** The figure is taken from Rodin's earlier *La Coquille et la Perle* (1889–90) and was originally modelled as seated on the ground.

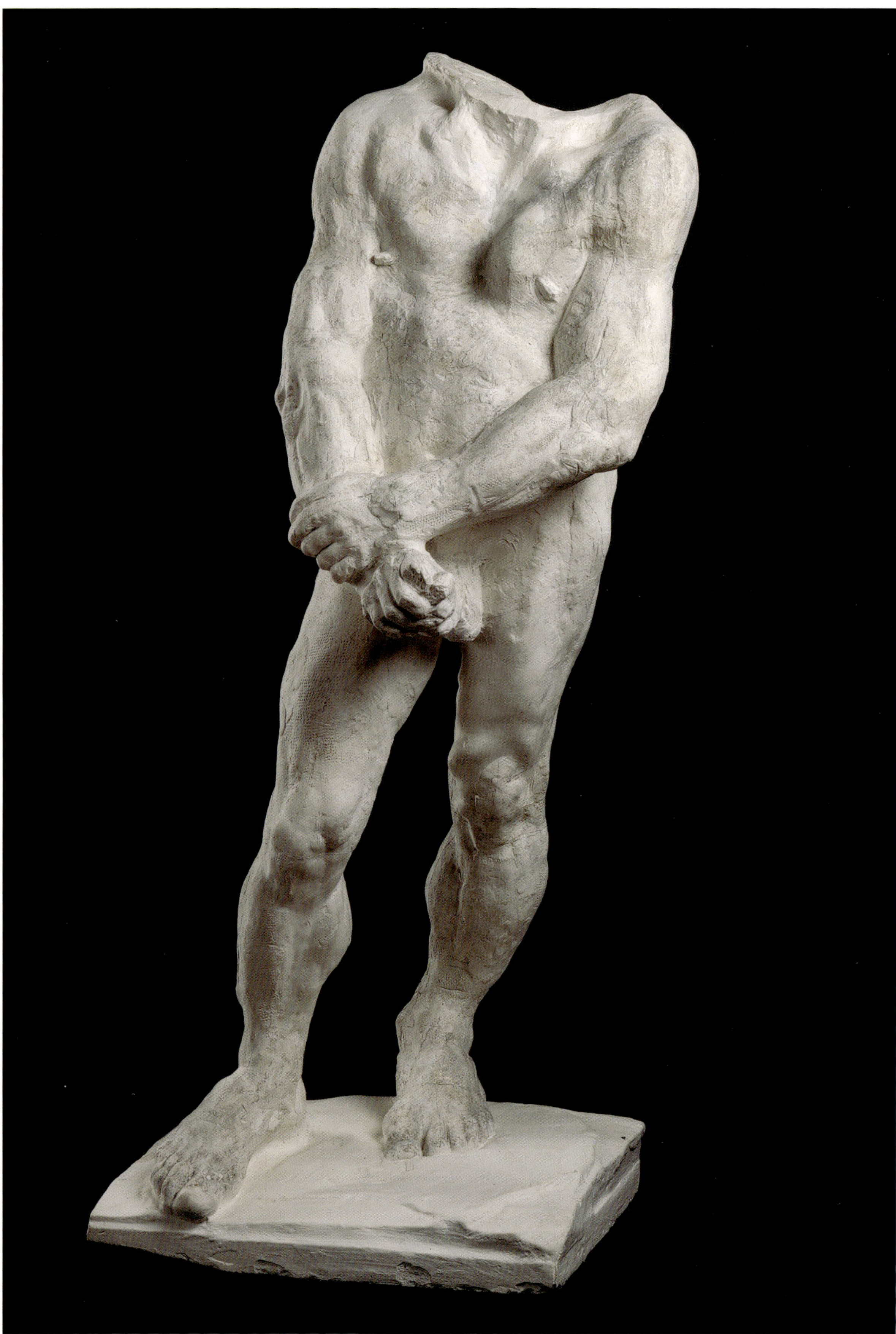

65

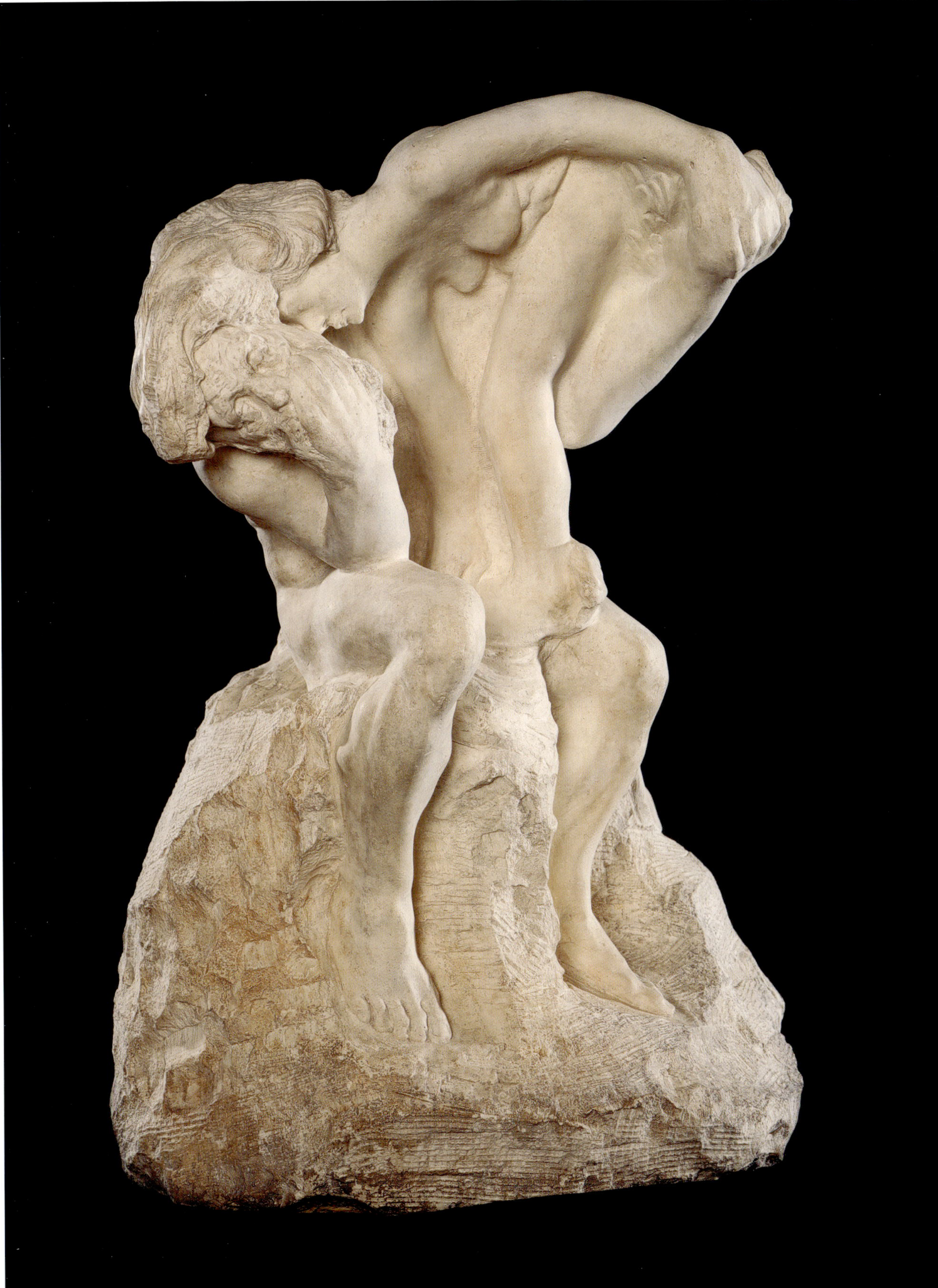

## 67. Lovis Corinth (1858–1925)

## *Self Portrait with a Model* 1903

Oil on canvas, 121 × 89 cm

Kunsthaus, Zurich (1951/17)

In this determinedly virile self portrait Lovis Corinth depicts himself as the forceful male artist, consoled and inspired by his model and muse. Centrally placed, his staring, full-frontal face at the apex of the picture's composition, Corinth holds the tools of his trade while his arms encircle his naked wife Charlotte Berend. She, by contrast, is essentially anonymous, her face hidden, her head on his shoulder which she clasps with one hand while the other is placed sustainingly on his heart.

The picture was painted three months after the couple's marriage in March 1903. Berend, 22 years Corinth's junior, had been one of his first pupils when in October 1901 he opened a private school for women artists in his Klopstockstrasse studio, shortly after his move to Berlin from Munich. Berend's own position as an artist is not reflected in any of Corinth's many portraits of her and, although she was a fellow member of the Berlin Secession from 1906 and exhibited with them, she essentially surrendered her own artistic ambitions to her husband's and her family's needs. The couple's daughter, Wilhelmine, later remembered a family life in which everything was directed towards the needs of her father, and every account suggests that Charlotte played an extraordinarily important role in giving Corinth a previously elusive emotional and psychological equilibrium, coaxing him from his frequent depressions with her tone of 'banter, irony and deep significance'.[1]

Corinth's psychological fragility and sense of mortality inform many of his self portraits, but neither is in evidence here. Instead, he assumes the role of the warrior artist, his brush and palette brandished like weapons, with Berend as the trophy of his art – Andromeda to his Perseus. The winged victories in the decorative border, extremely unusual for Corinth, perhaps support such a reading. Corinth was to repeat this juxtaposition of the vigorous clothed male with the naked damsel in even more extreme form in *The Victor* of 1910 (location unknown), in which the bare-breasted and smiling Berend leans back against the stern figure of the artist in full armour. Both pictures reflect the influence of the Nietzschean ideal of the warrior-like *Übermensch* (superman), and in his autobiography Corinth was to write of his artistic struggle in entirely Nietzschean tones:

> Since the battle for existence forces the artist to do his best, the competition is extreme. It does not matter whether his colleagues, even his best friends perish all around him, as long as he wins out as the strongest. As long as the strength of the victor remains decisive in this battle, nobody needs to be pitied, for it is the fate of the weak to succumb to the strong.[2]

For Nietzsche the power and creativity of the *Übermensch* lay in his natural, instinctual openness to Dionysian forces. Nietzsche located the 'genesis of art' in 'the cerebral system bursting with sexual energy', which he characterised as explicitly male, 'the creative instinct of the artist' born from 'the distribution of semen in his blood'.[3] Corinth cast himself as Dionysian in a number of self portraits[4] and Charlotte Berend in her memories of her husband suggests her role as Dionysian muse: 'When Corinth wound vine-leaves in his hair, when he lifted his glass and embraced his bacchic young wife, the world around him changed into the realm of Dionysus, to whom he felt closely allied.'[5] AS

**1** Charlotte Berend-Corinth, *Mein Leben mit Lovis Corinth*, Munich 1958, cited in Schuster et al. 1996–7, pp. 40–1.
**2** Cited in Uhr 1990, p. 175.
**3** Nietzsche 1968 edn, p. 424.
**4** For example, *Self Portrait as Howling Bacchant* (1905; Insel Hombroich; Berend-Corinth 1958, no. 400) and *Self Portrait with Glass* (1907; Národní Galerie, Prague; Berend-Corinth 1958, no. 344).
**5** C. Berend-Corinth, *Lovis*, Munich 1958, p. 103. Berend casts herself in a similar role in her account of Corinth's earlier portrait of himself with the – again naked – Berend. The account suggests the picture was painted in an almost Dionysian frenzy in which Berend – and wine – acted as enabling muses. C. Berend-Corinth, *Lovis Corinth: Bildnisse der Frau des Kunstlers*, Stuttgart 1958, p. 21, quoted in Uhr 1990, p. 139. Corinth's nickname for Berend, 'his Petermannchen', also suggests her wild, impulsive character: it derived from a story told by Charlotte that to ward off suitors she had pretended to be a gypsy orphan whose parents were members of the Petermann tribe.

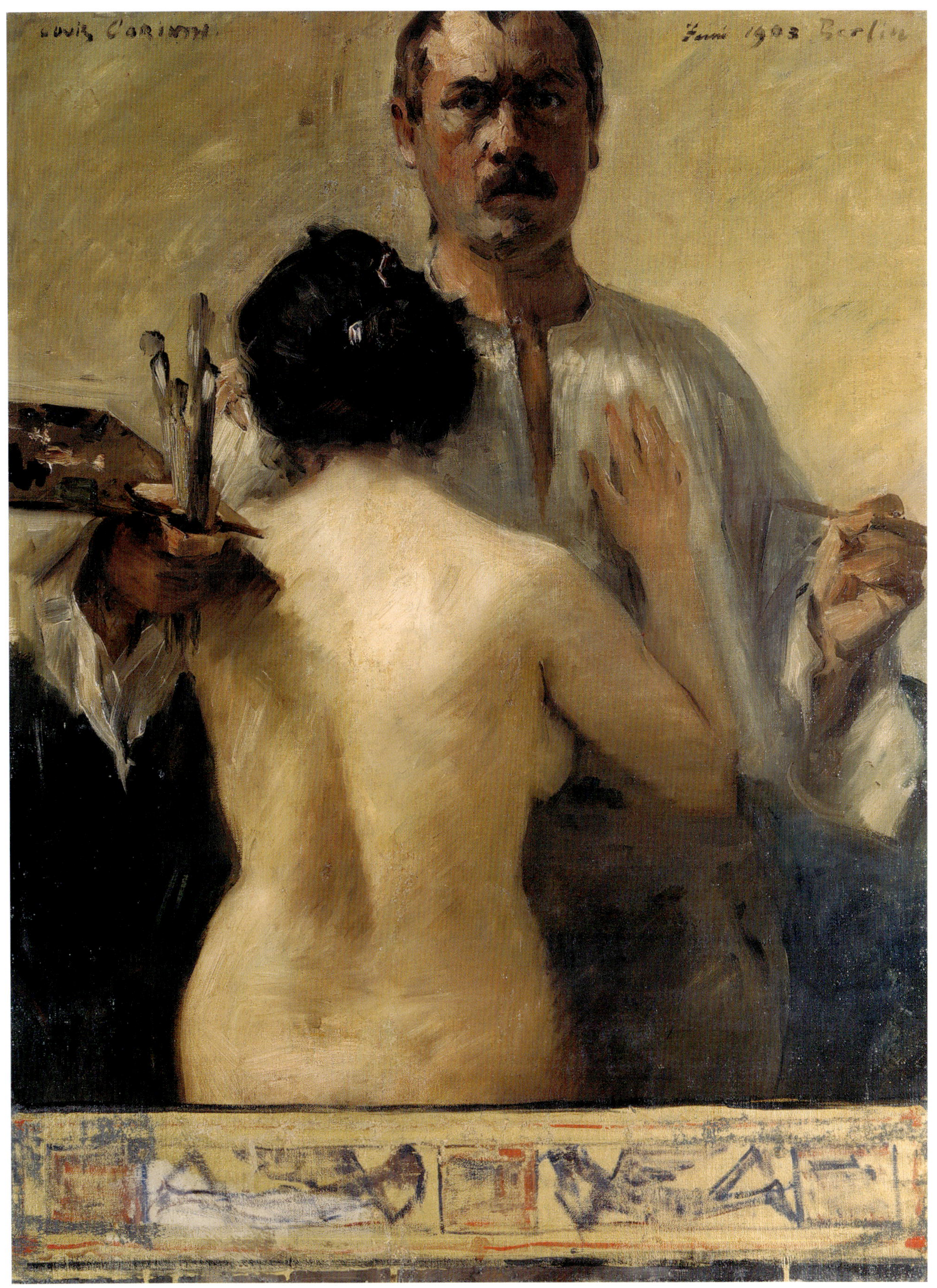
Lovis Corinth
Juni 1903 Berlin

## 68. Jacek Malczewski (1854–1926)

*The Inspiration of the Painter* 1897

Oil on canvas, 79.5 × 64 cm

National Museum, Cracow (MNK II-b-2543)

The scene is an artist's studio. In the background three figures sleep or cower at a long table on which sit paints and palettes. Beyond them more ghostly figures huddle in the corner behind a stove. In the foreground an artist is curled up on his chair, his head in his hand, his face hidden. He sits before a canvas that we cannot see, on the other side of which floats the huge and unnerving figure of a woman. Head held high, she occupies the entire height of the painting. She is encircled with ropes and wrapped in layers of cloth, including what appears to be an army greatcoat. A straw crown hangs on ropes from her head. Between her hands floats a glass sphere.

*The Inspiration of the Painter* is one of a number of works by the Polish Symbolist Malczewski in which he explored the nature of artistic creation and inspiration, and the role of the artist in the world. He first treated the figure of the artist in the 1880s, in works such as *Three Arts of Painting* (1886; whereabouts unknown) and *The Dream of the Painter* (1888; private collection), in which an artist sleeps in a landscape through which walks a procession of ghostly naked figures, and he returned to it throughout his career.[1]

Malczewski's conception of the artist, derived from Symbolist theory, was of someone who could intuitively reach beyond a material reality to the unchanging yet hidden essence of things. His elevated image of the figure of the artist was reflected in the many guises in which he depicted himself in his numerous self portraits, including those of Christ, Orpheus, Ezekiel, Don Quixote, a knight, pilgrim and faun. Great art was for Malczewski 'the unveiling of eternal harmonies taking their beginning in God'.[2] It was this process of unveiling, and the degree to which it was in the artist's control, that was the subject of many of his works. In *The Inspiration of the Painter*, the slumped figure of the artist is completely overwhelmed by the nightmarish figure of his imagination – although it is uncertain whether she has been called into being by the artist, or has imposed herself upon him.

The painting is linked thematically to Malczewski's series *Imaginary Scenes of the Artist* (1897–9), each of which shows the interior of an artist's studio in which the figure of the painter, sometimes naked and in shackles, is confronted by a chimera, half woman and half winged-beast, seductive and terrifying, who became a recurring symbol of art both for Malczewski and contemporary Polish Symbolist writers and artists. The chimera for Malczewski became an emblem of the conflict between the sensual and material, symbolised by female sexuality on the one hand, and the artist's yearning for the infinite and eternal on the other. The female figure in *The Inspiration of the Painter* seems to embody similar contradictions: the ropes that bind her and the weight of the clothes around her suggest an earthbound materiality, with the army coat perhaps alluding to Poland's struggles for independence, another recurring theme in Malczewski's paintings. On the other hand she floats free of the earth, while the mystical sphere she carries suggests the power of vision to a world beyond that of mere physical appearances. AS

**1** These include *Introduction: A Little Painter* (1890; National Museum, Cracow), *Melancholy* (1894; National Museum, Poznan), *Vicious Circle* (1895–7; National Museum, Poznan) and *Moment of Inspiration – The Harpy in Sleep* (1907; private collection, Poznan).

**2** J. Malczewski, 'On the Mission of Artists and the Goals of Art', speech of 1912 quoted in Lawniczakowa 1988, p. 46.

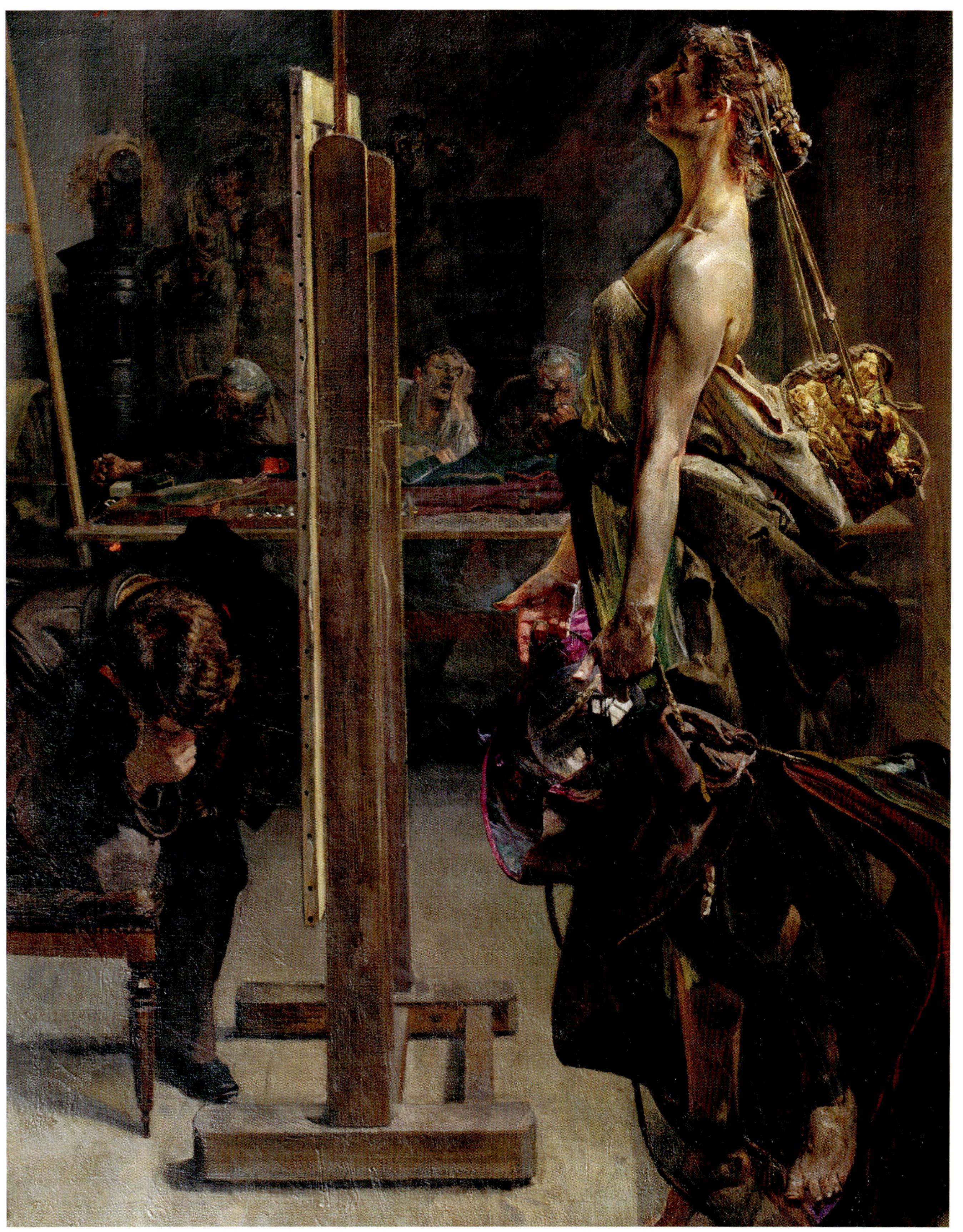

## 69. Gustave Moreau (1826–1898)

*The Poet and the Siren* 1894

Oil on canvas, 158 × 115 cm

Gustave Moreau Museum, Paris (66)

Moreau's late painting graphically encapsulates many Symbolist ideas about the creative individual and the threat posed to him by the femme fatale, emblem of perversity. Moreau had originally painted the subject in 1892–3 for the collector Francis Warrain (Matsuo Collection, Japan). At the same time he was being pressured by the Gobelins Tapestry Manufactory to provide a design for one of a proposed series of tapestries by contemporary artists. The project had been mooted some years earlier when, in September 1889, Edouard Gerspach at Gobelins had written to Moreau: 'Your painting is made for tapestry, its interpretation in textile would be a real pleasure for our weavers'. The commission was taken up in earnest by Gerspach's successor, Jules Guiffrey, in 1893, and the version shown here was probably the preliminary design shown to the Commission de Perfectionnement des Gobelins and approved by them at a meeting on 17 May 1894. A full-scale painted cartoon, with a different decorative border, was delivered to the Gobelins in 1896, although Moreau died before the tapestry's completion in 1899.[1]

Moreau's choice of subject for the Gobelins tapestry was clearly dictated in part by the timing of the request, but *The Poet and the Siren* must also have recommended itself as a summation of one of the abiding themes of his art: the position of the artist in the world. The young poet lies, in a pose that derives from Adam in Michelangelo's *Creation of Eve* on the Sistine chapel ceiling, at the feet of the huge fish-tailed siren who rises from the swamp-like sea, weeds clinging to her hair. Moreau's poet, like most of his heroes, is androgynous. The androgyne, an asexual embodiment of the male and female, was a prevailing type in Symbolist art, symbolic of purity and spirituality, and later came to represent the figure of the artist. Through the androgynous male – and he is always represented in a male body – Symbolist artists and writers could assert current notions of the 'feminine' as creative, while simultaneously excluding women themselves from the equation. In Moreau's painting the point is explicitly made, for towering above the pure and spiritual body of the slumped poet is the androgyne's antithesis, the femme fatale. Where the androgyne stood for spiritual purity, the femme fatale in any of her many guises – of harpy, vampire, sphinx or siren – was the embodiment of material perversity, the personification of voracious female sexuality.[2] The siren in Moreau's painting is explicitly an emblem of nature, half-animal; weeds still clinging to her, she is the inhabitant of a shadowy grotto, rendered in the oil study in abstract and vivid hues of blue and orange. Her earthy sexuality is both contrasted with and seen as fatal to the transcendent purity of the poet: she is the dominating, consuming woman who saps the strength of the passive and helpless poet, just as, for the Symbolist writer Albert Aurier, 'dirty sexuality' and 'filthy passion ... like a leper stalks and kills the artists of our villainous epoch'.[3] AS

**1** The cartoon is in the Musée de la Ville de Poitiers, the tapestry in Mobilier National, Paris.

**2** For a survey of the many guises of the femme fatale see Dijkstra 1986.

**3** A. Aurier, 'J-F. Henner' in *Oeuvres Posthumes*, Paris 1893, p. 289, quoted in Mathews 1999, p. 95.

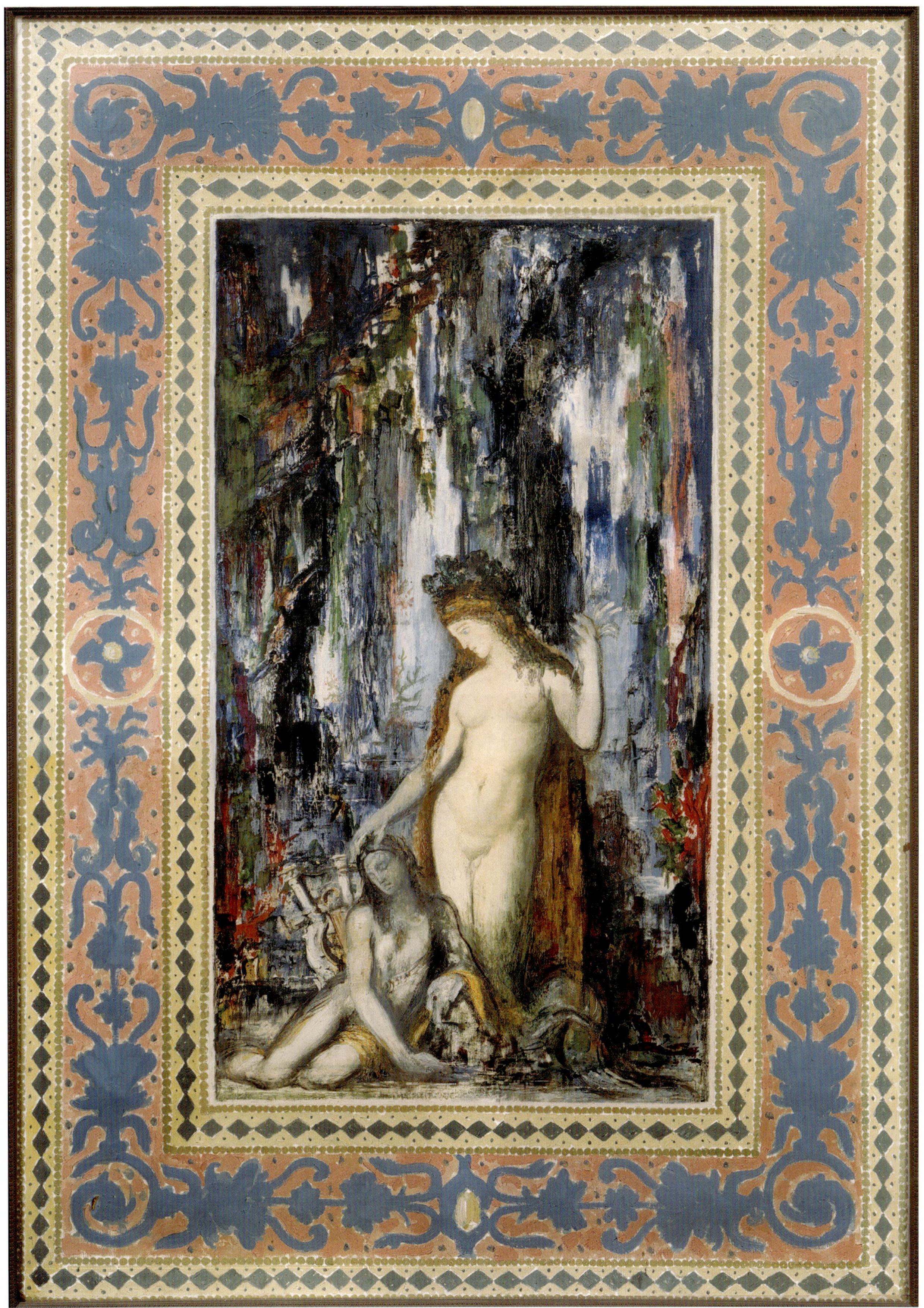

## 70. Edvard Munch (1863–1944)
### *Vampire* 1902

Lithographic print, 38 × 55cm

The British Museum, London (1970-7-11-8)

Munch's work in the 1890s was dominated by the theme of 'the battle, between man and woman, that is called love' and the image which came to be known as *Vampire* was central to this endeavour. Munch's first painting of the subject – then called *Love and Pain* – was the signature work of his ground-breaking *Frieze of Life* exhibition held at the end of 1893 at Unter den Linden 19, Berlin, and reproduced on the cover of the catalogue. It was one of the six paintings from a *Study for a Series on 'Love'* produced by Munch in a burst of extraordinary productivity that same year. These six works, which remain his most celebrated legacy, were to remain the central core of his *Frieze of Life* project, which he reproduced and reworked in paint and as prints over the succeeding years. Munch made the first black-and-white lithographs of *Vampire* in 1895 but returned to the motif again in 1902 to make a series of multi-coloured prints, using a combination of one or two lithographic stones and a woodblock cut into four separate pieces for the distinct areas of the composition.[1]

The title 'Vampire' was first used for the image for Munch's Stockholm exhibition of 1894, and was apparently derived from the description of the work by Munch's friend Stanislaw Przbyszewski:

> A broken man, and the face of a biting vampire on his neck … There is something terribly calm and passionless in this picture; an immeasurable, fatal quality of resignation. The man there rolls and rolls in abysmal depths, without will, powerless, and he is happy to be able to roll on with as little will as stone. Yet he cannot rid himself of the vampire, cannot rid himself of the pain either, and the woman will always sit there, biting forever with a thousand adders' tongues, with a thousand poison fangs.[2]

Munch's adoption of the new title suggests his sympathy for Przbyszewski's interpretation, but the image itself and Munch's own descriptions of it are more ambivalent. The enveloping figure of the woman, her red hair falling over the man's head, which is pressed to her breast, suggests her role as protector and consoler as well as consuming predator. The man buries his head, but she can also be read as bearing down upon him, a burden sapping the man of his (creative) powers. In a diary entry Munch describes the image in terms rather different from Przbyszewski's, suggesting the man's longing for intimacy as much as his fear of loss of control:

> And he laid his head on her breast – he felt the blood pulsing through her veins – he listened to the beat of her heart – he buried his face in her lap and felt two burning lips on his neck – a shiver shook his body – an icy feeling of ecstatic desire – and he pressed her to his body convulsively.[3]

Later still, Munch was to insist that the image 'is actually only a woman kissing a man on the neck'.[4]

Munch's attitude to women was coloured by his own experiences, most importantly his consuming love affair with his cousin by marriage, Millie Thaulow, embarked upon in the spirit of utopian free love preached by Hans Jaeger, the unofficial leader of the group of young artists and writers in Christiana, modern day Oslo, who called themselves the 'Christiana Bohême'. The affair ended in overwhelming jealousy and despair on Munch's part, and he recalled its effect in terms that also suggest the vampire image:

> What a deep mark she left on my mind, so deep that no other image can ever totally drive it away … Was it because she took my first kiss, that she took the sweetness of life from me? Was it because she lied, deceived, that one day she took the scales from my eyes so that I saw Medusa's head, saw life as a great horror?[5] AS

**1** Woll 2001, no. 41, pp. 73–4.
**2** *Das Werk des Edvard Munch*, Berlin 1894, p. 20, quoted in I. Müller-Westermann, '"The Age of Carmen": Gender Relationships in the Art of Edvard Munch, 1890–1920' in Schröder and Hoerschelmann 2003, pp. 67–82.
**3** Quoted in Eggum 2000, p. 181
**4** Letter from Munch to Jens Thiis, early 1930s, quoted in Schroder and Hoerschelmann 2003, p.193
**5** Munch Museum archives MS T 2770 (EM II), quoted in R. Heller, 'Form and Formation of Edvard Munch's Frieze of Life' in Wood 1992, pp. 25–37.

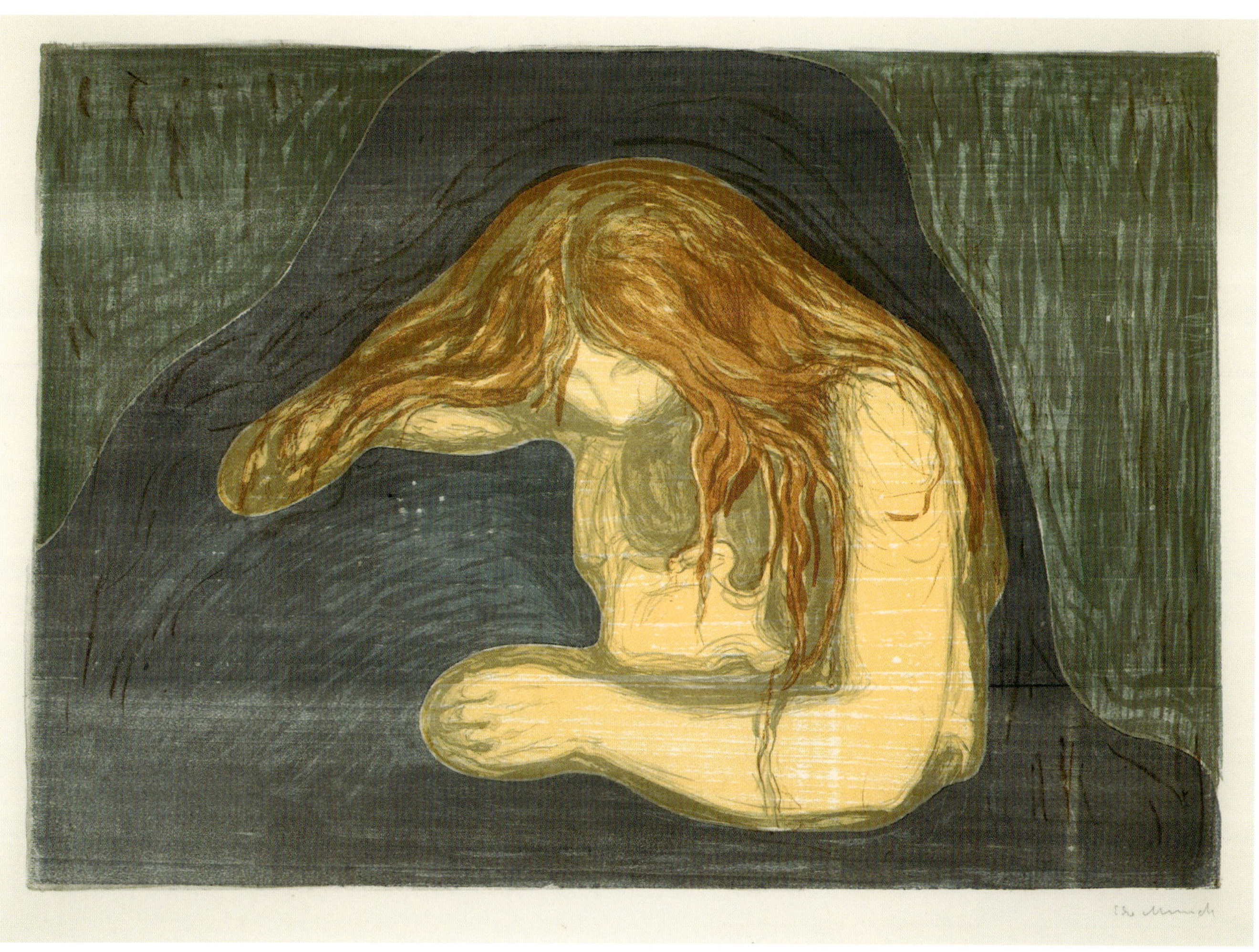

## 71. Egon Schiele (1890–1918)
## *Self Portrait as a Nude* 1912

Sketch for the Sema-album

Ink and black crayon on paper, 46.9 × 30.1 cm

Leopold Museum, Vienna (1440)

Between 1910 and 1912 Egon Schiele drew and painted an extraordinary series of nude self portraits. The drawings, remarkable for their variety of poses and moods, are swiftly executed in pen, pencil and watercolour. Their spontaneity implies that they were derived from direct observation in the same way as his contemporary drawings of nude models and children. But the extravagance of Schiele's poses – and the absolute absence of any indication of his role as a practising artist within the drawings – makes it evident that they are the product of memory or invention as much as scrutiny in front of the mirror. They are as much performances as they are exercises in observation.

The fact that Schiele was so often naked or semi-naked in his self portraits, at times adopting provocative poses or masturbating, suggests the adolescent's narcissistic self-absorption and the assertion of an emerging sexual identity. Schiele was 20 in 1910, but in many ways he remained a boy – even in 1913 he refused to go on holiday without packing his set of toy trains. The year 1912, when this drawing was made, was one of crisis for Schiele, and famously saw his imprisonment for three weeks in Neulenbach jail on the grounds of sexual immorality. His arrest was provoked by his use of child models; he was initially (and the surviving evidence suggests unjustifiably) charged with kidnap and rape before being convicted of the lesser charge of sexual immorality.

That Schiele saw his sexual urges as a wellspring of impulsive creativity is certain, apparently telling Arthur Roessler, the chronicler of his prison experiences, that 'I have doubtless painted "terrible" pictures, but do they believe I did it on purpose, just to shock the bourgeoisie? This has never been the case. But there are spectres brought forth by longing, and I have painted such spectres. Not because I enjoyed it – I just had to.'[1]

If Schiele's nudity is often explicitly linked to his sexual persona, in stripping himself bare in his self portraits he also exploits other associations of the naked figure, implying a desire to confront himself at his most vulnerable and exposed. In doing so he was continuing the tradition of Romantic self portraiture that had its origins a century earlier in portraits such as Janssen's (cat. 12), and had as an earlier model the nude self portrait drawings of Dürer. In the present drawing the gaunt, dark-eyed figure of the artist, described within an angular, undulating contour line of supreme economy, faces the viewer head-on. The beginnings of his outstretched arms might suggest the crucified Christ, but equally imply the performer's invitation to the viewer's voyeuristic gaze. As is true of so many of the Schiele's self portraits, the image treads a delicate and unnerving line between vulnerability and posturing. AS

**1** A. Roessler *Erinnerungen*, Vienna 1948, pp. 39–40, quoted in Kallir 1990, p. 123.

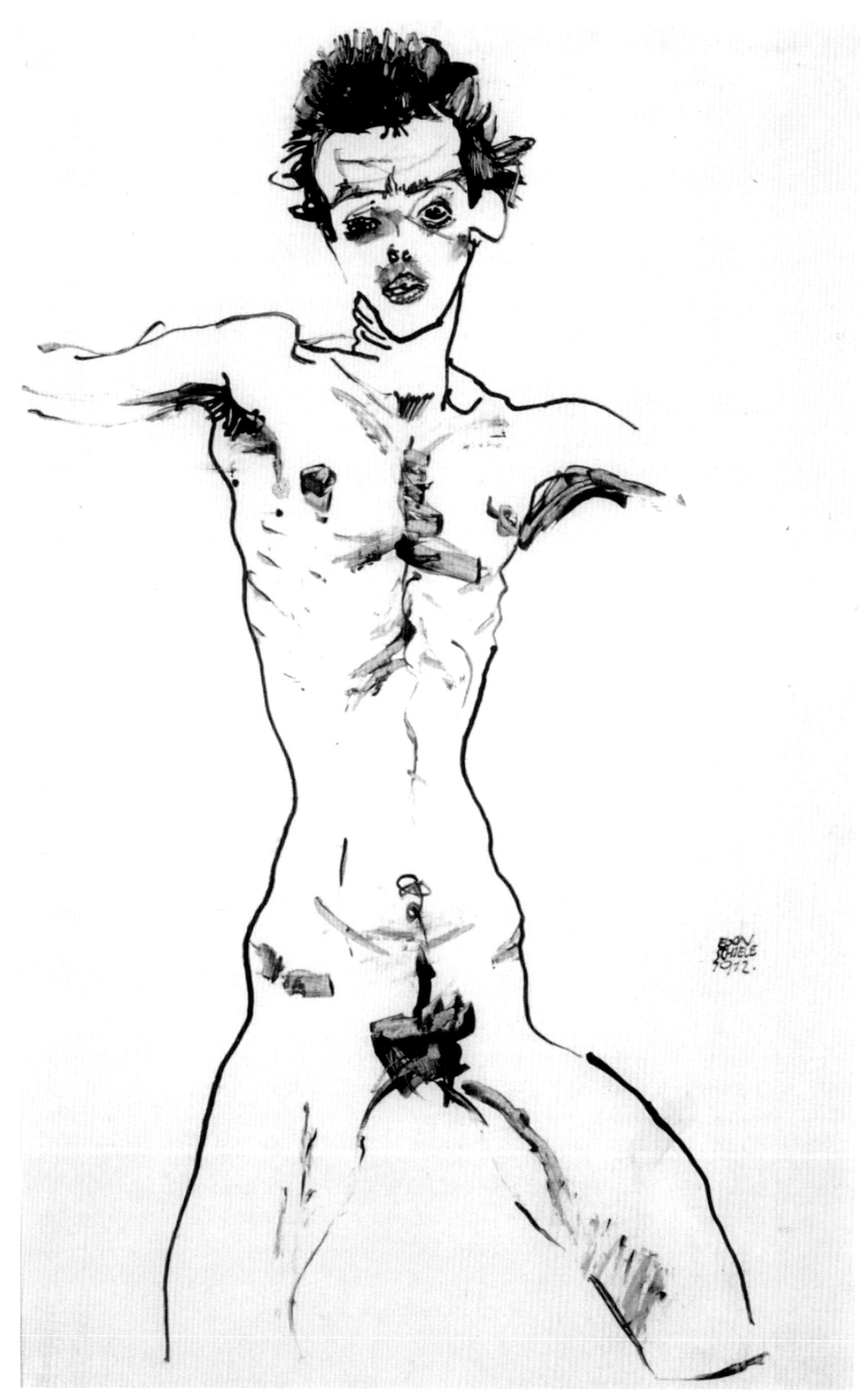
EGON
SCHIELE
1912.

## 72. Paula Modersohn-Becker (1876–1907)

*Self Portrait on her Sixth Wedding Anniversary* 1906

Oil on canvas, 61 × 50 cm

Kunstsammlungen/ Paula Modersohn-Becker Museum, Bremen

Most nineteenth-century self portraits by women betray the difficulty of asserting an identity as an artist in the face of prevailing notions of male genius. Only at the end of the century did women begin to declare the seriousness of their endeavour in their work by emphasising the craft of painting – showing themselves in the garb of a professional painter – but very few dramatised themselves as the creative individual in any of the many ways available to their male counterparts.

A profound exception from the early twentieth century is Paula Modersohn-Becker's *Self Portrait on her Sixth Wedding Anniversary.* This painting draws on and confronts the Romantic tradition of male self portraiture, and recognises the gendering of notions of creativity, while challenging and subverting them. It was painted during a brief period of optimistic and creative self-confidence, based above all on Modersohn-Becker's belief that she was at last finding herself as an independent, creative individual. The inscription states: 'I painted this age 30, on sixth wedding anniversary' (25 May). Although apparently defining her as a wife, this is in fact a proclamation of independence: the previous February she had left her husband, Otto, and travelled to Paris alone. She had done so in previous years, but this time she believed the rupture to be permanent: 'I couldn't stand it any longer and I'll probably never be able to stand it again either. It was all too confining for me and not what – and always less of what – I needed'.[1] By coming to Paris, Modersohn-Becker wished to assert her independent individuality: 'I am – Me – and hope to become Me more and more'.[2] She was, moreover, fully aware of the Romantic roots of her dilemma, referring to her separation as her '*Sturm and Drang* period'.[3]

She was initially unhappy in Paris, but in May her mood changed dramatically and she could write in letters to her mother and sister of 'living the most intensely happy period of my life', of 'beginning a new life' and 'living as if in ecstasy'.[4] The key to this change seems to have been the support she received from the German sculptor Bernhard Hoetger, the importance of which is revealed in an ecstatic letter: 'You've given me the most wonderful gift. You've given me myself. Now I have courage ... You are a great benefactor. Now I've come to believe that I shall become something'.[5] This courage and self-belief was to last a brief month (she became unwell at the beginning of June). [6]

If Modersohn-Becker's sense of confident independence is apparent from her letters and journals, her self portrait is both more suggestive and less explicit. She shows herself stripped to the waist, recalling Dürer's self-portraits just as Janssen had done seventy-five years earlier (cat. 12).[7] Dürer, Janssen and later still Gerstl (cat. 62) used the naked self-portrait to suggest parallels with Christ. Modersohn-Becker, with evident awareness, deliberately draws attention to her age of 30 in the inscription (the mythical age at which Christ was believed to have started his ministry), but in doing so only emphasises the different resonances of the female nude. She stares directly out of the painting but her face defies an easy reading. Most startling of all, her arms encircle her pregnant belly, yet she was not pregnant at the time. The previous month she had written to her husband explicitly (though not at that point irrevocably) putting her art before her expected role of wife and mother: 'I *cannot* come to you *now*, I *cannot* ... And I don't want a child from you, not *now*.'[8] Her decision to paint herself pregnant is certainly an acknowledgement of what were seen as 'natural' modes of female creativity, but also, by their invention within a self portrait, a direct challenge to them. Here Modersohn-Becker is model and engendering muse, her pregnancy a symbol of explicitly female creativity, but she is also defiantly the creative artist. AS

1 Letter to mother, 8 May 1906, Radycki 1980, p. 286.

2 Letter to Clara Rilke, 17 February 1906.

3 Letter to Otto Modersohn, 9 April 1906, Radycki op. cit. p. 283.

4 Letters to mother, 8 May 1906, and sister, May 1906, Radycki op. cit. p. 286.

5 Letter to Bernhard Hoetger, May 1906, Radycki op. cit. p. 285. Ironically, the following September it was Hoetger who was to persuade Paula to have a change of heart and invite Otto to join her in Paris, which led to their reconciliation.

6 Letter to Otto, 30 June 1906. By the end of summer Modersohn-Becker was resigned to Otto, writing to Clara Rilke (16 September) that she realised 'that I am not the sort of woman to stand alone in life'.

7 Although the comparison is extraordinarily suggestive, there is no evidence that Modersohn-Becker knew Janssen's self portrait.

8 Letter to Otto Modersohn, 9 April 1906. Modersohn-Becker became pregnant after her reconciliation with Otto, and was to die of an embolism less than three weeks after the birth of their daughter, Mathilde, on 21 November 1907.

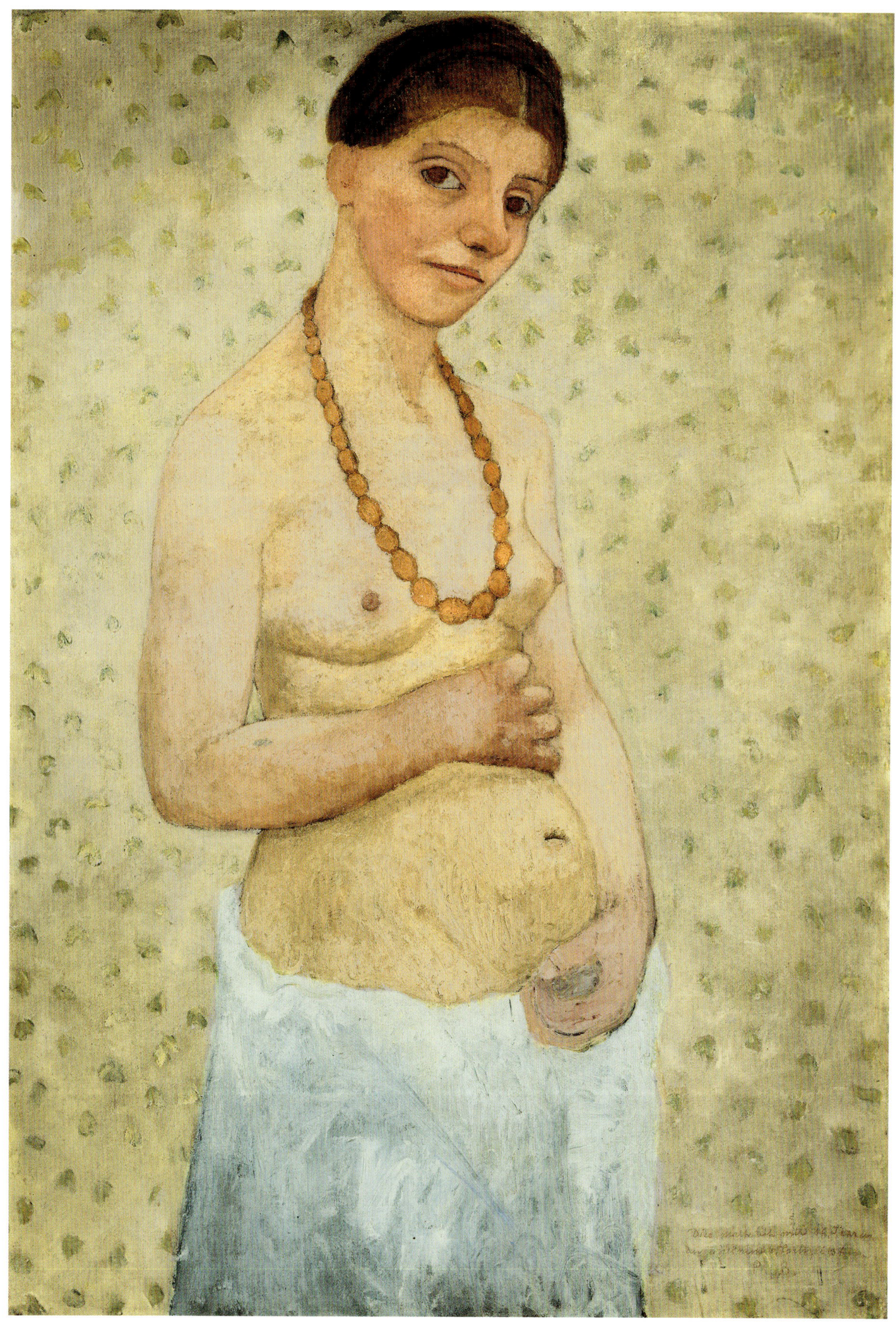

# Chronology

*Lois Oliver*

## History

**1789** French Revolution begins.

**1793** King Louis XVI and Queen Marie-Antoinette are guillotined. The moderate Girondins are overthrown by the Jacobins led by Maximilien Robespierre. Mass executions follow during the Reign of Terror.

**1794** Robespierre is ousted and the French Directory established.

**1799** Napoleon Bonaparte seizes power in France.

**1804** Napoleon I Bonaparte crowns himself Emperor of France; within a few years he has conquered most of Europe.

**1812** Napoleon's army suffers massive losses on the retreat from Moscow.

**1814** Napoleon is defeated by the allied armies of Britain, Russia and Austria, and exiled to Elba. Louis XVIII becomes King of France.

**1814–15** The Congress of Vienna redraws the political boundaries of Europe.

**1815** Following his escape from exile, Napoleon is finally defeated at the Battle of Waterloo by British, Dutch and German troops, and exiled to St Helena, where he dies in 1821.

**1821** Start of Greek War of Independence against Ottoman rule. One of the Greeks' most ardent supporters is British poet Lord Byron, who is mourned as a hero by the Greeks following his death in 1824. Prince Otto of Bavaria becomes king of an independent Greece in 1832.

**1830** July Revolution in Paris. Charles X is overthrown and Louis Philippe is enthroned as the 'Citizen King'.

**1831** Belgium becomes an independent nation under the sovereignty of Prince Léopold of Saxe-Coburg.

**1837** Queen Victoria ascends to the British throne.

**1848** Revolutions in many parts of Europe. In France, Louis Philippe is overthrown and the Second Republic established; in Germany and Italy, revolutions are violently suppressed within a few months.

**1852** Napoleon proclaims himself Emperor Napoleon III.

**1853–6** Crimean War.

**1857** Giuseppe Garibaldi forms the Italian National Association for the Unification of Italy.

**1861** Victor Emmanuel II of Sardinia is proclaimed King of Italy. The unification of Italy is completed when Rome is incorporated in 1870.

William I becomes King of Prussia and appoints Otto van Bismarck Prime Minister.

**1866** Bismarck takes Prussia to war with Austria, forcing Austria from the German Confederation.

**1870–1** Bismarck defeats Napoleon III in the Franco-Prussian War. William I, King of Prussia, is crowned Emperor of Germany. The Third Republic is established in France. A socialist Commune is set up in Paris (18 March–28 May 1871), in which artist Gustave Courbet plays an active role.

**1894** Captain Alfred Dreyfus, a Jewish French army officer, is wrongly convicted of passing French military secrets to Germany, sparking the 12-year Dreyfus affair and a national debate on anti-semitism. The pro-Dreyfus Emile Zola writes 'J'accuse', an open letter to the President of the French Republic and is tried for libel. Dreyfus is finally exonerated in 1906.

**1899–1902** Boer War.

**1901** Queen Victoria dies and Edward VII becomes King of Great Britain.

**1905** Norway becomes independent from Sweden.

**1907** The Triple Entente is signed by France, the United Kingdom, and Russia. These allies form the core of the forces that will oppose the Central Powers (Austria-Hungary and Germany) in the First World War.

**1914** First World War begins.

## Culture

**1791** Wolfgang Amadeus Mozart composes *The Magic Flute*.

**1798** William Wordsworth and Samuel Taylor Coleridge publish *Lyrical Ballads*, a key work of Romanticism, which is defined that year by German critic Friedrich Schlegel.

German Alois Senefelder invents lithography.

**1804** Ludwig van Beethoven completes his Third Symphony. On hearing that Napoleon has proclaimed himself Emperor he rejects the original title, 'Bonaparte', and the work becomes the 'Eroica'.

**1808** Johann Wolfgang von Goethe publishes the first part of his tragedy *Faust*.

**1811–20** The Regency period in Britain sees a flowering of Romantic literature in the poetry of John Keats, Percy Bysshe Shelley and Lord Byron and the novels of Sir Walter Scott. Their work inspires visual artists throughout Europe, in particular the French painter Eugène Delacroix.

**1812** Jacob and Wilhelm Grimm publish their *Fairy Tales*.

**1813** The waltz dance-craze sweeps Europe's ballrooms.

**1816** French chemist Nicéphore Niépce produces the first photographic negative.

**1825** The first public railway, the Stockton to Darlington, opens in Britain.

**1830** Hector Berlioz composes his autobiographical *Symphonie Fantastique*, subtitled 'Episodes in the Life of an artist'.

**1830s** The Can-Can becomes popular in Paris dance-halls.

**1840** First postage stamp in Great Britain.

**1846** Belgian Adolphe Sax patents the saxophone.

**1845** Henry Murger publishes the first of his stories about a band of writers, musicians and artists; later instalments appear under the title *Scenes of Bohemian Life*.

**1851** The Great Exhibition opens in the Crystal Palace, Hyde Park, London.

**1853** Baron Georges-Eugène Haussmann becomes prefect of the Seine département, Paris and (until 1870) directs projects that transform the city.

**1854** Japan is opened to trade with the West. In the following decades, Japanese wares are avidly collected by artists including Edgar Degas, James Tissot and James Abbott McNeill Whistler, and writers including Charles Baudelaire and Emile Zola.

**1855** Exposition Universelle, Paris. Robert Browning publishes *Men and Women*.

**1857** Baudelaire publishes *Les fleurs du mal*, Gustave Flaubert publishes *Madame Bovary* and Charles Dickens publishes *Little Dorrit*.

**1859** Charles Darwin publishes *On the Origin of Species*.

**1859–60** Baudelaire writes *The Painter of Modern Life*.

**1862** Victor Hugo publishes *Les Misérables*.

**1863** London Underground opens.

**1864–9** Tolstoy publishes *War and Peace*.

**1867** Karl Marx publishes first volume of *Das Kapital*.

**1871** Friedrich Nietzsche publishes *The Birth of Tragedy*.

**1872** George Eliot publishes *Middlemarch*.

**1877** First complete performance of Richard Wagner's operatic *Ring Cycle*.

**1879** First performance of Piotr Ilyich Tchaikovsky's *Eugene Onegin*.

**1881** Gilbert and Sullivan operettas delight audiences at the newly opened Savoy Theatre in London.

**1886** Emile Zola publishes *L'Oeuvre* (*The Masterpiece*), causing a permanent rift with his childhood friend, Paul Cézanne, who recognises himself in the principal character, a failed artist who commits suicide.

**1889** Exposition Universelle, Paris. The Eiffel Tower is erected and the Moulin Rouge opens.

**1894** Oscar Wilde's play *Salome* is published, translated from French by Lord Alfred Douglas, with illustrations by Aubrey Beardsley. The eroticism of the play and illustrations causes a scandal.

Claude Debussy composes *Prélude à l'après-midi d'un faune*, inspired by the work of symbolist poet Stéphane Mallarmé.

**1895** The world's first cinema opens in Paris.

Oscar Wilde is charged with engaging in homosexual activity with Lord Alfred Douglas.

**1896** Premiere of Giacomo Puccini's opera *La Bohème*.

**1898** The Paris Metro opens.

**1900** Exposition Universelle, Paris.

Sigmund Freud publishes *Interpretation of Dreams*, establishing the new discipline of psychoanalysis.

**1901** The first Nobel Prizes are awarded.

Guglielmo Marconi transmits the first telegraphic radio messages.

**1905** Albert Einstein proposes his Theory of Relativity.

**1908** Henry Ford produces the Model T motorcar.

**1909** French aviator Louis Blériot crosses the English Channel by aeroplane.

**1913** The premiere of Igor Stravinsky's ballet *The Rite of Spring* by the Ballet Russes in Paris causes a riot.

Marcel Proust publishes *Swann's Way*, the first volume of his larger project, *Remembrance of Things Past*.

## Art

**1804–14** Napoleon I Bonaparte is glorified in Neoclassical works by painter Jacques-Louis David and sculptor Antonio Canova.

**1810** A group of artists from Vienna settle in an abandoned monastery in Rome, where their simple lifestyle and spiritual subject matter earn them the name the 'Nazarenes'.

**1819** Théodore Gericault sparks controversy with *The Raft of the Medusa*, showing the desperate survivors of a French government frigate wrecked off the coast of Africa in 1816.

**1830–70** The Barbizon school of landscape painters flourishes in France.

**1840s** Café Momus, Paris, becomes the meeting place for a group of artists and writers, including Jules Husson Champfleury and Gustave Courbet.

**1848** The Pre-Raphaelite Brotherhood is founded in England.

**1855** Rejected by the art selectors for the Paris Exposition Universelle, Courbet sets up his 'Pavilion of Realism' outside the entrance.

**1860s** Growth of the Arts and Crafts Movement in England.

**1862** The Tuileries Gardens in Paris is the meeting place for artists, critics and writers, including Edouard Manet, Baudelaire and Fantin Latour, as recorded in Manet's *Music in the Tuileries Gardens*.

**1863** Manet's *Le Déjeuner sur l'herbe* creates a sensation at the Salon des Refusés, established after the conservative Paris Salon jury rejects over half the submissions for the year. It hangs alongside pictures by Camille Pissarro, Paul Cézanne and James Abbott McNeill Whistler.

**1865** Manet's *Olympia* creates a scandal at the Paris Salon.

**1874** First Impressionist Exhibition features works by Claude Monet, Pierre-Auguste Renoir, Berthe Morisot, Alfred Sisley, Camille Pissarro and Edgar Degas.

**1877** Whistler's *Nocturne in Black and Gold: The Falling Rocket* causes controversy at the first Grosvenor Gallery exhibition in London. The critic Ruskin accuses Whistler of 'flinging a pot of paint in the public's face'; Whistler sues for libel.

**1878** Cézanne withdraws from the Impressionists, marking the beginnings of Post-Impressionism.

**1884** Avant-garde artists including James Ensor and Théo van Rysselberghe set up the exhibition society 'Les XX' (Les Vingt) in Belgium. Later members include Auguste Rodin and Jan Toorop.

**1886** Jean Moréas publishes a Symbolist manifesto in *Le Figaro*, arguing for an art that expresses the subjective world of dreams and the imagination.

**1888** Gauguin and Van Gogh spend nine weeks painting together in Arles, South France. The collaboration collapses when Van Gogh suffers a breakdown, in which he cuts off part of his ear.

**1889** A small group of French artists influenced by Paul Gauguin and led by Paul Sérusier form a Symbolist group, the 'Nabis'.

**1890s** The Art Nouveau style dominates design and architecture in Europe.

**1892** The Munich Secession is founded, the first of several split-away groups of artists in Germany determined to set up exhibition opportunities outside the control of the ruling academies.

**1893** Norwegian artist Edvard Munch paints *The Scream*.

**1894** First Salon des Cent Exhibition, Paris.

**1897–1903** Els Quatre Gats café in Barcelona is the meeting place for bohemian writers and artists, including the young Picasso, who has his first exhibition at the café in 1900.

**1907** Picasso paints *Les Demoiselles d'Avignon*; the first exhibition of Cubist art is held in Paris.

# Bibliography

**J. Adhémar**, *Gavarni*, exh. cat., Bibliothèque Nationale, Paris 1954

**P. Alechinsky et al**, *James Ensor (1860–1949)*, exh. cat., Musées Royaux des Beaux-Arts de Belgique, Brussels, 1999

**R. Asleson, S.P. Casteras and P. Cormac** (eds), *Pre-Raphaelite and Other Masters: The Andrew Lloyd Webber Collection*, Royal Academy of Arts, London 2003

**C.B. Bailey**, *Renoir's Portraits: Impressions of an Age*, exh. cat., National Gallery of Canada, Ottawa / Art Institute of Chicago / the Kimbell Art Museum, Fort Worth 1997

**J. Baillio**, *Elisabeth Louise Vigée Le Brun*, exh. cat., Kimbell Art Museum, Fort Worth 1982

**C. Baudelaire**, *The Mirror of Art: Critical Studies by Charles Baudelaire*, ed. Jonathan Mayne, London 1955

**C. Baudelaire**, 'The Painter of Modern Life' in *The Painter of Modern Life and Other Essays*, trans. and ed. J. Mayne, London 1964a

**C. Baudelaire**, *Art in Paris 1845–1862: Reviews of Salons and Other Exhibitions*, trans. and ed. J. Mayne, London 1964b

**C. Berend-Corinth**, *Die Gemälde von Lovis Corinth*, Munich 1958

**J. Block**, *From Les XX and Belgian Avant-Gardism 1868–1894*, Ann Arbor 1984

**A. Boime**, *Thomas Couture and the Eclectic Vision*, New Haven and London 1980

**P. Bordes**, *Courbet à Montpellier*, exh. cat., Musée Fabre, Montpellier 1985

**C. Boyle-Turner**, *Paul Sérusier*, Ann Arbor 1980

**R. Brettell, F. Cachin and C. Stuckley**, *The Art of Paul Gauguin*, exh. cat., National Gallery of Art, Washington DC and Art Institute of Chicago 1988

**A. Brookner**, *Romanticism and its Discontents*, London 2000

**M.R. Brown**, *Gypsies and Bohemians: The Myth of the Artist in Nineteenth-Century France*, Anne Arbor 1985

**J. Brüschweiler and G. Magnaguagno** (eds), *Ferdinand Hodler*, exh. cat., Nationalgalerie, Berlin, Musée du Petit Palais, Paris and Kunsthaus, Zurich 1983

**H. Buchanan**, *Edgar Degas and Ludovic Lepic: An Impressionist Friendship*, Cleveland Studies in the History of Art, vol. 2, Cleveland 1997

**T. Burollet and L.M.A. Schoonbaert** (eds), *James Ensor*, exh. cat., Musée du Petit Palais, Paris 1990

**F. Cachin, C. Moffett and J. Wilson-Bareau**, *Edouard Manet, 1832–1883*, exh. cat., Grand Palais, Paris and Metropolitan Museum of Art, New York 1983

**P.D. Cate and P.E. Boyer**, *The Circle of Toulouse Lautrec: An Exhibition of the Artist and his Close Associates*, exh. cat., Jane Voorhees Zimmerli Art Museum, New Brunswick, NJ 1985

**T. Chang**, 'The Meeting': Gustave Courbet and Alfred Bruyas' in *Burlington Magazine* CXXXVIII (September 1996), pp. 586–91

**J. Cladel**, *Rodin: The Man and his Art*, trans. S.K. Star, New York 1917

**K. Clark** (ed.), *Ruskin Today*, London 1964

**T.J. Clark**, *Image of the People: Gustave Courbet and the 1848 Revolution*, London 1973

**P. Conisbee, K. Monrad and L. Bøgh Rønberg**, *Christoffer Wilhelm Eckersberg, 1783–1853*, exh. cat., National Gallery of Art, Washington DC 2003

**E.T. Cook and A.D.O. Wedderburn** (eds), *The Works of John Ruskin*, 39 vols, London 1902–12

**D. Cooper**, 'Renoir, Lise and the Le Coeur Family: A Study of Renoir's Early Development', *Burlington Magazine* CI (1959), pp. 163–71, 322–8

**D. Cooper** (ed.), *Paul Gauguin: 45 Lettres à Vincent, Théo et Jo van Gogh*, The Hague 1983

**P. Courthion**, *Courbet raconté par lui-même et par ses amis*, 2 vols, Geneva 1948 and 1950

**M. Davies and C. Gould**, *National Gallery Catalogues: French School, Early Nineteenth Century*, London 1970

**A. Derbes and M. Sandona** (eds), *The Cambridge Companion to Giotto*, Cambridge 2004

**B. Dijkstra**, *Idols of Perversity: Fantasies of Feminine Evil in Fin-de-Siècle Culture*, Oxford 1986

**D. Druick** (ed.), *Van Gogh and Gauguin: The Studio of the South*, exh. cat., Art Institute of Chicago and Van Gogh Museum, Amsterdam 2001

**D. Druick and M. Hoog** (eds), *Fantin-Latour*, exh. cat., National Gallery of Canada, Ottawa

**A. Eggum**, *Edvard Munch: The Frieze of Life from Painting to Graphic Art*, Oslo 2000

**A.E. Elsen**, *Rodin's Art: The Rodin Collection of the Iris & B. Gerald Cantor Center for Visual Arts at Stanford University*, Stanford 2003

**M. Forster-Hahn, C. Keisch, P.-K. Schuster, A. Wesenberg et al**, *Spirit of an Age: Paintings from the Nationalgalerie, Berlin*, exh. cat., National Gallery of Art, Washington DC and National Gallery, London 2001

**M.B. Frank**, *German Romantic Painting Redefined*, Aldershot 2001

**C. Fréches and A. Tarrasse**, *The Nabis: Bonnard, Vuillard and their Culture*, Paris 1990

**C. Fréches and A. Tarrasse**, *Les Nabis*, exh. cat., Galeries Nationales du Grand Palais, Paris 1993

**F. Fredericks**, *The First Gothics*, New York 1987

**V. Frisch and J.T. Shipley**, *Auguste Rodin: A Biography*, New York 1939

**P. Gauguin**, *Lettres de Paul Gauguin à Emile Bernard, 1888–1891*, Geneva 1954

**S. Giesen**, *Victor Emil Janssen. Selbstbildnis vor der Staffelei*, Hamburg 2001

**S. Geist**, *Interpreting Cézanne*, London and Cambridge 1988

**E. and J. de Goncourt**, *Journal: Mémoires de la vie littéraire*, ed. R. Ricatte. 3 vols, Paris 1989

**P. Gsell**, *L'Art: Entretiens réunis par Paul Gsell*, Paris 1911; English trans. Berkeley 1984

**P. Hasse**, 'Aus dem Leben Friedrich Overbecks: Briefe an Eltern und Geschwester' in *Allgemeine Konservative Monatsschrift für das Christliche Deutschland* 44 (1887)

**J. Herbert**, *The New Painting: Impressionism 1874–1886*, National Gallery of Art, Washington DC 1986

**R.L. Herbert**, *Impressionism: Art, Leisure and Parisian Society*, New Haven and London 1988

**K. Hiesinger** (ed.), *Art Nouveau in Munich: Masters of Jugendstil*, exh. cat., Philadelphia Museum of Art 1988

**J. Hone**, *The Life of George Moore*, London 1936

**H. Honour**, *Romanticism*, London 1981

**L. Johnson**, *The Paintings of Eugène Delacroix: A Critical Catalogue*, 6 vols, Oxford 1981–9

**A. Joubin** (ed.), *Correspondance générale d'Eugène Delacroix*, 5 vols, Paris 1935–8

**A. Joubin** (ed.), *Journal d'Eugène Delacroix*, 3 vols, Paris 1950

**J. Kallir**, *Egon Schiele: The Complete Works*, New York 1990

**J. Knowles**, *The life and writings of Henry Fuseli, Esq. M.A. R.A.*, 3 vols (1831), repr. with a new introduction by D.H. Weinglass, New York 1982

**E. Kris and O. Kurz**, *Legend, Myth and Magic in the Image of the Artist* (1934), rev. edn New Haven 1979

**A. Lawniczakowa**, 'In the Mirror of a Well: On Jacek Malczewski's Self-Portraits', *Bulletin du Musée National de Varsovie* XXIX, 1988, pp. 33–60

**F.H. Lehr**, *Die Blütezeit romantischer Bildkunst. Franz Pforr der Meister des Lukasbundes*, Marburg 1924

**R. Leslie and T. Taylor**, *The Life and Times of Sir Joshua Reynolds*, 2 vols, London 1865

**M. MacDonald, S. Galassi and A. Ribeiro**, *Whistler, Women and Fashion*, exh. cat., Frick Collection, New York 2003

**A. McLaren Young, M. MacDonald, R. Spencer and H. Miles**, *The Paintings of James McNeill Whistler*, New Haven and London 1980

**R. McMullen**, *Victorian Outsider*, London 1974

**M McCully** (ed.), *A Picasso Anthology: Documents, Criticism, Reminiscences*, London 1981

**M. Malingue** (ed.), *Lettres de Gauguin à sa femme et à ses amis*, Paris 1949

**D. Mannings**, *Sir Joshua Reynolds: A Complete Catalogue of his Paintings*, New Haven and London 2000

**N. Margolis Maurer**, *The Pursuit of Spiritual Wisdom: The thought and art of Vincent Van Gogh and Gauguin*, London 1998

**P. Mathews**, *Passionate Discontent: Creativity, Gender, and French Symbolist Art*, Chicago and London 1999

**P.L. Mathieu**, *Gustave Moreau*, Boston 1976

**V. Merlhès** (ed.), *Correspondence de Paul Gauguin: Documents, témoignes*, Paris 1948, rev. edn 1984

**L. Merrill**, *The Peacock Room: A Cultural Biography*, Freer Gallery of Art, New Haven and London 1998

**E. Moers**, *The Dandy, Brummell to Beerbohm*, London 1960

**G. Moore**, *'Hail and Farewell!' Vale*, London 1914

**L. Morowitz and W. Vaughan** (eds), *Artistic Brotherhoods in the Nineteenth Century*, Burlington, VT 2000

**F. Nietzsche**, *The Will to Power*, trans. and ed. W. Kaufmann and R.J. Hollingdale, London 1968

**L. Nochlin**, 'Gustave Courbet's *Meeting*: A Portrait of the Artist as a Wandering Jew', *Art Bulletin* 49 (1967), pp. 209–22

***Oxford Dictionary of National Biography*** (ODNB), Oxford 2004

**L. Parris**, *The Pre-Raphaelites*, exh. cat., Tate, London 1984

**N. Penny** (ed.), *Reynolds*, exh. cat., Royal Academy of Arts, London 1986

**R. Pickvance** (ed.), *Edouard Manet*, exh. cat., Fondation Pierre Gianadda, Martigny, Switzerland 1996

**M. Postle** (ed.), *Joshua Reynolds: The Creation of Celebrity*, exh. cat., Tate, London 2005

**W.L. Pressly**, *The Life and Art of James Barry*, New Haven and London 1981

**A. Proust**, *Edouard Manet: Souvenirs*, Paris 1913

**J. D. Radycki** (trans.), *The Letters and Journals of Paula Modersohn-Becker*, Metuchen and London 1980

**T. Reff**, 'Pissarro's Portrait of Cézanne', *Burlington Magazine* CIX (1967), pp. 627–33

**T. Reff**, 'Manet's portrait of Zola', *Burlington Magazine* CXVII (1975), pp. 34–44

**T. Reff**, *Degas: The Artist's Mind*, London 1976a

**T. Reff**, *The Notebooks of Degas: A Catalogue of the 38 Notebooks in the Bibliothèque Nationale and other Collections*, Oxford 1976b

**J. Rewald**, *The History of Impressionism*, New York 1955

**J. Rewald**, *Camille Pissarro*, New York 1963

**J. Rewald**, *Post-Impressionism*, London 1978

**J. Rewald**, *Cézanne: A Biography*, New York 1986

**J. Reynolds**, *Fifteen Discourses*, London and New York 1906

**J. Richardson**, *A Life of Picasso*, vol. 1: *1881–1906*, London 1991

**G. Rivière**, *M. Degas, bourgeois de Paris*, Paris 1935

**D. Rouart and D. Wildenstein**, *Edouard Manet: Catalogue Raisonné*, 2 vols, Geneva 1975

**G. Schiff and W. Hofman**, *Henry Fuseli, 1741–1825*, trans. S. Twohig, exh. cat., Tate, London 1975

**L. Schneider** (ed.), *Giotto in Perspective*, Englewood Cliff 1974

**K.A. Schröder and A. Hoerschelmann** (eds), *Edvard Munch: Theme and Variation*, exh. cat., Albertina, Vienna 2003

**K.A. Schröder and H. Szeemann** (eds), *Egon Schiele and his Contemporaries: Austrian Painting and Drawing from 1900 to 1930 from the Leopold Collectiom, Vienna*, Munich 1989

**P.-K. Schuster, C. Vitali and B. Butts**, *Lovis Corinth*, exh. cat., Tate, London 1996–7

**M.V. Schwarz and P. Theis**, 'Giotto's father: Old stories and new documents', *Burlington Magazine* CXLI (1999), pp. 676–7

**J. Seigel**, *Bohemian Paris: Culture Politics and the Boundaries of Bourgeois Life, 1830–1930*, Baltimore and London 1986, rev. edn 1999

**A. Sérullaz, V. Pomerède, J.J. Rishel et al.**, *Delacroix: The Late Work*, exh. cat., Philadelphia Museum of Art 1998

**P. Sérusier**, *ABC de la peinture* (2nd edn), Paris 1942

**G. Solana, R. Shiff, G. Cogeval and M.D. Jiménez-Blanco**, *Gauguin and the Origins of Symbolism*, exh. cat., Museo Thyssen-Bornemisza, Madrid 2004

**M.A. Stevens** (ed.), *Emile Bernard 1868–1941: A Pioneer of Modern Art*, exh. cat., Rijksmuseum Vincent Van Gogh, Amsterdam and Stadtische Kunsthalle, Mannheim 1990

**M. Sturgis**, *Passionate Attitudes: The English Decadence of the 1890s*, London 1995

**B. Stutzer** (ed.), *Blicke ins Licht: Neue Betrachtungen zum Werk von Giovanni Segantini*, Segantini Museum, St Moritz 2004

**A. Tabarant**, *Manet et ses oeuvres*, 4th edn, Paris 1947

**G. Tinterow and H. Loyrette**, *Origins of Impressionism*, exh. cat., Metropolitan Museum of Art, New York 1994

**H. Toussaint and M.-T. de Forges**, *Gustave Courbet, 1819–1877*, exh. cat., Petit Palais, Paris and Royal Academy of Arts, London 1977

**H. Uhr**, *Lovis Corinth*, Berkeley 1990

**J. Van Deputte** (ed.), *Le Salon des Cent: affiches d'artistes*, exh. cat., Musée Carnavalet, Paris 1994

**V. van Gogh**, *The Complete Letters of Vincent van Gogh*, 3 vols (1958), 3rd edn, Boston 2000

**G. Vasari**, *Lives of the Painters, Sculptors and Architects*, trans. G. du C. de Vere, intro. and notes by D. Ekserdjian, 2 vols, Everyman's Library, London 1996

**W. Vaughan**, *Caspar David Friedrich 1774–1840: Romantic Painting in Dresden*, exh. cat., Tate, London 1972

**W. Vaughan**, *German Romantic Painting*, New Haven and London 1980

**W. Vaughan**, *Samuel Palmer, Vision and Landscape*, exh. cat., British Museum, London 2005

**E. Waterhouse**, *Painting in Britain, 1530–1790*, London 1953

**G.P. Weisberg**, *The Realist Tradition: French Painting and Drawing 1830–1900*, exh. cat., Cleveland Museum of Art 1981

**J. Weiss**, 'Bohemian Nostalgia: Picasso in Villon's Paris' in *Picasso: The Early Years 1892–1906*, ed. M. McCully, Washington and Boston 1997

**S. Wildman** (ed.), *Visions of Love and Life: Pre-Raphaelite Art from the Birmingham Collection*, touring exh. cat., Art Services International, USA, 1995

**M. Wilson**, *Manet at Work: An exhibition to mark the centenary of the death of Edouard Manet 1832–1883*, exh. cat., The National Gallery, London 1983

**A. Wohlgemuth**, *Honoré Daumier: Kunst im Spiegel der Karikatur von 1830–1870*, Frankfurt 1996

**G. Woll**, *Edvard Munch: The Complete Graphic Works*, London 2001

**M.H. Wood** (ed.), *The Frieze of Life*, exh. cat., The National Gallery, London 1992

# Photographic credits

**Amsterdam:** © Van Gogh Museum, Amsterdam: cat. 37. © Van Gogh Museum (Vincent van Gogh Foundation): cat. 53, fig. 11

**Baltimore:** © The Walters Art Museum, Baltimore, Maryland: fig. 13

**Berlin:** Staatliche Museen zu Berlin, Nationalgalerie © Bildarchiv Preussischer Kulturbesitz. Nationalgalerie, Staatliche Museen zu Berlin. Photo Jörg P. Anders: cats. 9, 10

**Birmingham:** City Museum and Art Gallery © Birmingham Museums and Art Gallery: cat. 16. The Trustees of the Barber Institute of Fine Arts, University of Birmingham © Birmingham Museums and Art Gallery: cat. 50

**Bremen:** © Kunstsammlugen Böttcherstrasse/Paula Modersohn-Becker Museum, Bremen: cat. 72

**Cambridge, Massachusetts (MA):** Courtesy of Fogg Art Museum, Harvard University Art Museums © 2004 President and Fellows of Harvard College. Photo David Mathews: fig. 10

**Chicago, Illinois (IL):** © 2002 The Art Institute of Chicago, All Rights Reserved: cat. 40

**Cleveland, Ohio (OH):** © The Cleveland Museum of Art, Cleveland, Ohio: fig. 15

**Copenhagen:** © Ny Carlsberg Glyptotek, Copenhagen. Photo Ole Haupt: cat. 4

**Cracow:** © National Museum in Kracow: cat. 68

**Dublin:** © Dublin City Gallery, The Hugh Lane: cat. 44. © The National Gallery of Ireland, Dublin: cat. 30

**Florence:** Galleria degli Uffizi, Firenze © 2000. Photo Scala, Firenze – su concessione Ministero Beni e Attività Culturali: cat. 3

**Graff Diamonds Ltd**: cat. 34

**Grenoble:** © Musée de Grenoble: cat. 14

**Hamburg:** Hamburger Kunsthalle © Bildarchiv Preussischer Kulturbesitz, Berlin. Photo Christoph Irrgang: cat. 8. Photo Elke Walford: cats. 12, 49. Hamburger Kunsthalle © Bridgeman Art Library, London: fig. 3

**London:** © The British Museum: cats. 11, 24. © The British Museum and DACS 2006: cat. 58. © The British Museum and Munch-Ellingsen Group, BONO, Oslo / DACS, London 2006: cat. 70. © The National Gallery, London: cats. 2, 19, 32, 41, fig. 12. The National Portrait Gallery, London © By Courtesy of the National Portrait Gallery, London: cat. 45. © By Courtesy of the National Portrait Gallery, London and ADAGP, Paris and DACS, London 2006: cat. 46. © Royal Academy of Arts, London: cat. 1. Sir Andrew Lloyd Webber Art Foundation © Succession Picasso \ DACS 2006: cat. 39. Tate, London © Tate 2006: cat. 21. The Victoria and Albert Museum © V&A Images \ V&A Museum, London: cats. 5, 6, 38, 47, 48. © V&A Images \ V&A Museum, London and DACS 2006: cats. 59, 64

**Los Angeles:** © Hammer Museum, Los Angeles, CA. Photo Robert Wedemeyer: cat. 52

**Madrid:** © Museo Romantico: cat. 22

**Montpellier:** © Musée Fabre, Montpellier Agglomeration. Photo Frédéric Jaulmes: cats. 18, 29, fig. 9

**Munich:** Bayerische Staatsgemäldesammlungen © Artothek Weilheim and Ingeborg & Dr. Wolfgang Henze-Ketterer, Wichtrach/Bern: fig. 17

**New York:** © 1980 The Metropolitan Museum of Art, New York: cat. 43. © 1992 The Metropolitan Museum of Art, New York: cat. 42

**Nice:** © Musée des Beaux-Arts Jules Chéret de Nice, on deposit from the Musée d'Orsay. Photo Muriel Anssens: cat. 36

**Oslo:** Munch Museum. Photo Andersen/de Jong © Munch Museum/Munch-Ellingsen Group / DACS 2006: fig. 16

**Oxford:** © Copyright in this Photograph Reserved to the Ashmolean Museum, Oxford: fig. 2

**Paris:** © Bibliothèque Nationale de France, Paris: cats. 23, 25, 26, 27, fig. 7. © Centre Georges Pompidou, Paris, Musée national d'art moderne / Centre de création industrielle. Photo CNAC/MNAM Dist. RMN Jacqueline Hyde and ADAGP, Paris and DACS, London 2006: fig. 1. © Galérie Cazeau-Béraudière, Paris and ADAGP, Paris and DACS, London, 2006: cat. 57. Musée d'Orsay, Paris © RMN, Paris Photo Hervé Lewandowski: cat. 54, figs. 8, 19. Photo Jean-Gilles Berizzi: cat. 15. © RMN, Paris and ADAGP, Paris and DACS, London 2006. Photo Hervé Lewandowski: fig. 14. Musée du Louvre, Paris © RMN, Paris. Photo Droits réservés: fig. 4. Photo Gérard Blot: figs. 5, 6. Photo Hervé Lewandowski: cat. 33. Photo Jean-Gilles Berizzi: cat. 28. Musée National Gustave Moreau Paris © Photo RMN, Paris. Droits réservés: cat. 20. Photo Christian Jean: cat. 69. Musée Rodin, Paris © Musée Rodin, Paris. Photo Adam Rzepka: cats. 65, 66. Petit Palais, Musée des Beaux-Arts de la Ville de Paris © Photothèque des musées de la ville de Paris. Photo Pierrain: cat. 13

**Saint Germain en Laye:** © Musée Départemental Maurice Denis, Saint Germain en Laye, France: cat. 55. © Musée Départemental Maurice Denis, Saint Germain en Laye, France and ADAGP, Paris and DACS, London 2006: cat. 56

**St Moritz:** © Segantini Museum, St Moritz: cat. 60

**São Paulo:** © Museu de Arte de São Paulo Assis Chateaubriand, São Paulo, Brazil. Photo Luiz Hossaka: cat. 35

**Stockholm:** Nationalmuseum, Stockholm © The National Museums of Fine Arts, Stockholm: cat. 31

**Stuttgart:** © Staatsgalerie Stuttgart: cat. 61

**Valenciennes:** © Musée des Beaux-Arts de Valenciennes. Photo Claude Thériez: cat. 7

**Vienna:** © Leopold Museum, Vienna: cats. 62, 63, 71

**West Palm Beach:** © Norton Museum of Art, West Palm Beach, Florida: cat. 51

**Zurich:** © 2002 Kunsthaus Zürich. All rights reserved: cat. 67

**Private collection**: fig 18

**Private collection** © Courtesy Nathan Fine Art Berlin/Zurich: cat. 17

# Index